PandoraHearts

Jun Mochizuki

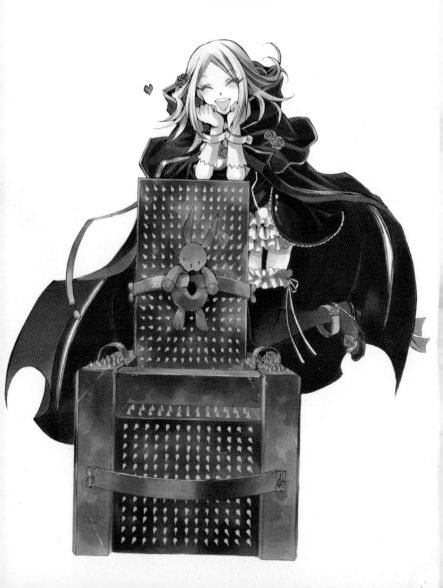

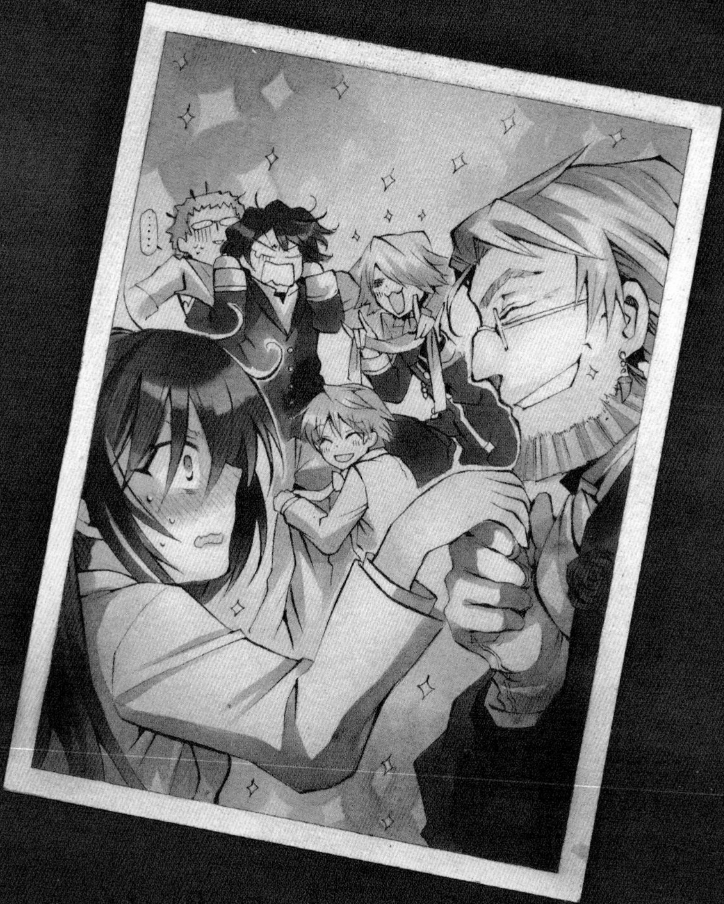

CONTENTS

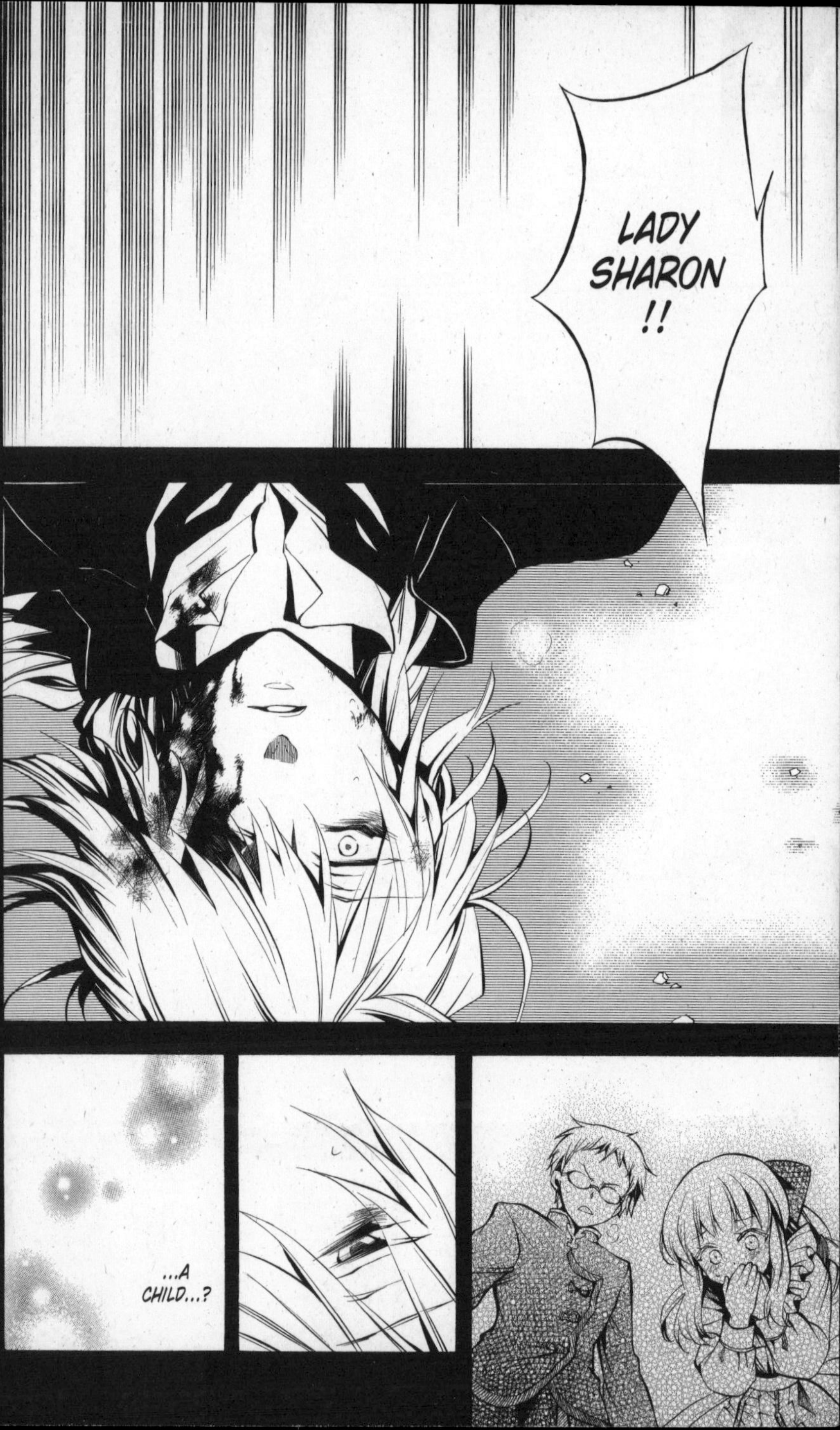
LADY SHARON !!
...A CHILD...?

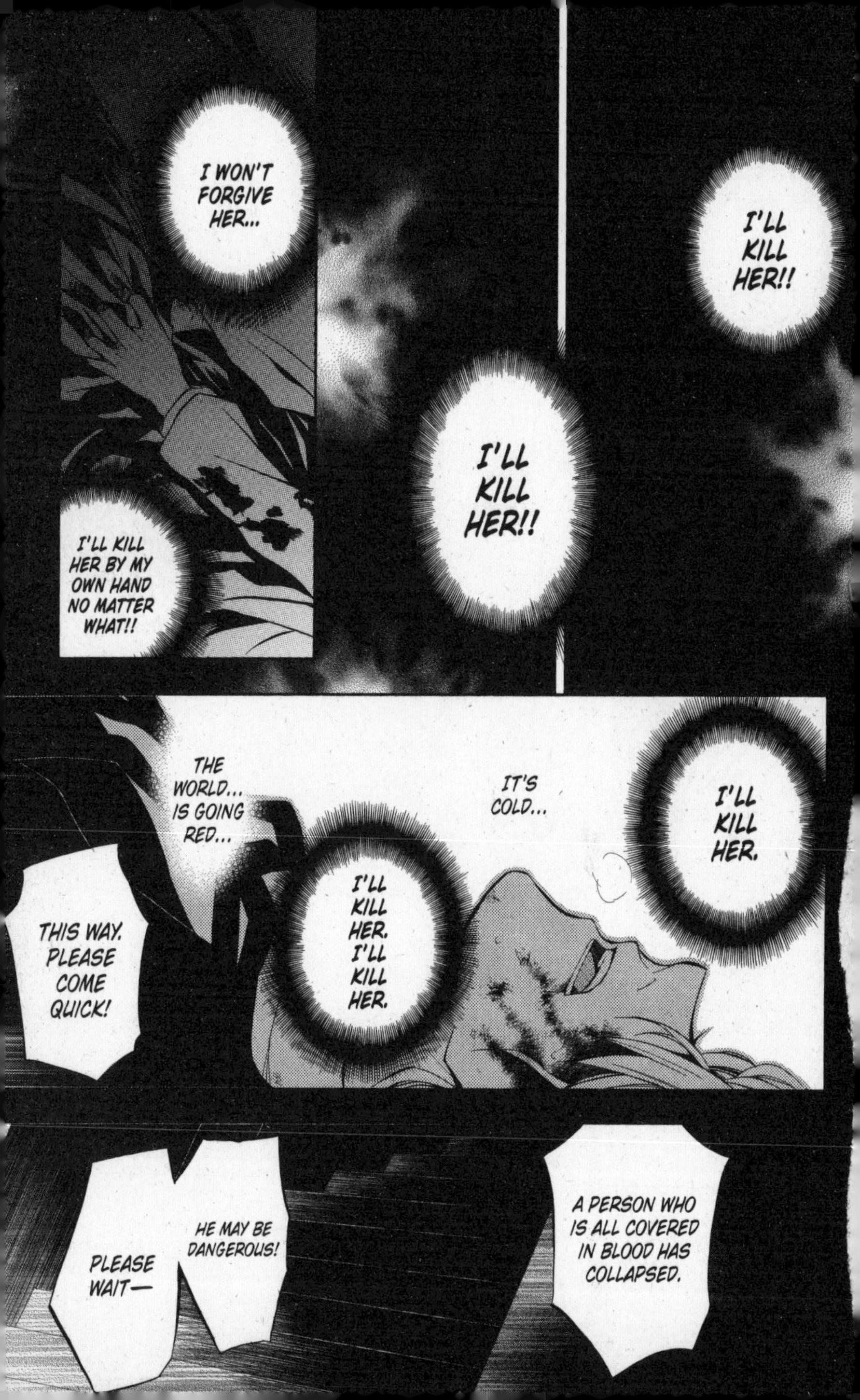
I'LL KILL HER!!
I'LL KILL HER!!
I WON'T FORGIVE HER...
I'LL KILL HER BY MY OWN HAND NO MATTER WHAT!!
I'LL KILL HER.
IT'S COLD...
I'LL KILL HER. I'LL KILL HER.
THE WORLD... IS GOING RED...
THIS WAY. PLEASE COME QUICK!
A PERSON WHO IS ALL COVERED IN BLOOD HAS COLLAPSED.
HE MAY BE DANGEROUS!
PLEASE WAIT—

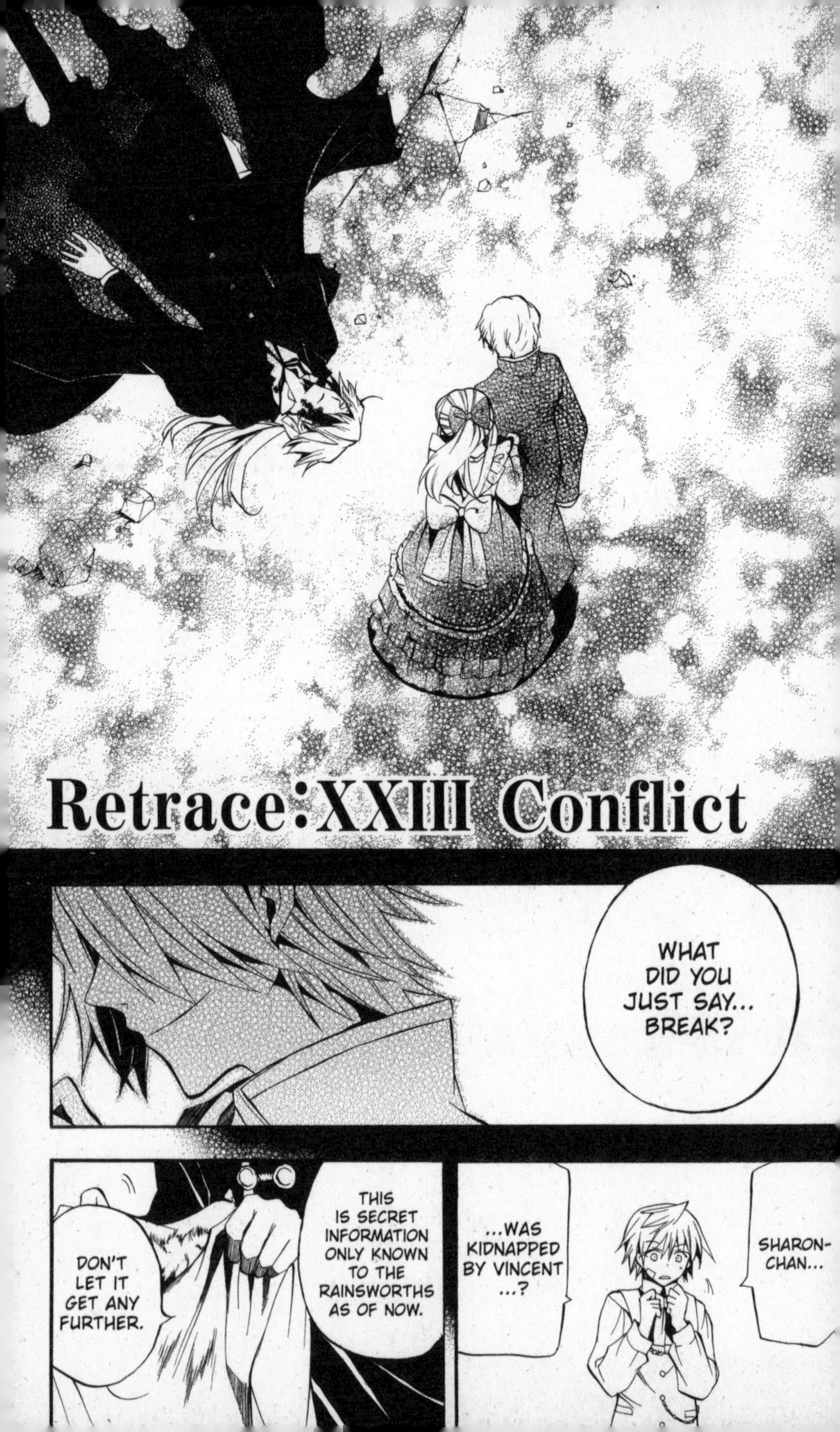
Retrace:XXIII Conflict
WHAT DID YOU JUST SAY... BREAK?
SHARON-CHAN...
...WAS KIDNAPPED BY VINCENT ...?
THIS IS SECRET INFORMATION ONLY KNOWN TO THE RAINSWORTHS AS OF NOW.
DON'T LET IT GET ANY FURTHER.

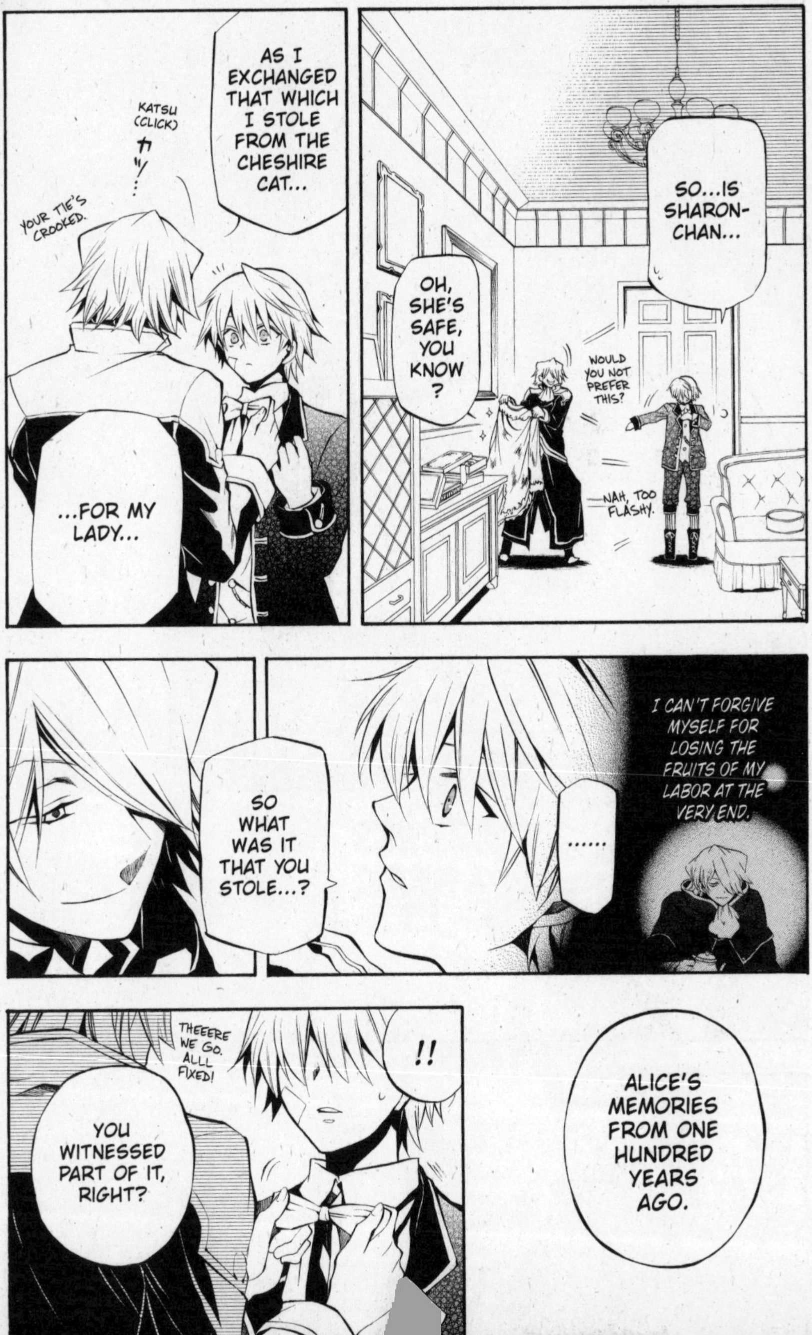
SO...IS SHARON-CHAN...
OH, SHE'S SAFE, YOU KNOW?
WOULD YOU NOT PREFER THIS?
NAH, TOO FLASHY.
AS I EXCHANGED THAT WHICH I STOLE FROM THE CHESHIRE CAT...
KATSU (CLICK)
カッ…
YOUR TIE'S CROOKED.
...FOR MY LADY...
I CAN'T FORGIVE MYSELF FOR LOSING THE FRUITS OF MY LABOR AT THE VERY END.
......
SO WHAT WAS IT THAT YOU STOLE...?
ALICE'S MEMORIES FROM ONE HUNDRED YEARS AGO.
!!
THEEERE WE GO. ALLL FIXED!
YOU WITNESSED PART OF IT, RIGHT?

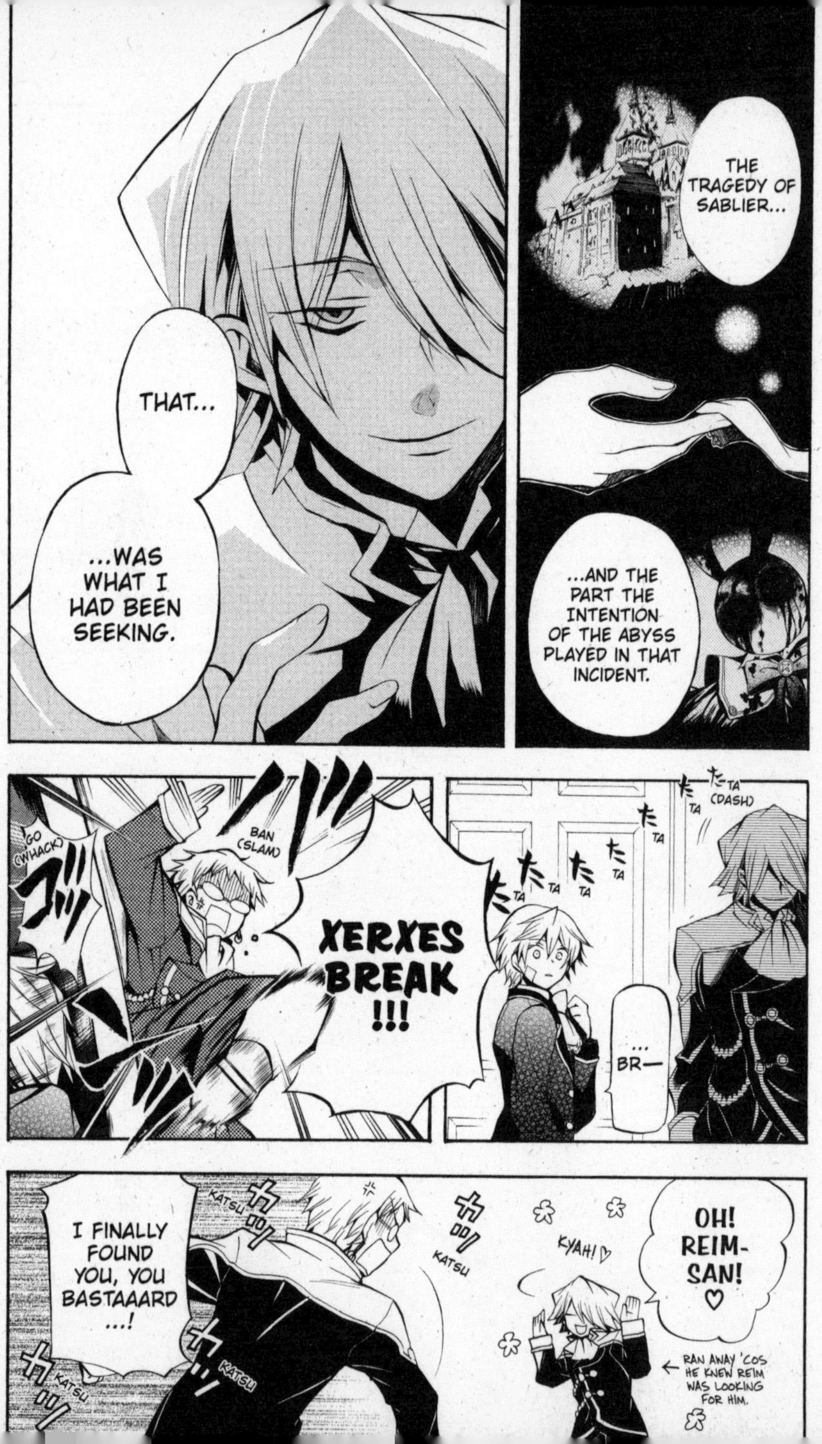
THE TRAGEDY OF SABLIER...
...AND THE PART THE INTENTION OF THE ABYSS PLAYED IN THAT INCIDENT.
THAT...
...WAS WHAT I HAD BEEN SEEKING.
TA TA (DASH)
TA
TA
TA
TA
TA
TA
... BR—
BAN (SLAM)
GO (WHACK)
XERXES BREAK !!!
OH! REIM-SAN! ♥
KYAH! ♥
RAN AWAY 'COS HE KNEW REIM WAS LOOKING FOR HIM.
KATSU
KATSU
I FINALLY FOUND YOU, YOU BASTAAARD ...!
KATSU
KATSU

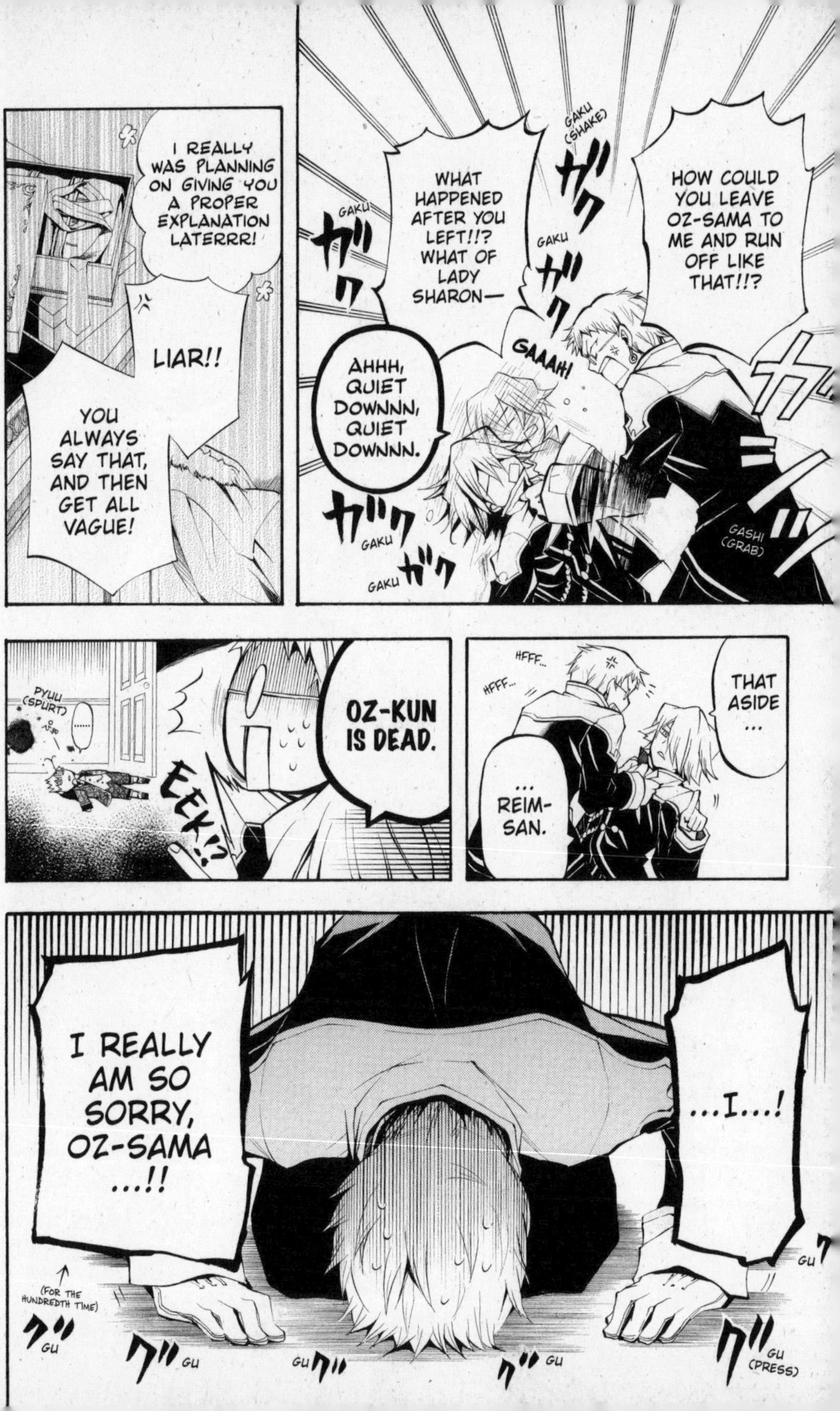
HOW COULD YOU LEAVE OZ-SAMA TO ME AND RUN OFF LIKE THAT!!?
GASHI (GRAB)
GAKU (SHAKE)
GAKU
WHAT HAPPENED AFTER YOU LEFT!!? WHAT OF LADY SHARON—
GAKU
GAAAH!
AHHH, QUIET DOWNNN, QUIET DOWNNN.
GAKU
GAKU
I REALLY WAS PLANNING ON GIVING YOU A PROPER EXPLANATION LATERRR!
LIAR!!
YOU ALWAYS SAY THAT, AND THEN GET ALL VAGUE!
HFFF...
HFFF...
THAT ASIDE ...
... REIM-SAN.
OZ-KUN IS DEAD.
EEK!!?
PYULI (SPURT)
......
...I...!
GU
GU (PRESS)
GU
GU
GU
I REALLY AM SO SORRY, OZ-SAMA ...!!
(FOR THE HUNDREDTH TIME)
GU

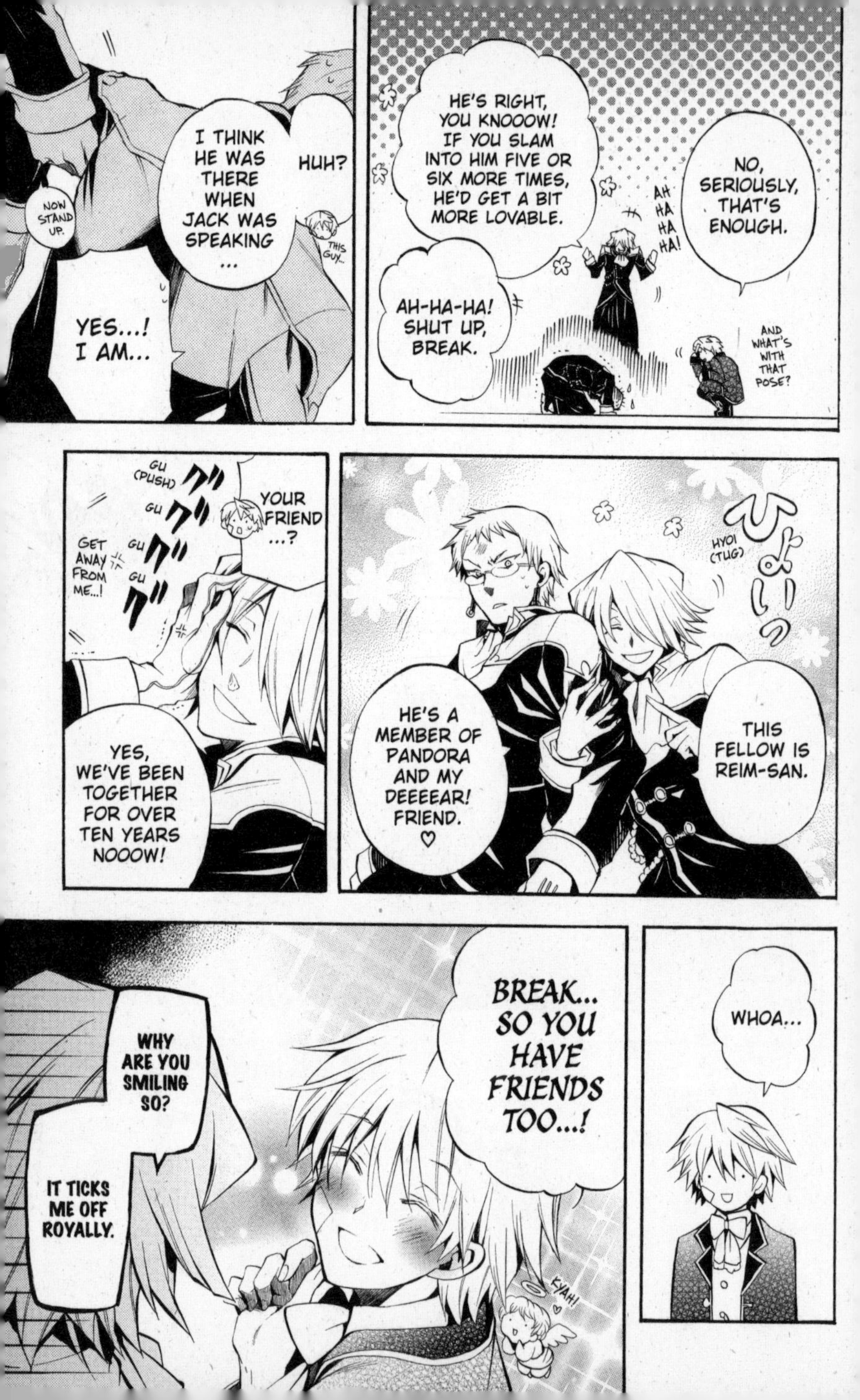
NO, SERIOUSLY, THAT'S ENOUGH.
HE'S RIGHT, YOU KNOOOW! IF YOU SLAM INTO HIM FIVE OR SIX MORE TIMES, HE'D GET A BIT MORE LOVABLE.
AH HA HA HA!
AH-HA-HA! SHUT UP, BREAK.
AND WHAT'S WITH THAT POSE?
HUH?
I THINK HE WAS THERE WHEN JACK WAS SPEAKING ...
THIS GUY...
NOW STAND UP.
YES...! I AM...
ひょいっ
HYOI (TUG)
THIS FELLOW IS REIM-SAN.
HE'S A MEMBER OF PANDORA AND MY DEEEEAR! FRIEND. ♡
YOUR FRIEND ...?
GU (PUSH) グ
GU グ
GU グ
GU グ
GET AWAY FROM ME...!
YES, WE'VE BEEN TOGETHER FOR OVER TEN YEARS NOOOW!
WHOA...
BREAK... SO YOU HAVE FRIENDS TOO...!
KYAH!
WHY ARE YOU SMILING SO?
IT TICKS ME OFF ROYALLY.

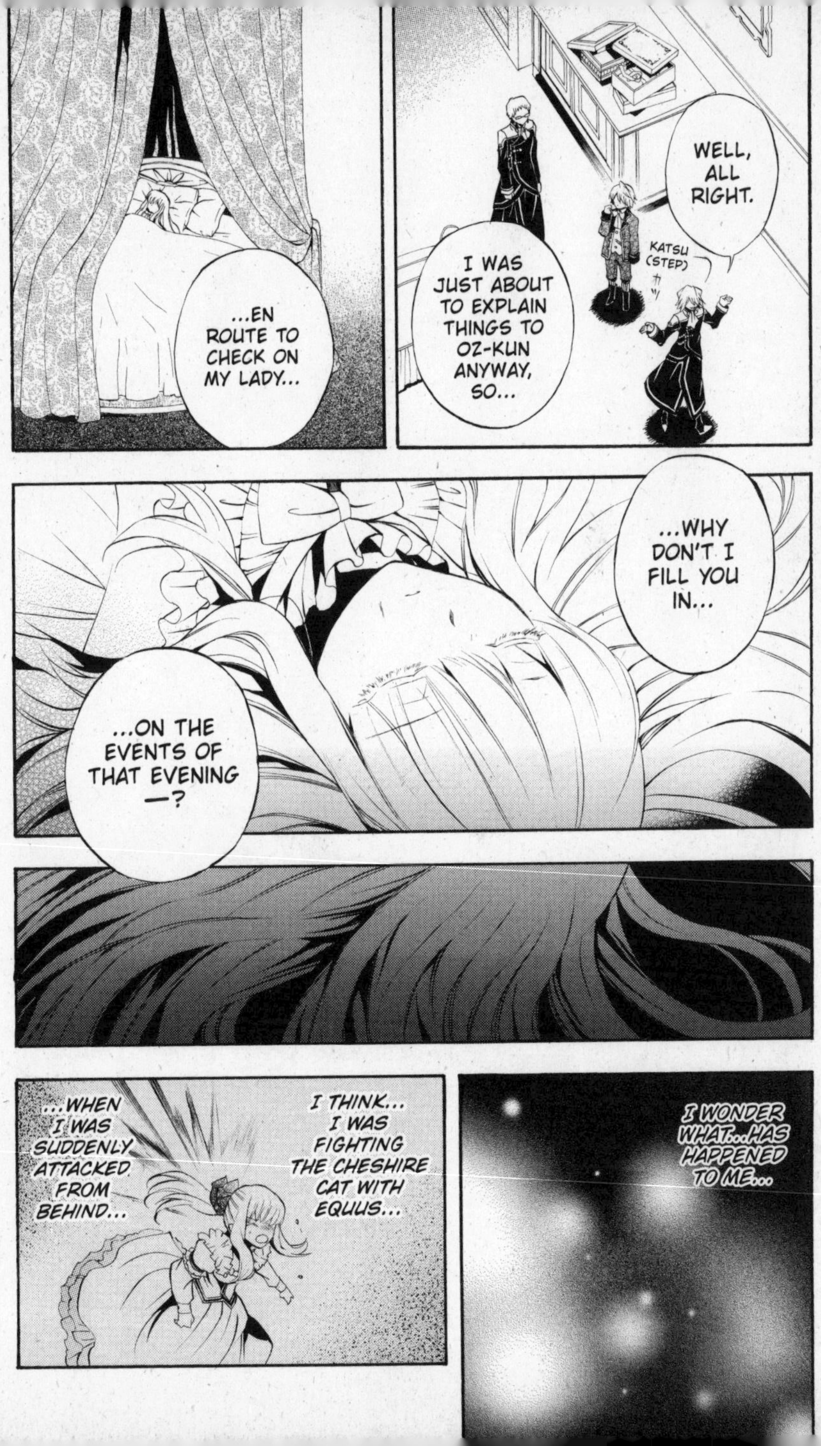
WELL, ALL RIGHT.
KATSU (STEP)
カツ
I WAS JUST ABOUT TO EXPLAIN THINGS TO OZ-KUN ANYWAY, SO...
...EN ROUTE TO CHECK ON MY LADY...
...WHY DON'T I FILL YOU IN...
...ON THE EVENTS OF THAT EVENING—?
I WONDER WHAT...HAS HAPPENED TO ME...
I THINK... I WAS FIGHTING THE CHESHIRE CAT WITH EQUUS...
...WHEN I WAS SUDDENLY ATTACKED FROM BEHIND...

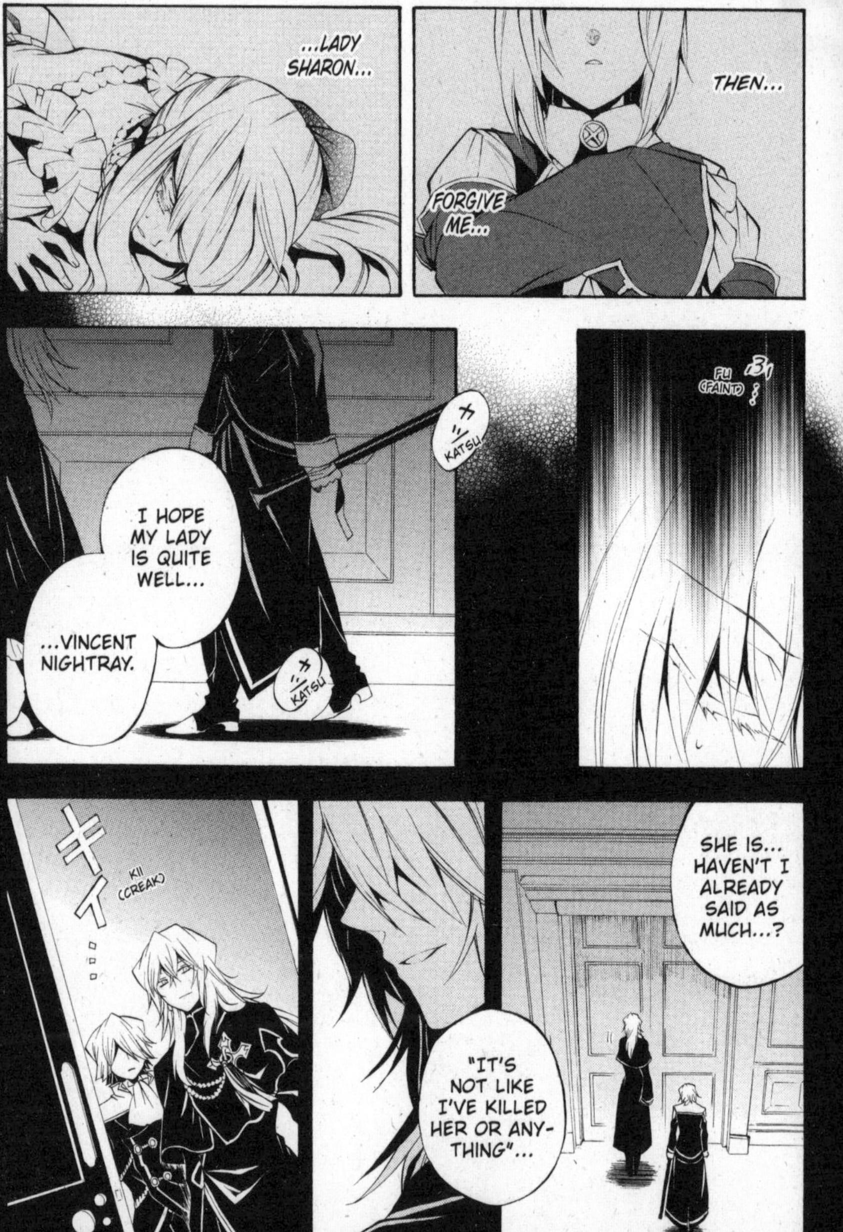
THEN...
FORGIVE ME...
...LADY SHARON...
FU (FAINT)
KATSU
I HOPE MY LADY IS QUITE WELL...
...VINCENT NIGHTRAY.
KATSU
SHE IS... HAVEN'T I ALREADY SAID AS MUCH...?
"IT'S NOT LIKE I'VE KILLED HER OR ANYTHING"...
KII (CREAK)

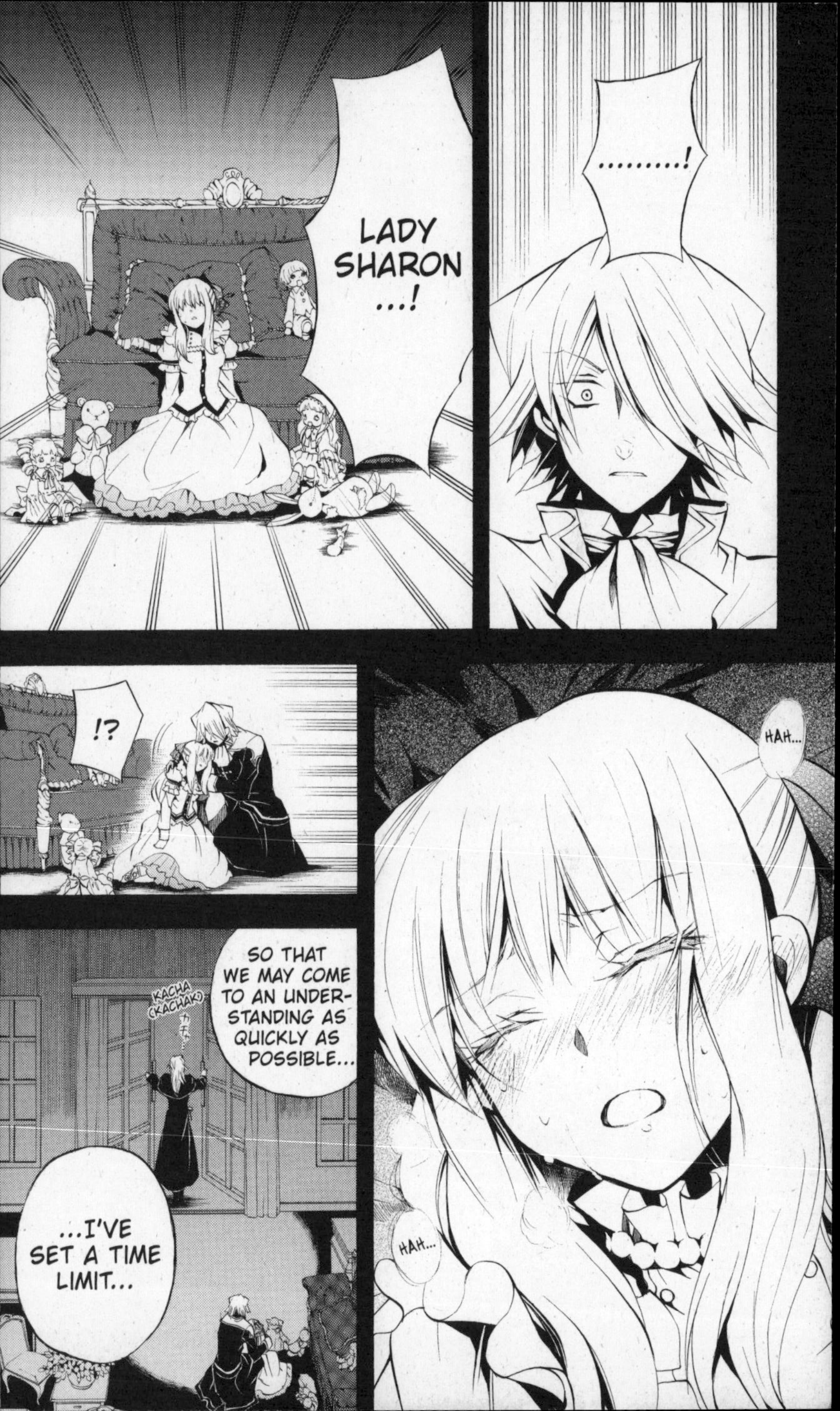
..........!
LADY SHARON ...!
HAH...
HAH...
!?
SO THAT WE MAY COME TO AN UNDER-STANDING AS QUICKLY AS POSSIBLE...
KACHA (KACHAK)
...I'VE SET A TIME LIMIT...

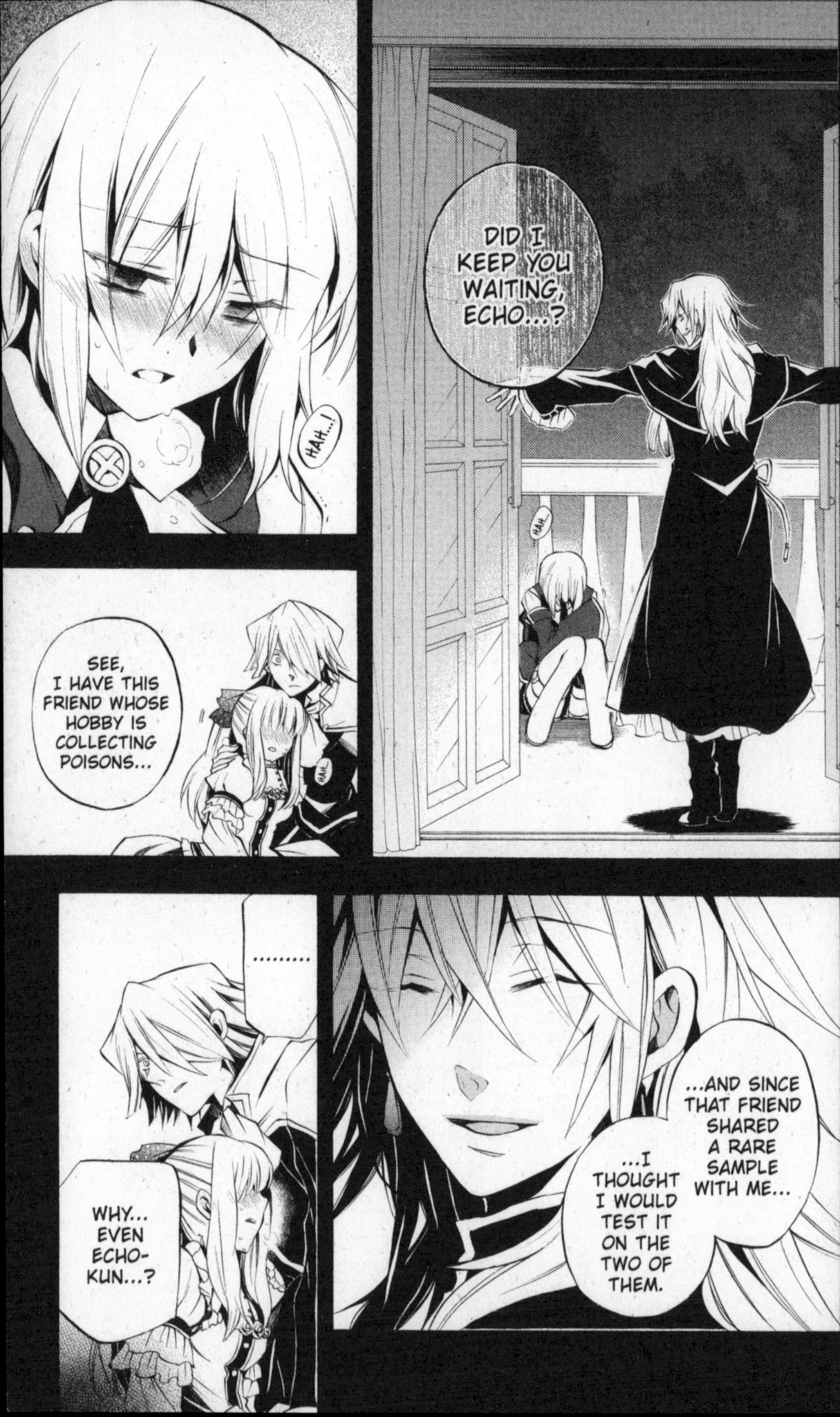
DID I KEEP YOU WAITING, ECHO...?
HAH...
HAH...!
...
SEE, I HAVE THIS FRIEND WHOSE HOBBY IS COLLECTING POISONS...
HAH...
...AND SINCE THAT FRIEND SHARED A RARE SAMPLE WITH ME...
...I THOUGHT I WOULD TEST IT ON THE TWO OF THEM.
....
WHY... EVEN ECHO-KUN...?

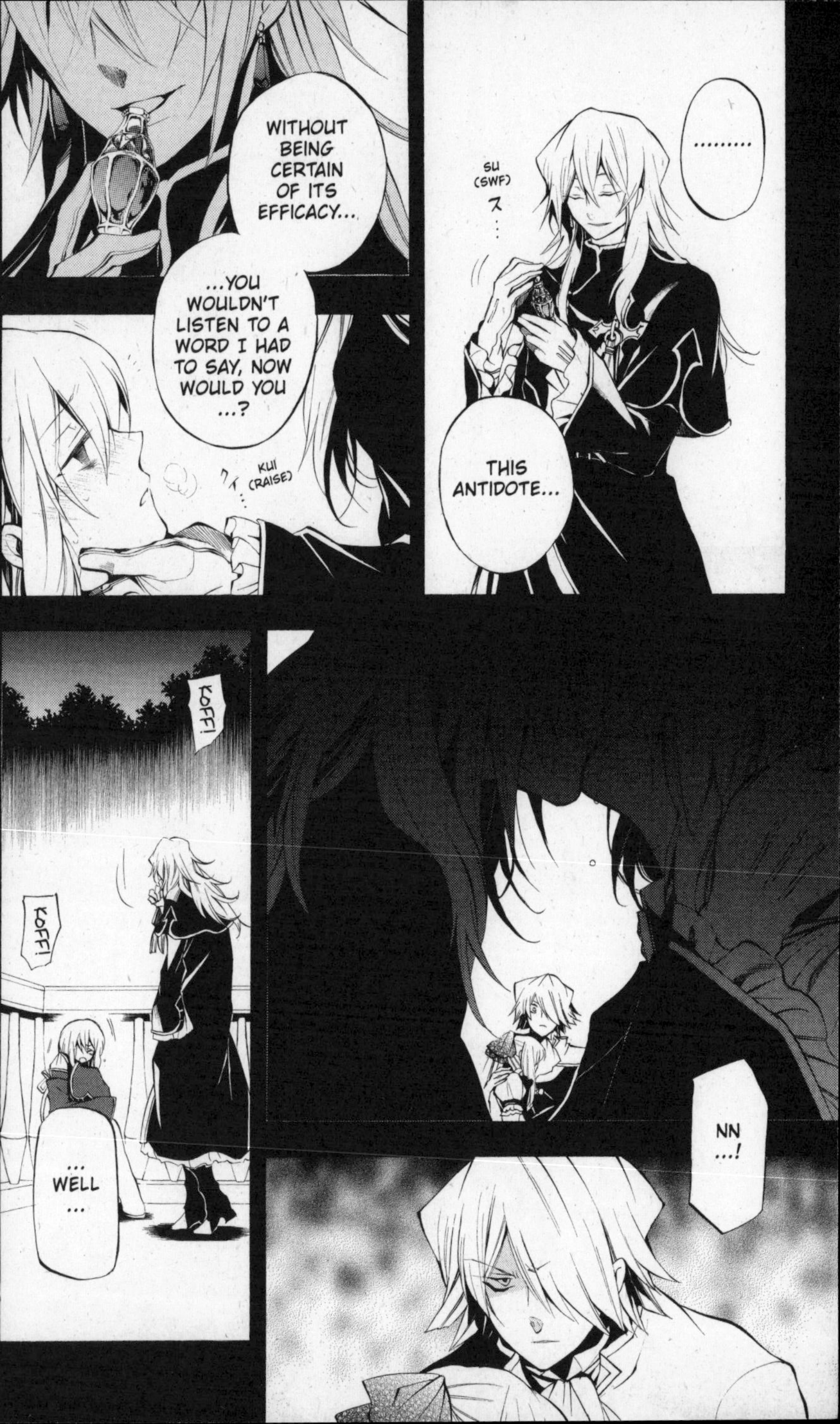
....
SU (SWF) ス...
THIS ANTIDOTE...
WITHOUT BEING CERTAIN OF ITS EFFICACY...
...YOU WOULDN'T LISTEN TO A WORD I HAD TO SAY, NOW WOULD YOU ...?
KUI (RAISE) クイ...
NN ...!
KOFF!
KOFF!
... WELL ...

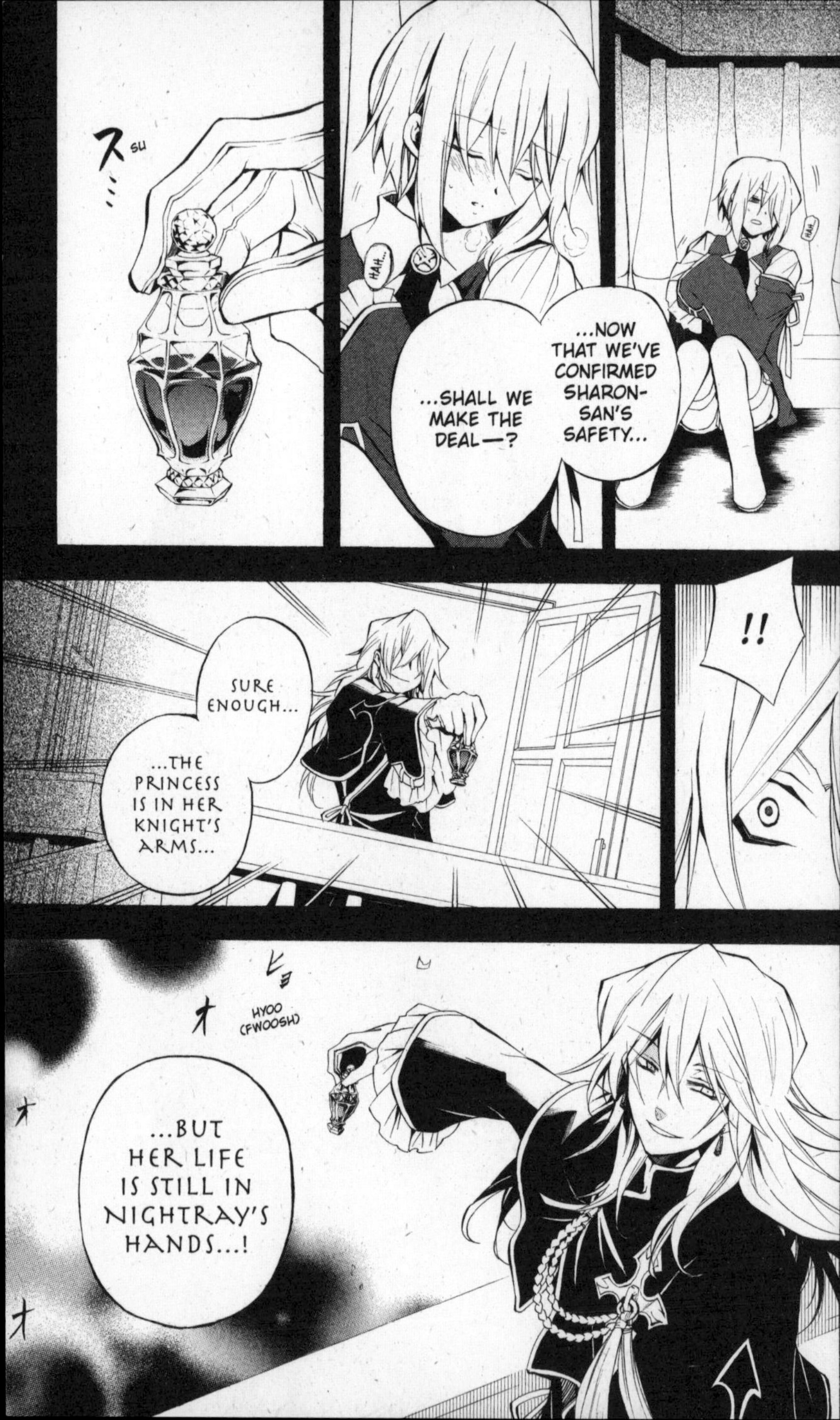
HAH...
HAH...
...NOW THAT WE'VE CONFIRMED SHARON-SAN'S SAFETY...
...SHALL WE MAKE THE DEAL—?
ス SU
!!
SURE ENOUGH...
...THE PRINCESS IS IN HER KNIGHT'S ARMS...
ヒョ HYOO (FWOOSH)
オ
オ
オ
...BUT HER LIFE IS STILL IN NIGHTRAY'S HANDS...!

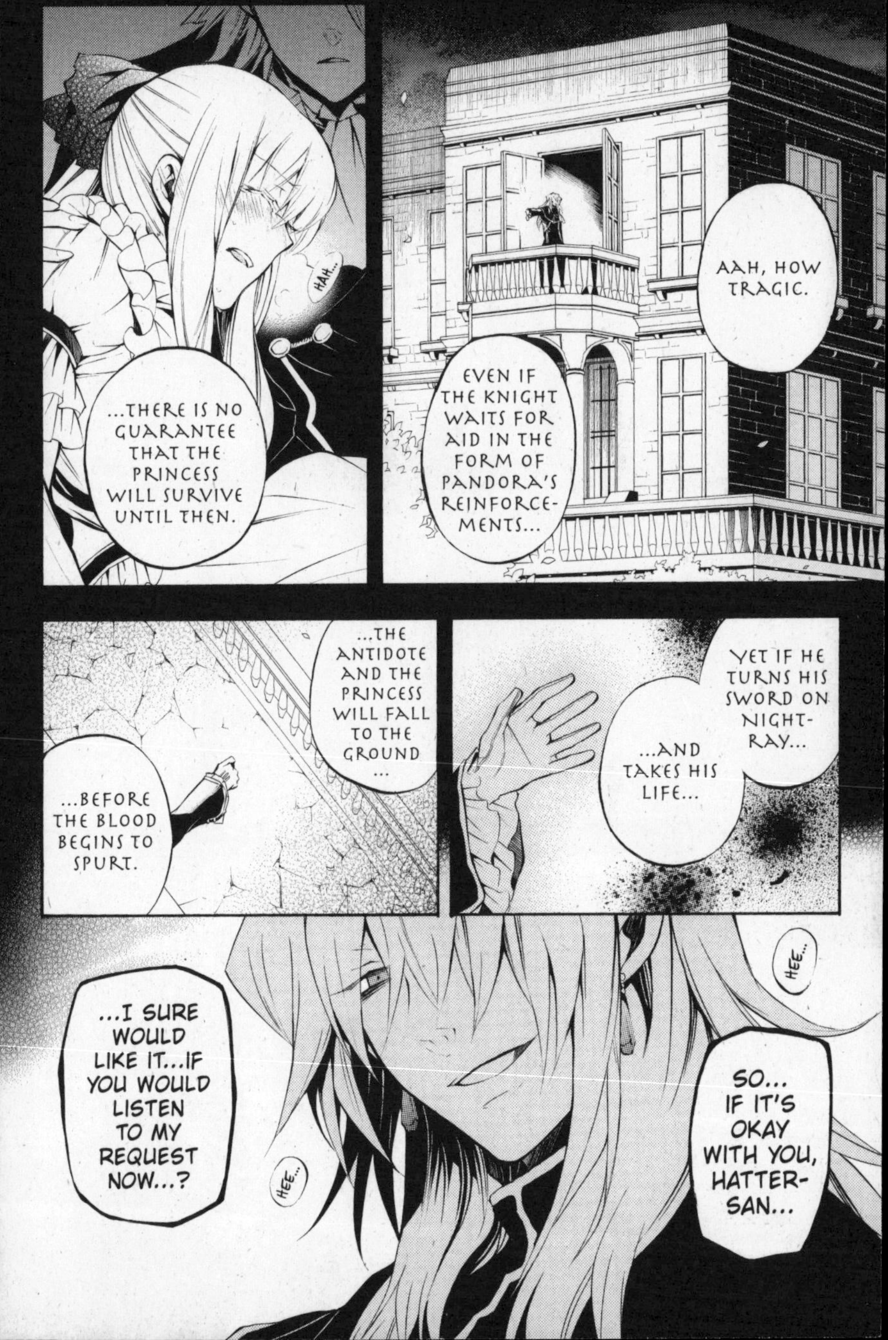
AAH, HOW TRAGIC.
EVEN IF THE KNIGHT WAITS FOR AID IN THE FORM OF PANDORA'S REINFORCE-MENTS...
HAH...
...THERE IS NO GUARANTEE THAT THE PRINCESS WILL SURVIVE UNTIL THEN.
YET IF HE TURNS HIS SWORD ON NIGHT-RAY...
...AND TAKES HIS LIFE...
...THE ANTIDOTE AND THE PRINCESS WILL FALL TO THE GROUND...
...BEFORE THE BLOOD BEGINS TO SPURT.
HEE...
SO... IF IT'S OKAY WITH YOU, HATTER-SAN...
...I SURE WOULD LIKE IT...IF YOU WOULD LISTEN TO MY REQUEST NOW...?
HEE...

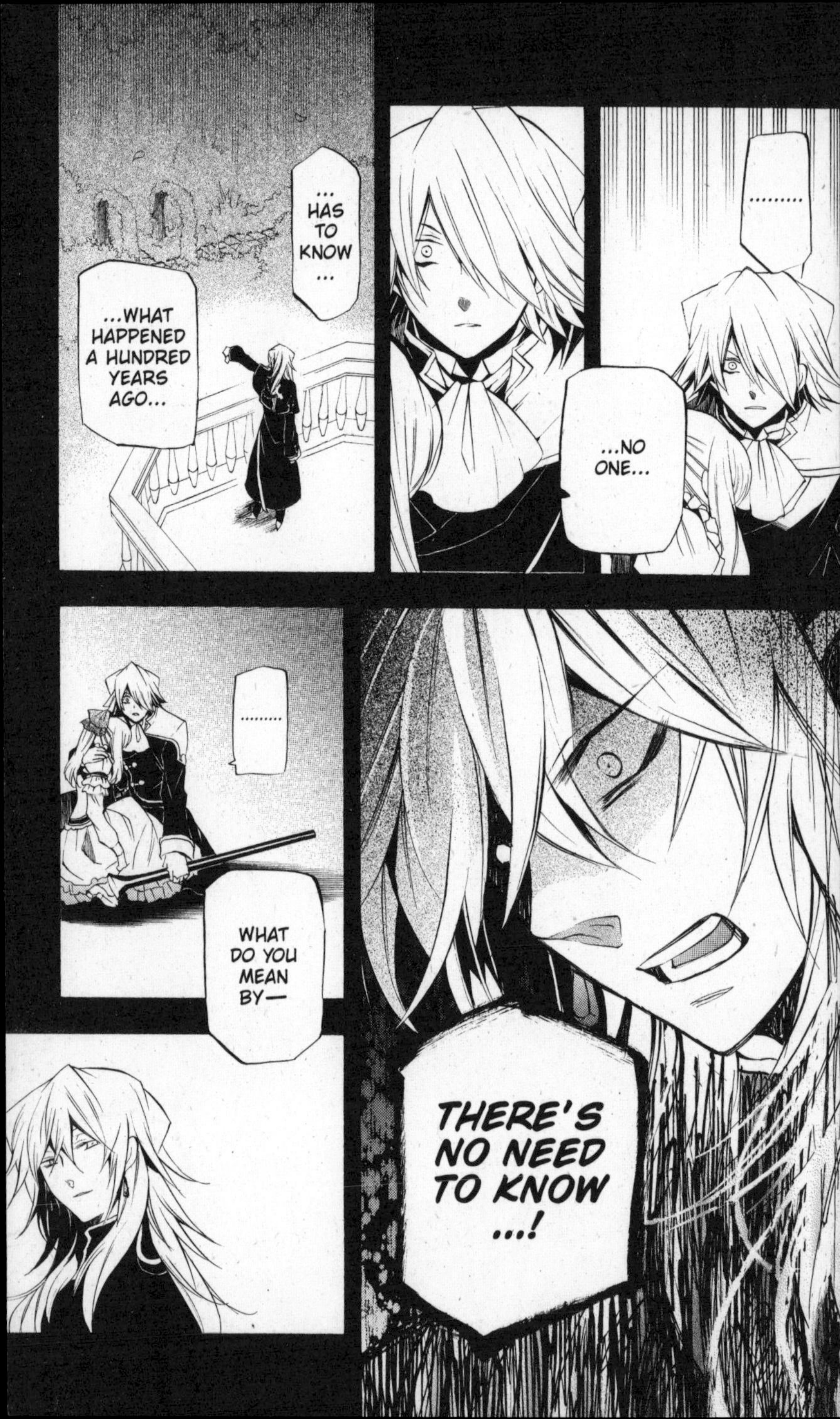
....
...NO ONE...
...HAS TO KNOW...
...WHAT HAPPENED A HUNDRED YEARS AGO...
THERE'S NO NEED TO KNOW ...!
....
WHAT DO YOU MEAN BY—

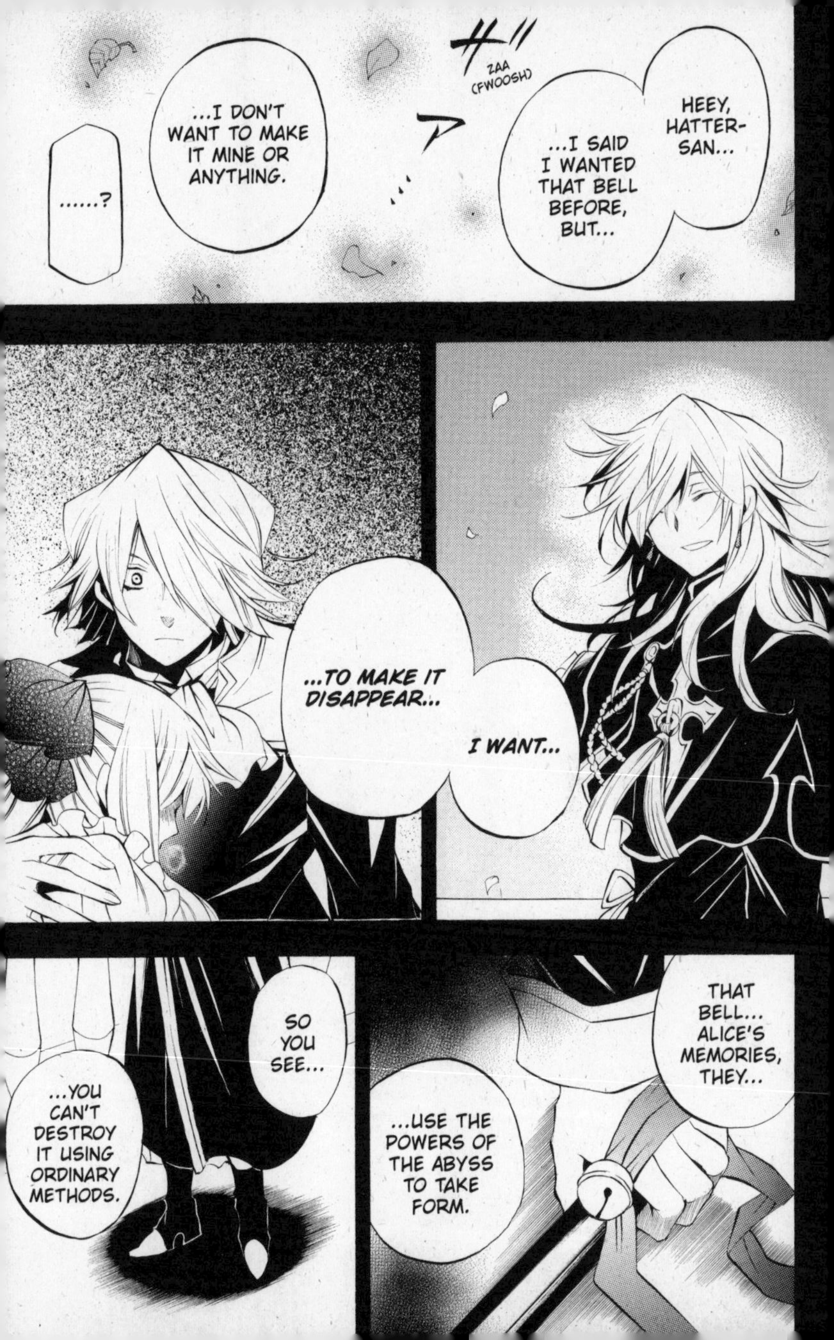
HEEY, HATTER-SAN...
...I SAID I WANTED THAT BELL BEFORE, BUT...
ZAA (FWOOSH)
...I DON'T WANT TO MAKE IT MINE OR ANYTHING.
......?
I WANT...
...TO MAKE IT DISAPPEAR...
THAT BELL... ALICE'S MEMORIES, THEY...
...USE THE POWERS OF THE ABYSS TO TAKE FORM.
SO YOU SEE...
...YOU CAN'T DESTROY IT USING ORDINARY METHODS.

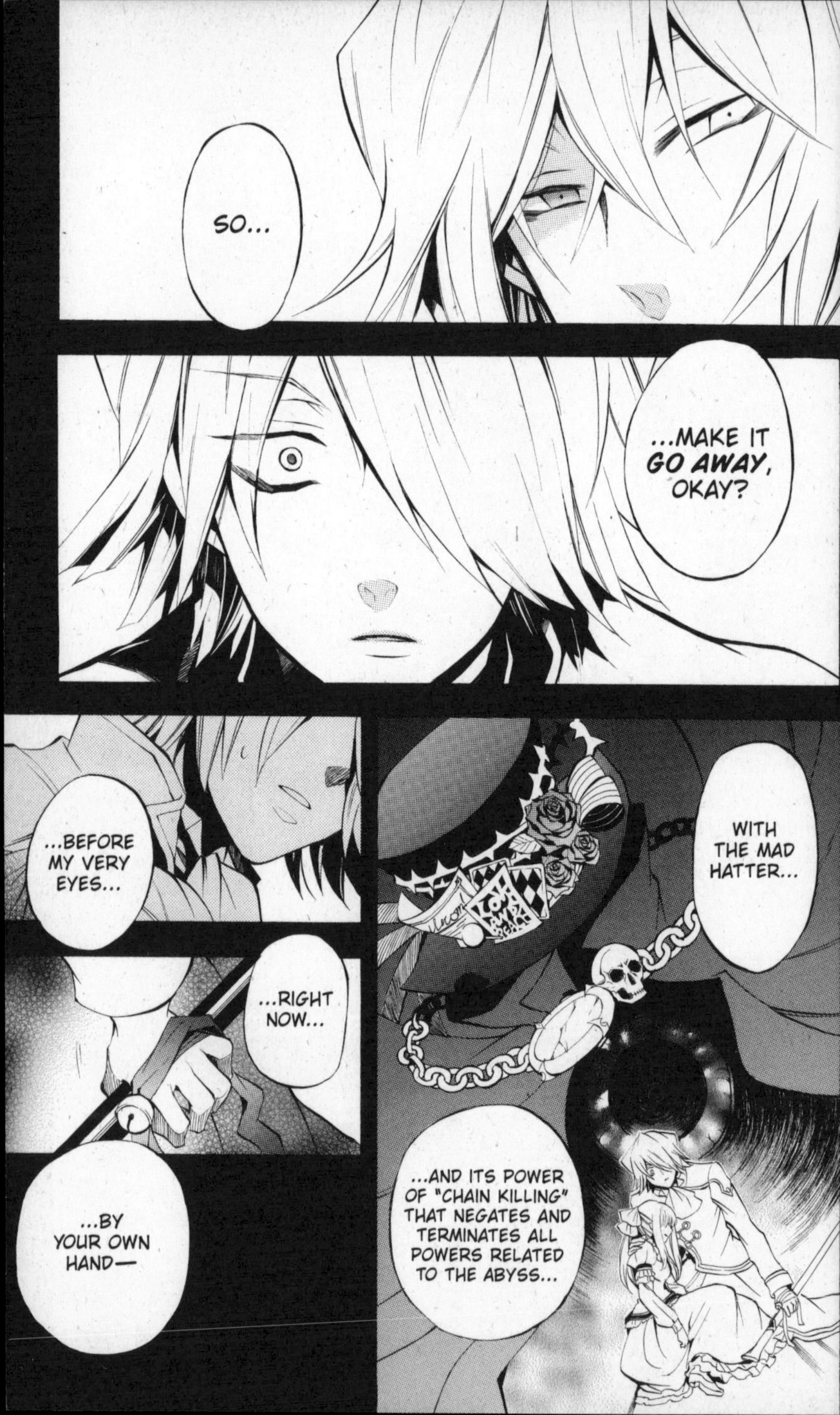
SO...
...MAKE IT GO AWAY, OKAY?
WITH THE MAD HATTER...
...AND ITS POWER OF "CHAIN KILLING" THAT NEGATES AND TERMINATES ALL POWERS RELATED TO THE ABYSS...
...BEFORE MY VERY EYES...
...RIGHT NOW...
...BY YOUR OWN HAND—

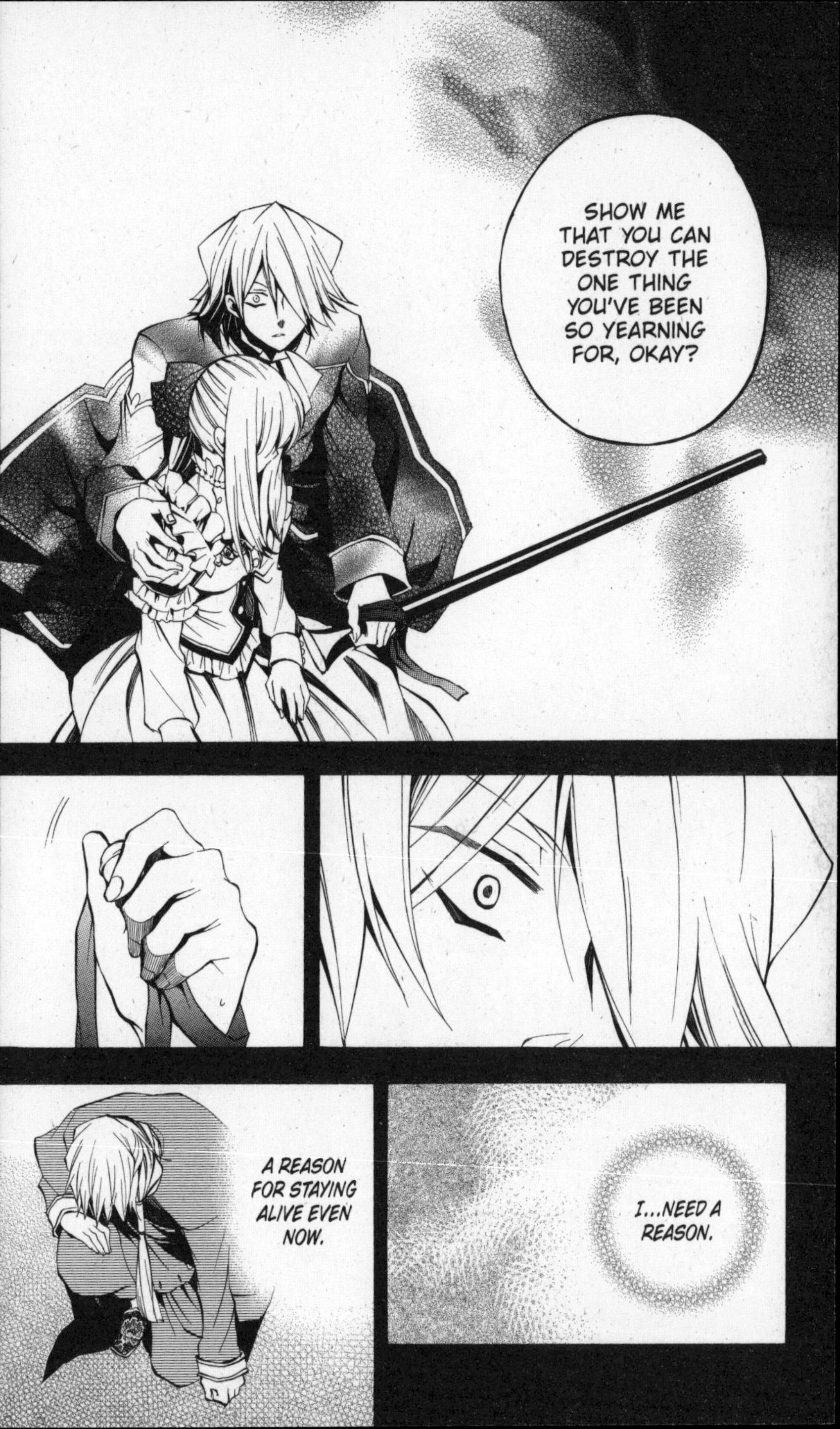
SHOW ME THAT YOU CAN DESTROY THE ONE THING YOU'VE BEEN SO YEARNING FOR, OKAY?
I...NEED A REASON.
A REASON FOR STAYING ALIVE EVEN NOW.

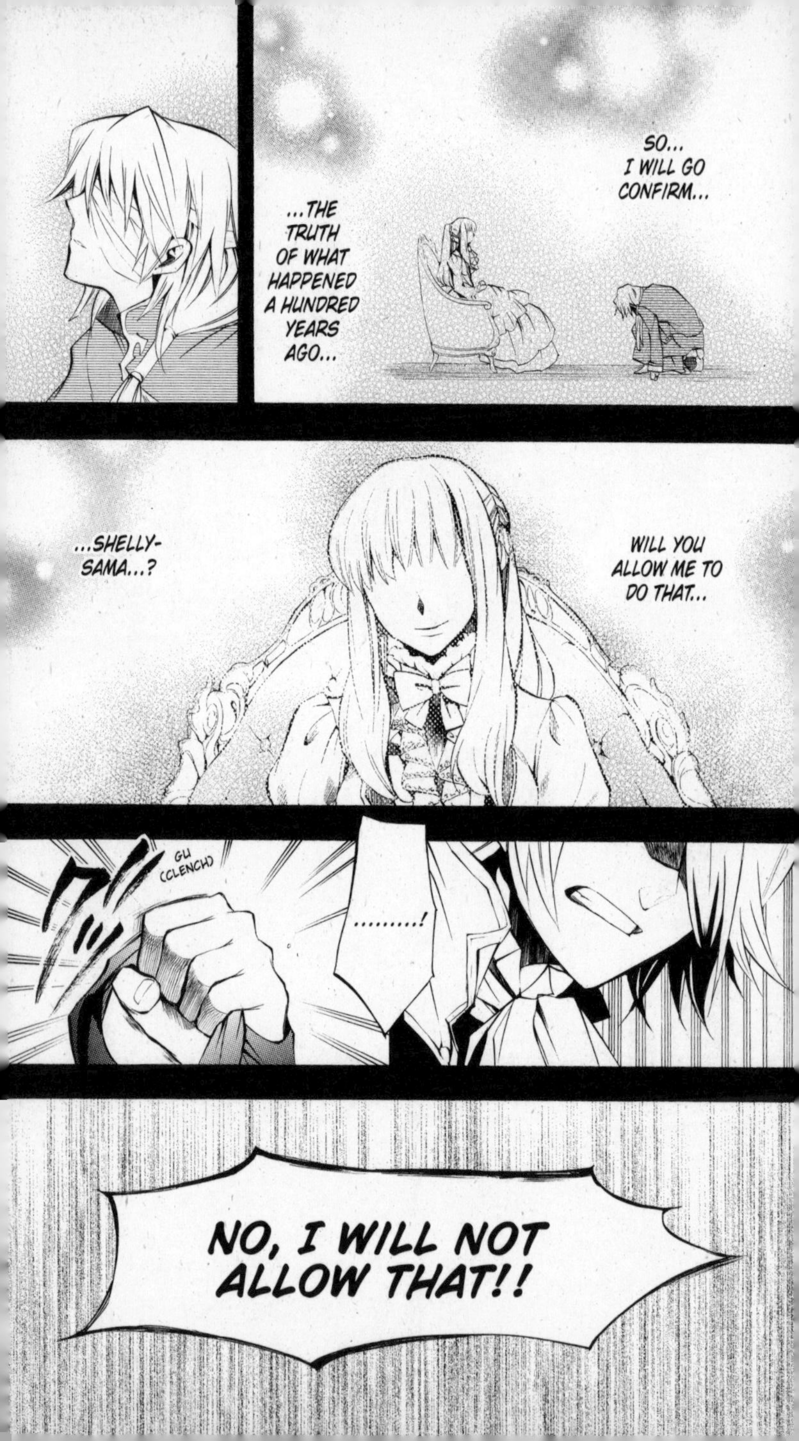
SO... I WILL GO CONFIRM...
...THE TRUTH OF WHAT HAPPENED A HUNDRED YEARS AGO...
WILL YOU ALLOW ME TO DO THAT...
...SHELLY-SAMA...?
.........!
GU (CLENCH)
NO, I WILL NOT ALLOW THAT!!

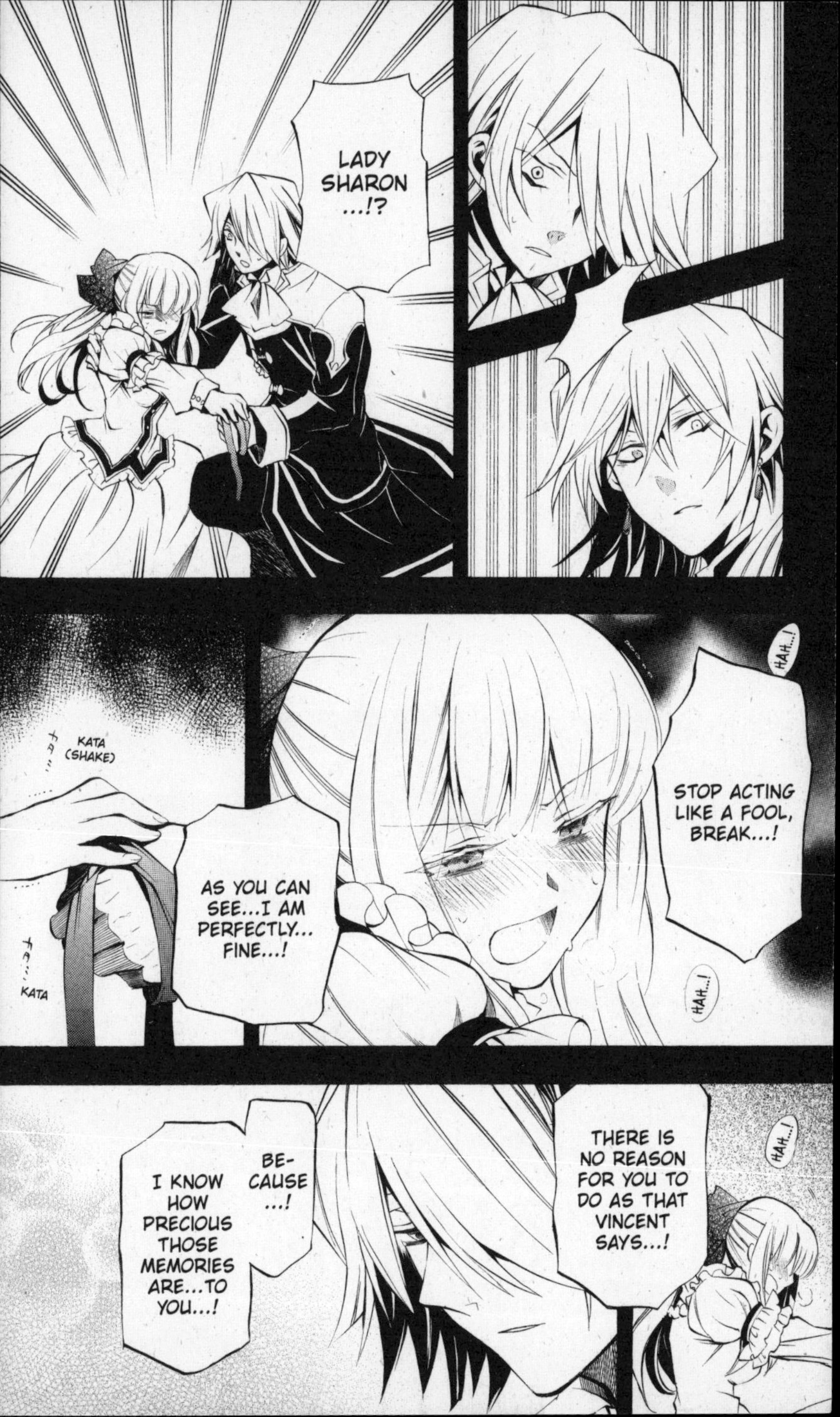
LADY SHARON ...!?
HAH...!
STOP ACTING LIKE A FOOL, BREAK...!
HAH...!
AS YOU CAN SEE...I AM PERFECTLY... FINE...!
KATA (SHAKE)
KATA
HAH...!
THERE IS NO REASON FOR YOU TO DO AS THAT VINCENT SAYS...!
BE-CAUSE ...!
I KNOW HOW PRECIOUS THOSE MEMORIES ARE...TO YOU...!

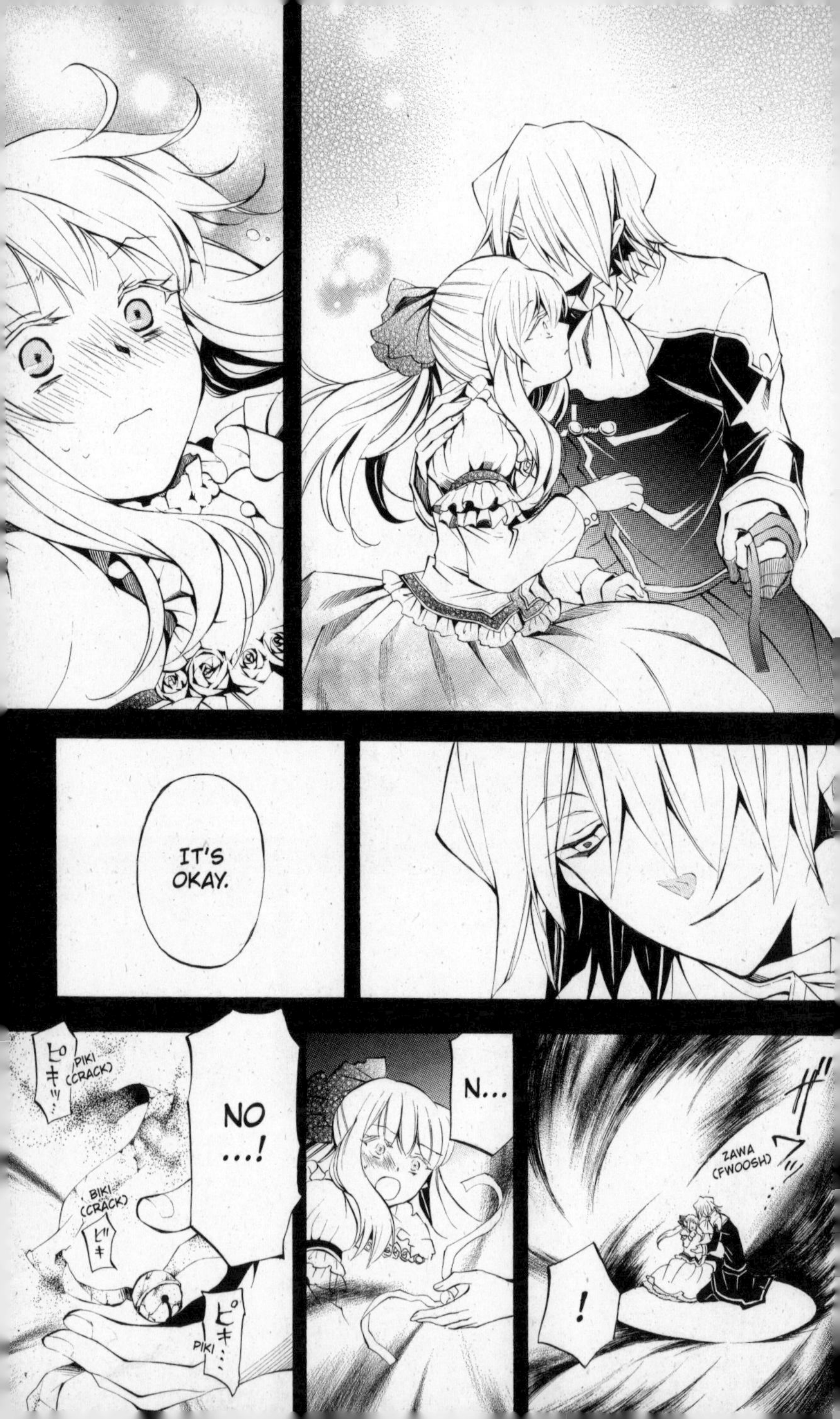
IT'S OKAY.
ザワッ
ZAWA (FWOOSH)
!
N...
NO ...!
ピキッ
PIKI (CRACK)
BIKI (CRACK)
ビキ
ピキ...
PIKI

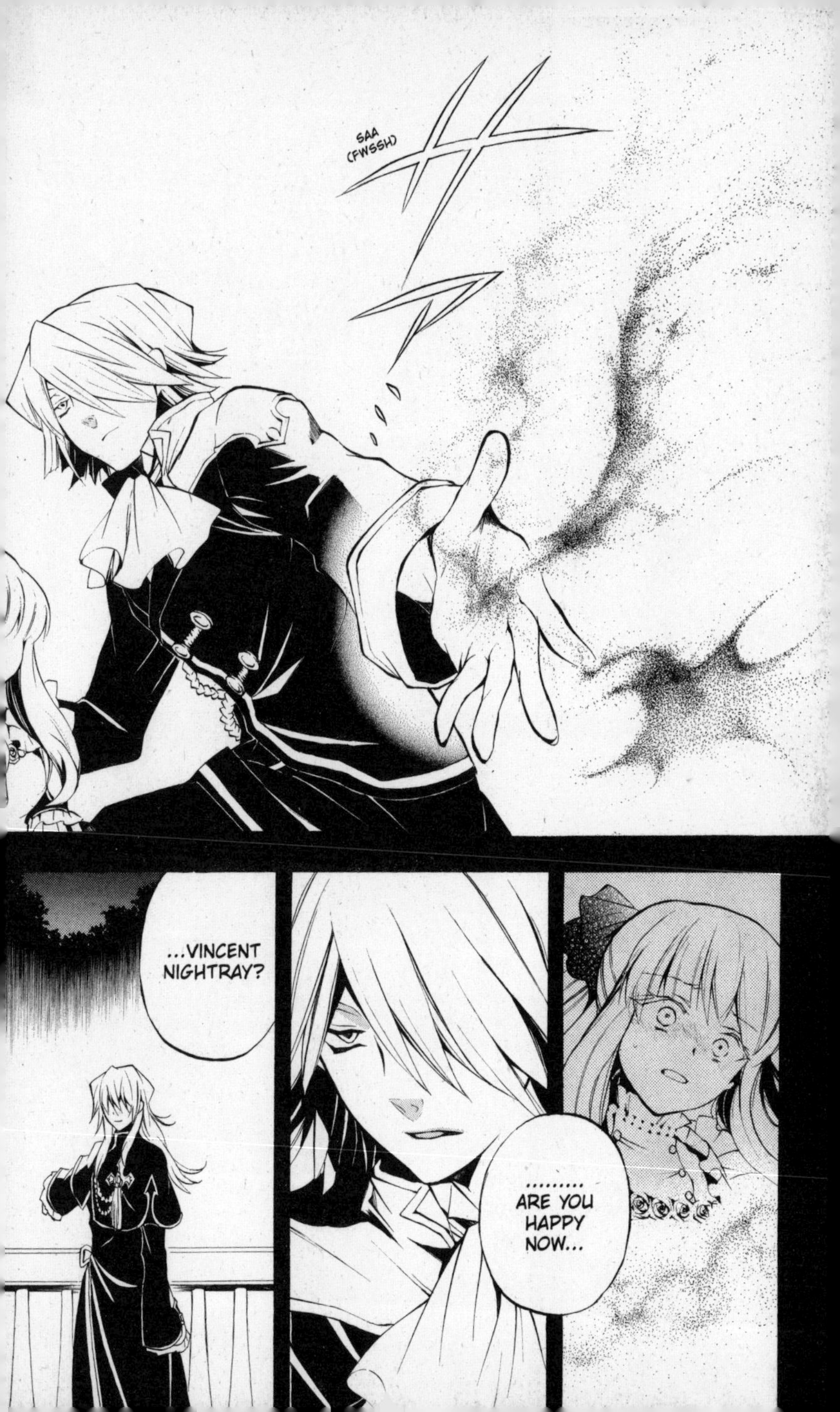
SAA (FWSSH)
....
ARE YOU HAPPY NOW...
...VINCENT NIGHTRAY?

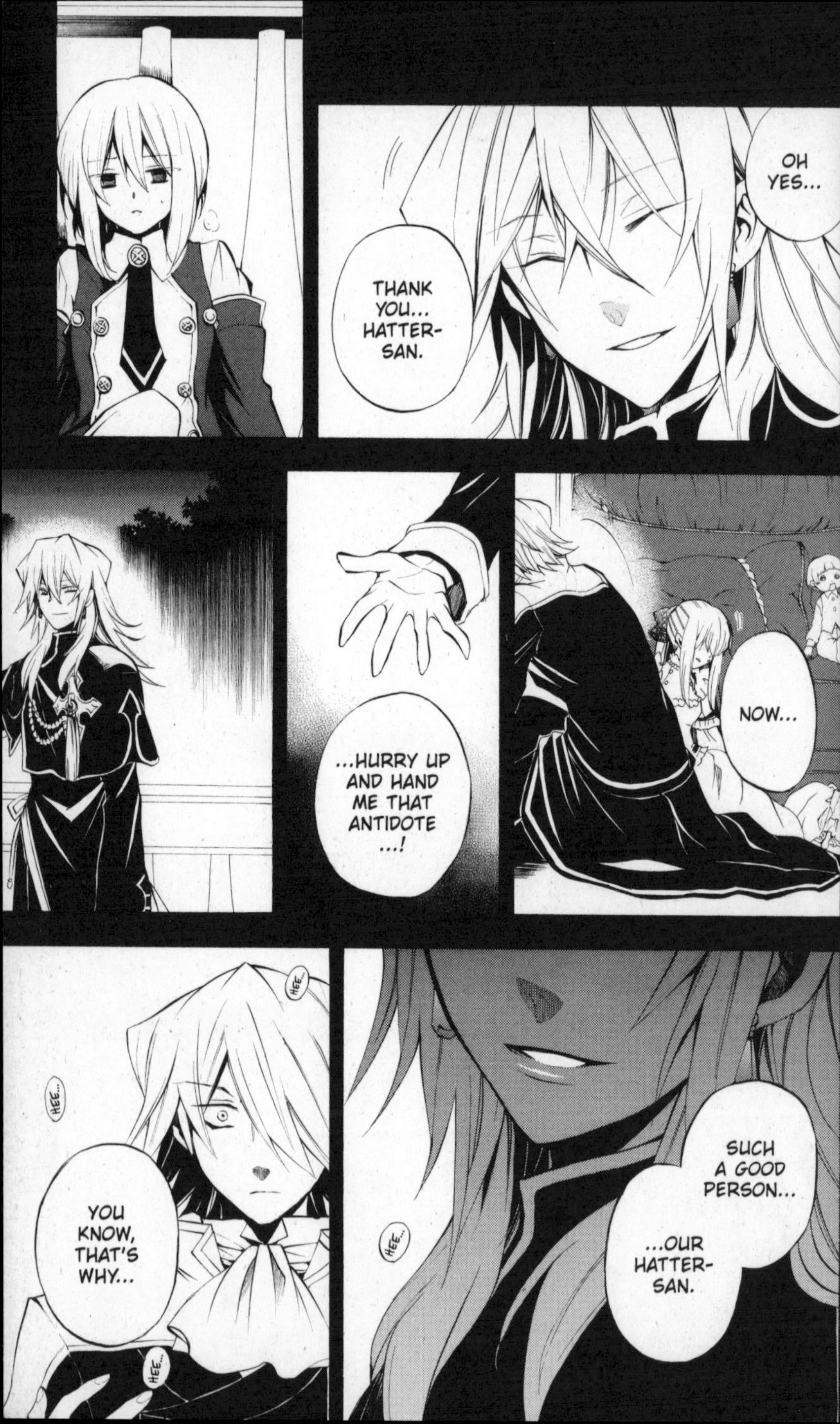
OH YES...
THANK YOU... HATTER-SAN.
NOW...
...HURRY UP AND HAND ME THAT ANTIDOTE ...!
SUCH A GOOD PERSON...
...OUR HATTER-SAN.
HEE...
HEE...
HEE...
YOU KNOW, THAT'S WHY...
HEE...

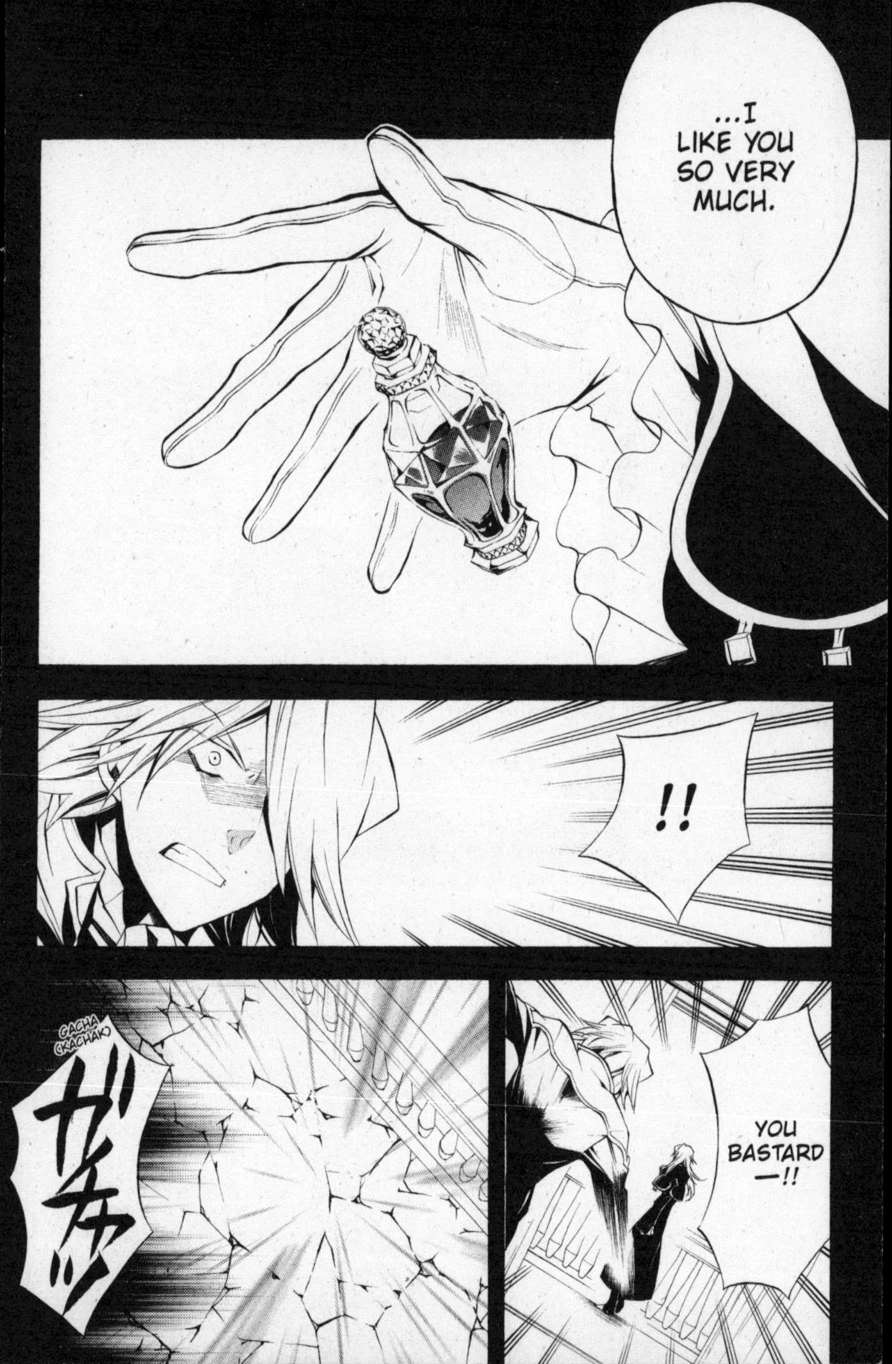
...I LIKE YOU SO VERY MUCH.
!!
YOU BASTARD—!!
GACHA (KACHAK)
ガチャ!!

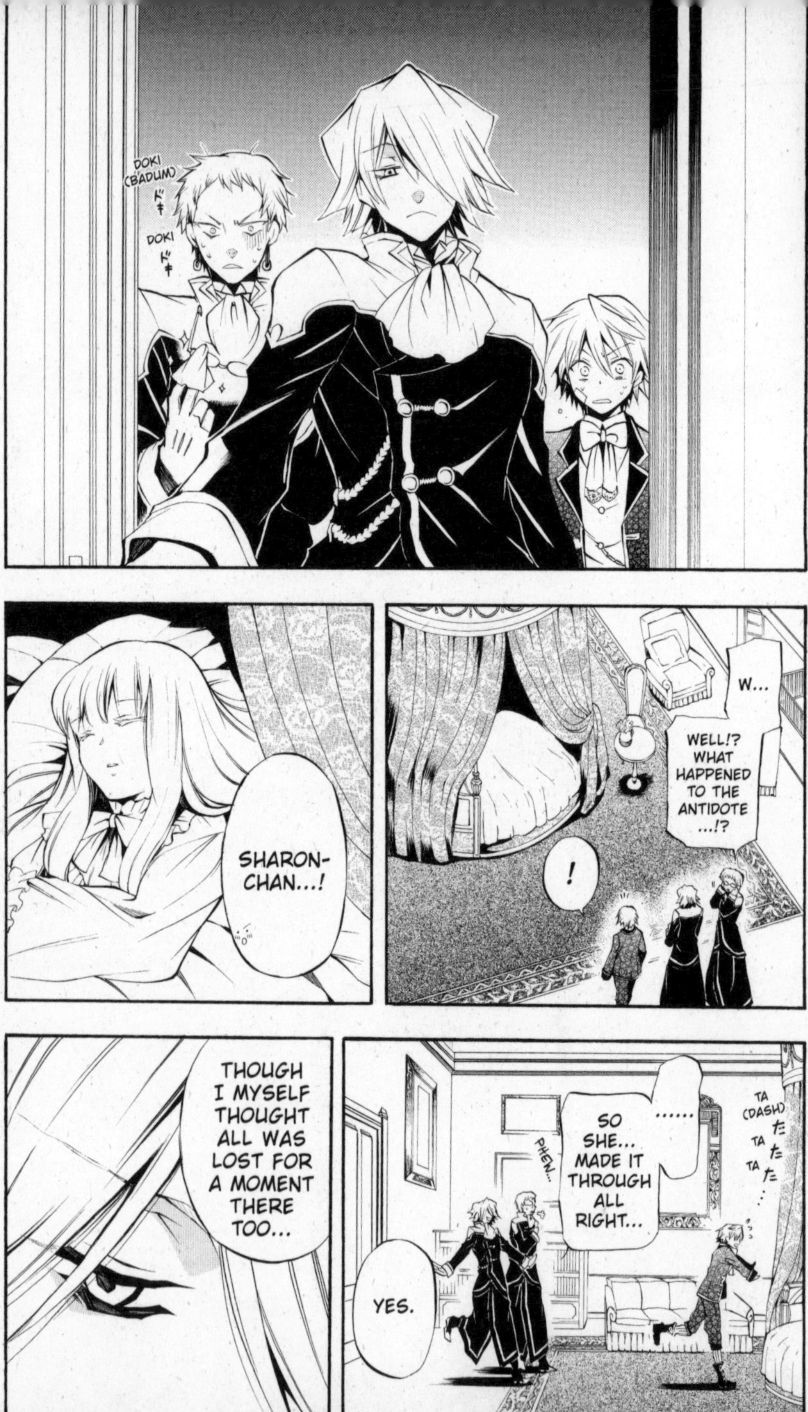
DOKI (BADUM)
ドキ
DOKI
ドキ
W...
WELL!? WHAT HAPPENED TO THE ANTIDOTE ...!?
!
SHARON-CHAN...!
TA (DASH)
たたた
TA
TA
......
SO SHE... MADE IT THROUGH ALL RIGHT...
PHEW...
YES.
THOUGH I MYSELF THOUGHT ALL WAS LOST FOR A MOMENT THERE TOO...

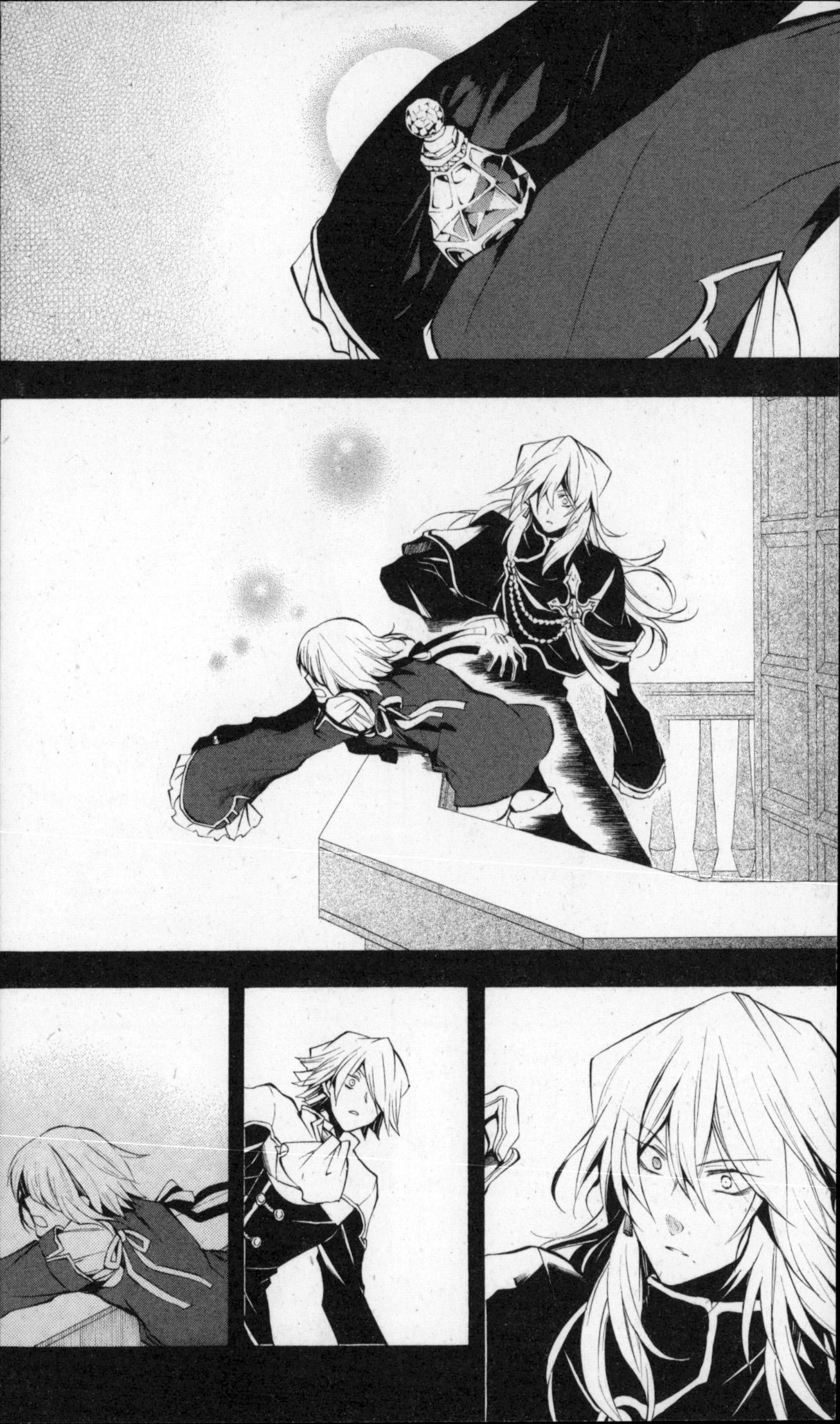

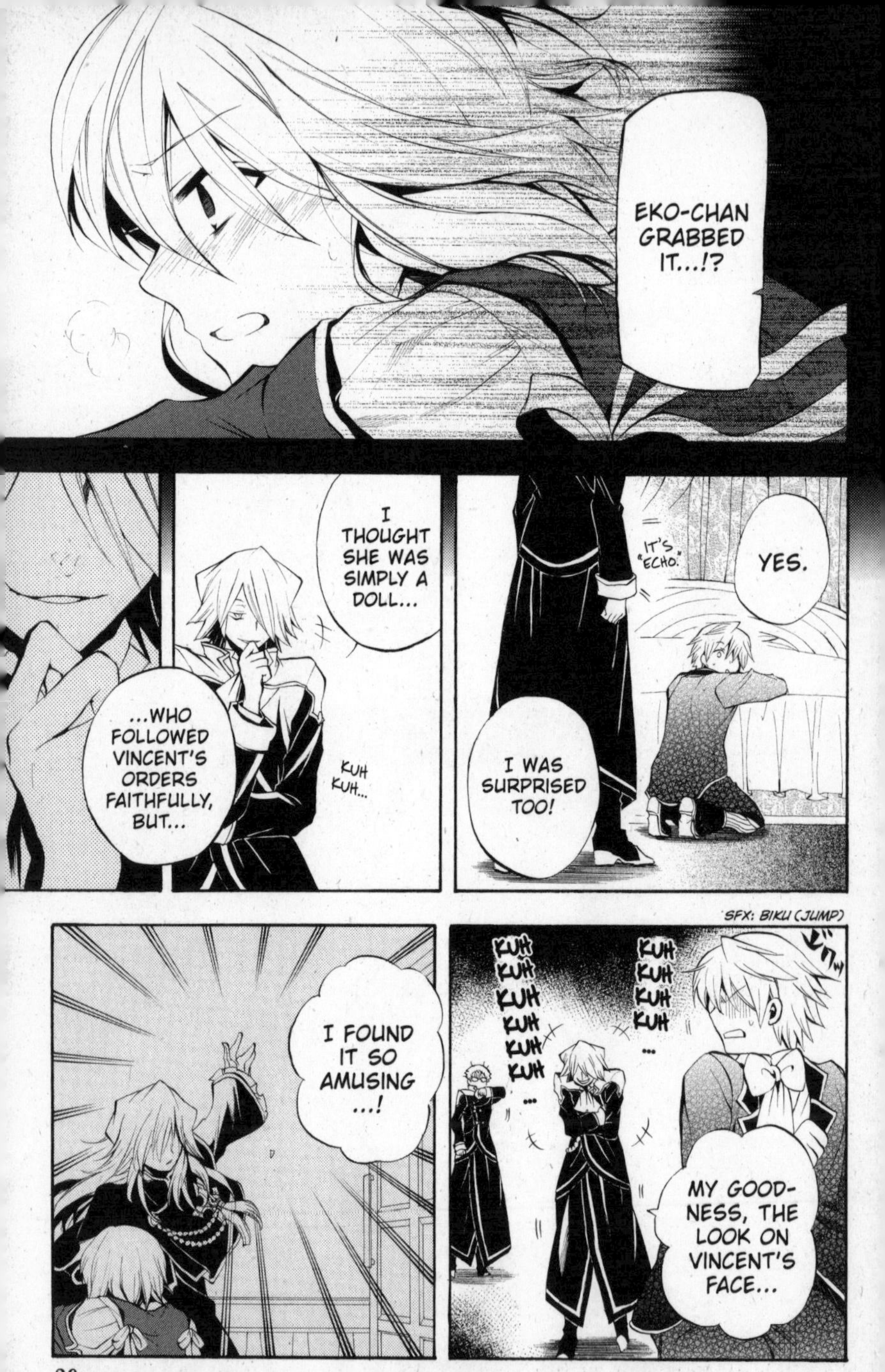
EKO-CHAN GRABBED IT...!?
YES.
IT'S "ECHO."
I WAS SURPRISED TOO!
I THOUGHT SHE WAS SIMPLY A DOLL...
KUH KUH...
...WHO FOLLOWED VINCENT'S ORDERS FAITHFULLY, BUT...
SFX: BIKU (JUMP)
KUH KUH KUH KUH ...
KUH KUH KUH KUH KUH KUH ...
MY GOOD-NESS, THE LOOK ON VINCENT'S FACE...
I FOUND IT SO AMUSING ...!

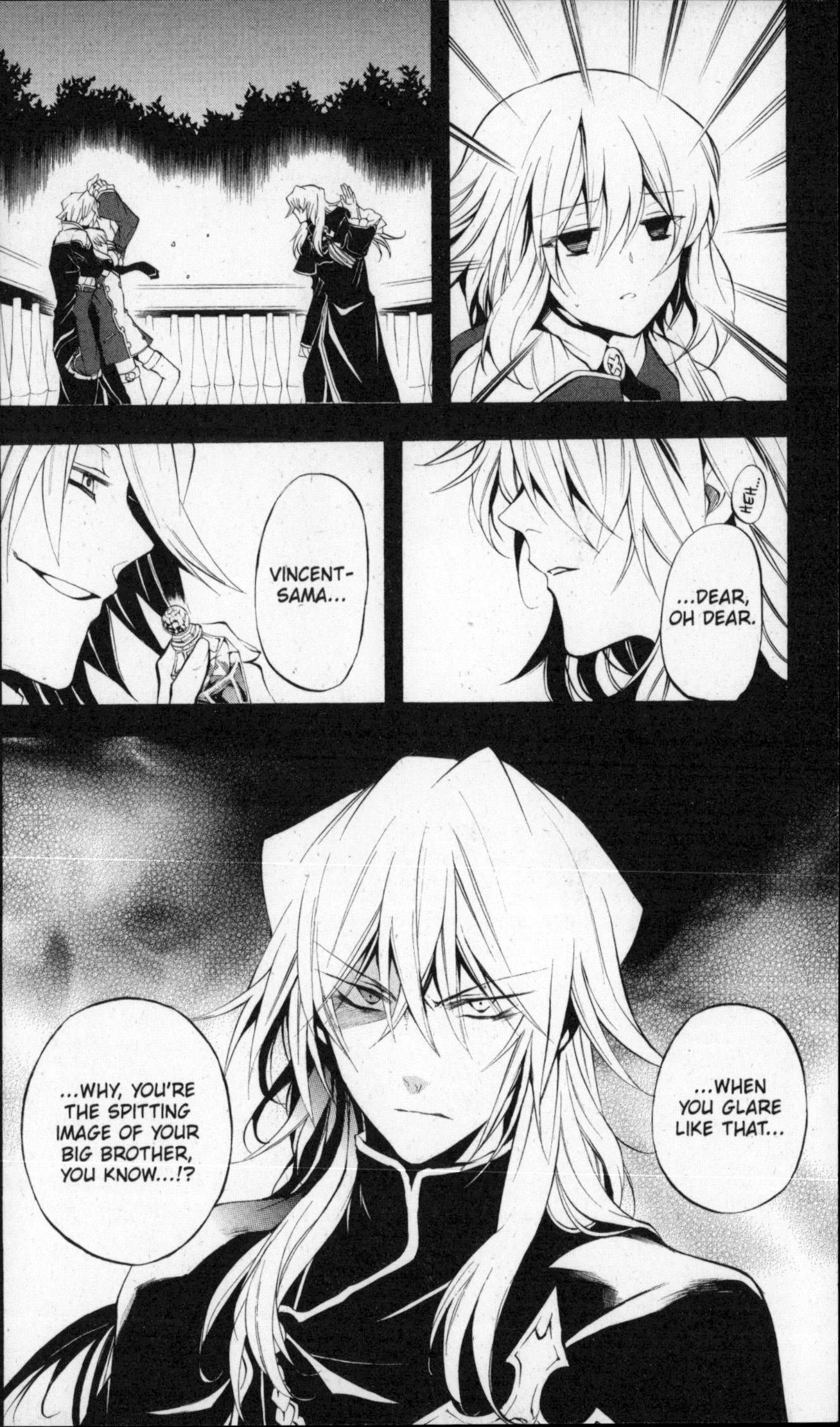
HEH...
...DEAR, OH DEAR.
VINCENT-SAMA...
...WHEN YOU GLARE LIKE THAT...
...WHY, YOU'RE THE SPITTING IMAGE OF YOUR BIG BROTHER, YOU KNOW...!?

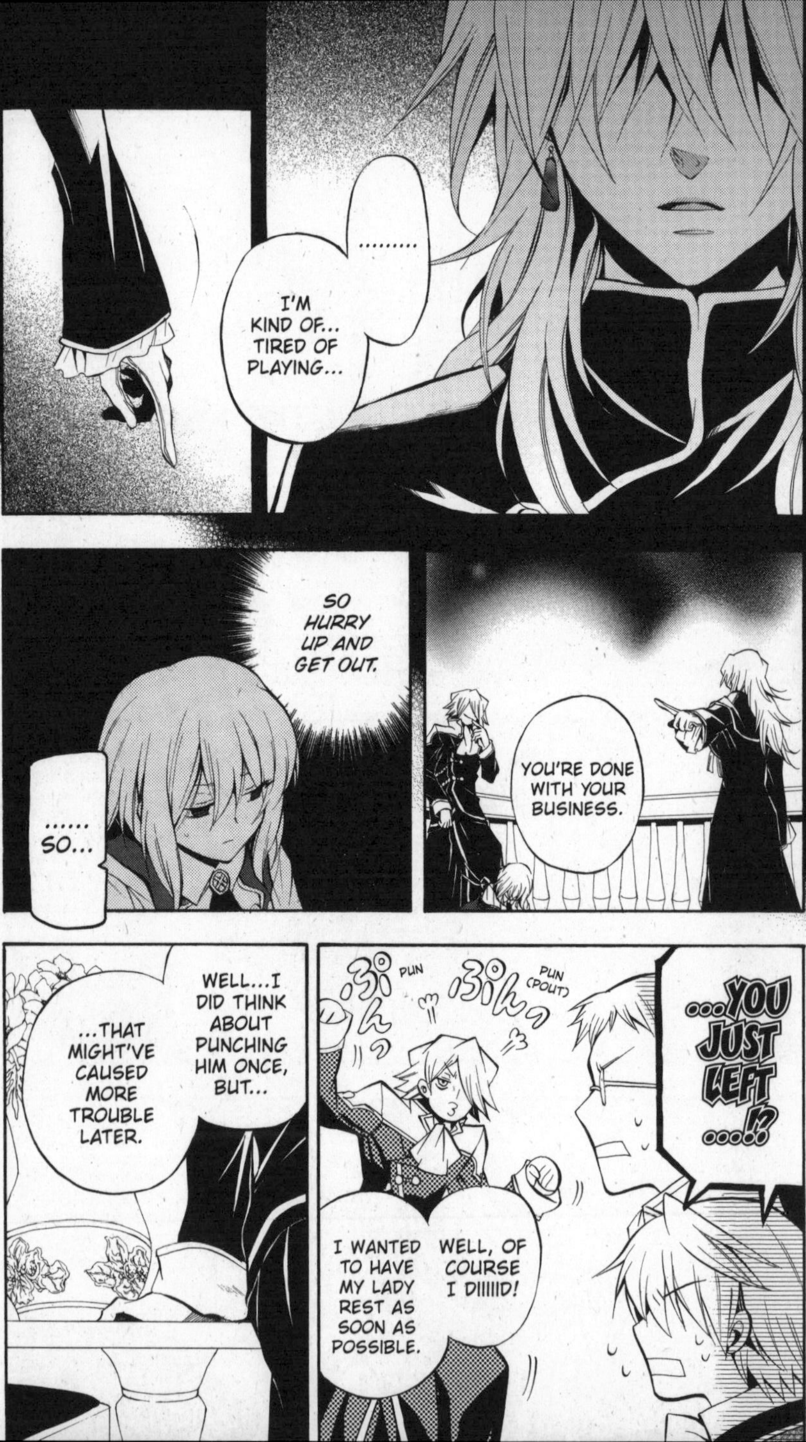
....
I'M KIND OF... TIRED OF PLAYING...
YOU'RE DONE WITH YOUR BUSINESS.
SO HURRY UP AND GET OUT.
...... SO...
...YOU JUST LEFT...!?
PUN
PUN (POUT)
WELL, OF COURSE I DIIIIID!
I WANTED TO HAVE MY LADY REST AS SOON AS POSSIBLE.
WELL...I DID THINK ABOUT PUNCHING HIM ONCE, BUT...
...THAT MIGHT'VE CAUSED MORE TROUBLE LATER.

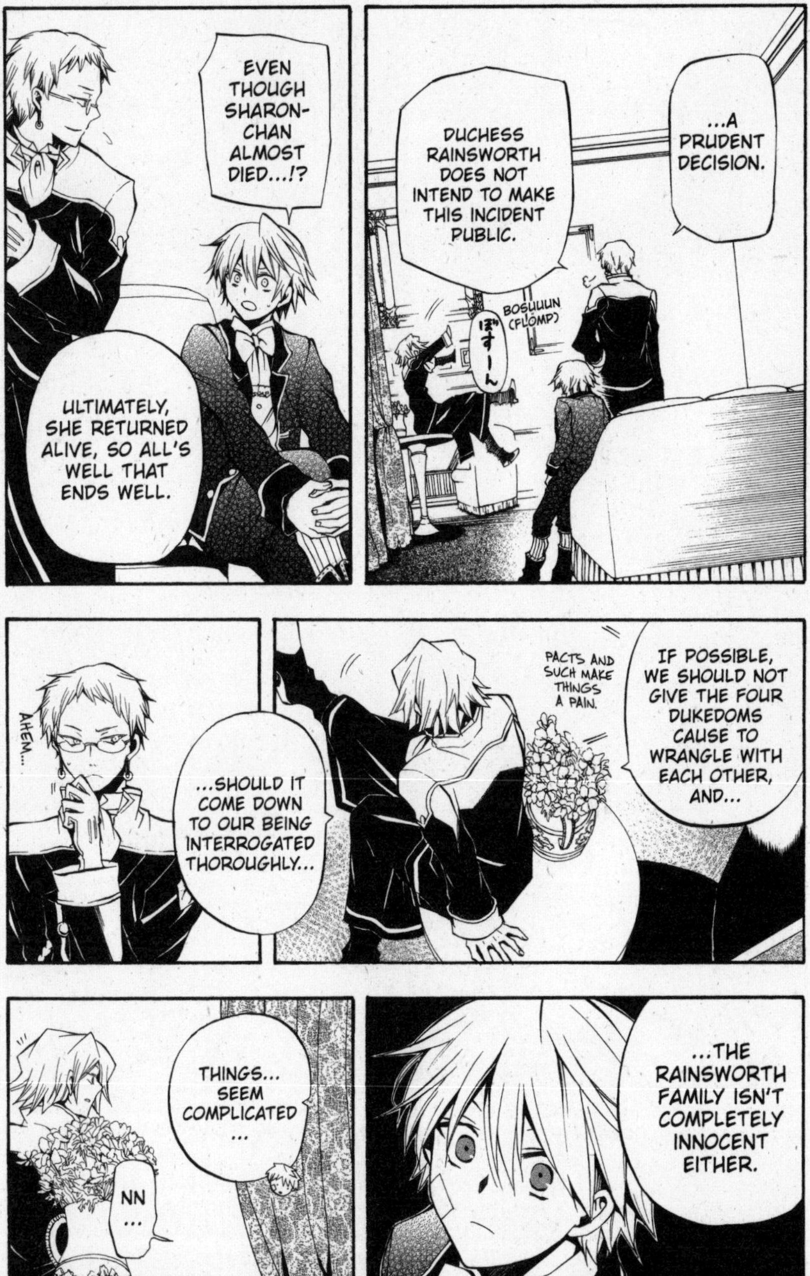
...A PRUDENT DECISION.
DUCHESS RAINSWORTH DOES NOT INTEND TO MAKE THIS INCIDENT PUBLIC.
BOSUUN (FLOMP)
ぼすーん
EVEN THOUGH SHARON-CHAN ALMOST DIED...!?
ULTIMATELY, SHE RETURNED ALIVE, SO ALL'S WELL THAT ENDS WELL.
IF POSSIBLE, WE SHOULD NOT GIVE THE FOUR DUKEDOMS CAUSE TO WRANGLE WITH EACH OTHER, AND...
PACTS AND SUCH MAKE THINGS A PAIN.
AHEM...
...SHOULD IT COME DOWN TO OUR BEING INTERROGATED THOROUGHLY...
...THE RAINSWORTH FAMILY ISN'T COMPLETELY INNOCENT EITHER.
THINGS... SEEM COMPLICATED...
NN...

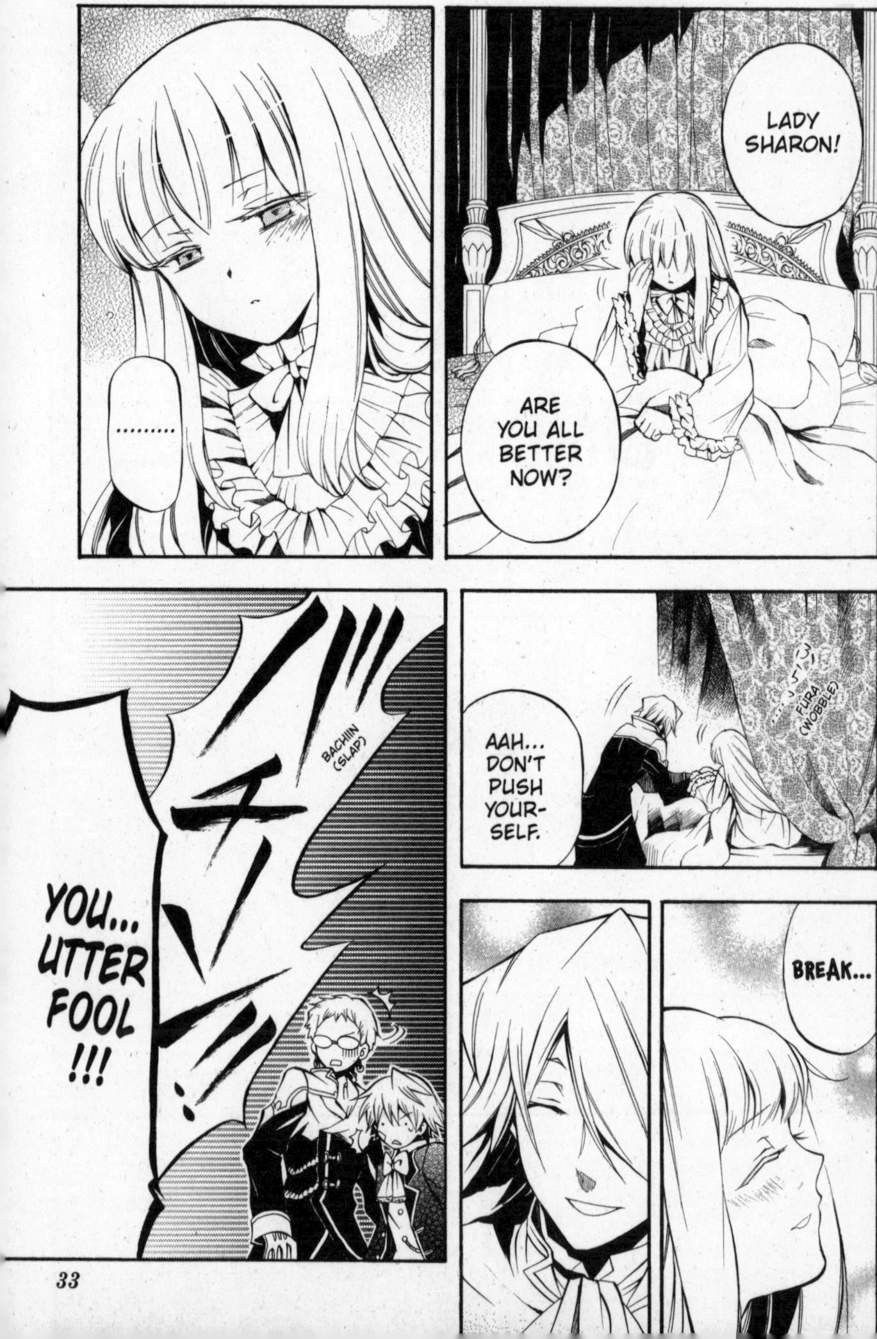
LADY SHARON!
ARE YOU ALL BETTER NOW?
....
FURA (WOBBLE)
AAH... DON'T PUSH YOURSELF.
BREAK...
BACHIIN (SLAP)
YOU... UTTER FOOL!!!

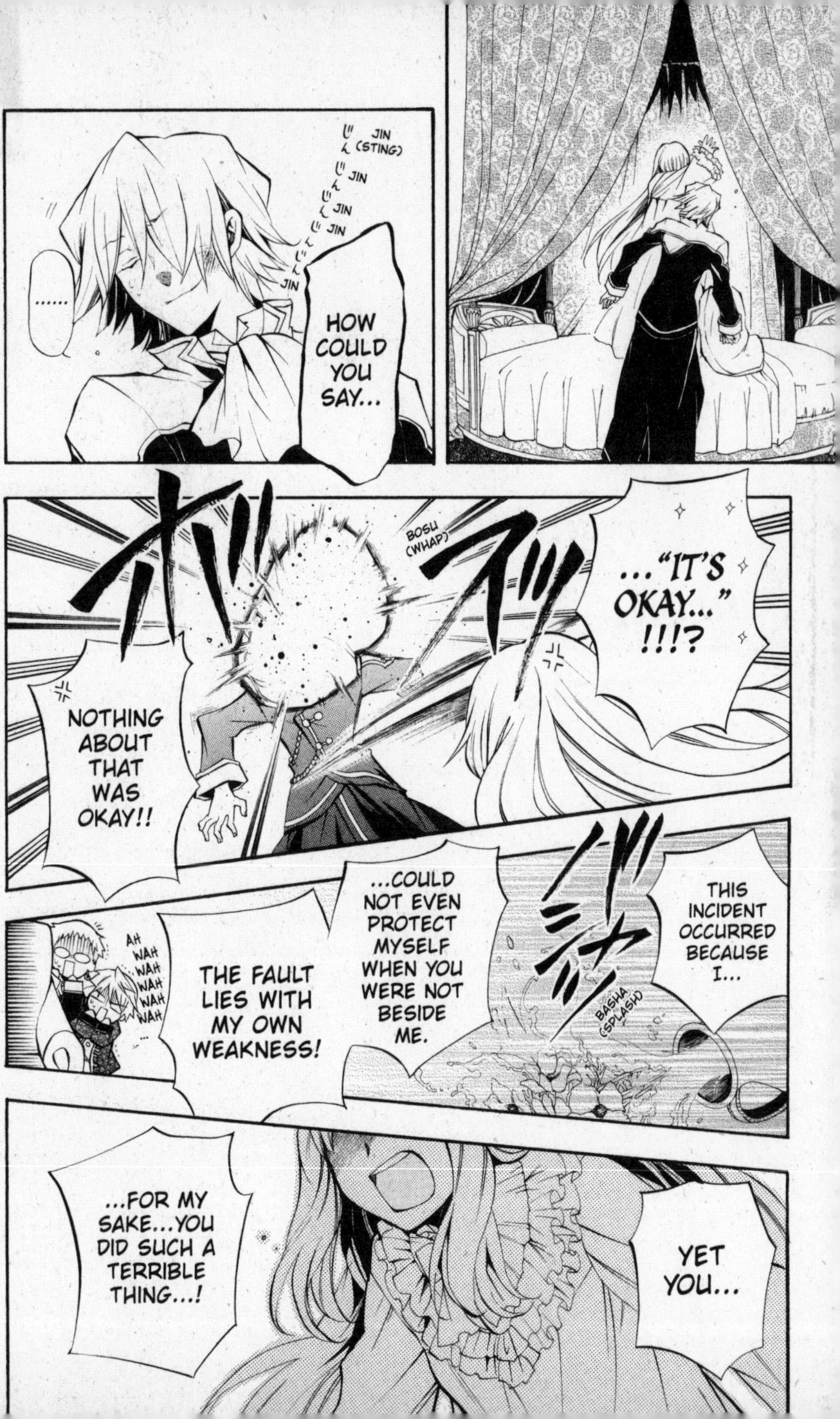

JIN (STING) JIN JIN JIN JIN
HOW COULD YOU SAY...
......
..."IT'S OKAY..." !!!?
BOSU (WHAP)
NOTHING ABOUT THAT WAS OKAY!!
THIS INCIDENT OCCURRED BECAUSE I...
BASHA (SPLASH)
...COULD NOT EVEN PROTECT MYSELF WHEN YOU WERE NOT BESIDE ME.
THE FAULT LIES WITH MY OWN WEAKNESS!
AH WAH WAH WAH WAH WAH ...
YET YOU...
...FOR MY SAKE...YOU DID SUCH A TERRIBLE THING...!

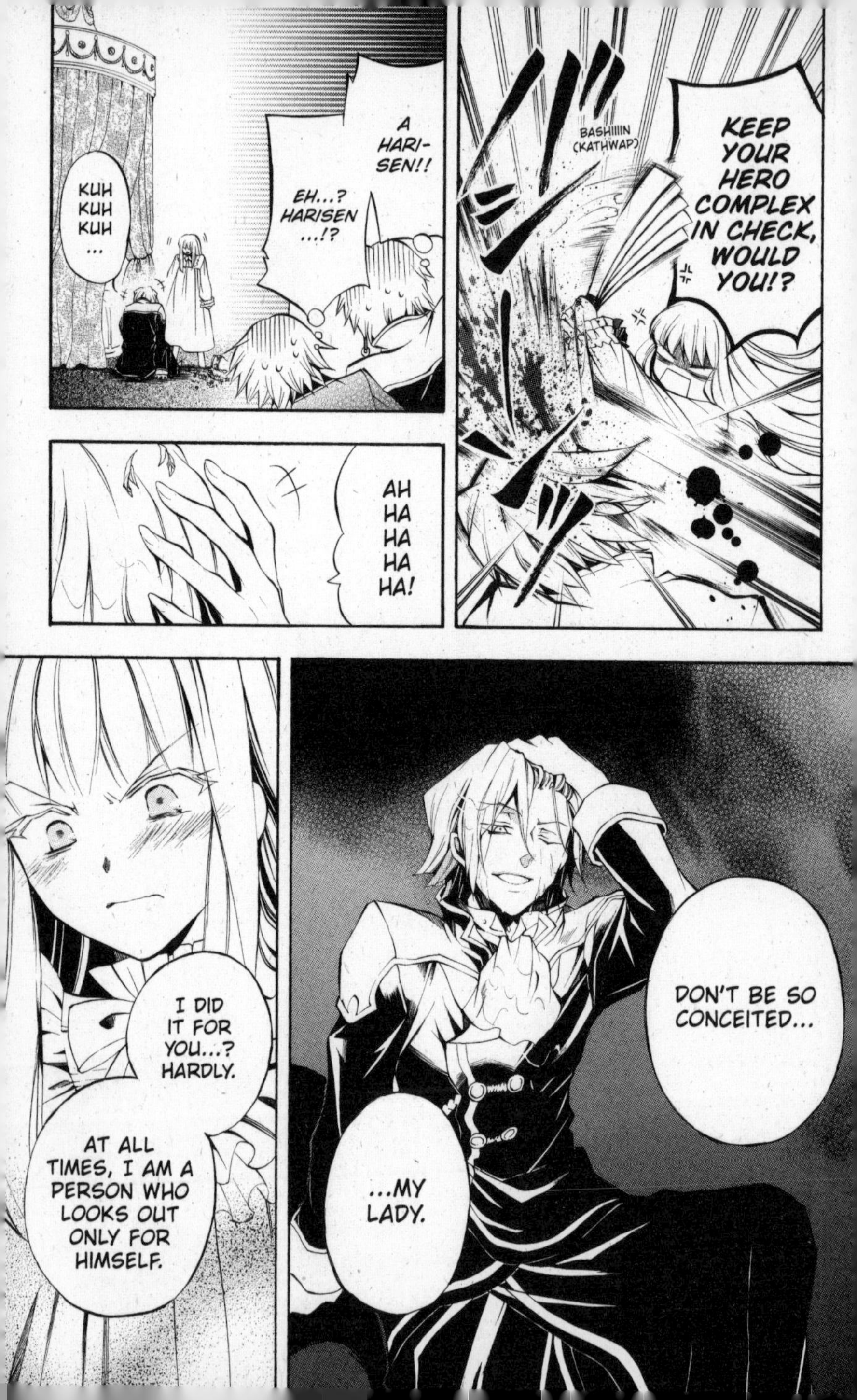
BASHIIIIN (KATHWAP)
KEEP YOUR HERO COMPLEX IN CHECK, WOULD YOU!?
A HARI-SEN!!
EH...? HARISEN ...!?
KUH KUH KUH ...
AH HA HA HA HA!
DON'T BE SO CONCEITED...
...MY LADY.
I DID IT FOR YOU...? HARDLY.
AT ALL TIMES, I AM A PERSON WHO LOOKS OUT ONLY FOR HIMSELF.

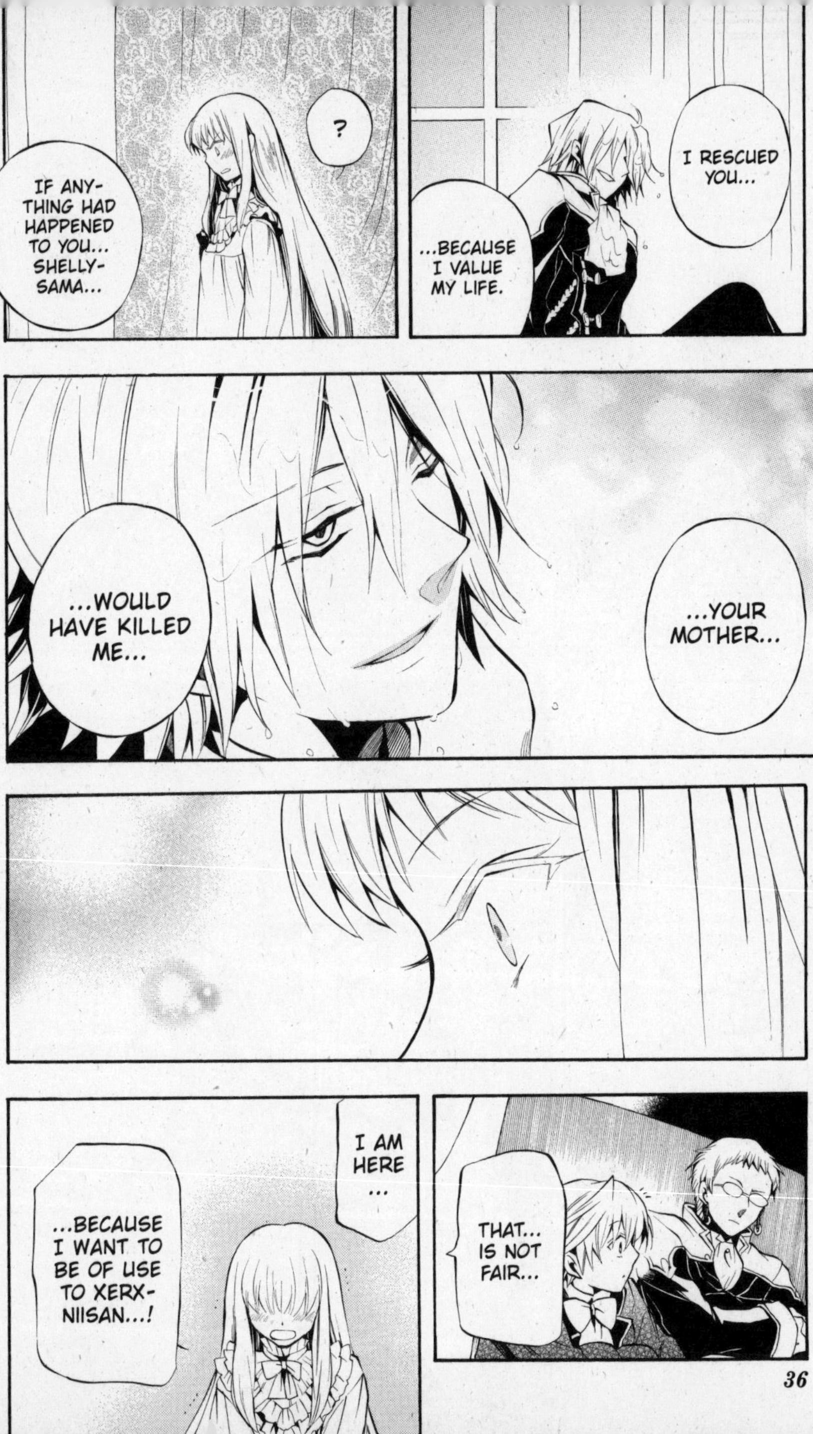
I RESCUED YOU...
...BECAUSE I VALUE MY LIFE.
?
IF ANY-THING HAD HAPPENED TO YOU... SHELLY-SAMA...
...YOUR MOTHER...
...WOULD HAVE KILLED ME...
THAT... IS NOT FAIR...
I AM HERE...
...BECAUSE I WANT TO BE OF USE TO XERX-NIISAN...!

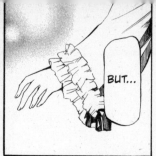

BUT...
UU...
UU...!
......
WAAAAAAAAH!
COME. THERE, THERE NOW.
SHOO!
SHOO!
SO (SNEAK) SO
KII (CREAK)
—"XERX-NIISAN"?
AAH... SHE IS REFERRING TO XERXES.
SHE USED TO CALL HIM THAT WHEN SHE WAS LITTLE.

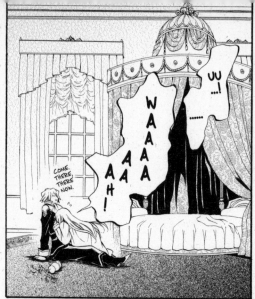

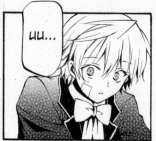

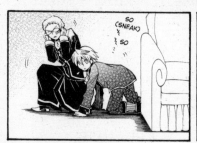

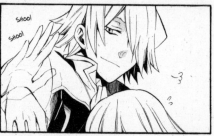

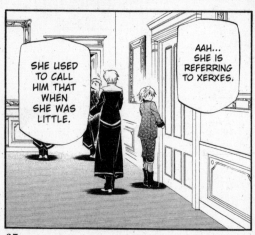

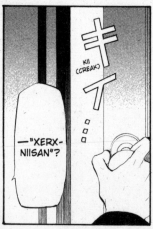

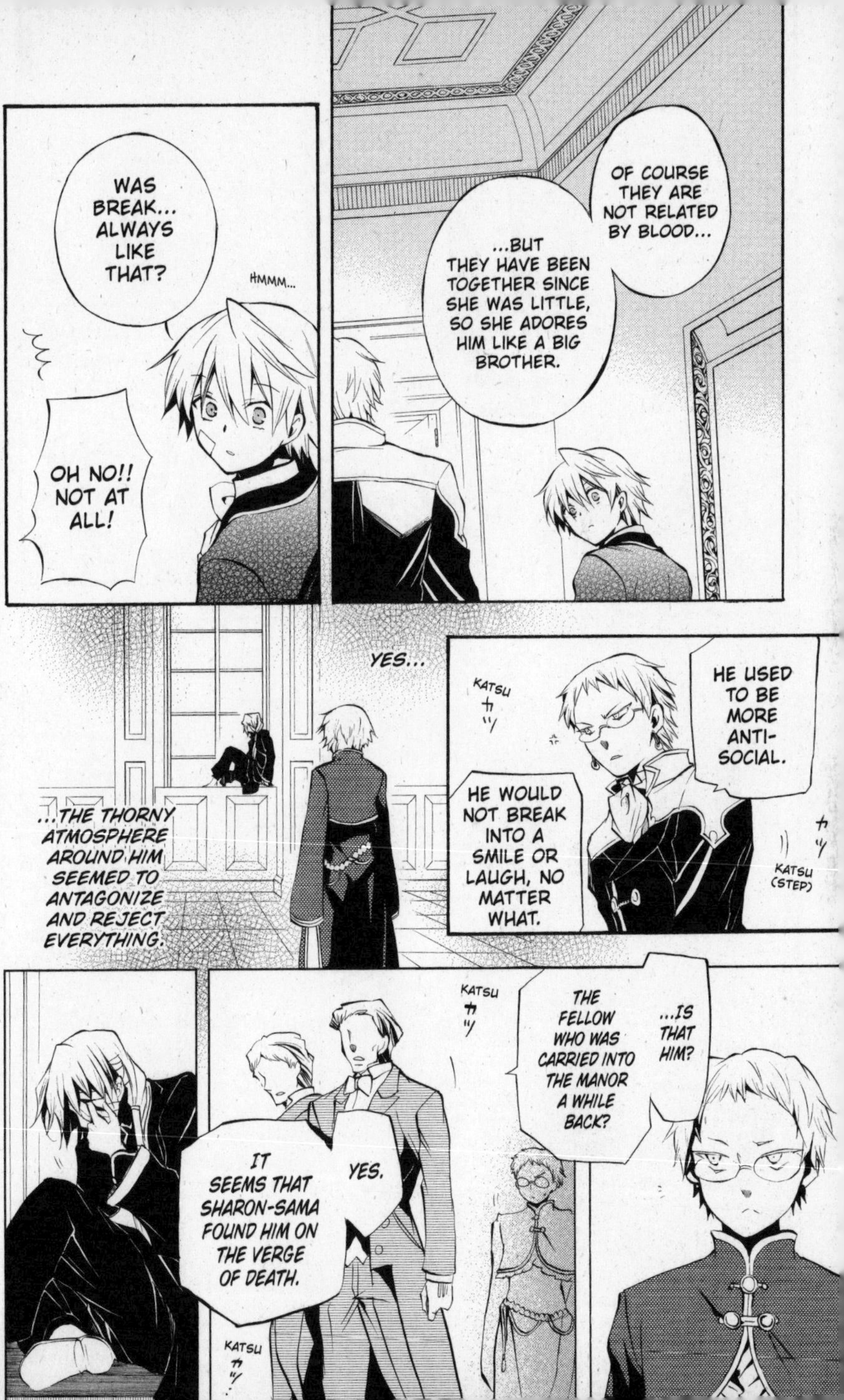
OF COURSE THEY ARE NOT RELATED BY BLOOD...
...BUT THEY HAVE BEEN TOGETHER SINCE SHE WAS LITTLE, SO SHE ADORES HIM LIKE A BIG BROTHER.
WAS BREAK... ALWAYS LIKE THAT?
HMMM...
OH NO!! NOT AT ALL!
HE USED TO BE MORE ANTI-SOCIAL.
カツ KATSU (STEP)
KATSU カツ
HE WOULD NOT BREAK INTO A SMILE OR LAUGH, NO MATTER WHAT.
YES...
...THE THORNY ATMOSPHERE AROUND HIM SEEMED TO ANTAGONIZE AND REJECT EVERYTHING.
...IS THAT HIM?
THE FELLOW WHO WAS CARRIED INTO THE MANOR A WHILE BACK?
KATSU カツ
YES.
IT SEEMS THAT SHARON-SAMA FOUND HIM ON THE VERGE OF DEATH.
KATSU カツ

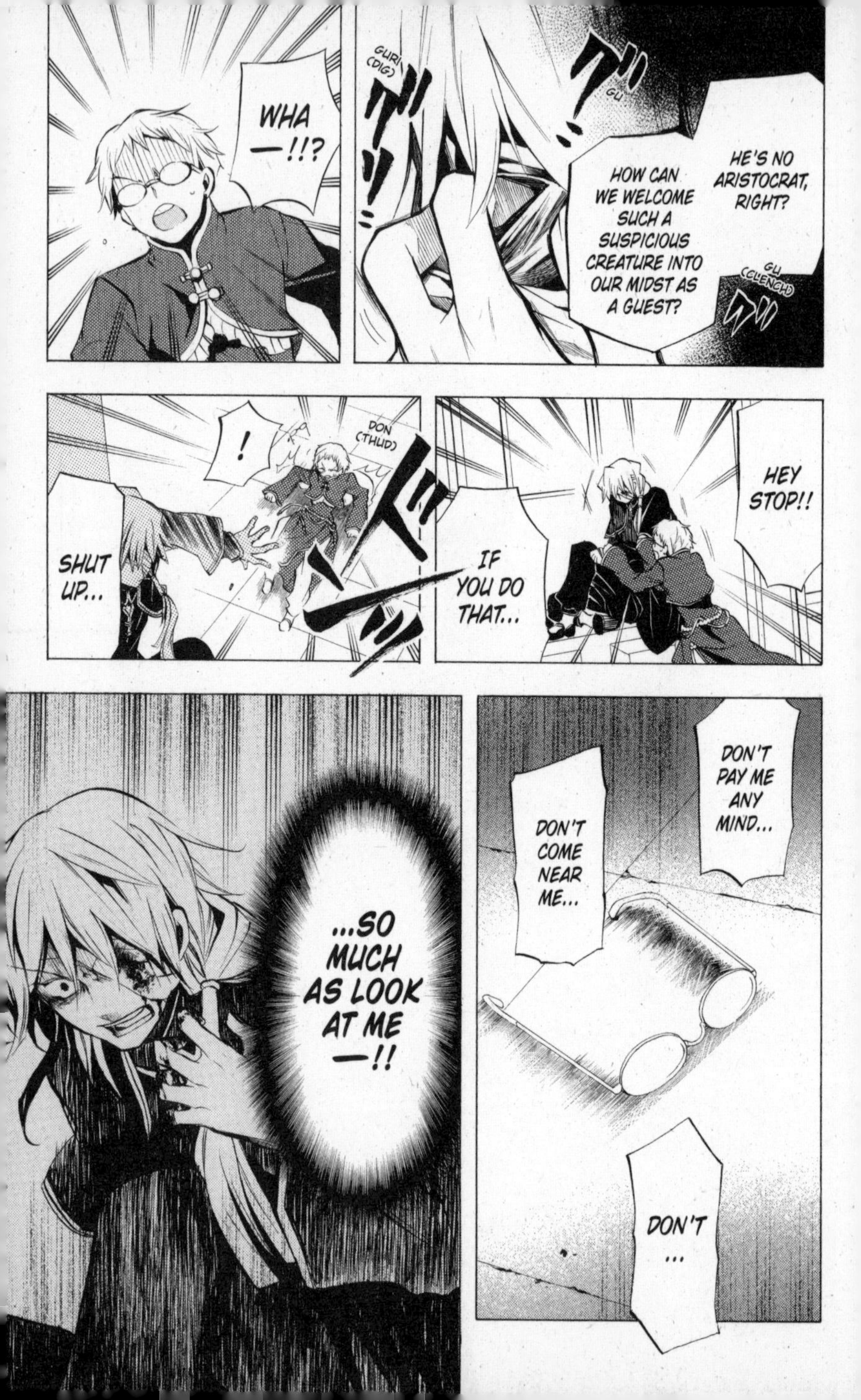
GU
GURI (DIG)
HE'S NO ARISTOCRAT, RIGHT?
HOW CAN WE WELCOME SUCH A SUSPICIOUS CREATURE INTO OUR MIDST AS A GUEST?
GU (CLENCH)
WHA —!!?
HEY STOP!!
IF YOU DO THAT...
DON (THUD)
!
SHUT UP...
DON'T PAY ME ANY MIND...
DON'T COME NEAR ME...
DON'T ...
...SO MUCH AS LOOK AT ME —!!

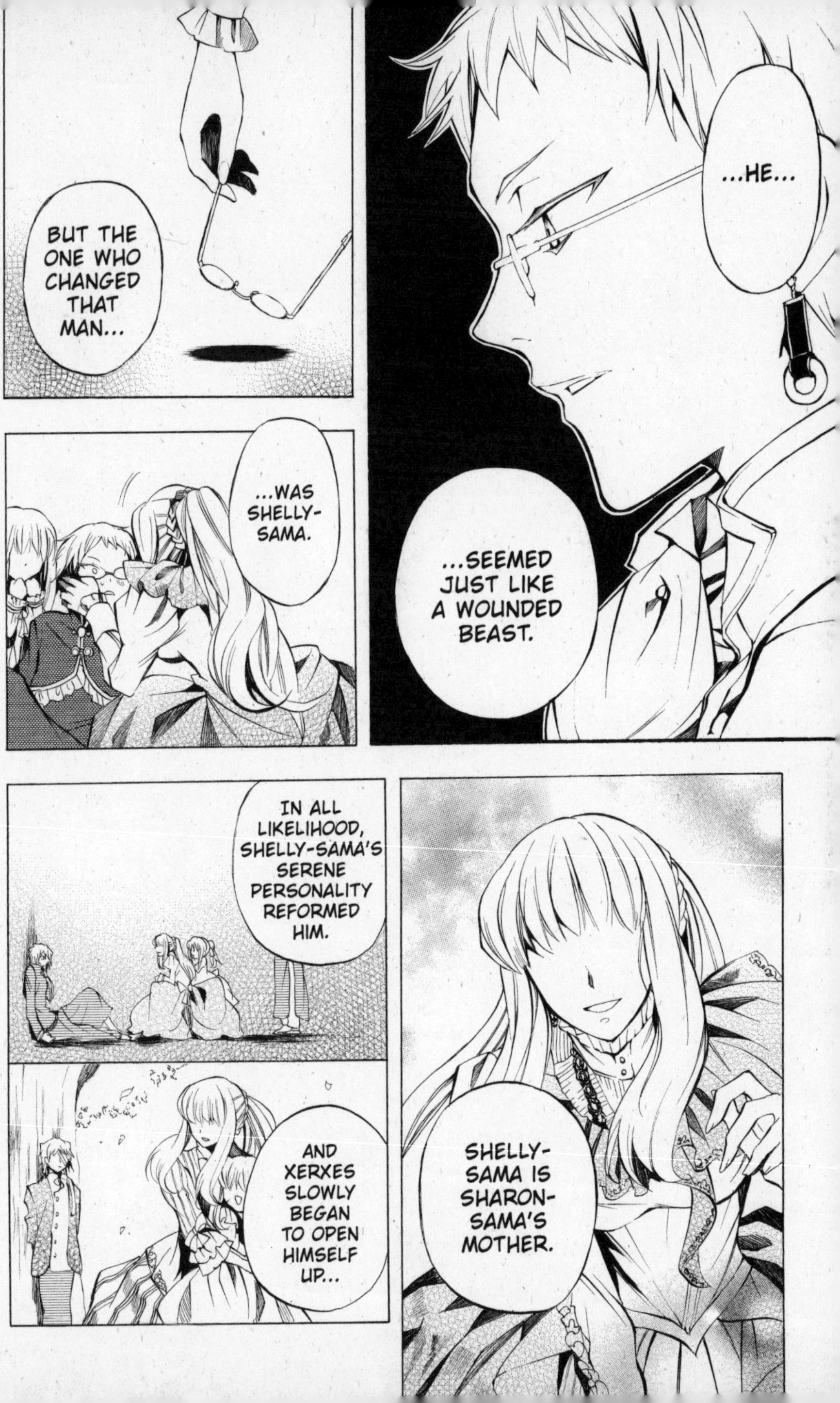
...HE...
...SEEMED JUST LIKE A WOUNDED BEAST.
BUT THE ONE WHO CHANGED THAT MAN...
...WAS SHELLY-SAMA.
SHELLY-SAMA IS SHARON-SAMA'S MOTHER.
IN ALL LIKELIHOOD, SHELLY-SAMA'S SERENE PERSONALITY REFORMED HIM.
AND XERXES SLOWLY BEGAN TO OPEN HIMSELF UP...

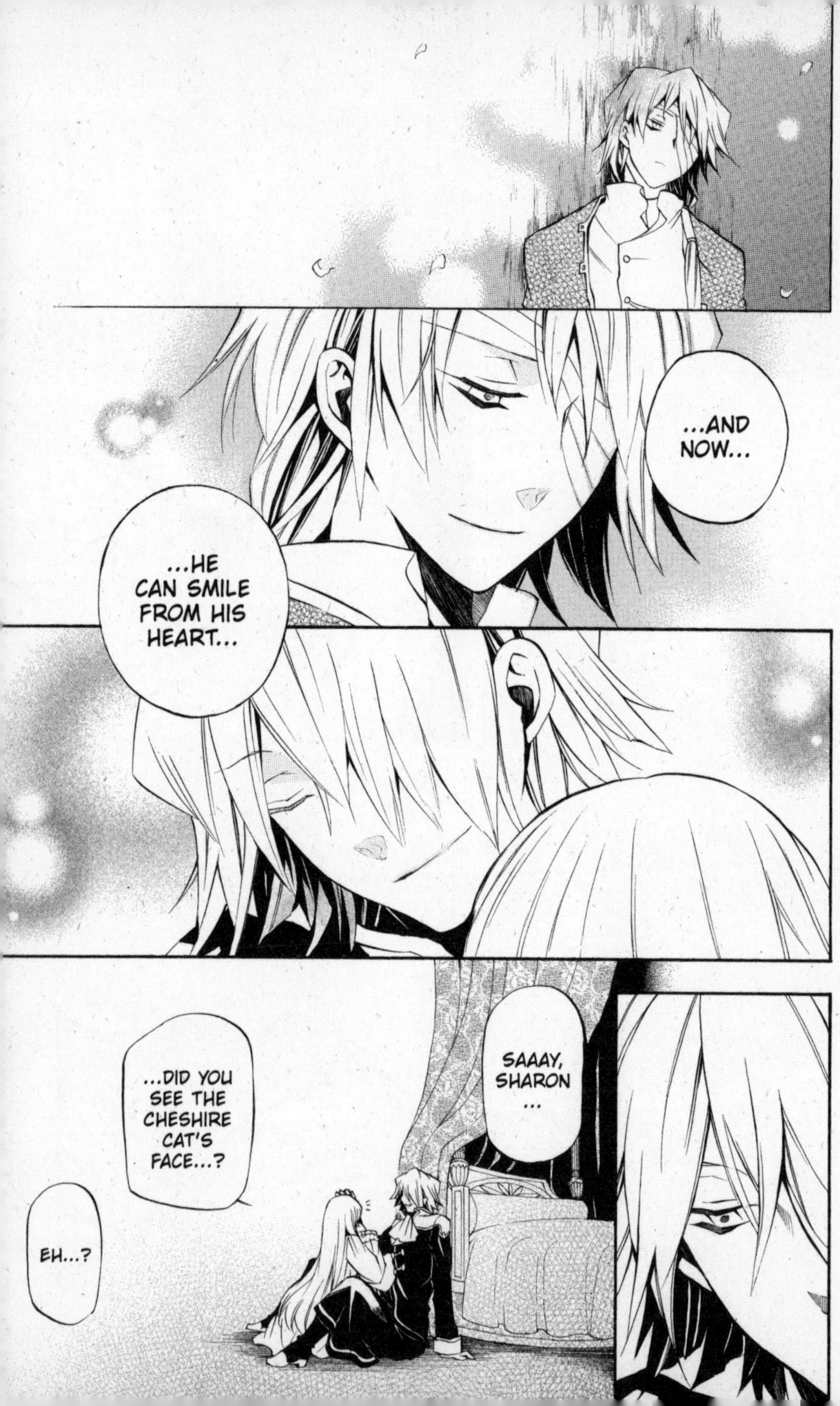
...AND NOW...
...HE CAN SMILE FROM HIS HEART...
SAAAY, SHARON ...
...DID YOU SEE THE CHESHIRE CAT'S FACE...?
EH...?

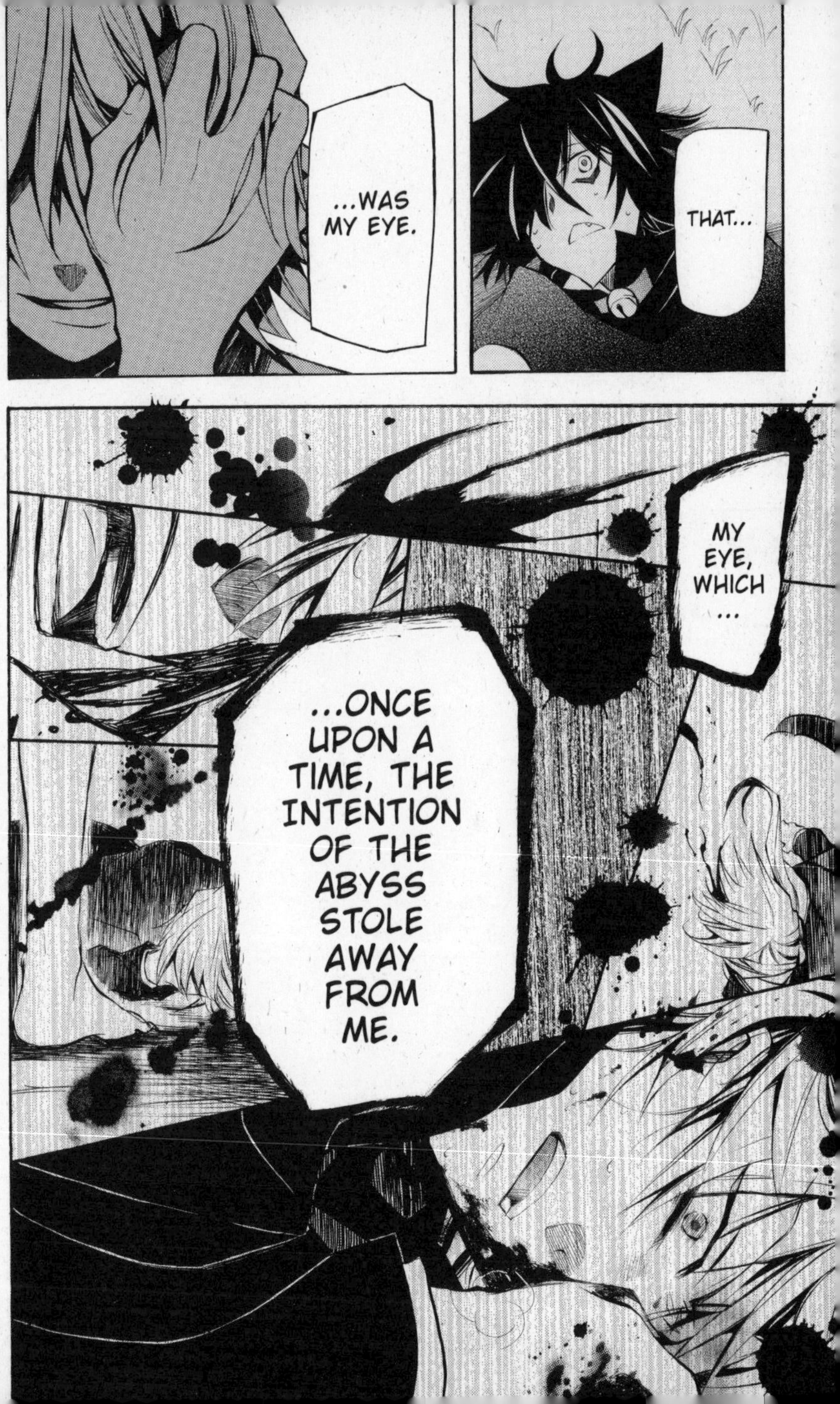
THAT...
...WAS MY EYE.
MY EYE, WHICH...
...ONCE UPON A TIME, THE INTENTION OF THE ABYSS STOLE AWAY FROM ME.

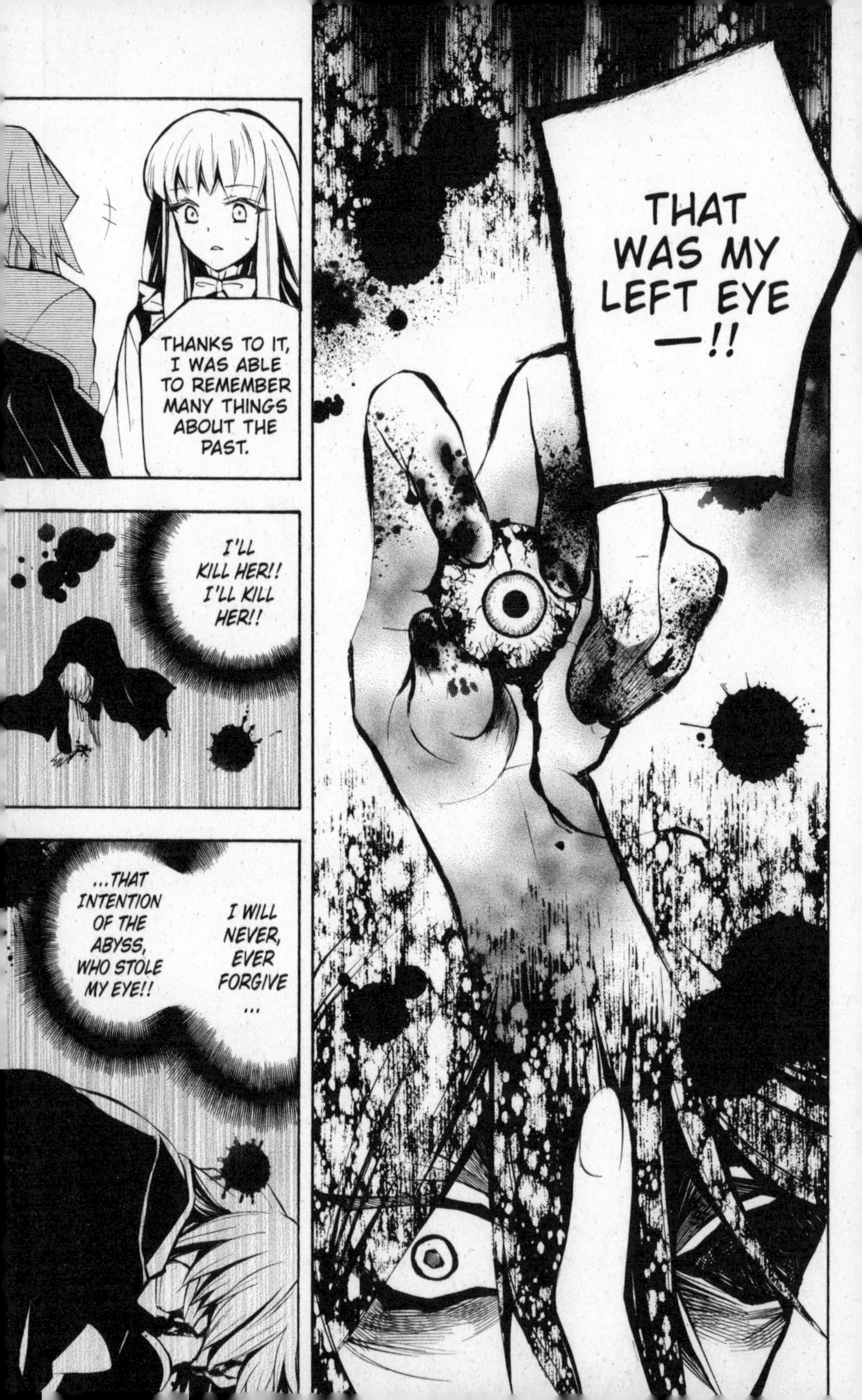
THAT WAS MY LEFT EYE —!!
THANKS TO IT, I WAS ABLE TO REMEMBER MANY THINGS ABOUT THE PAST.
I'LL KILL HER!! I'LL KILL HER!!
I WILL NEVER, EVER FORGIVE ...
...THAT INTENTION OF THE ABYSS, WHO STOLE MY EYE!!

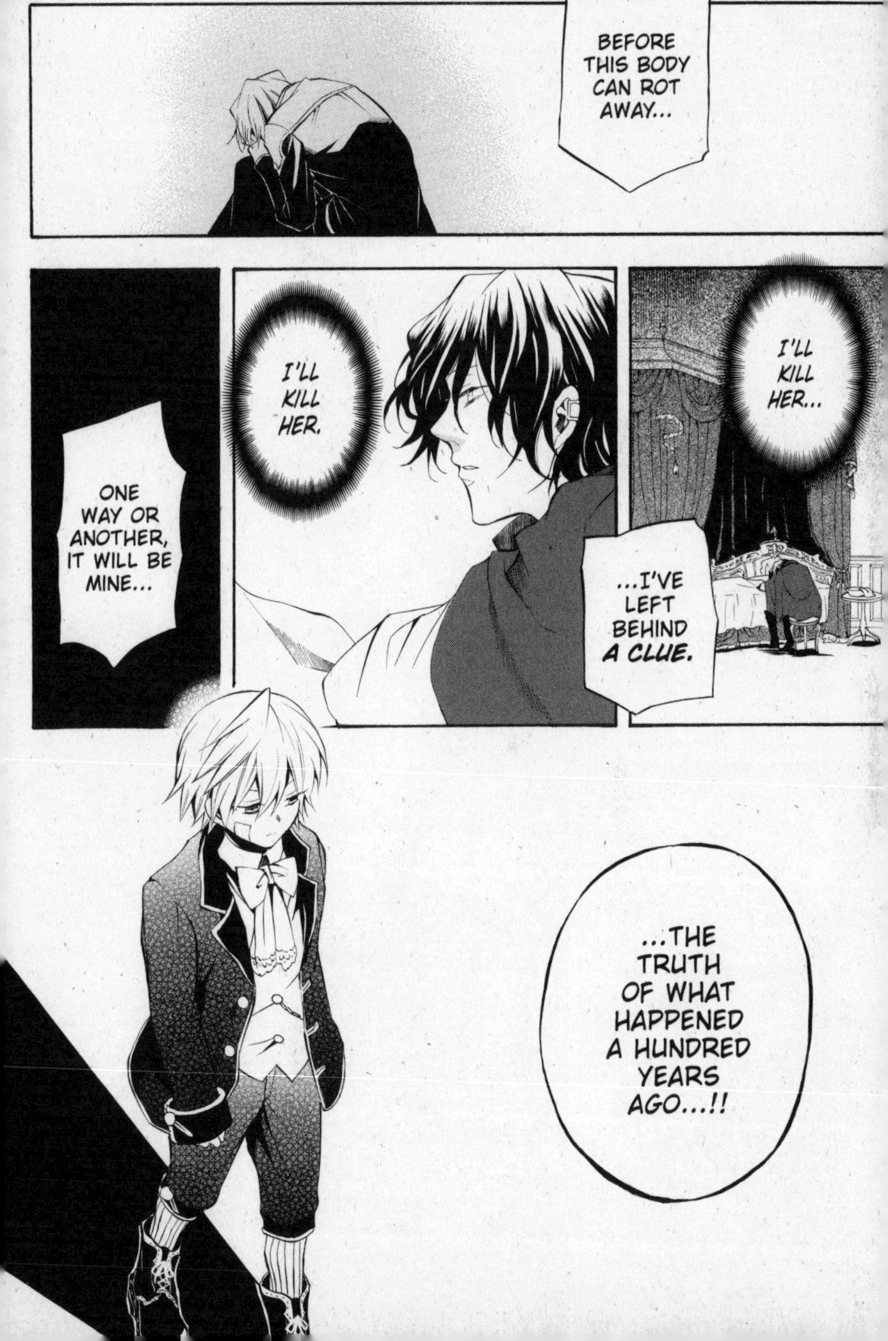
BEFORE THIS BODY CAN ROT AWAY...
I'LL KILL HER...
...I'VE LEFT BEHIND A CLUE.
I'LL KILL HER.
ONE WAY OR ANOTHER, IT WILL BE MINE...
...THE TRUTH OF WHAT HAPPENED A HUNDRED YEARS AGO...!!

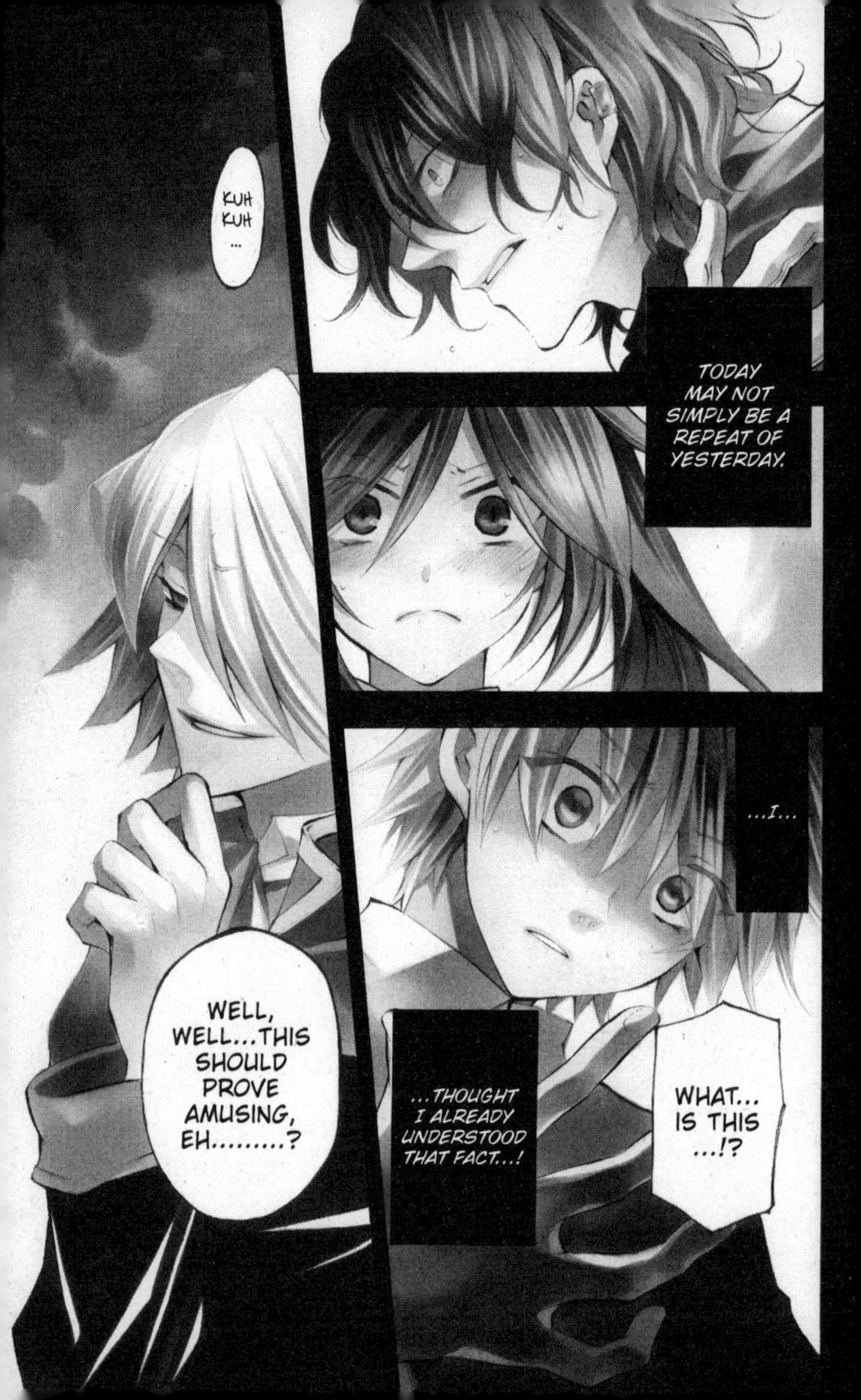
TODAY MAY NOT SIMPLY BE A REPEAT OF YESTERDAY.
...I...
WHAT... IS THIS ...!?
...THOUGHT I ALREADY UNDERSTOOD THAT FACT...!
KUH KUH ...
WELL, WELL...THIS SHOULD PROVE AMUSING, EH.........?

BONUS MANGA IT'S WRITTEN "CLOWN," BUT YOU SOMETIMES READ IT AS "MAGICIAN," YOU KNOOOOW!?

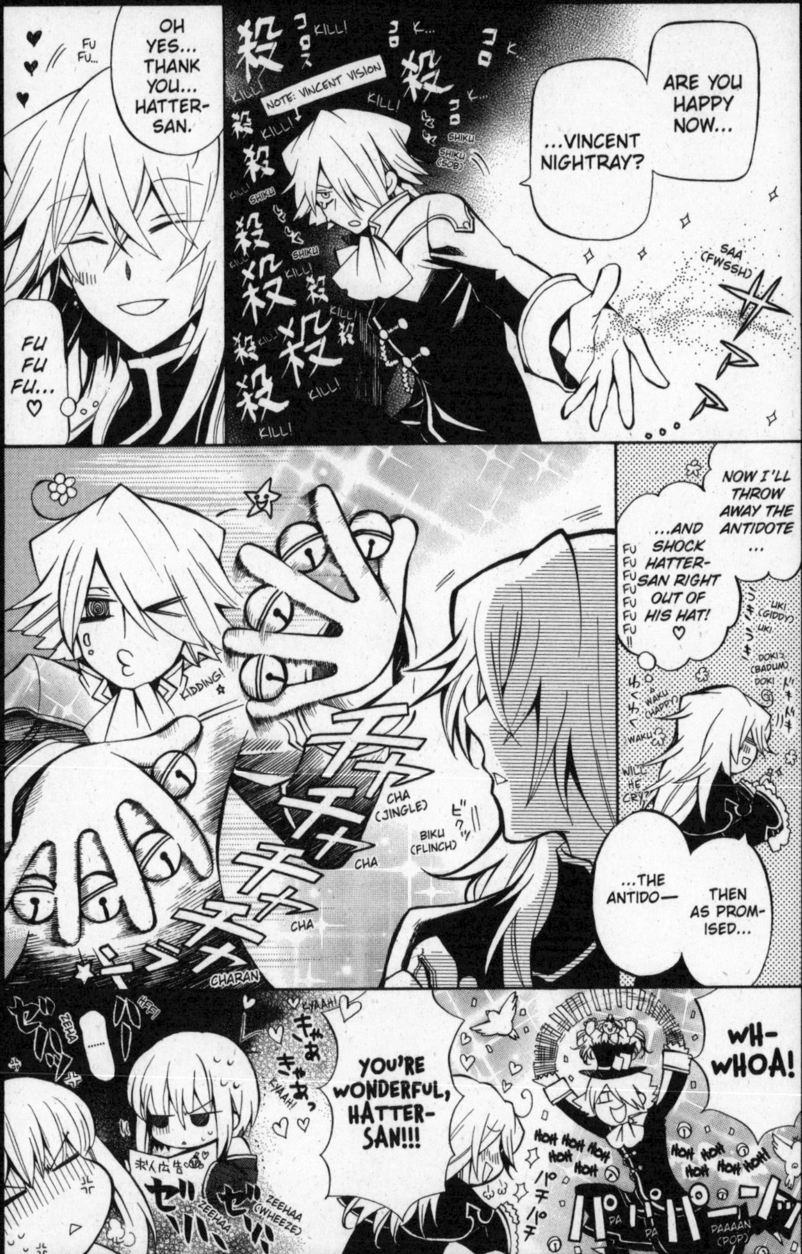

ARE YOU HAPPY NOW...
...VINCENT NIGHTRAY?
SAA (FWSSH)
NOTE: VINCENT VISION
KILL!
SHIKU SHIKU (SOB)
OH YES... THANK YOU... HATTER-SAN.
FU FU...
FU FU FU... ♡
NOW I'LL THROW AWAY THE ANTIDOTE...
...AND SHOCK HATTER-SAN RIGHT OUT OF HIS HAT! ♡
FU FU FU FU FU FU FU!!
UKI (GIDDY) UKI
DOKI (BADUMP) DOKI
WAKU (HAPPY) WAKU
WILL HE CRY?
THEN AS PROMISED...
...THE ANTIDO—
BIKU (FLINCH)
CHA (JINGLE)
CHA
CHA
CHARAN
KIDDING! ☆
WH-WHOA!
HOH HOH HOH HOH HOH
PAAAAN (POP)
YOU'RE WONDERFUL, HATTER-SAN!!!
KYAAH!
ZEEHAA (WHEEZE)
ZEEHAA
ZEEHA
......

PAPER: WANT ADS

SFX: PACHI (CLAP) PACHI

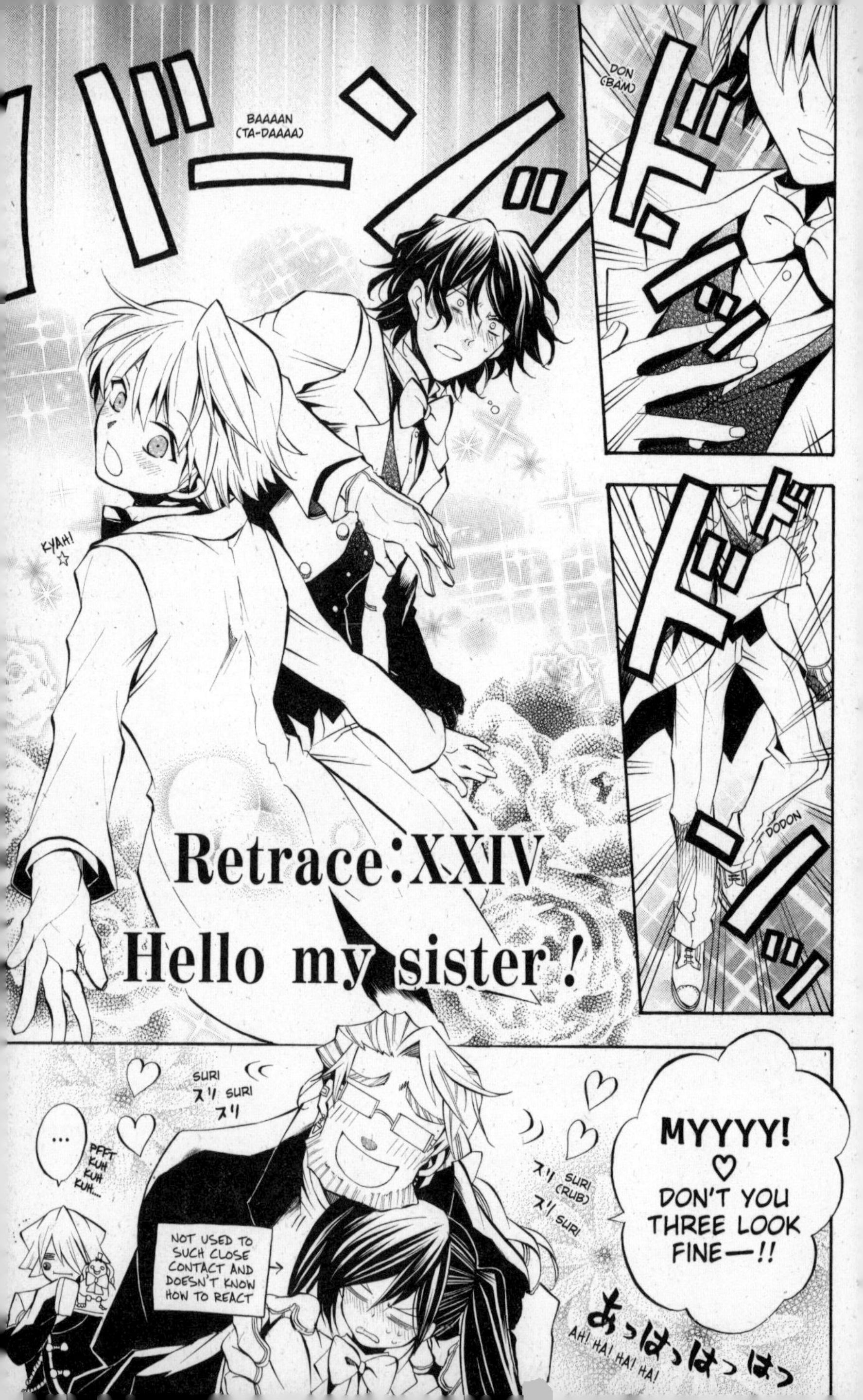
DON (BAM)
DODON
BAAAAN (TA-DAAAA)
KYAH! ☆
Retrace:XXIV
Hello my sister!
MYYYY! ♡ DON'T YOU THREE LOOK FINE—!!
スリ SURI スリ SURI
スリ SURI (RUB) スリ SURI
あっはっはっはっ
AH! HA! HA! HA!
...
PFFT KUH KUH KUH...
NOT USED TO SUCH CLOSE CONTACT AND DOESN'T KNOW HOW TO REACT

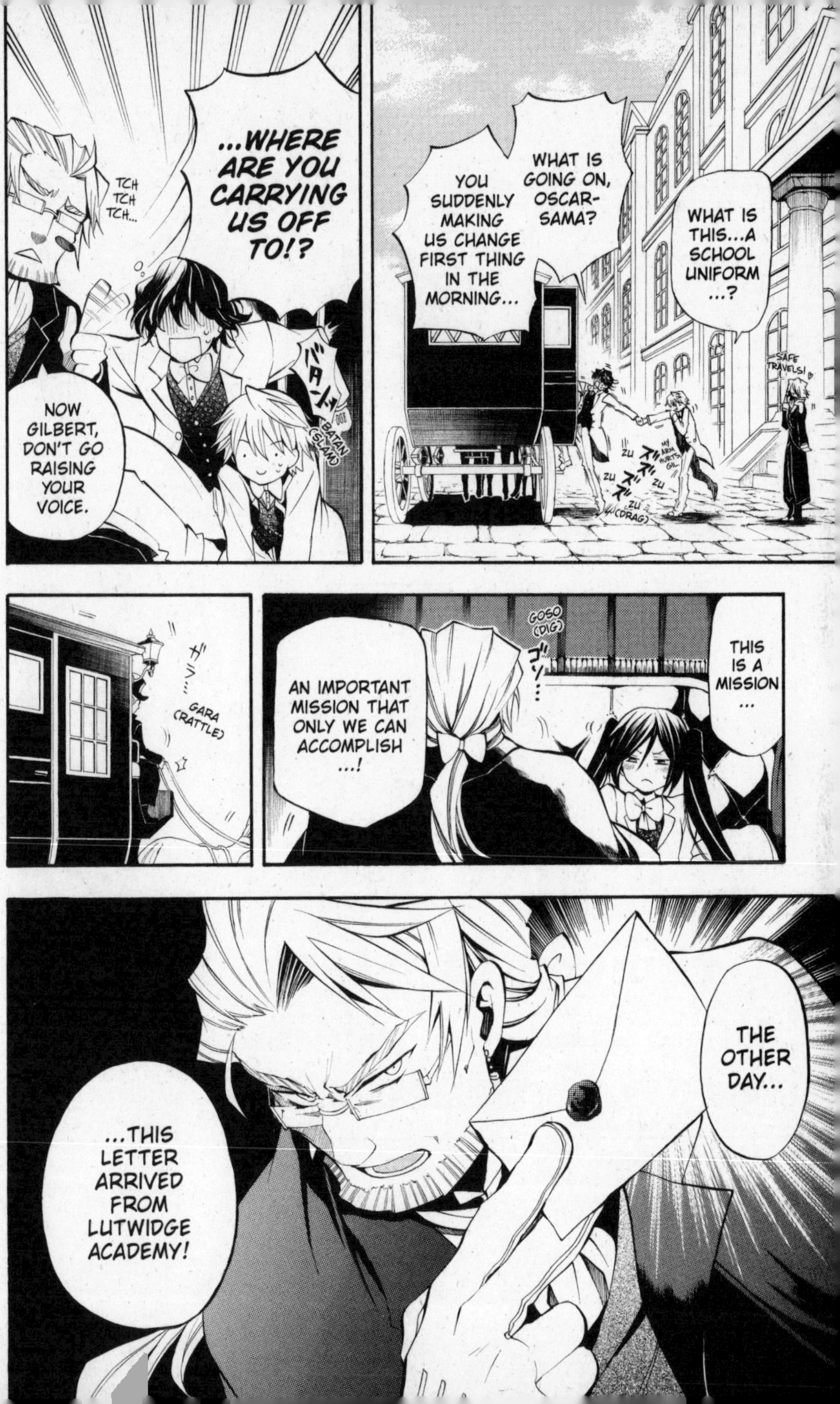
WHAT IS THIS...A SCHOOL UNIFORM ...?
SAFE TRAVELS!
WHAT IS GOING ON, OSCAR-SAMA?
YOU SUDDENLY MAKING US CHANGE FIRST THING IN THE MORNING...
MY ARM HURTS, GIL.
ZU ZU ZU ZU (DRAG)
...WHERE ARE YOU CARRYING US OFF TO!?
TCH TCH TCH...
BATAN (SLAM)
NOW GILBERT, DON'T GO RAISING YOUR VOICE.
THIS IS A MISSION ...
GOSO (DIG)
AN IMPORTANT MISSION THAT ONLY WE CAN ACCOMPLISH ...!
GARA (RATTLE)
THE OTHER DAY...
...THIS LETTER ARRIVED FROM LUTWIDGE ACADEMY!

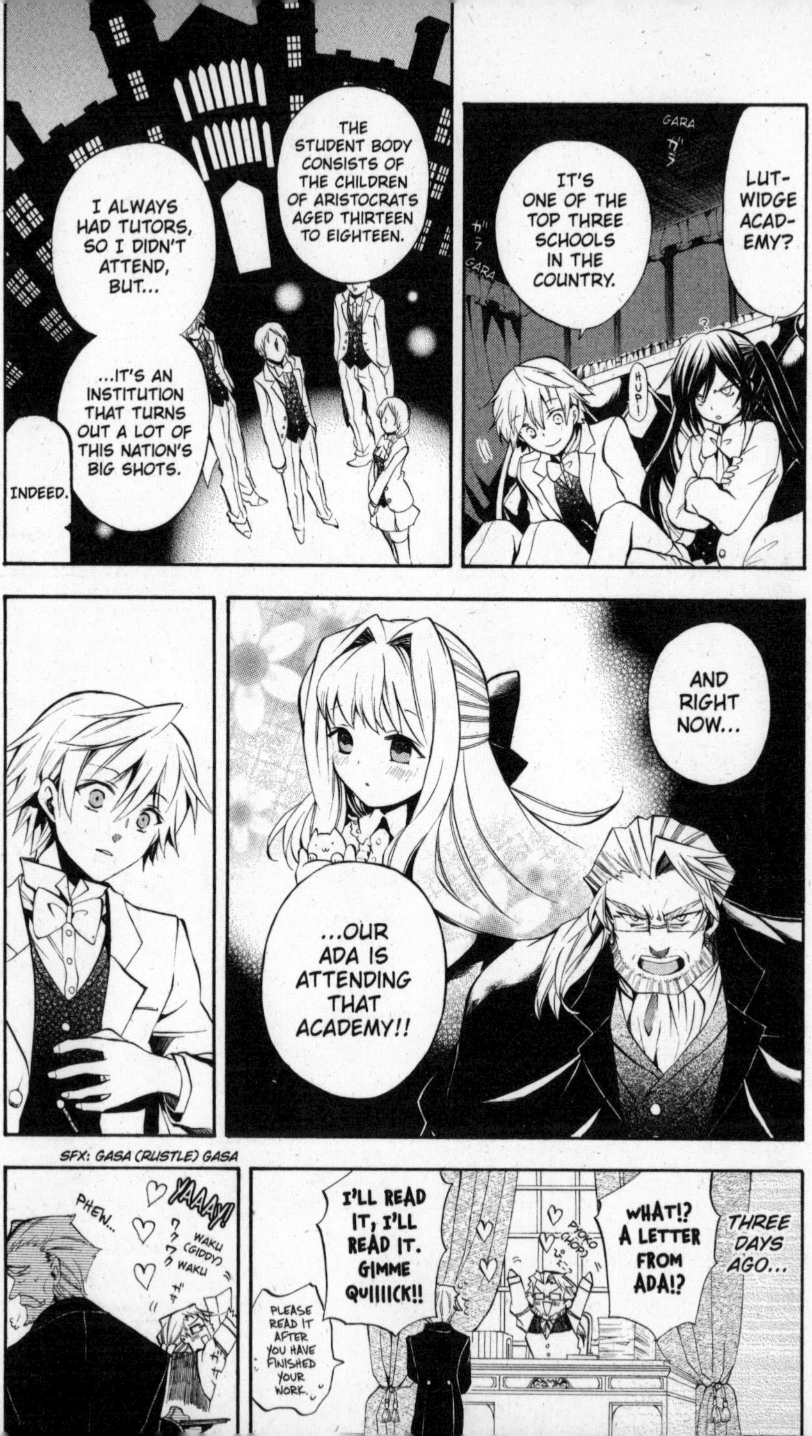
LUT-WIDGE ACAD-EMY?
GARA
IT'S ONE OF THE TOP THREE SCHOOLS IN THE COUNTRY.
GARA
HUP!
THE STUDENT BODY CONSISTS OF THE CHILDREN OF ARISTOCRATS AGED THIRTEEN TO EIGHTEEN.
I ALWAYS HAD TUTORS, SO I DIDN'T ATTEND, BUT...
...IT'S AN INSTITUTION THAT TURNS OUT A LOT OF THIS NATION'S BIG SHOTS.
INDEED.
AND RIGHT NOW...
...OUR ADA IS ATTENDING THAT ACADEMY!!
SFX: GASA (RUSTLE) GASA
THREE DAYS AGO...
WHAT!? A LETTER FROM ADA!?
PYOKO (HOP)
I'LL READ IT, I'LL READ IT. GIMME QUIIIICK!!
PLEASE READ IT AFTER YOU HAVE FINISHED YOUR WORK.
YAAAY!
WAKU (GIDDY) WAKU
PHEW...

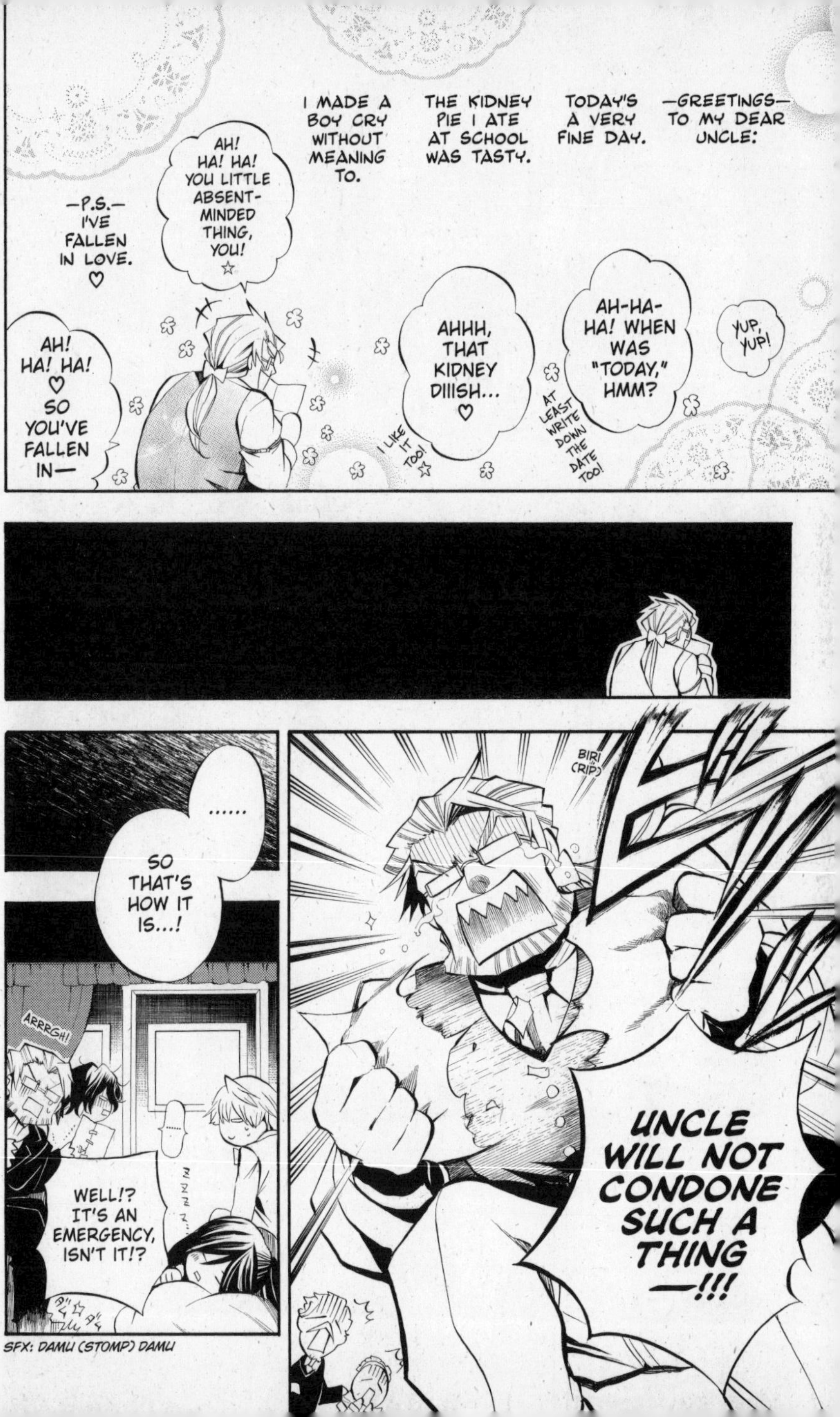
—GREETINGS— TO MY DEAR UNCLE:
TODAY'S A VERY FINE DAY.
THE KIDNEY PIE I ATE AT SCHOOL WAS TASTY.
I MADE A BOY CRY WITHOUT MEANING TO.
YUP, YUP!
AH-HA-HA! WHEN WAS "TODAY," HMM?
AT LEAST WRITE DOWN THE DATE TOO!
AHHH, THAT KIDNEY DIIISH... ♡
I LIKE IT TOO! ☆
AH! HA! HA! YOU LITTLE ABSENT-MINDED THING, YOU! ☆
—P.S.— I'VE FALLEN IN LOVE. ♡
AH! HA! HA! ♡ SO YOU'VE FALLEN IN—
BIRI (RIP)
UNCLE WILL NOT CONDONE SUCH A THING —!!!
......
SO THAT'S HOW IT IS...!
ARRRGH!
WELL!? IT'S AN EMERGENCY, ISN'T IT!?

SFX: DAMU (STOMP) DAMU

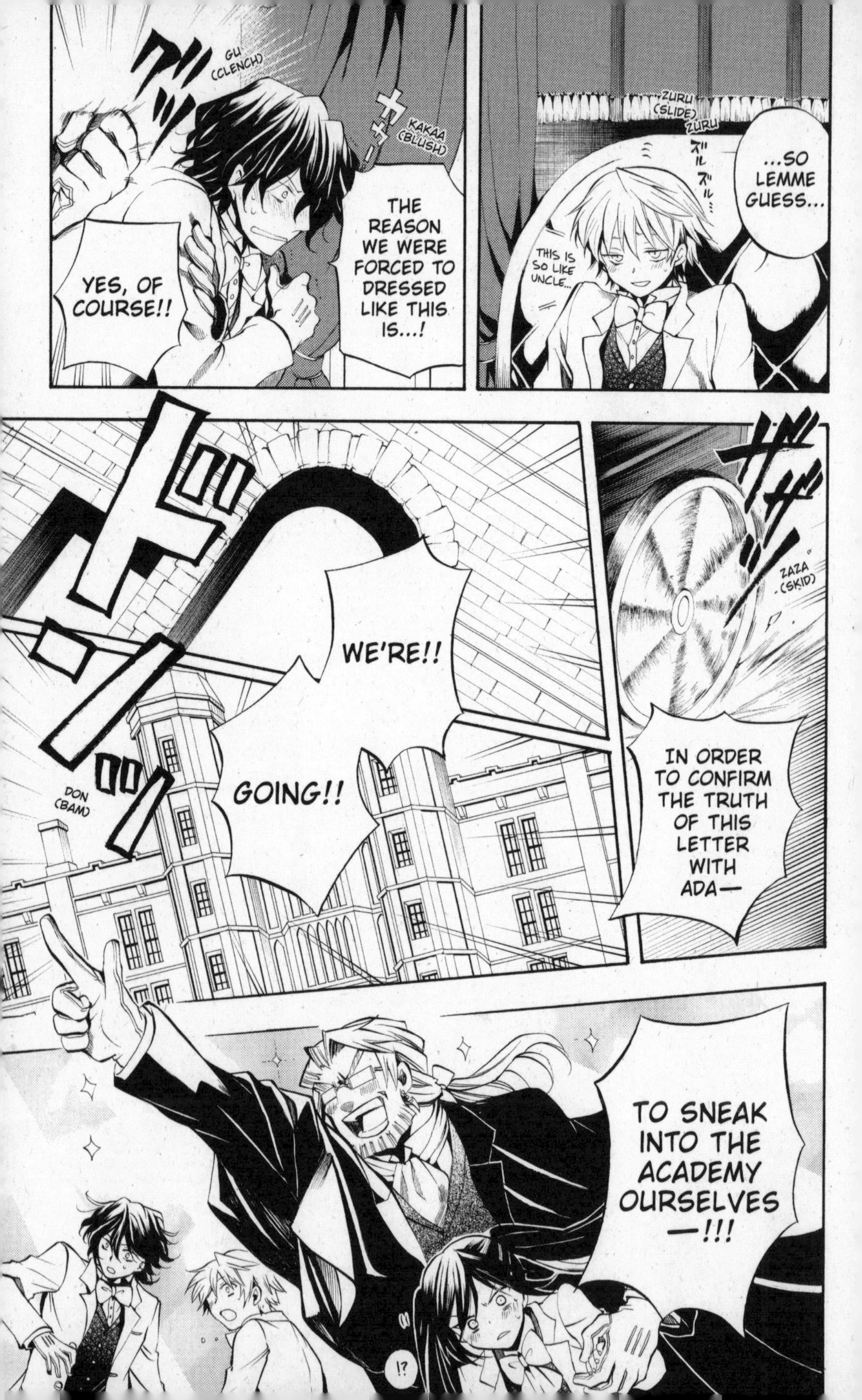
ZURU (SLIDE) ZURU
...SO LEMME GUESS...
THIS IS SO LIKE UNCLE...
GU (CLENCH)
KAKAA (BLUSH)
THE REASON WE WERE FORCED TO DRESSED LIKE THIS IS...!
YES, OF COURSE!!
ZAZA (SKID)
IN ORDER TO CONFIRM THE TRUTH OF THIS LETTER WITH ADA—
DON (BAM)
WE'RE!!
GOING!!
TO SNEAK INTO THE ACADEMY OURSELVES—!!!
!?

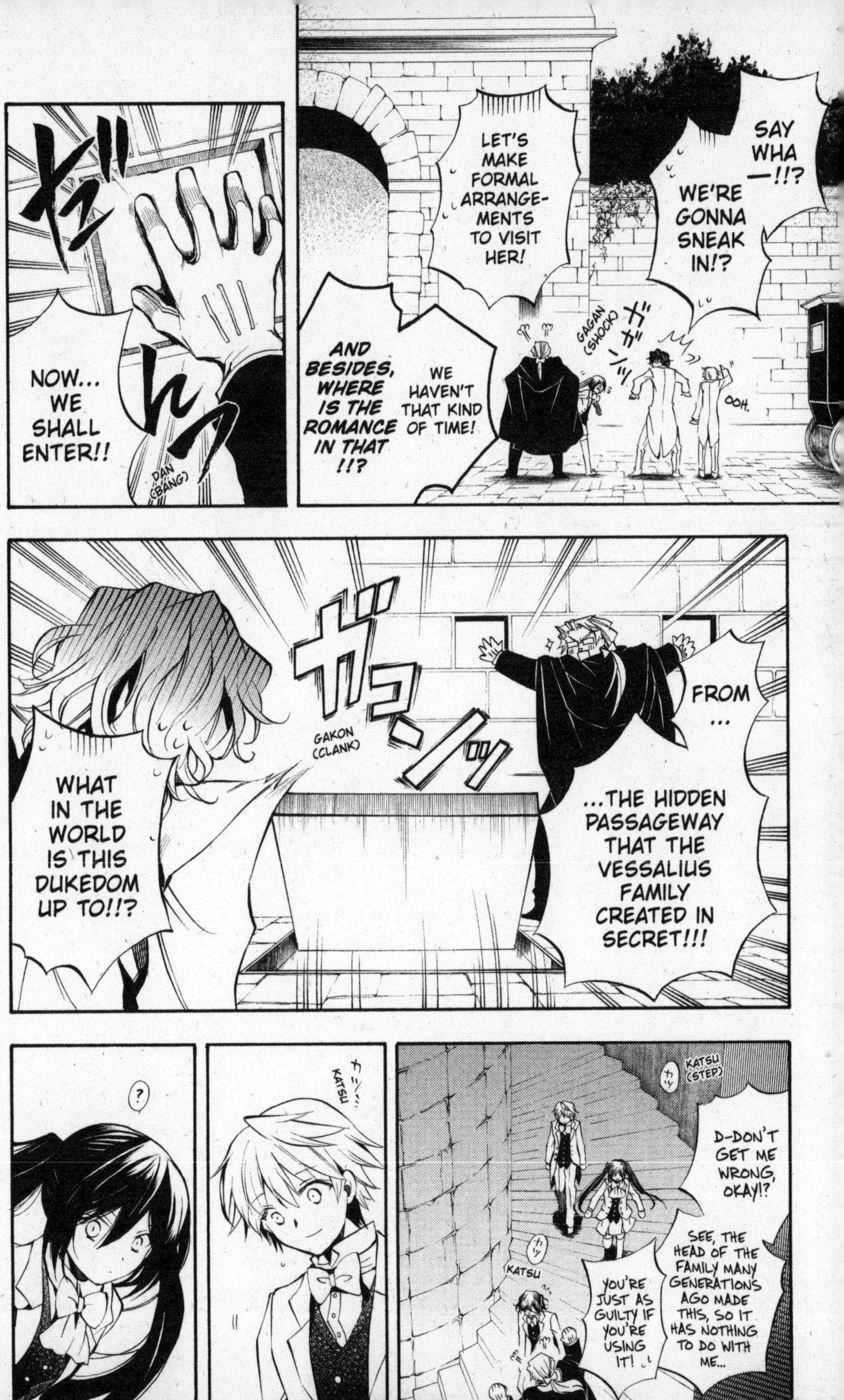
SAY WHA—!!? WE'RE GONNA SNEAK IN!?
LET'S MAKE FORMAL ARRANGEMENTS TO VISIT HER!
GAGAN (SHOCK)
OOH.
WE HAVEN'T THAT KIND OF TIME!
AND BESIDES, WHERE IS THE ROMANCE IN THAT!!?
DAN (BANG)
NOW... WE SHALL ENTER!!
FROM...
...THE HIDDEN PASSAGEWAY THAT THE VESSALIUS FAMILY CREATED IN SECRET!!!
GAKON (CLANK)
WHAT IN THE WORLD IS THIS DUKEDOM UP TO!!?
KATSU (STEP)
D-DON'T GET ME WRONG, OKAY!?
SEE, THE HEAD OF THE FAMILY MANY GENERATIONS AGO MADE THIS, SO IT HAS NOTHING TO DO WITH ME...
YOU'RE JUST AS GUILTY IF YOU'RE USING IT!
KATSU
KATSU
?

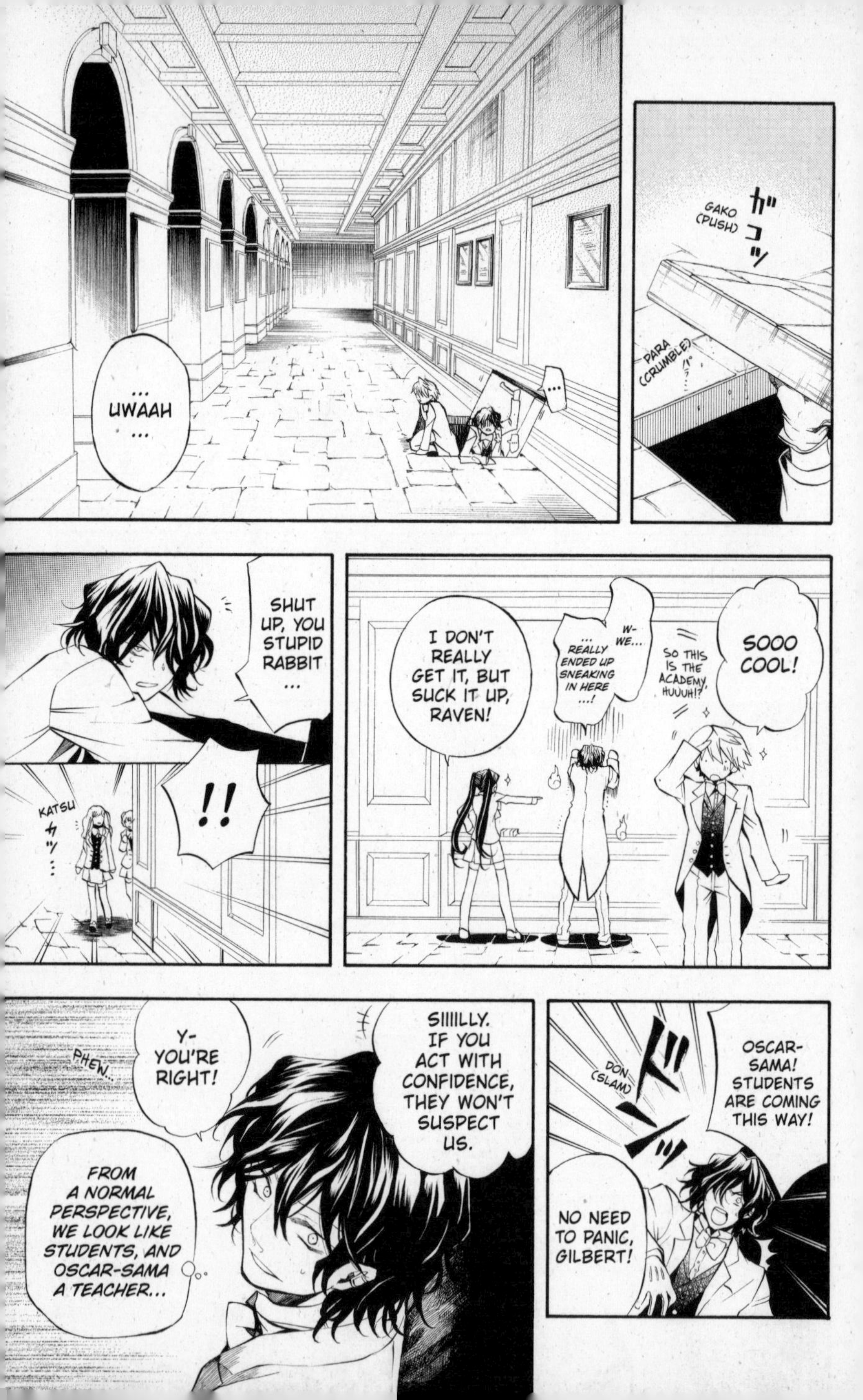
GAKO (PUSH)
ガコッ
PARA (CRUMBLE)
パラ…
... UWAAH ...
...
SOOO COOL!
SO THIS IS THE ACADEMY, HUUUH!?
W-WE...
... REALLY ENDED UP SNEAKING IN HERE ...!
I DON'T REALLY GET IT, BUT SUCK IT UP, RAVEN!
SHUT UP, YOU STUPID RABBIT ...
!!
KATSU
カッ…
OSCAR-SAMA! STUDENTS ARE COMING THIS WAY!
DON (SLAM)
ド
NO NEED TO PANIC, GILBERT!
SIIIILLY. IF YOU ACT WITH CONFIDENCE, THEY WON'T SUSPECT US.
Y-YOU'RE RIGHT!
PHEW...
FROM A NORMAL PERSPECTIVE, WE LOOK LIKE STUDENTS, AND OSCAR-SAMA A TEACHER...

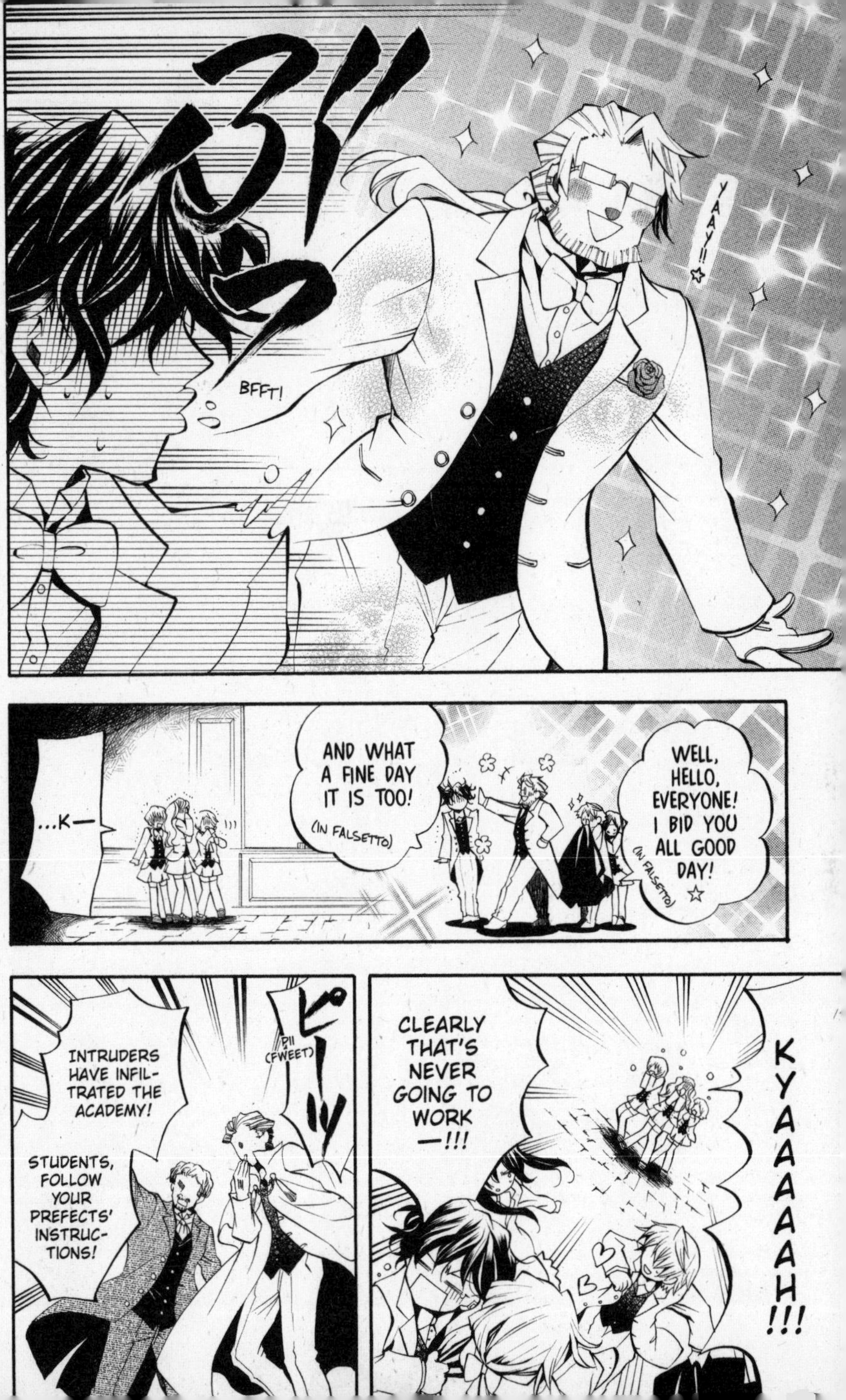
YAAY!!☆
BFFT!
WELL, HELLO, EVERYONE! I BID YOU ALL GOOD DAY! ☆
(IN FALSETTO)
AND WHAT A FINE DAY IT IS TOO!
(IN FALSETTO)
...K—
KYAAAAAAH!!!
CLEARLY THAT'S NEVER GOING TO WORK—!!!
PII (FWEET)
INTRUDERS HAVE INFILTRATED THE ACADEMY!
STUDENTS, FOLLOW YOUR PREFECTS' INSTRUCTIONS!

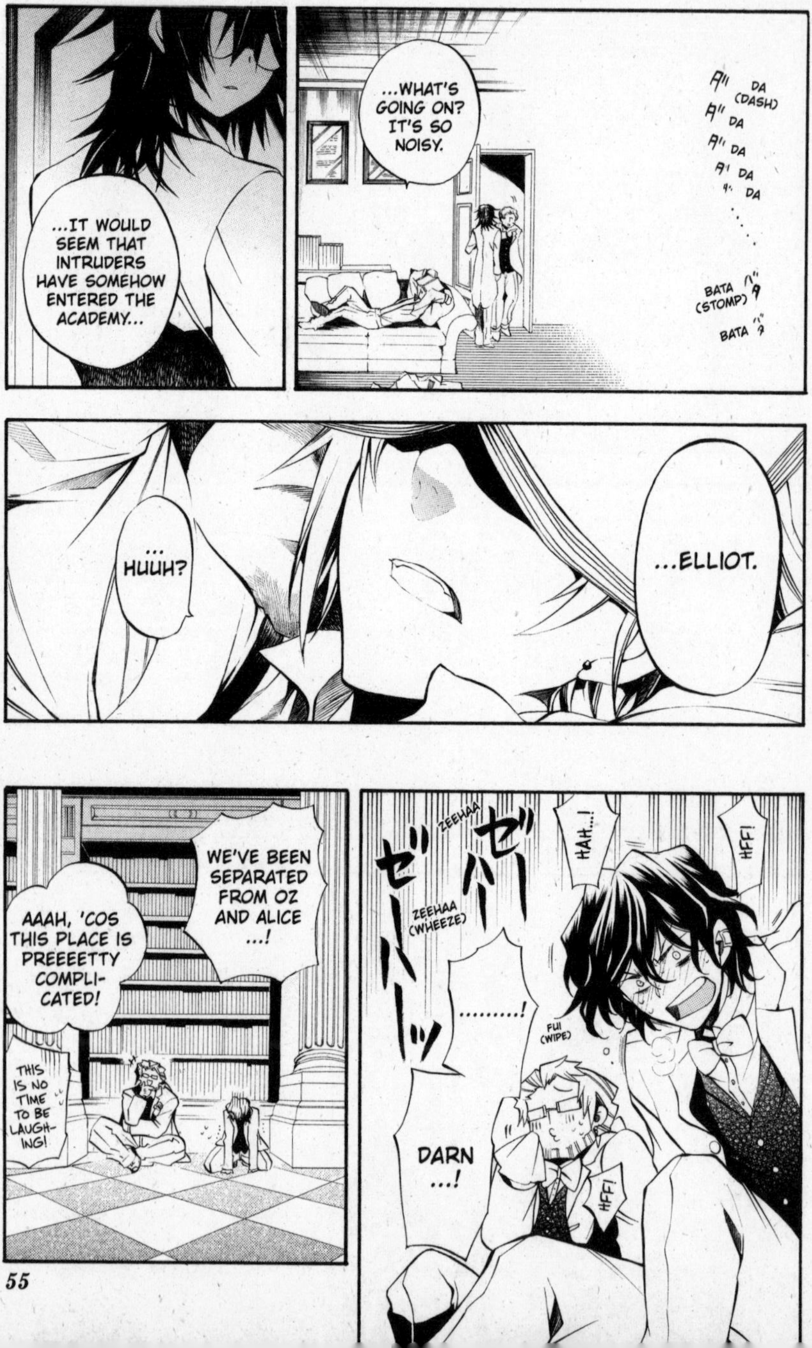
...WHAT'S GOING ON? IT'S SO NOISY.
DA (DASH)
DA
DA
DA
DA
BATA (STOMP)
BATA
...IT WOULD SEEM THAT INTRUDERS HAVE SOMEHOW ENTERED THE ACADEMY...
...ELLIOT.
... HUUH?
HFF!
HAH...!
ZEEHAA
ZEEHAA (WHEEZE)
.........!
FUI (WIPE)
DARN ...!
HFF!
WE'VE BEEN SEPARATED FROM OZ AND ALICE ...!
AAAH, 'COS THIS PLACE IS PREEEETTY COMPLI-CATED!
THIS IS NO TIME TO BE LAUGH-ING!

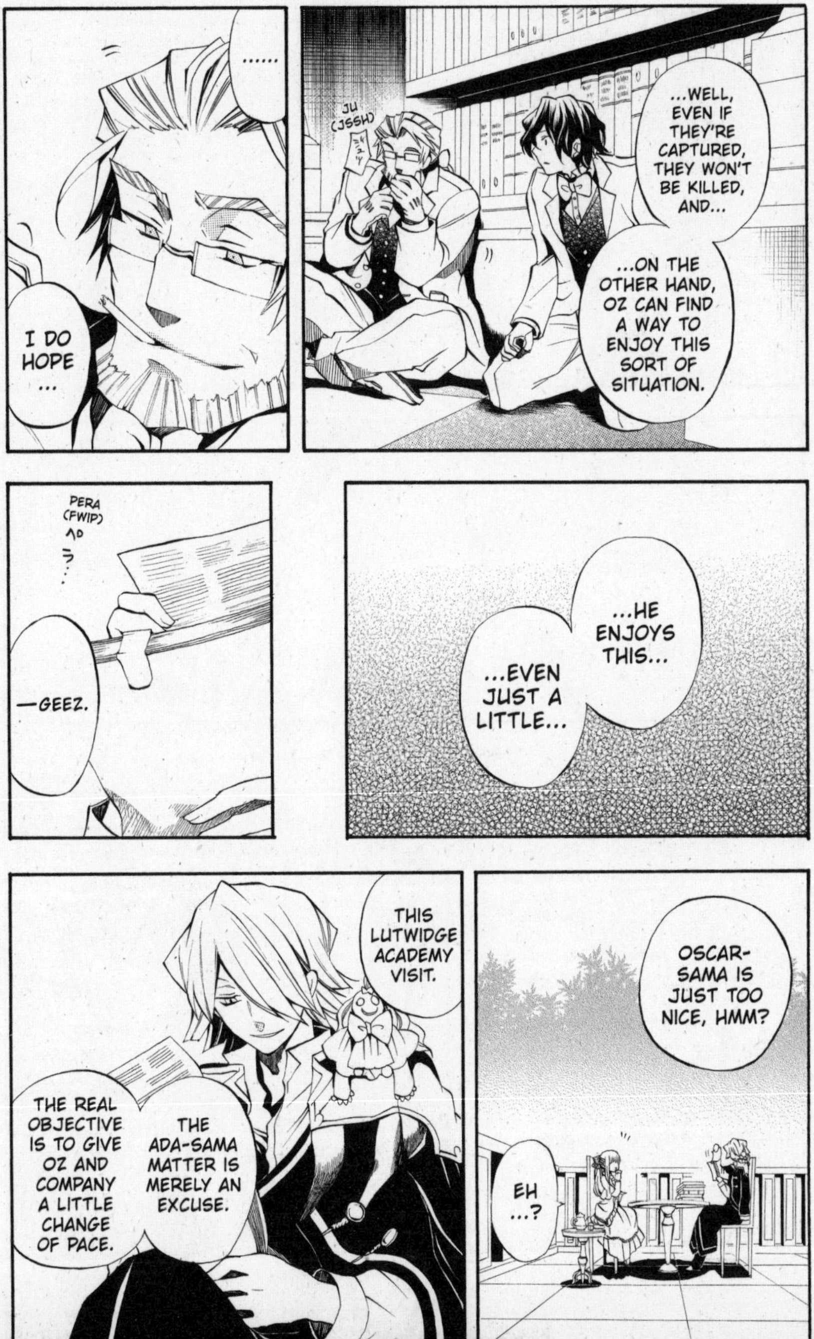
...WELL, EVEN IF THEY'RE CAPTURED, THEY WON'T BE KILLED, AND...
JU (JSSH)
...ON THE OTHER HAND, OZ CAN FIND A WAY TO ENJOY THIS SORT OF SITUATION.
......
I DO HOPE ...
...HE ENJOYS THIS...
...EVEN JUST A LITTLE...
PERA (FWIP)
—GEEZ.
OSCAR-SAMA IS JUST TOO NICE, HMM?
EH ...?
THIS LUTWIDGE ACADEMY VISIT.
THE ADA-SAMA MATTER IS MERELY AN EXCUSE.
THE REAL OBJECTIVE IS TO GIVE OZ AND COMPANY A LITTLE CHANGE OF PACE.

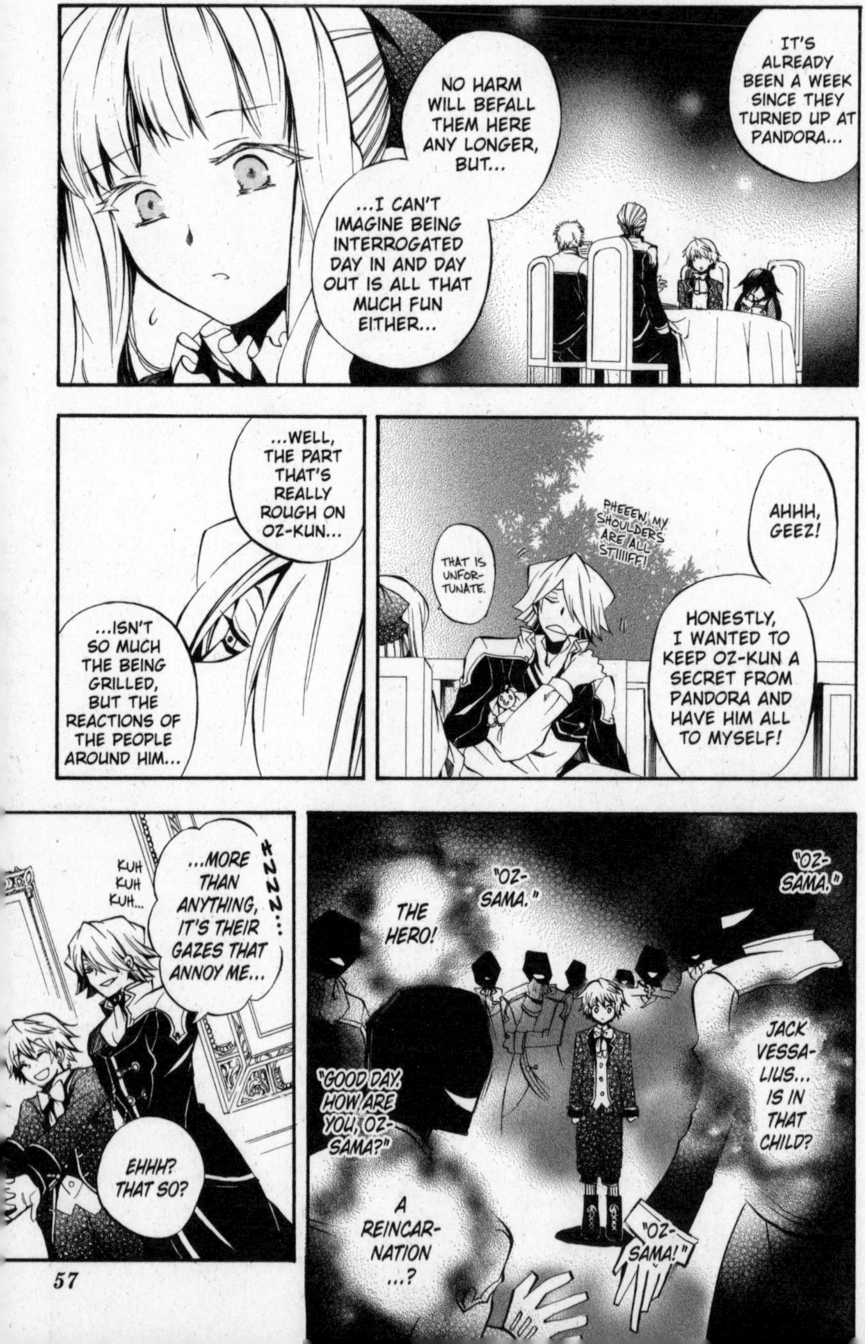
IT'S ALREADY BEEN A WEEK SINCE THEY TURNED UP AT PANDORA...
NO HARM WILL BEFALL THEM HERE ANY LONGER, BUT...
...I CAN'T IMAGINE BEING INTERROGATED DAY IN AND DAY OUT IS ALL THAT MUCH FUN EITHER...
AHHH, GEEZ!
HONESTLY, I WANTED TO KEEP OZ-KUN A SECRET FROM PANDORA AND HAVE HIM ALL TO MYSELF!
PHEEEW, MY SHOULDERS ARE ALL STIIIIFF!
THAT IS UNFORTUNATE.
...WELL, THE PART THAT'S REALLY ROUGH ON OZ-KUN...
...ISN'T SO MUCH THE BEING GRILLED, BUT THE REACTIONS OF THE PEOPLE AROUND HIM...
"OZ-SAMA."
"OZ-SAMA."
THE HERO!
JACK VESSALIUS... IS IN THAT CHILD?
"GOOD DAY. HOW ARE YOU, OZ-SAMA?"
A REINCARNATION...?
"OZ-SAMA!"
...MORE THAN ANYTHING, IT'S THEIR GAZES THAT ANNOY ME...
HNNN...
KUH KUH KUH...
EHHH? THAT SO?

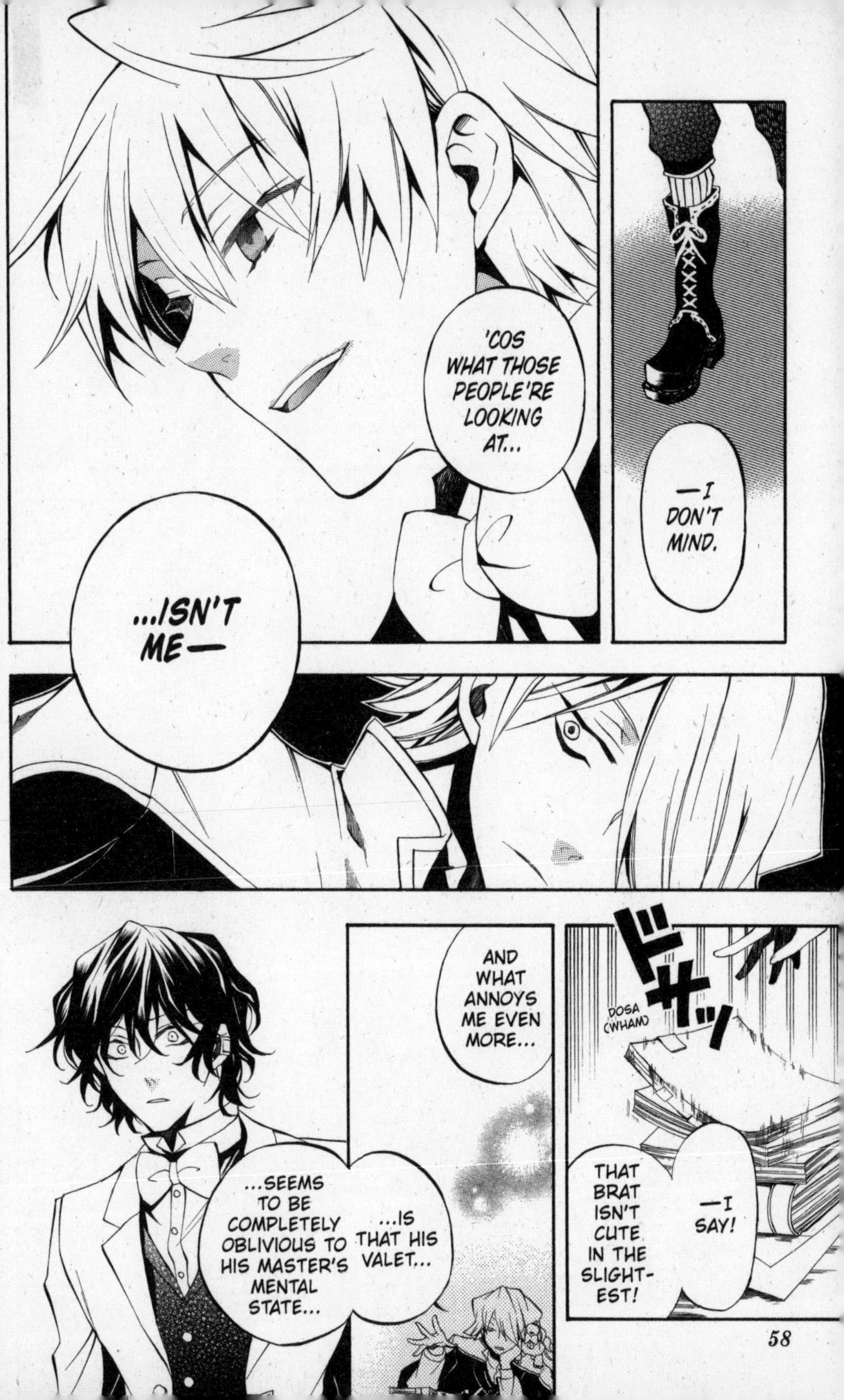
—I DON'T MIND.
'COS WHAT THOSE PEOPLE'RE LOOKING AT...
...ISN'T ME—
DOSA (WHAM)
THAT BRAT ISN'T CUTE IN THE SLIGHT-EST!
—I SAY!
AND WHAT ANNOYS ME EVEN MORE...
...IS THAT HIS VALET...
...SEEMS TO BE COMPLETELY OBLIVIOUS TO HIS MASTER'S MENTAL STATE...

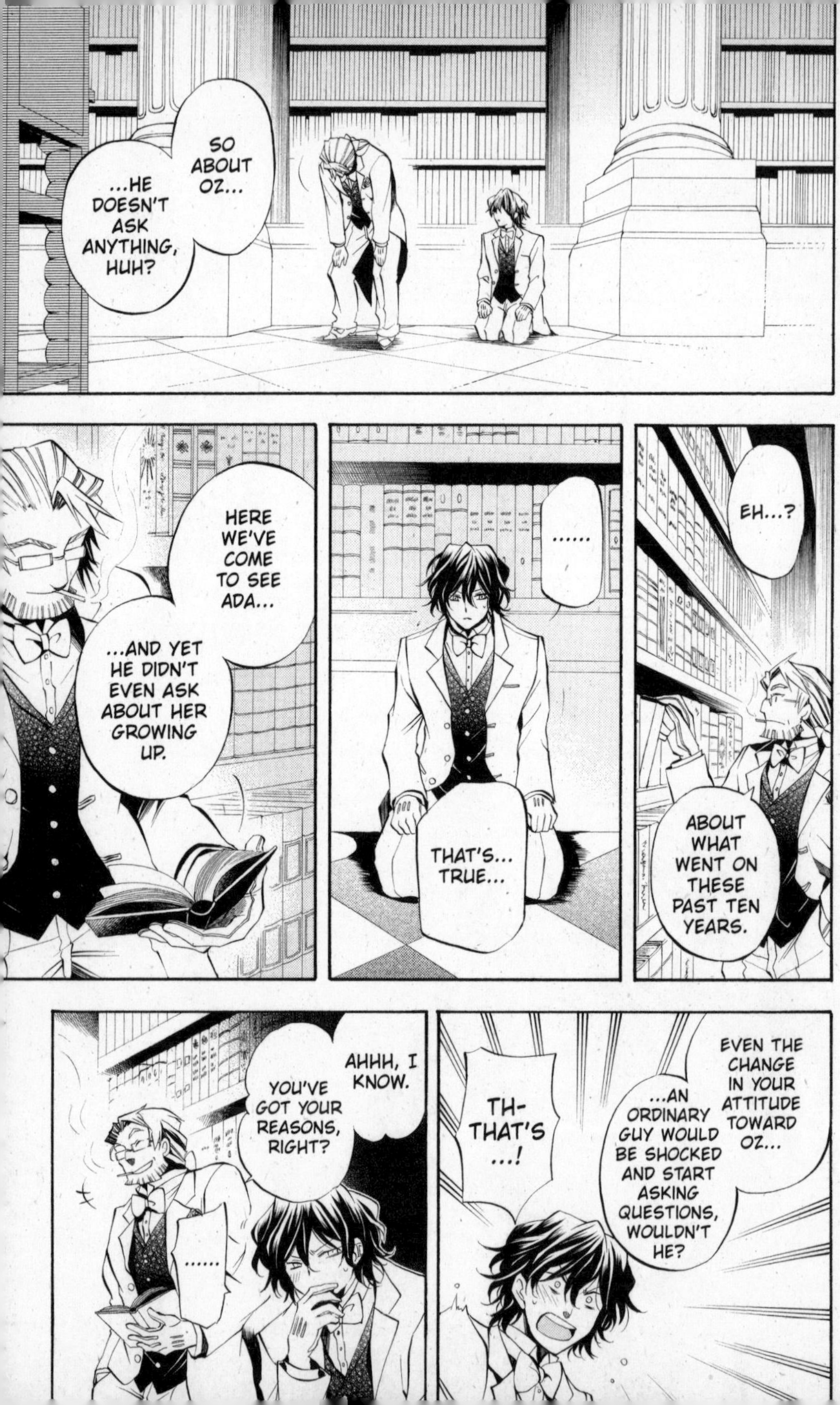
SO ABOUT OZ...
...HE DOESN'T ASK ANYTHING, HUH?
EH...?
ABOUT WHAT WENT ON THESE PAST TEN YEARS.
......
THAT'S... TRUE...
HERE WE'VE COME TO SEE ADA...
...AND YET HE DIDN'T EVEN ASK ABOUT HER GROWING UP.
EVEN THE CHANGE IN YOUR ATTITUDE TOWARD OZ...
...AN ORDINARY GUY WOULD BE SHOCKED AND START ASKING QUESTIONS, WOULDN'T HE?
TH-THAT'S ...!
AHHH, I KNOW.
YOU'VE GOT YOUR REASONS, RIGHT?
......

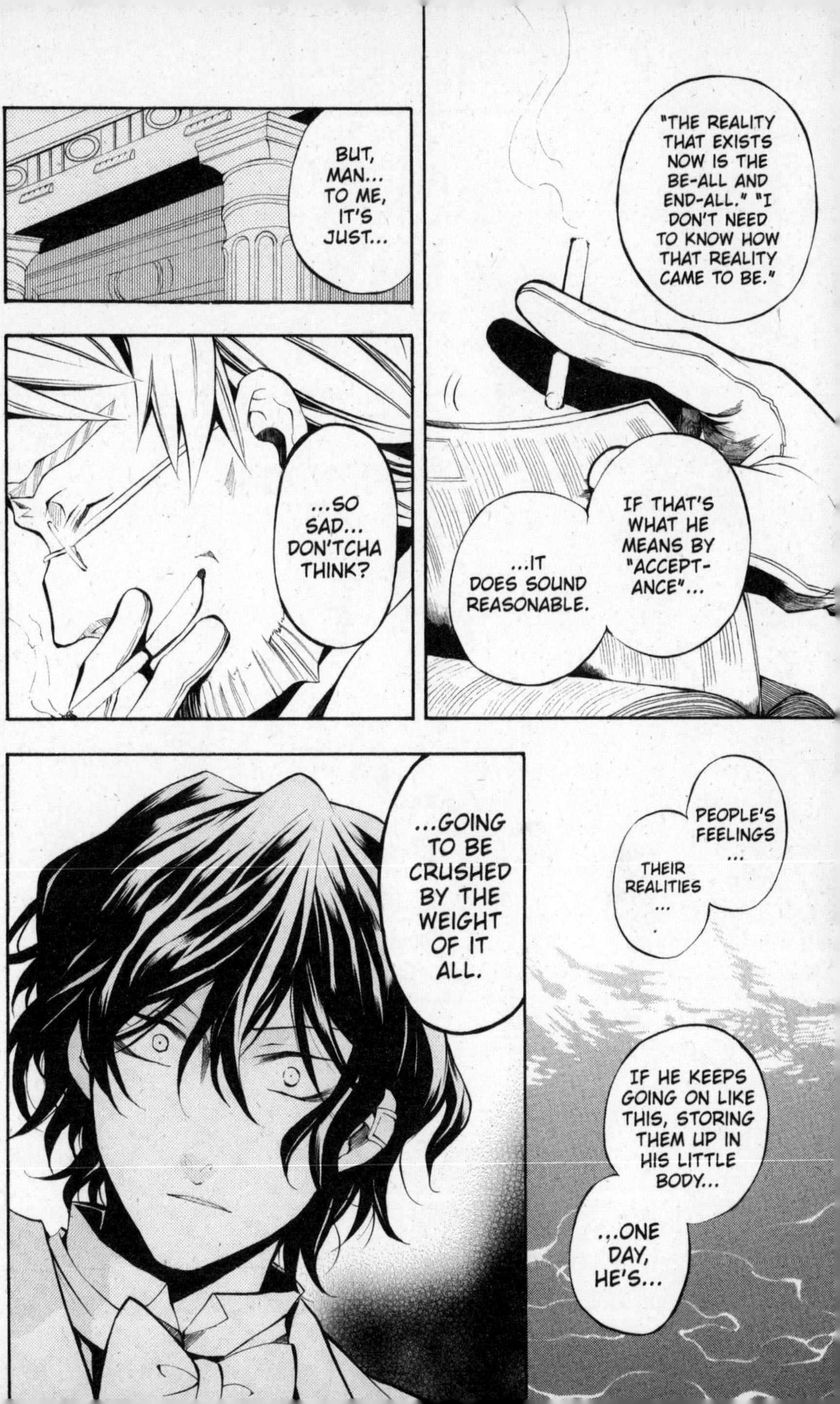
"THE REALITY THAT EXISTS NOW IS THE BE-ALL AND END-ALL." "I DON'T NEED TO KNOW HOW THAT REALITY CAME TO BE."
IF THAT'S WHAT HE MEANS BY "ACCEPT-ANCE"...
...IT DOES SOUND REASONABLE.
BUT, MAN... TO ME, IT'S JUST...
...SO SAD... DON'TCHA THINK?
PEOPLE'S FEELINGS...
THEIR REALITIES...
IF HE KEEPS GOING ON LIKE THIS, STORING THEM UP IN HIS LITTLE BODY...
...ONE DAY, HE'S...
...GOING TO BE CRUSHED BY THE WEIGHT OF IT ALL.

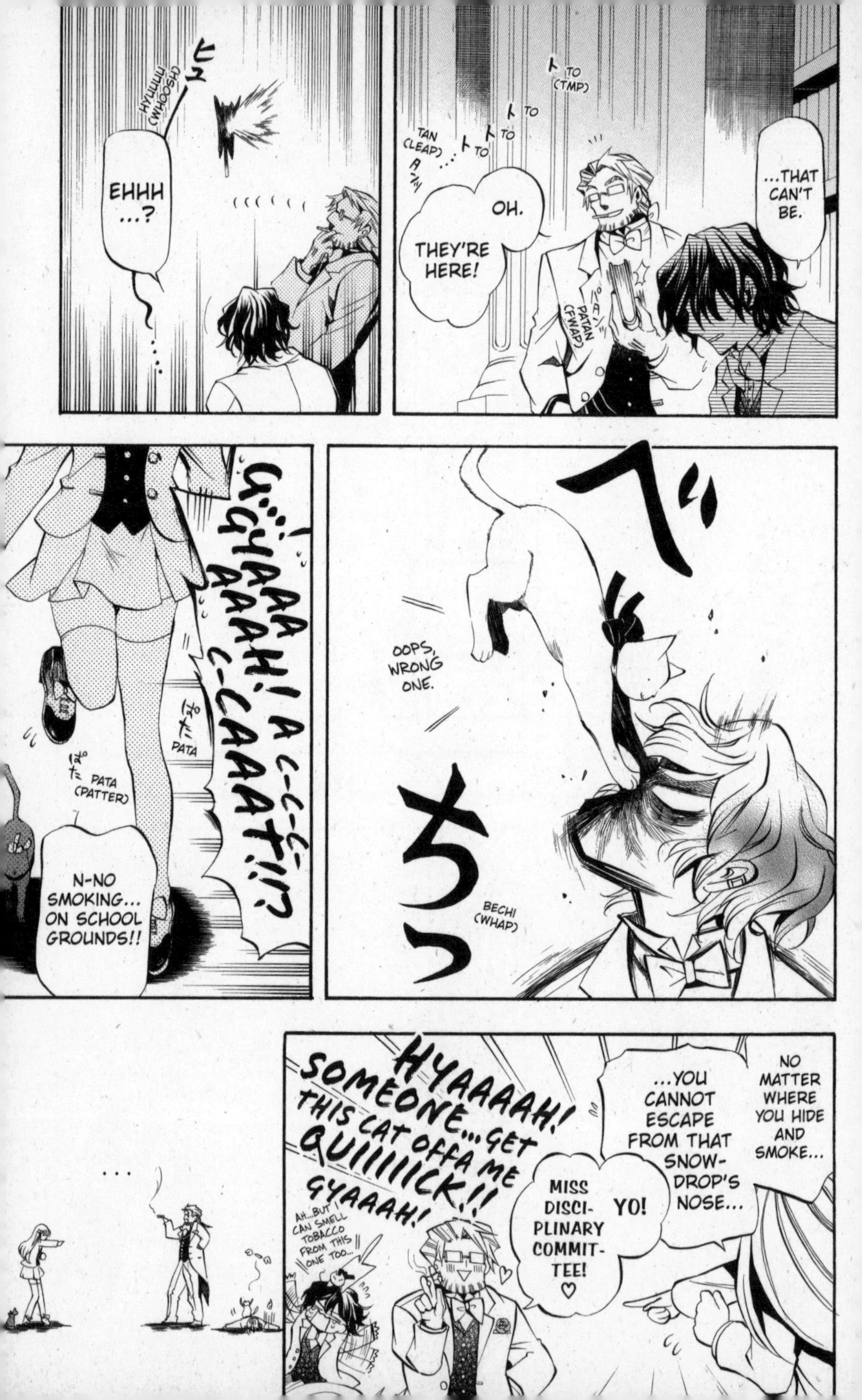
...THAT CAN'T BE.
TO (TMP)
TO
TO
TO
TAN (LEAP)
OH.
THEY'RE HERE!
PATAN (FWAP)
EHHH ...?
OOPS, WRONG ONE.
BECHI (WHAP)
GYAAAAAAAH! A C-C-C-C-CAAAT!!!?
PATA
PATA (PATTER)
N-NO SMOKING... ON SCHOOL GROUNDS!!
NO MATTER WHERE YOU HIDE AND SMOKE...
...YOU CANNOT ESCAPE FROM THAT SNOW-DROP'S NOSE...
YO!
MISS DISCI-PLINARY COMMIT-TEE! ♡
HYAAAAAH!
SOMEONE...GET THIS CAT OFFA ME QUIIIIICK!!
GYAAAH!
AH...BUT I CAN SMELL TOBACCO FROM THIS ONE TOO...
...

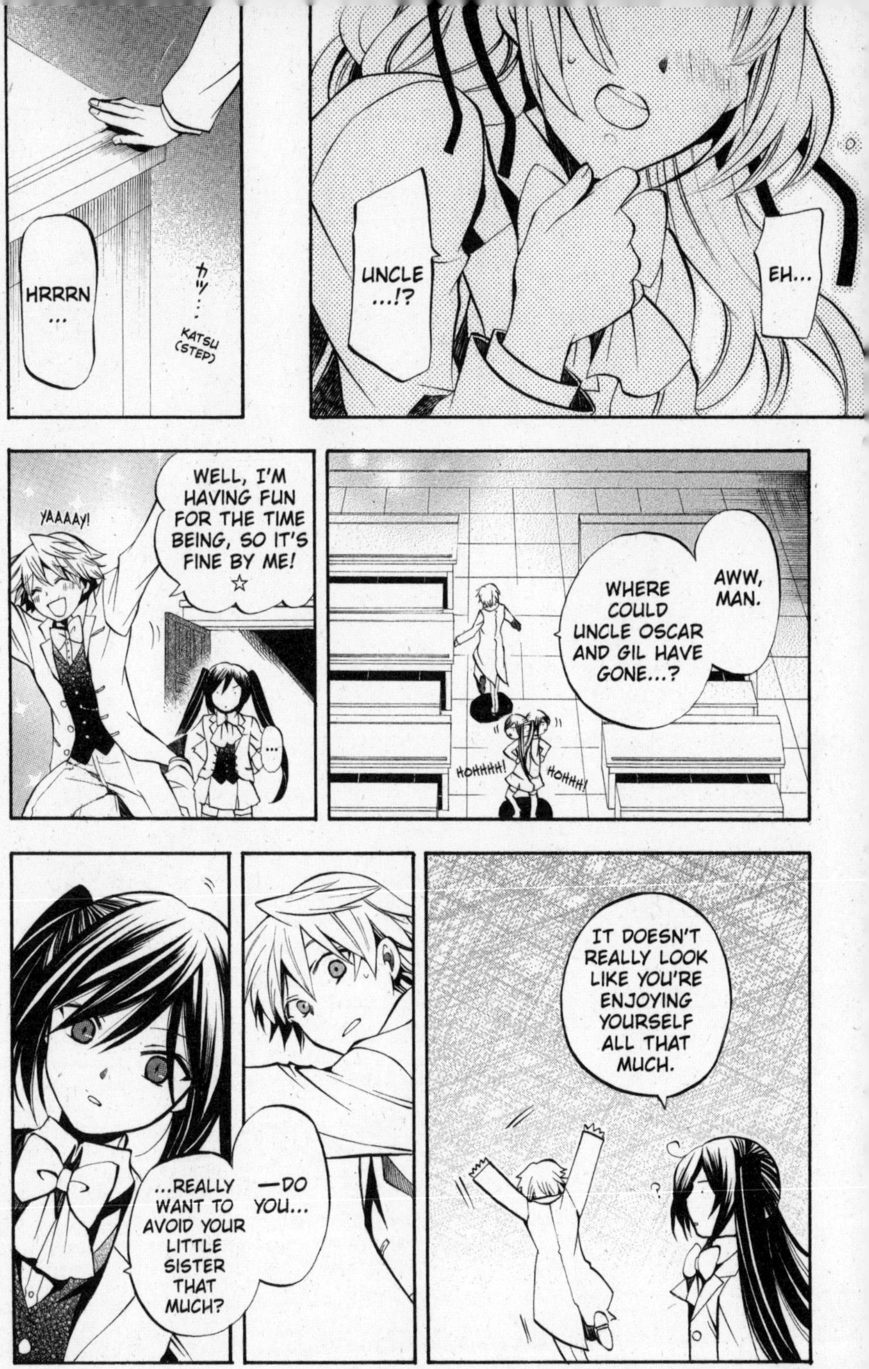
EH...
UNCLE ...!?
カッ...
KATSU (STEP)
HRRRN ...
AWW, MAN.
WHERE COULD UNCLE OSCAR AND GIL HAVE GONE...?
HOHHH!
HOHHHH!
WELL, I'M HAVING FUN FOR THE TIME BEING, SO IT'S FINE BY ME! ☆
YAAAAY!
...
IT DOESN'T REALLY LOOK LIKE YOU'RE ENJOYING YOURSELF ALL THAT MUCH.
—DO YOU...
...REALLY WANT TO AVOID YOUR LITTLE SISTER THAT MUCH?

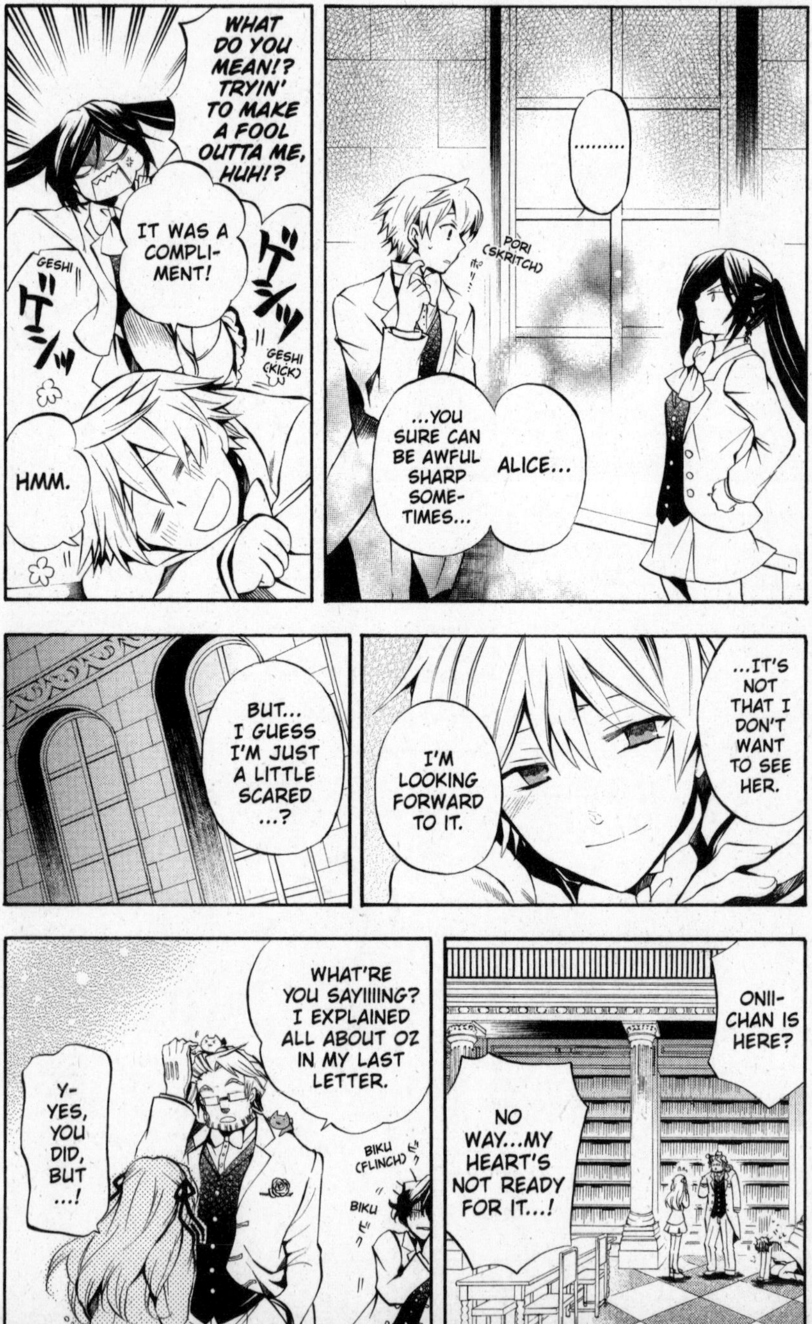
....
PORI (SKRITCH)
ALICE...
...YOU SURE CAN BE AWFUL SHARP SOMETIMES...
WHAT DO YOU MEAN!? TRYIN' TO MAKE A FOOL OUTTA ME, HUH!?
IT WAS A COMPLIMENT!
GESHI (KICK)
GESHI
HMM.
...IT'S NOT THAT I DON'T WANT TO SEE HER.
I'M LOOKING FORWARD TO IT.
BUT... I GUESS I'M JUST A LITTLE SCARED ...?
ONII-CHAN IS HERE?
NO WAY...MY HEART'S NOT READY FOR IT...!
WHAT'RE YOU SAYIIIING? I EXPLAINED ALL ABOUT OZ IN MY LAST LETTER.
BIKU (FLINCH)
BIKU
Y-YES, YOU DID, BUT ...!

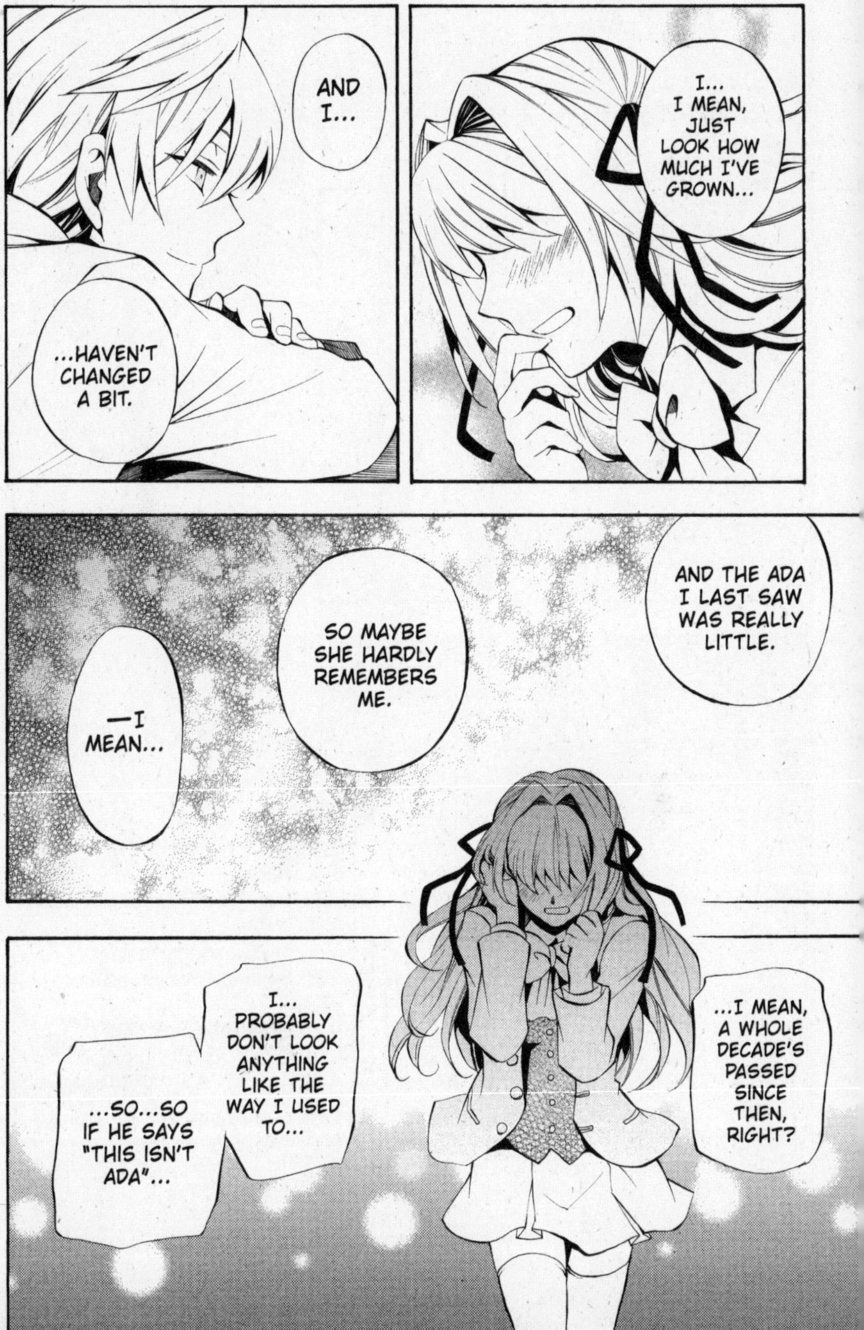
I... I MEAN, JUST LOOK HOW MUCH I'VE GROWN...
AND I...
...HAVEN'T CHANGED A BIT.
AND THE ADA I LAST SAW WAS REALLY LITTLE.
SO MAYBE SHE HARDLY REMEMBERS ME.
—I MEAN...
...I MEAN, A WHOLE DECADE'S PASSED SINCE THEN, RIGHT?
I... PROBABLY DON'T LOOK ANYTHING LIKE THE WAY I USED TO...
...SO...SO IF HE SAYS "THIS ISN'T ADA"...

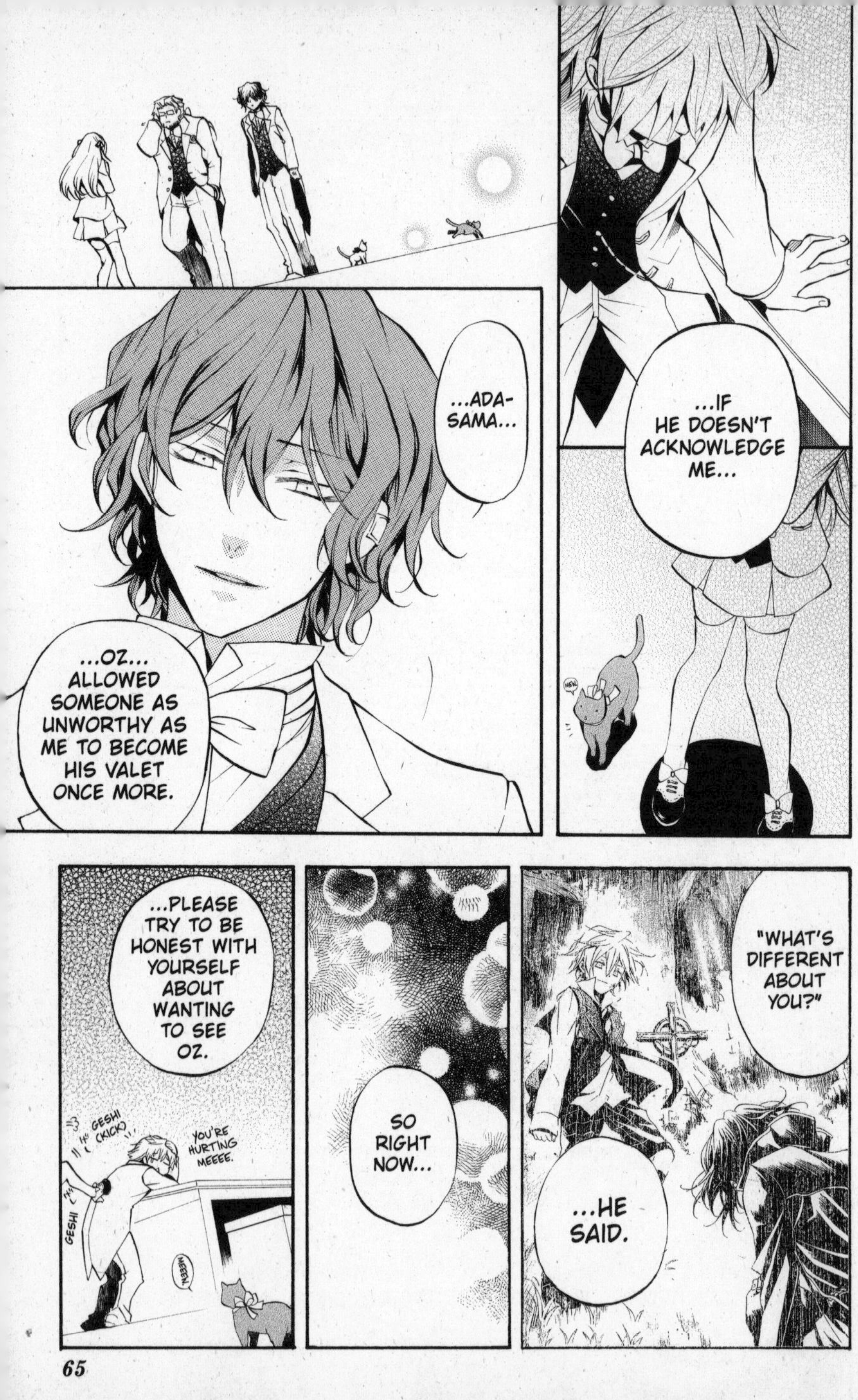
...IF HE DOESN'T ACKNOWLEDGE ME...
MEW
...ADA-SAMA...
...OZ... ALLOWED SOMEONE AS UNWORTHY AS ME TO BECOME HIS VALET ONCE MORE.
"WHAT'S DIFFERENT ABOUT YOU?"
...HE SAID.
SO RIGHT NOW...
...PLEASE TRY TO BE HONEST WITH YOURSELF ABOUT WANTING TO SEE OZ.
GESHI (KICK)
YOU'RE HURTING MEEEE.
GESHI
MEEEW.

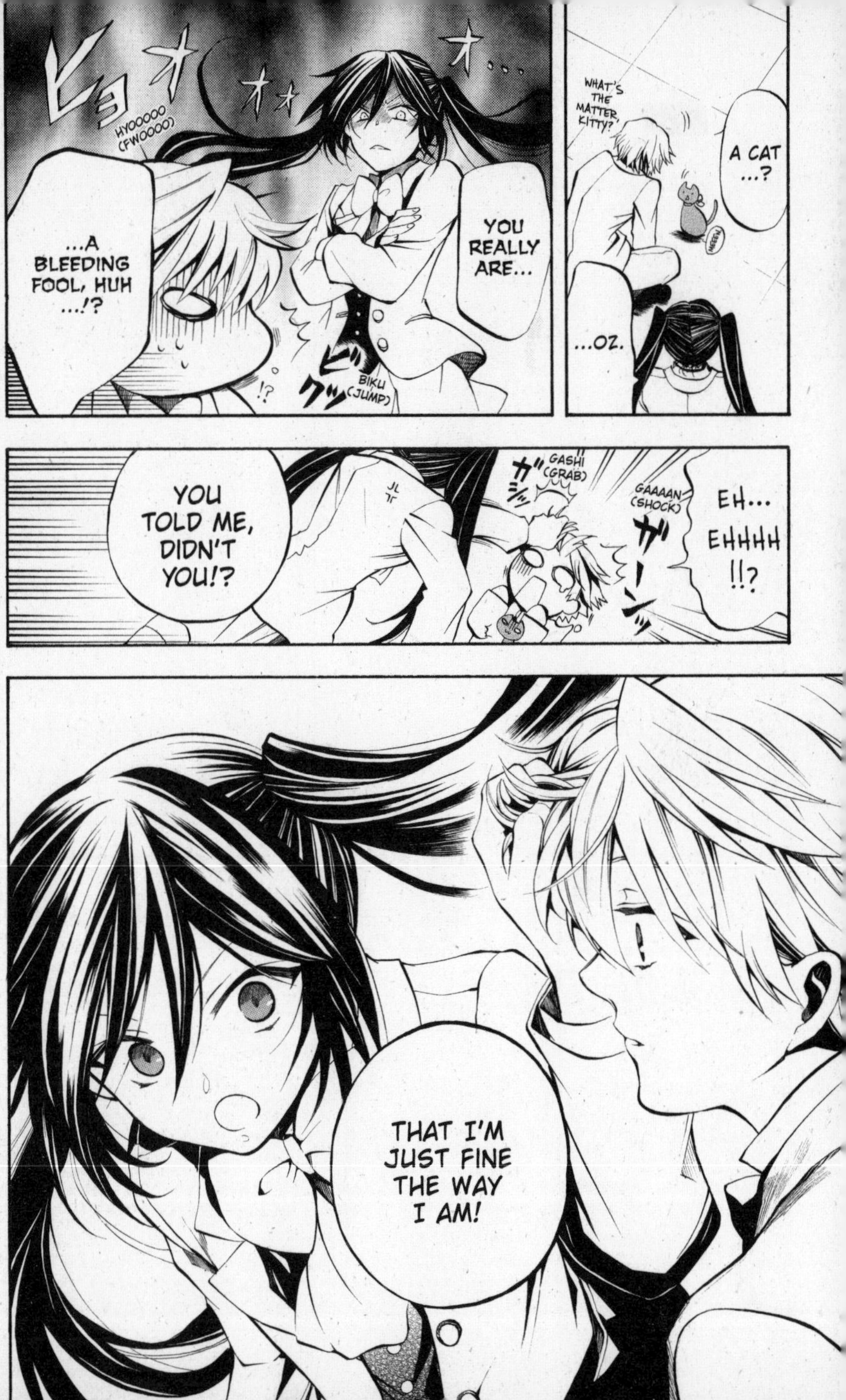
A CAT ...?
WHAT'S THE MATTER, KITTY?
MEEEW.
...OZ.
HYOOOOO (FWOOOO)
YOU REALLY ARE...
...A BLEEDING FOOL, HUH ...!?
BIKU (JUMP)
!?
EH... EHHHH !!?
GAAAAN (SHOCK)
GASHI (GRAB)
YOU TOLD ME, DIDN'T YOU!?
THAT I'M JUST FINE THE WAY I AM!

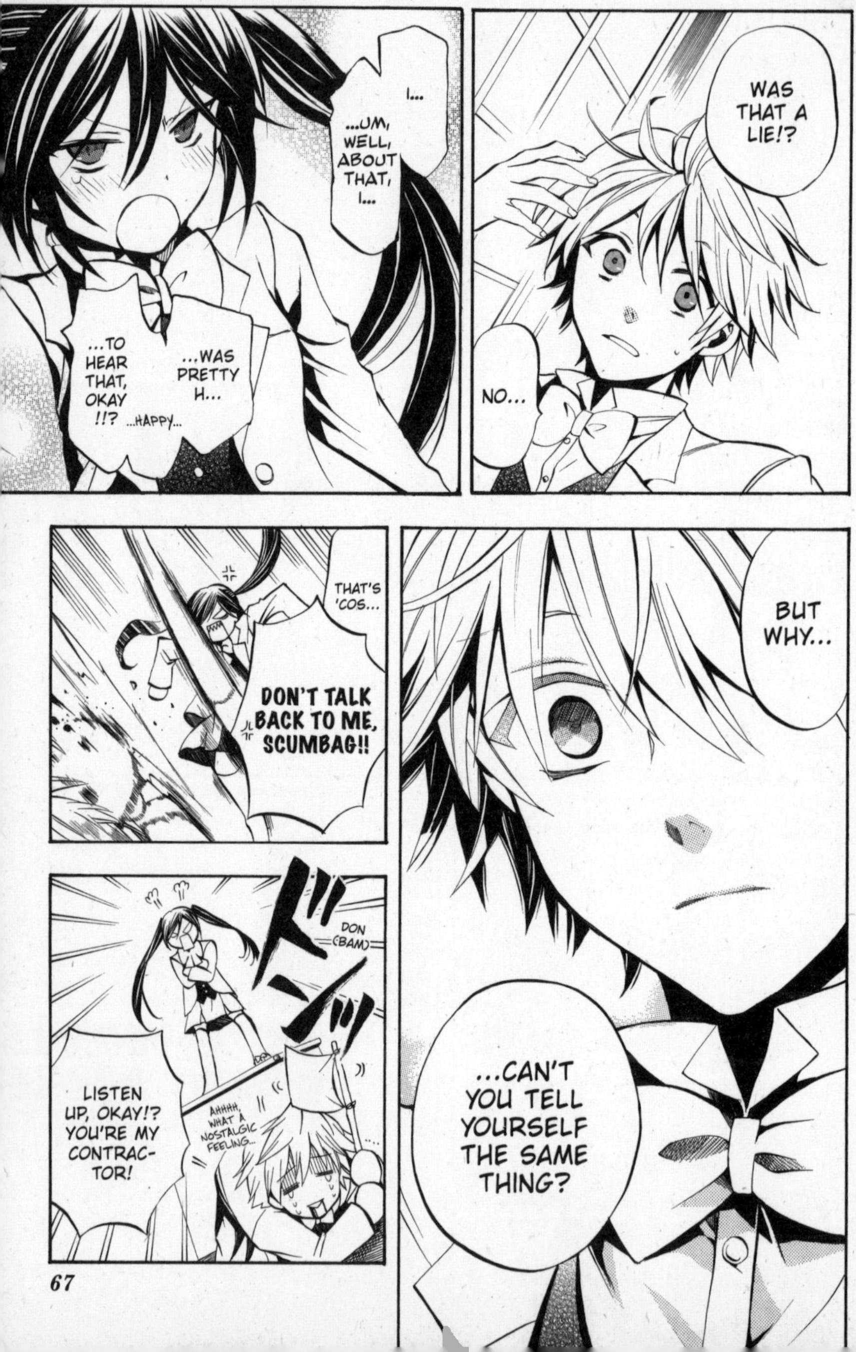
WAS THAT A LIE!?
NO...
I...
...UM, WELL, ABOUT THAT, I...
...WAS PRETTY H...
...HAPPY...
...TO HEAR THAT, OKAY!!?
BUT WHY...
...CAN'T YOU TELL YOURSELF THE SAME THING?
THAT'S 'COS...
DON'T TALK BACK TO ME, SCUMBAG!!
DON (BAM)
LISTEN UP, OKAY!? YOU'RE MY CONTRACTOR!
AHHHH, WHAT A NOSTALGIC FEELING...
...

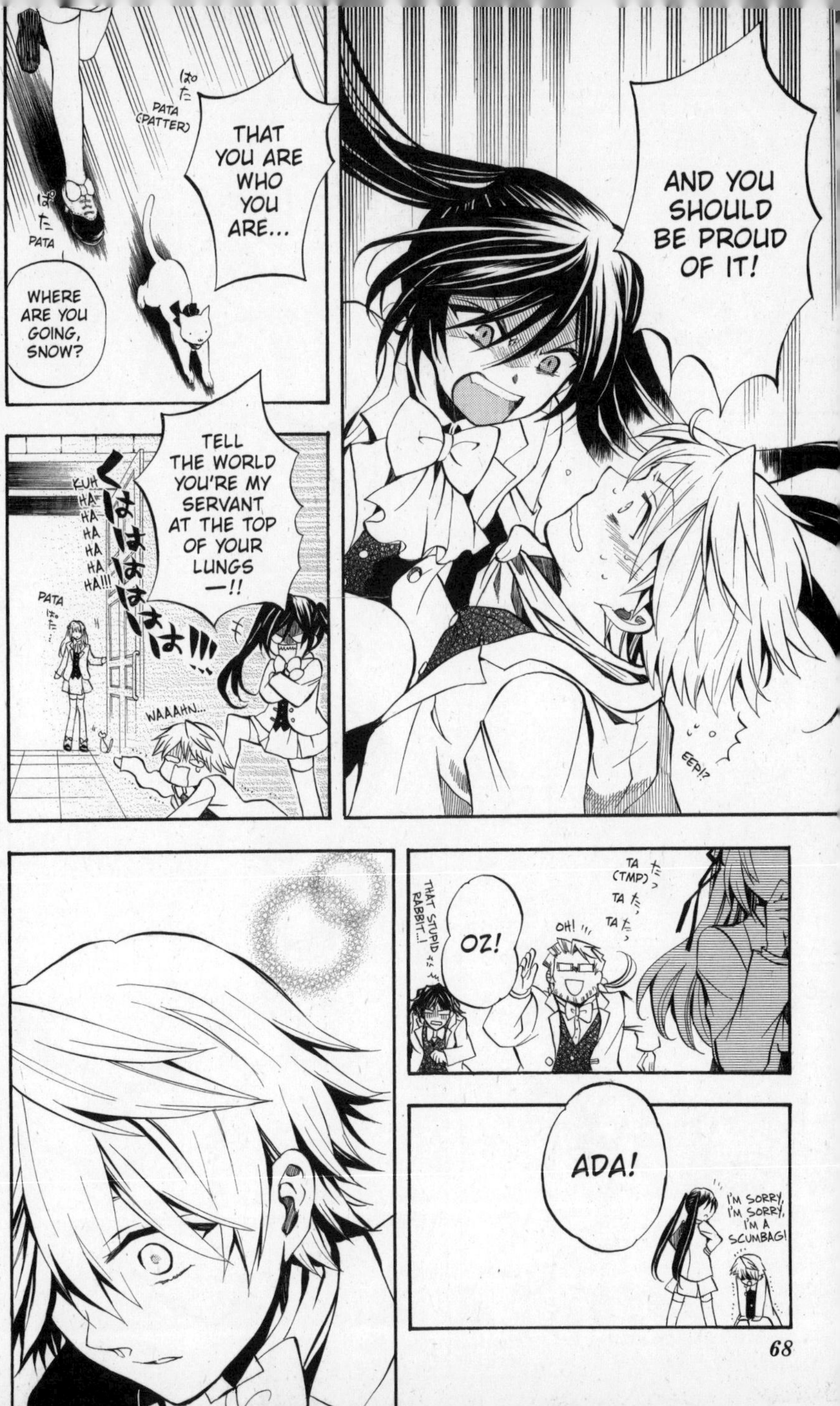
AND YOU SHOULD BE PROUD OF IT!
EEP!?
ぱた PATA (PATTER)
THAT YOU ARE WHO YOU ARE...
ぱた PATA
WHERE ARE YOU GOING, SNOW?
TELL THE WORLD YOU'RE MY SERVANT AT THE TOP OF YOUR LUNGS ー!!
くはははははは!!! KUH HA HA HA HA HA HA!!!
PATA ぱた...
WAAAHN...
TA たっ (TMP)
TA た,
TA た,
OH! !!
OZ!
THAT STUPID RABBIT...!
ADA!
I'M SORRY, I'M SORRY, I'M A SCUMBAG!

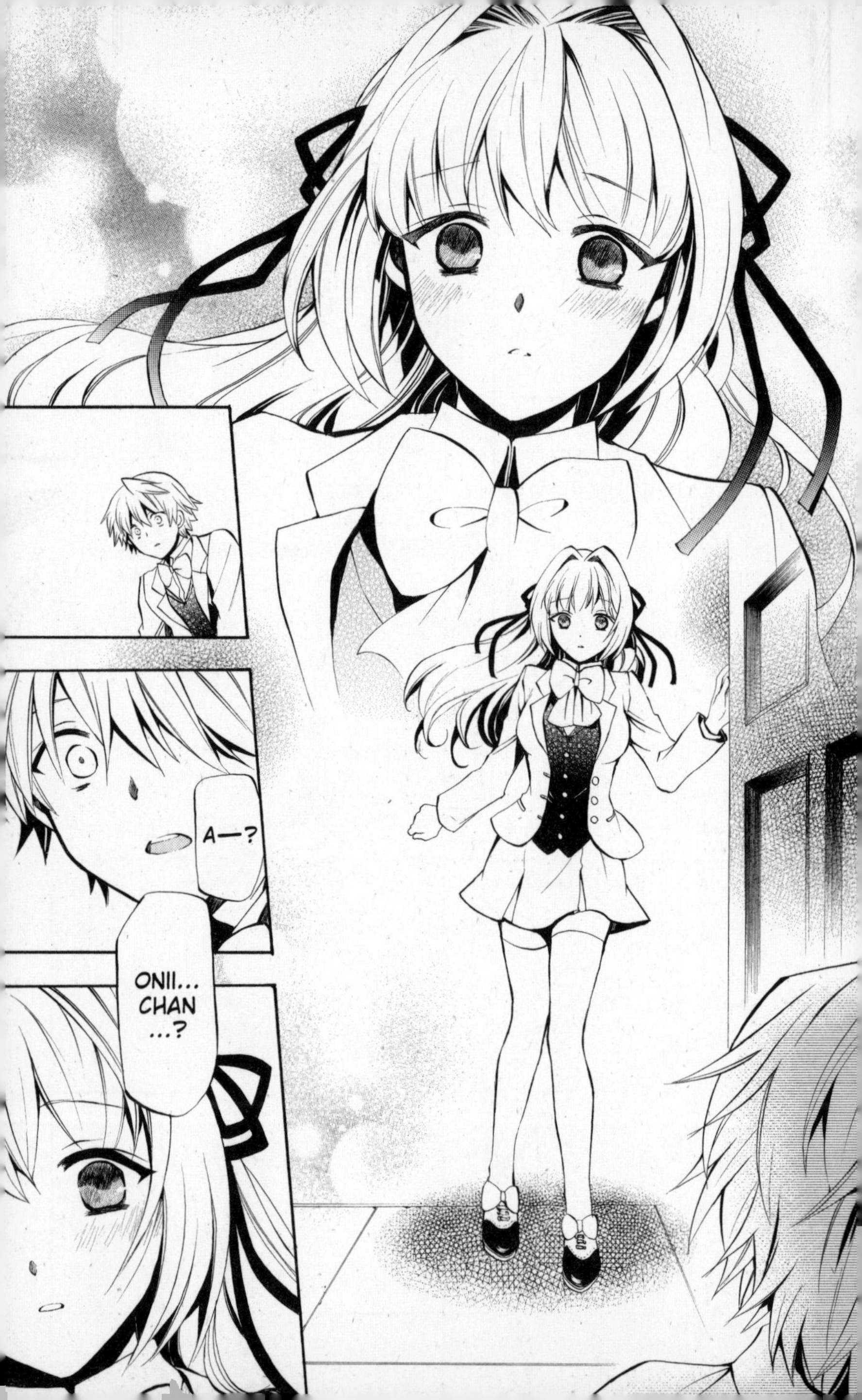
A—?
ONII... CHAN ...?

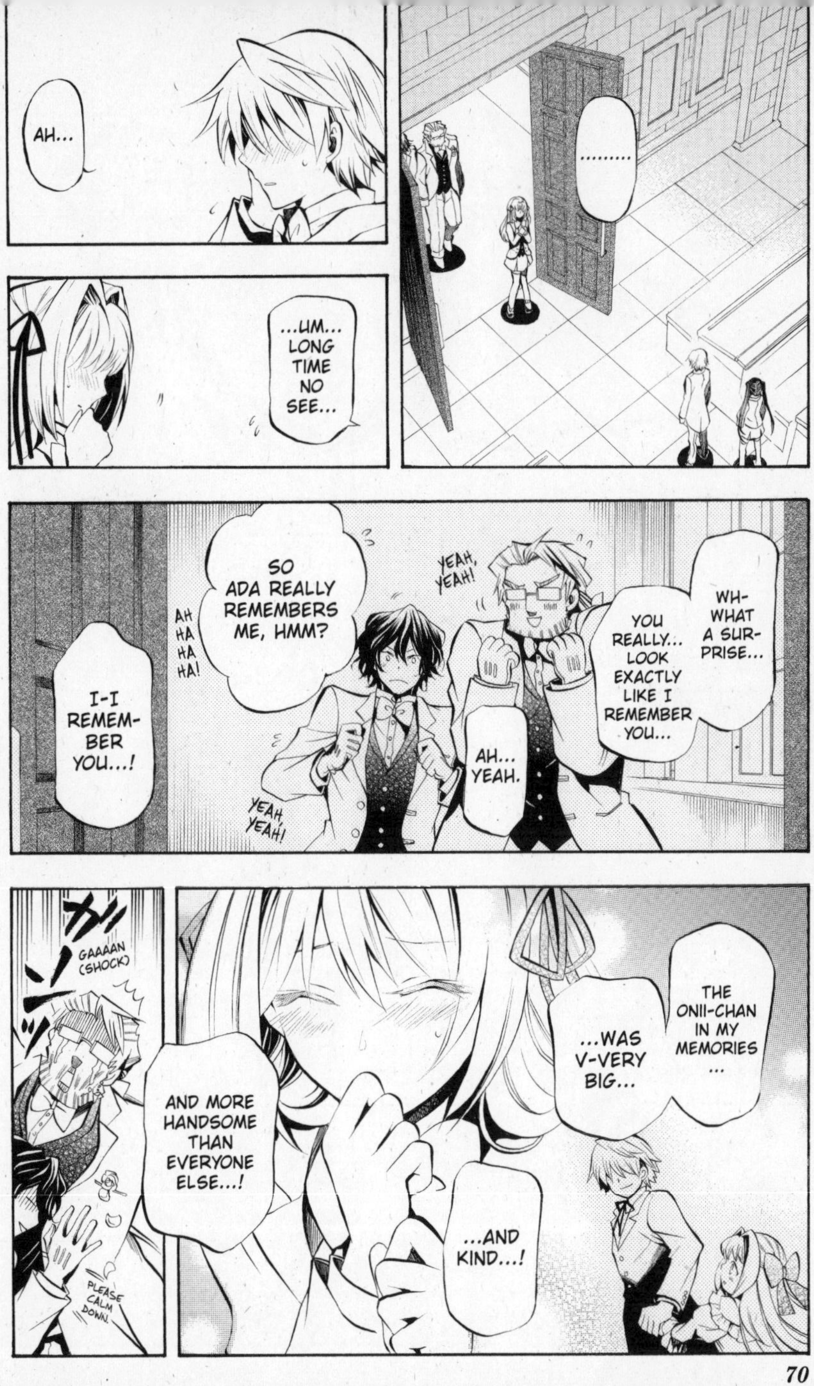
....
AH...
...UM... LONG TIME NO SEE...
WH-WHAT A SURPRISE...
YOU REALLY... LOOK EXACTLY LIKE I REMEMBER YOU...
YEAH, YEAH!
AH... YEAH.
SO ADA REALLY REMEMBERS ME, HMM?
AH HA HA HA!
YEAH, YEAH!
I-I REMEMBER YOU...!
THE ONII-CHAN IN MY MEMORIES...
...WAS V-VERY BIG...
AND MORE HANDSOME THAN EVERYONE ELSE...!
...AND KIND...!
GAAAAN (SHOCK)
PLEASE CALM DOWN.

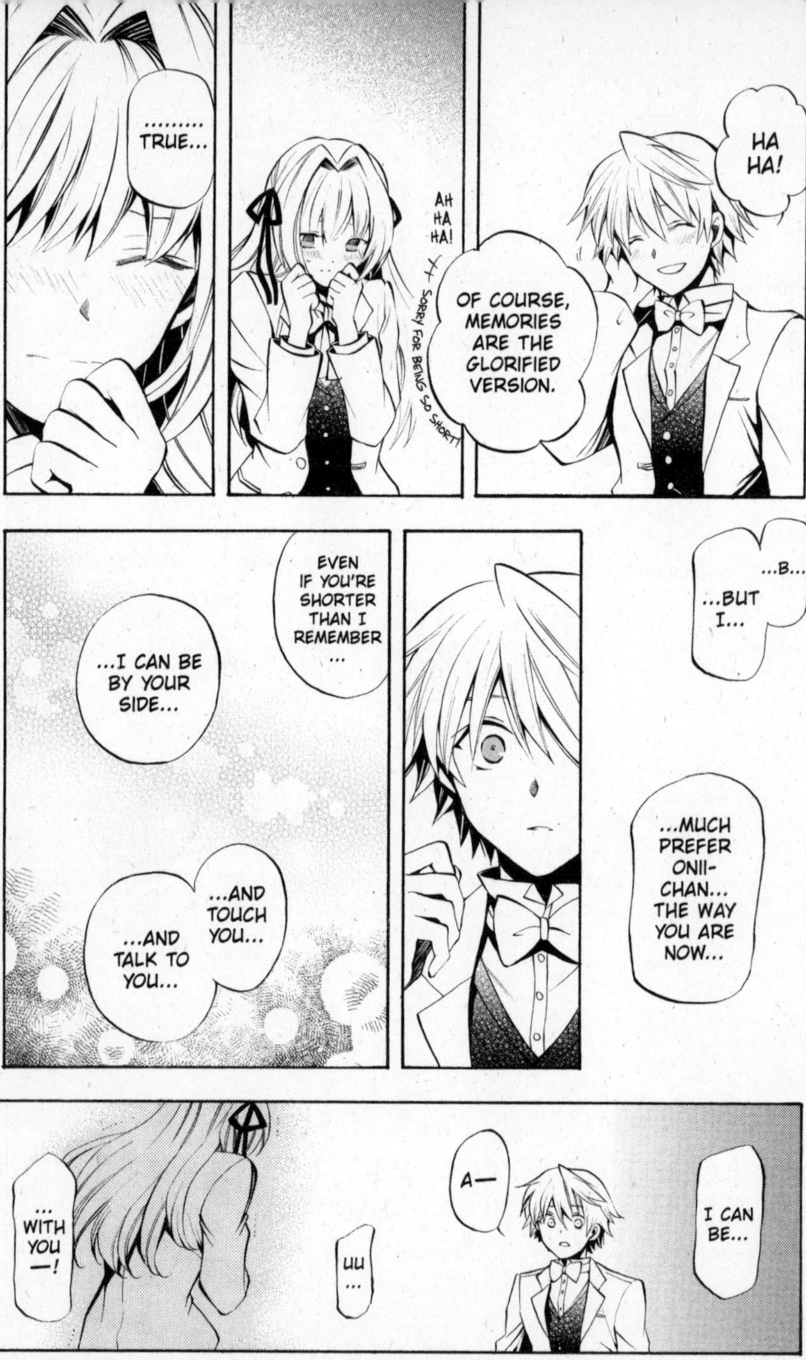
HA HA!
OF COURSE, MEMORIES ARE THE GLORIFIED VERSION.
AH HA HA!
SORRY FOR BEING SO SHORT!
.... TRUE...
...B... ...BUT I...
...MUCH PREFER ONII-CHAN... THE WAY YOU ARE NOW...
EVEN IF YOU'RE SHORTER THAN I REMEMBER...
...I CAN BE BY YOUR SIDE...
...AND TOUCH YOU...
...AND TALK TO YOU...
I CAN BE...
A—
UU...
...WITH YOU—!

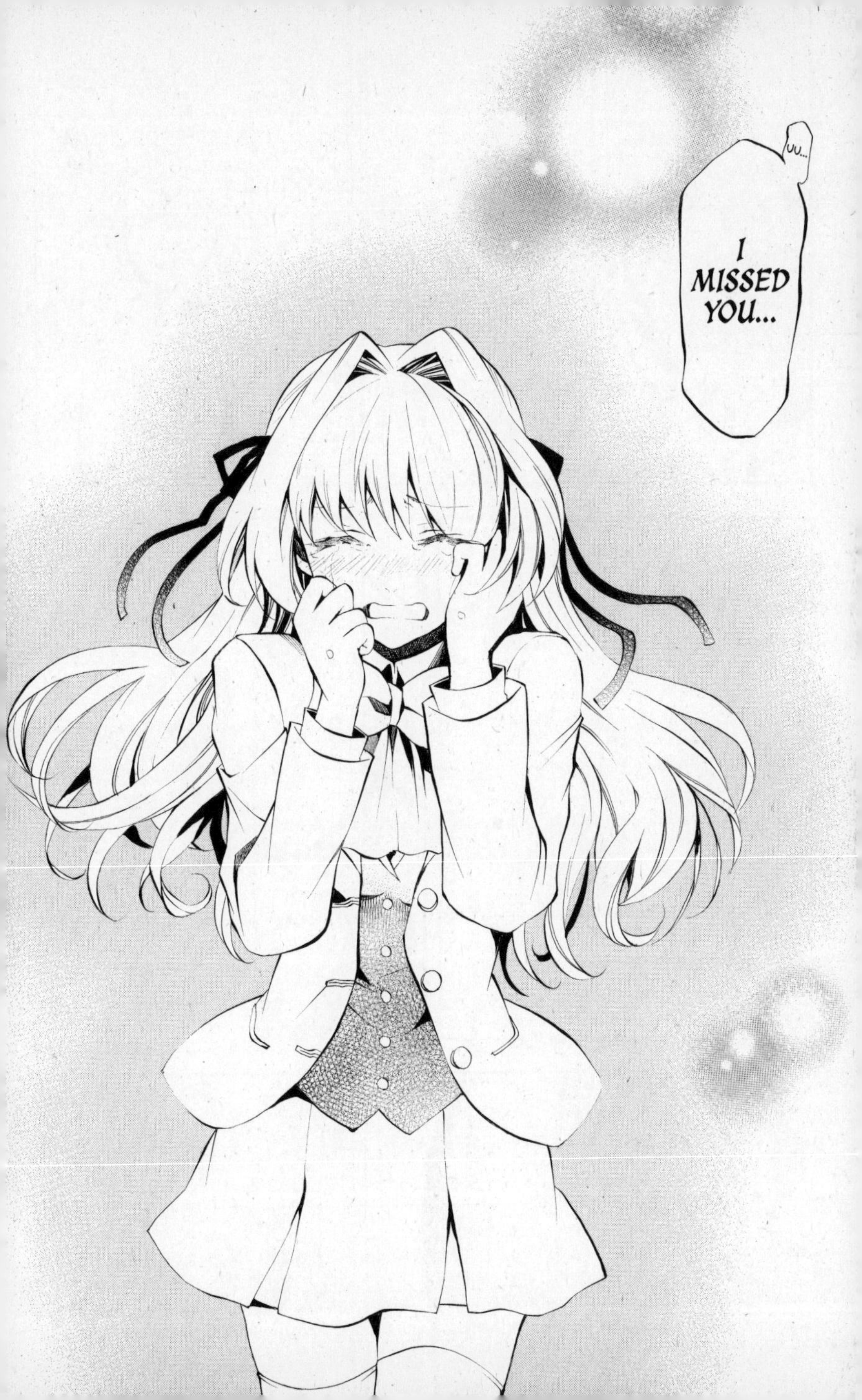
UU...
I MISSED YOU...

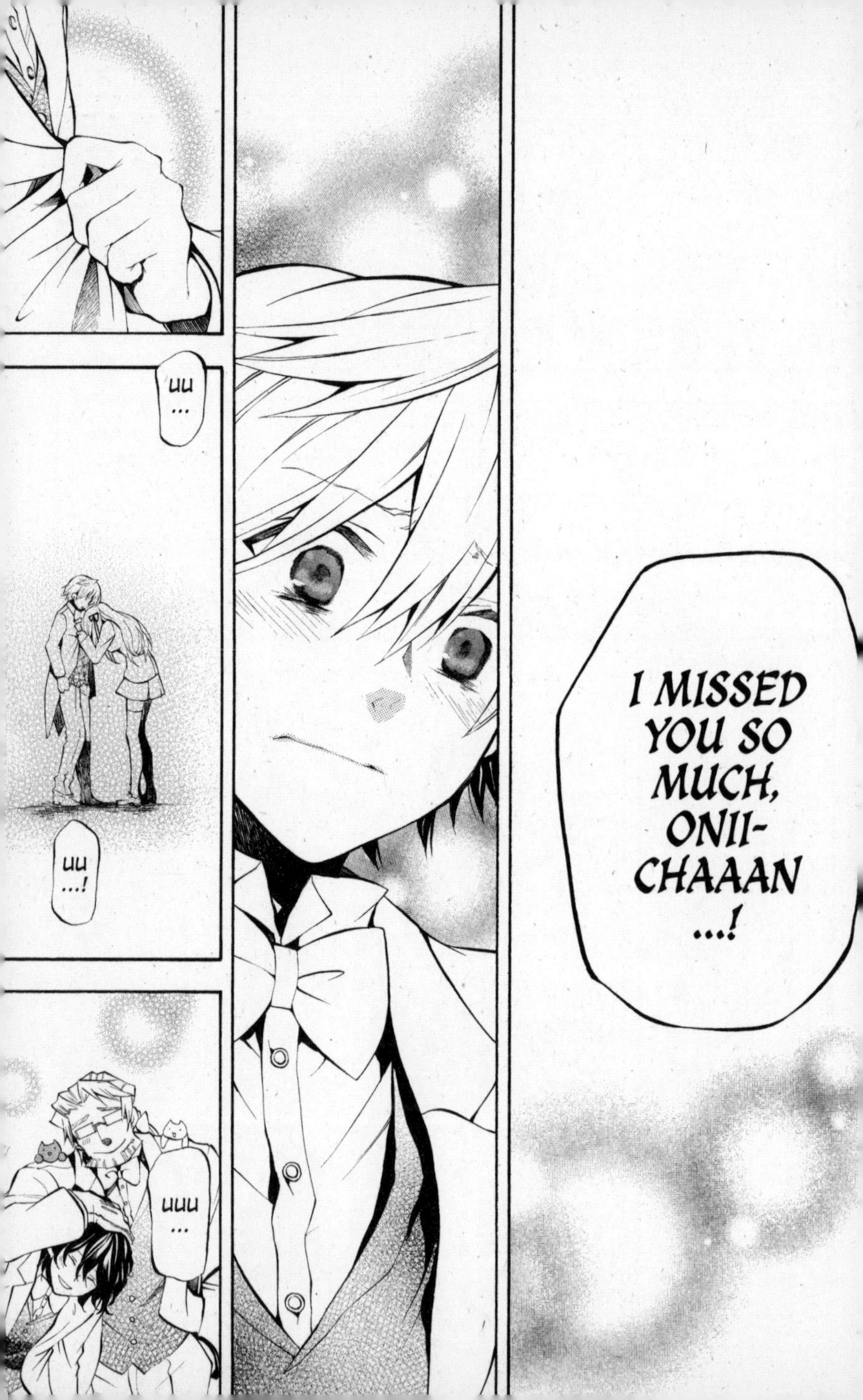
I MISSED YOU SO MUCH, ONII-CHAAAN ...!
UU ...
UU ...!
UUU ...

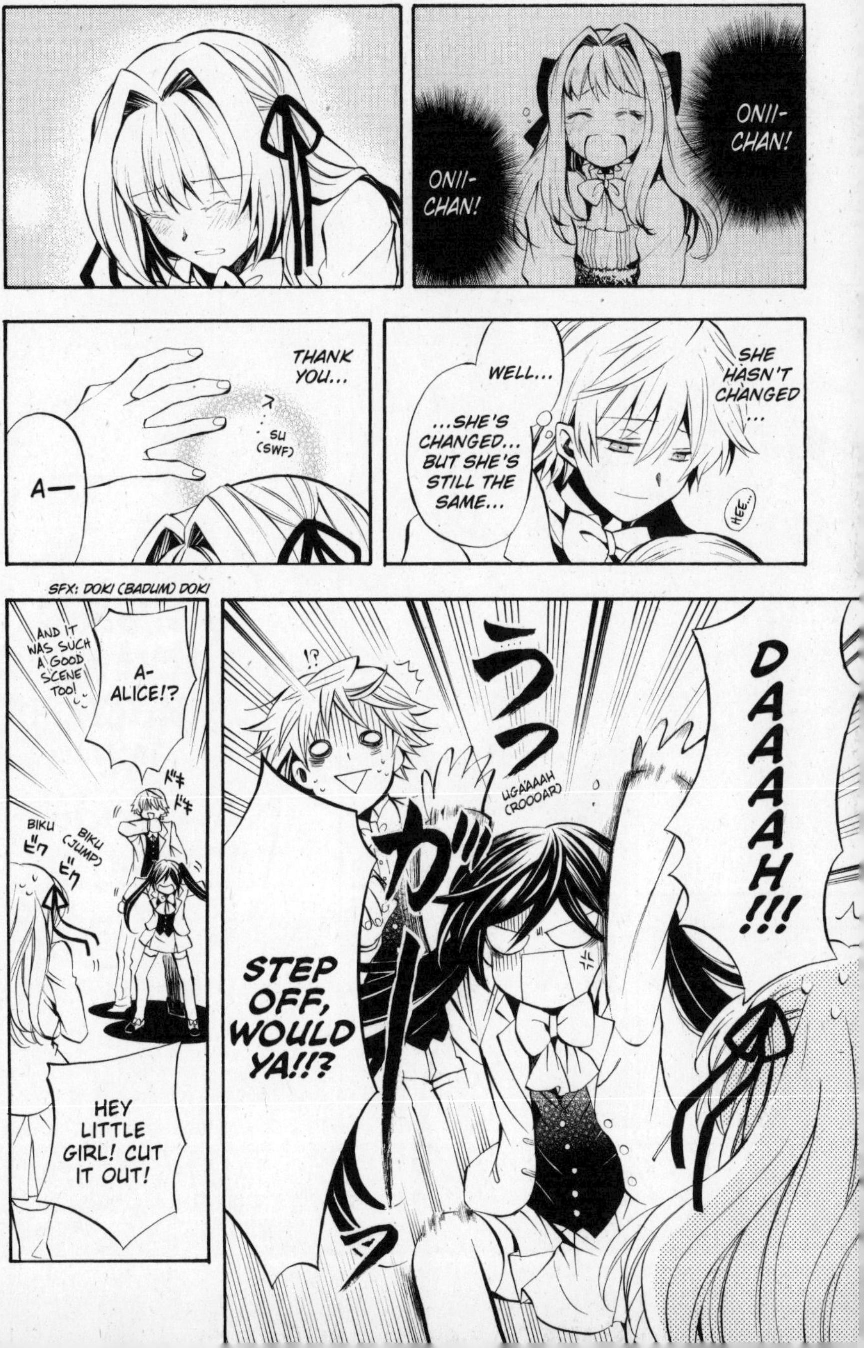
ONII-CHAN!
ONII-CHAN!
SHE HASN'T CHANGED...
WELL...
...SHE'S CHANGED... BUT SHE'S STILL THE SAME...
HEE...
THANK YOU...
SU (SWF)
A—
SFX: DOKI (BADUM) DOKI
DAAAAAH!!!
UGAAAAH (ROOOAR)
STEP OFF, WOULD YA!!?
!?
A- ALICE!?
AND IT WAS SUCH A GOOD SCENE TOO!
ドキ ドキ
BIKU (JUMP) ビク
BIKU ビク
HEY LITTLE GIRL! CUT IT OUT!

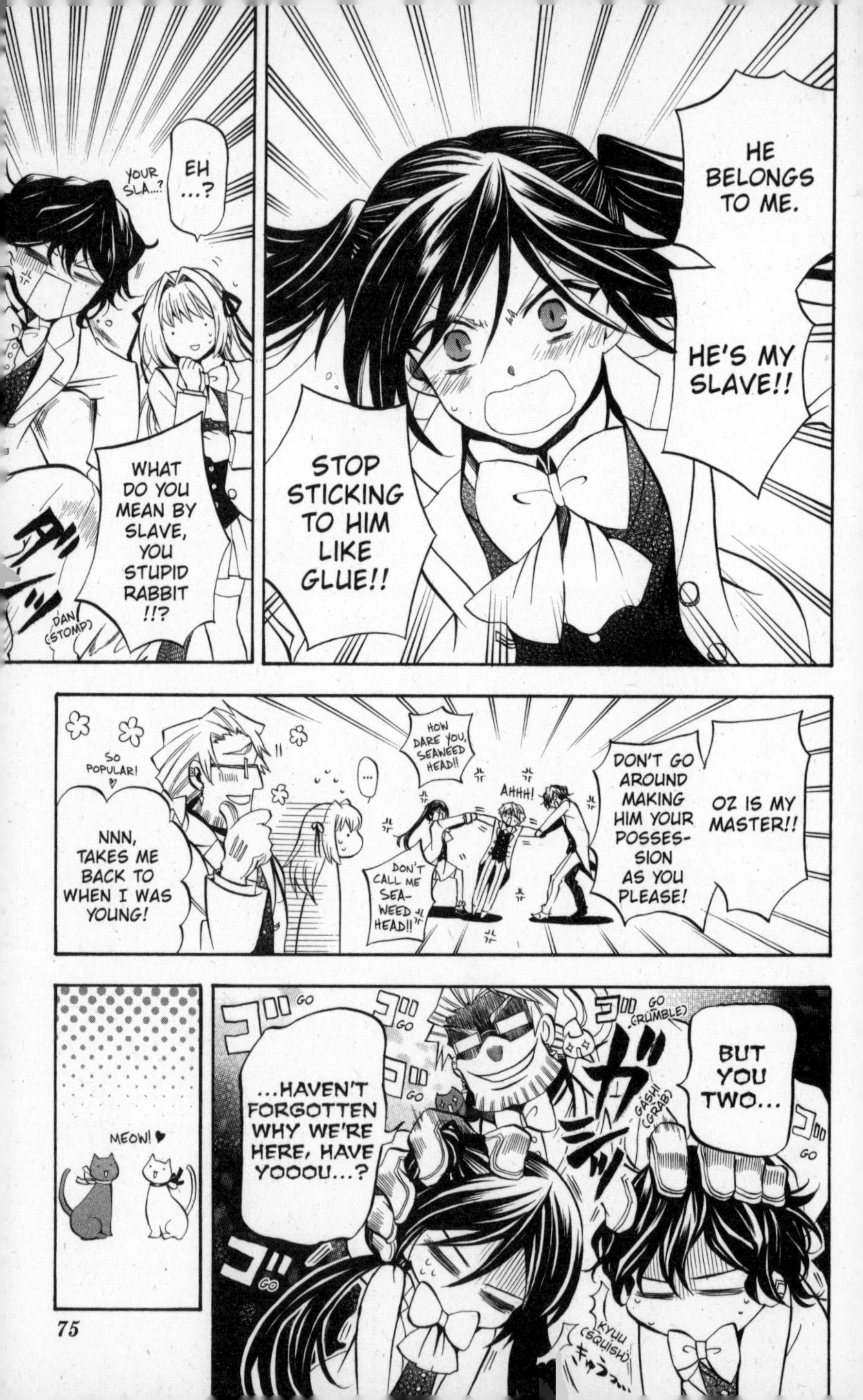
HE BELONGS TO ME.
HE'S MY SLAVE!!
STOP STICKING TO HIM LIKE GLUE!!
EH ...?
YOUR SLA...?
WHAT DO YOU MEAN BY SLAVE, YOU STUPID RABBIT !!?
DAN (STOMP)
OZ IS MY MASTER!!
DON'T GO AROUND MAKING HIM YOUR POSSES-SION AS YOU PLEASE!
HOW DARE YOU, SEAWEED HEAD!!
AHHH!
DON'T CALL ME SEA-WEED HEAD!!
...
SO POPULAR!
NNN, TAKES ME BACK TO WHEN I WAS YOUNG!
GO
GO (RUMBLE)
BUT YOU TWO...
GASH! (GRAB)
...HAVEN'T FORGOTTEN WHY WE'RE HERE, HAVE YOOOU...?
KYUU (SQUISH)
MEOW!

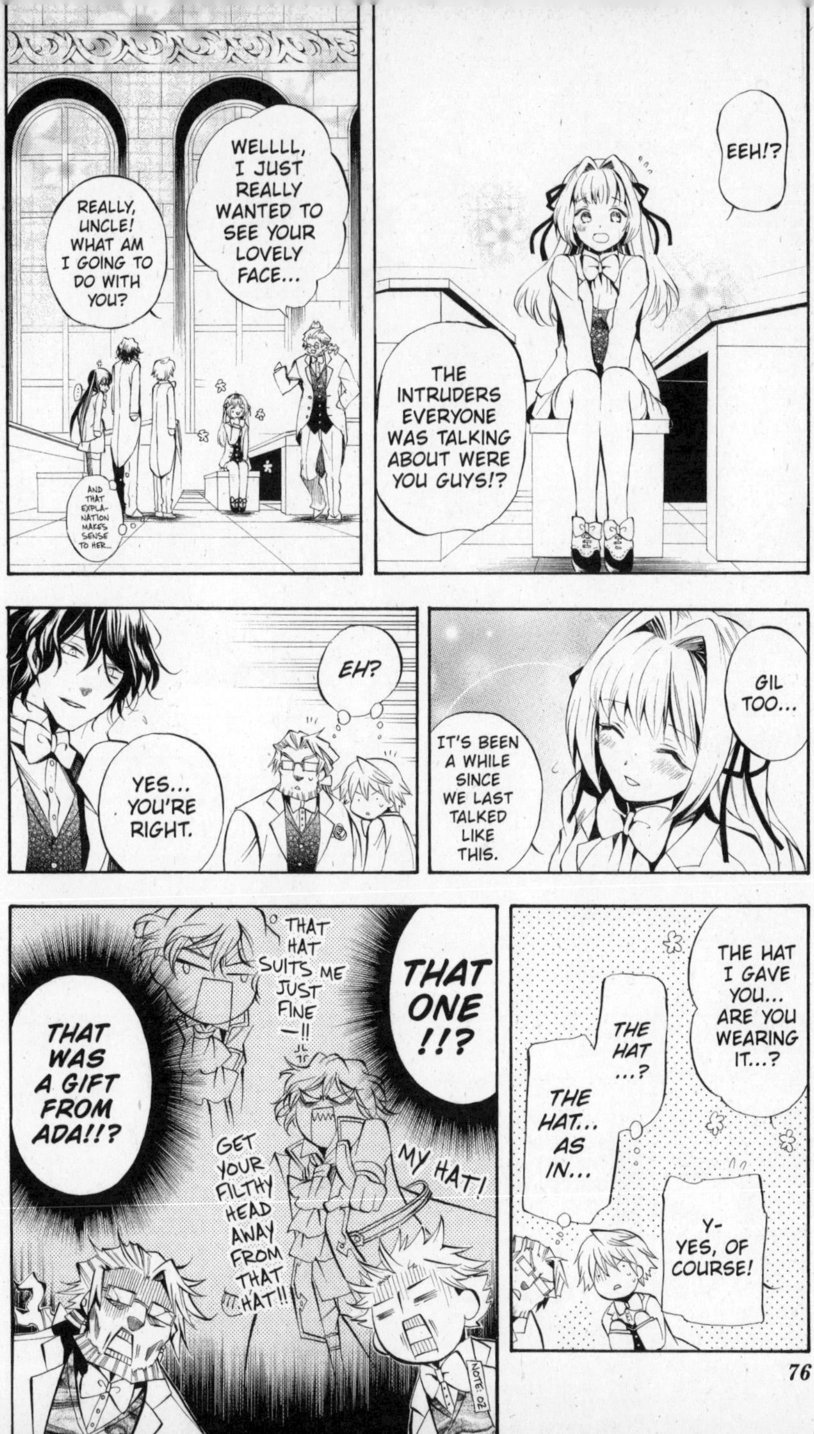
EEH!?
THE INTRUDERS EVERYONE WAS TALKING ABOUT WERE YOU GUYS!?
WELLLL, I JUST REALLY WANTED TO SEE YOUR LOVELY FACE...
REALLY, UNCLE! WHAT AM I GOING TO DO WITH YOU?
AND THAT EXPLANATION MAKES SENSE TO HER...
GIL TOO...
IT'S BEEN A WHILE SINCE WE LAST TALKED LIKE THIS.
EH?
YES... YOU'RE RIGHT.
THE HAT I GAVE YOU... ARE YOU WEARING IT...?
THE HAT ...?
THE HAT... AS IN...
Y- YES, OF COURSE!
THAT ONE!!?
THAT HAT SUITS ME JUST FINE—!!
MY HAT!
GET YOUR FILTHY HEAD AWAY FROM THAT HAT!!
THAT WAS A GIFT FROM ADA!!?
NOTE: 02

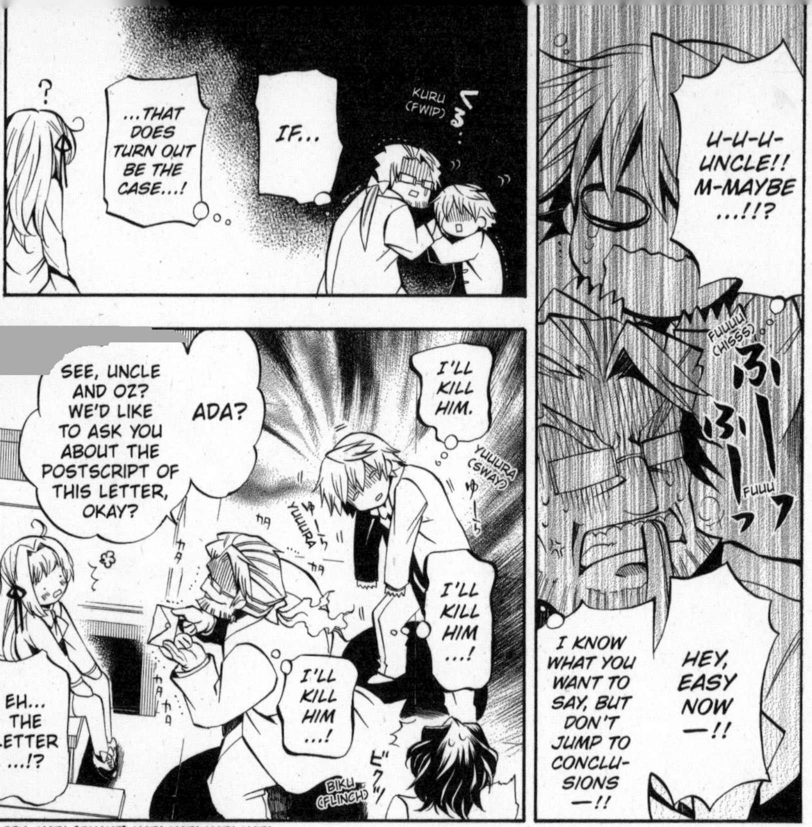
U-U-U-UNCLE!! M-MAYBE ...!!?
FUUUU (HISSS)
FUUU
HEY, EASY NOW—!!
I KNOW WHAT YOU WANT TO SAY, BUT DON'T JUMP TO CONCLUSIONS—!!
KURU (FWIP)
IF...
...THAT DOES TURN OUT BE THE CASE...!
I'LL KILL HIM.
YUUURA (SWAY)
ADA?
SEE, UNCLE AND OZ? WE'D LIKE TO ASK YOU ABOUT THE POSTSCRIPT OF THIS LETTER, OKAY?
YUUURA
I'LL KILL HIM...!
I'LL KILL HIM...!
BIKU (FLINCH)
EH... THE LETTER ...!?

SFX: KATA (SHAKE) KATA KATA KATA KATA

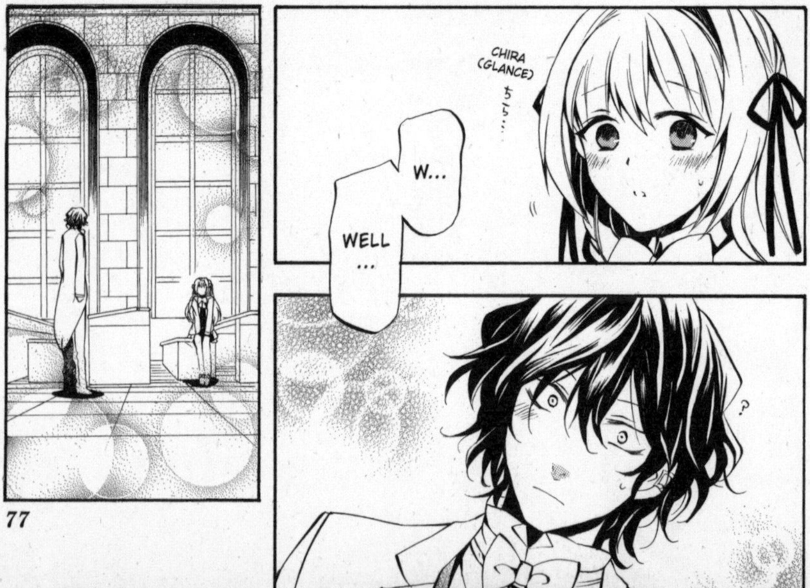
CHIRA (GLANCE)
W...
WELL ...
?

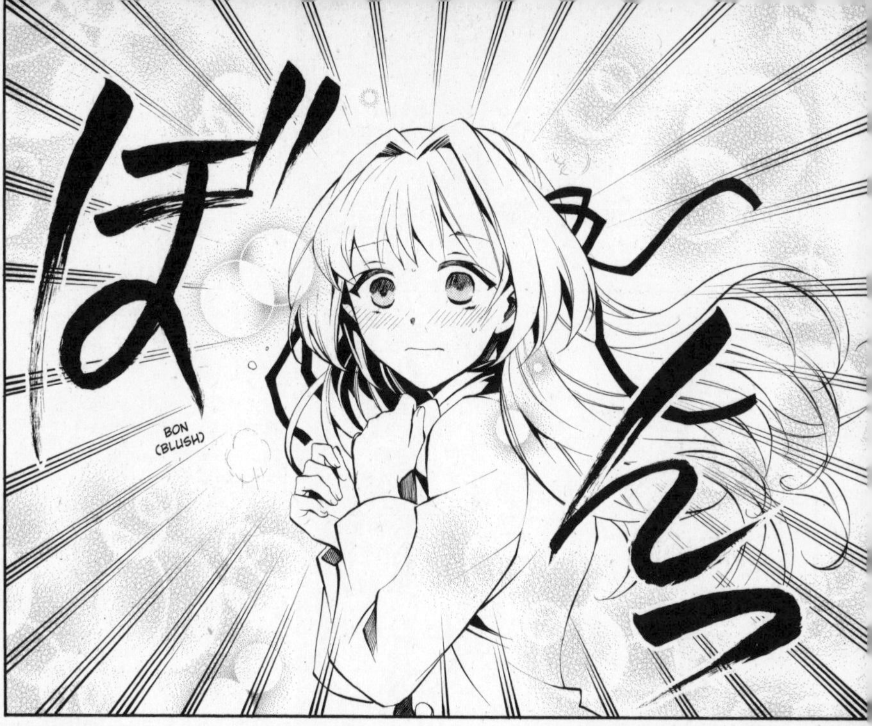
ぼん
BON (BLUSH)

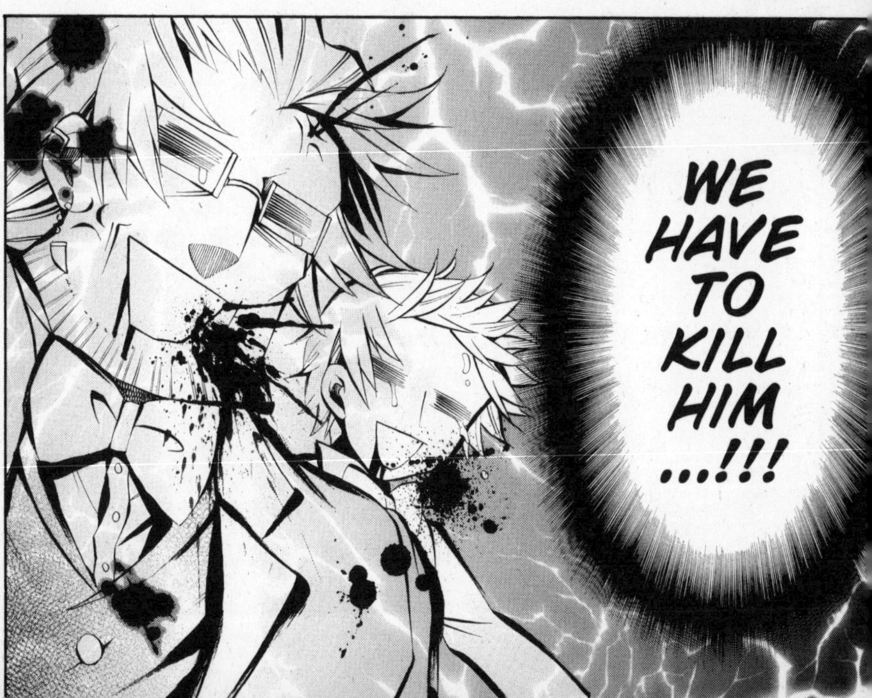
WE HAVE TO KILL HIM ...!!!

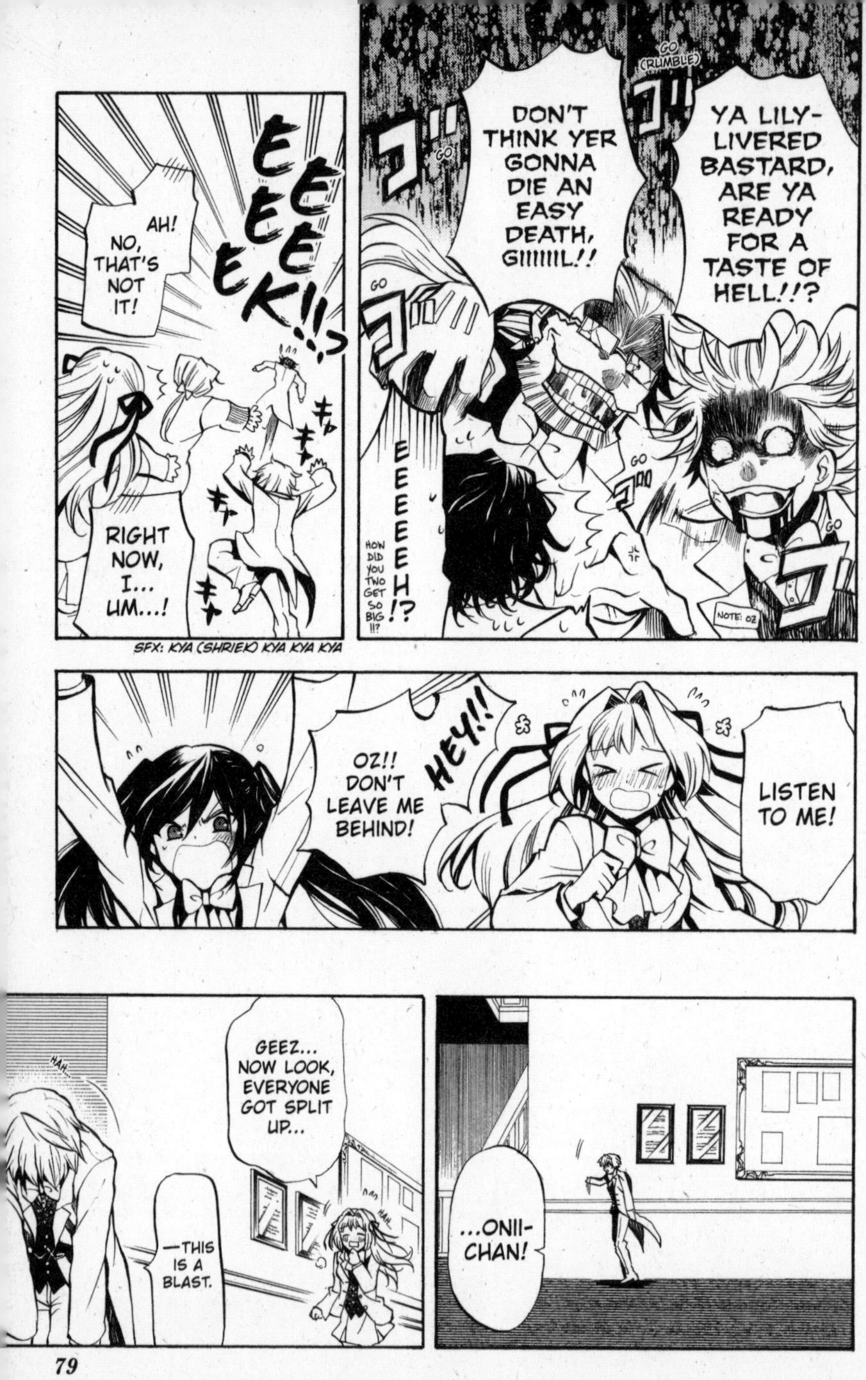
GO (RUMBLE)
YA LILY-LIVERED BASTARD, ARE YA READY FOR A TASTE OF HELL!!?
GO
DON'T THINK YER GONNA DIE AN EASY DEATH, GIIIIIIL!!
GO
GO
GO
EEEEEEEH!?
HOW DID YOU TWO GET SO BIG!!?
NOTE: OZ
EEEEEEK!!?
AH! NO, THAT'S NOT IT!
RIGHT NOW, I... UM...!
SFX: KYA (SHRIEK) KYA KYA KYA
LISTEN TO ME!
HEY!!
OZ!! DON'T LEAVE ME BEHIND!
...ONII-CHAN!
GEEZ... NOW LOOK, EVERYONE GOT SPLIT UP...
HAH
—THIS IS A BLAST.
HAH...

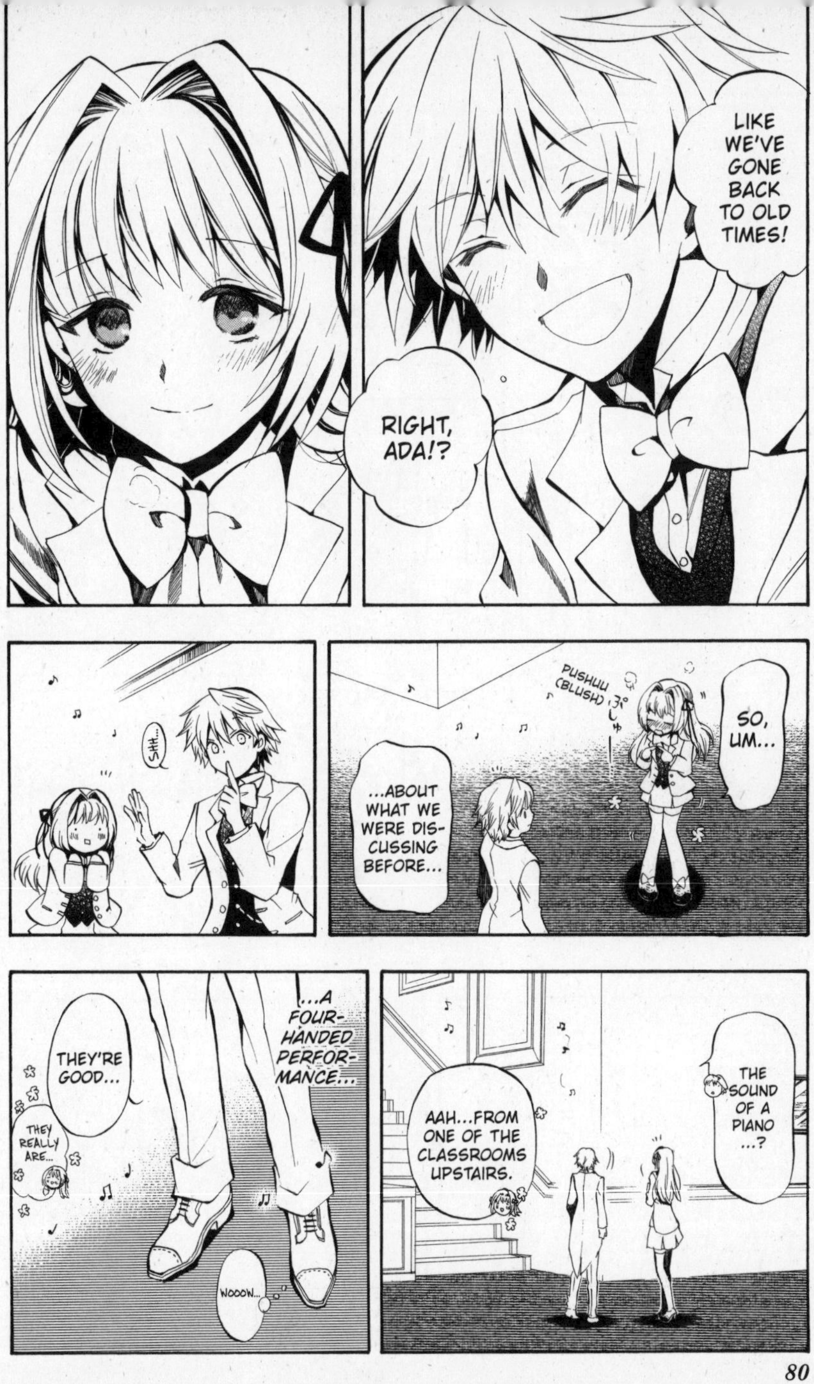
LIKE WE'VE GONE BACK TO OLD TIMES!
RIGHT, ADA!?
SO, UM...
PUSHUU (BLUSH)
ぷしゅー
...ABOUT WHAT WE WERE DISCUSSING BEFORE...
SHH...
THE SOUND OF A PIANO ...?
AAH...FROM ONE OF THE CLASSROOMS UPSTAIRS.
...A FOUR-HANDED PERFORMANCE...
THEY'RE GOOD...
THEY REALLY ARE...
WOOOW...

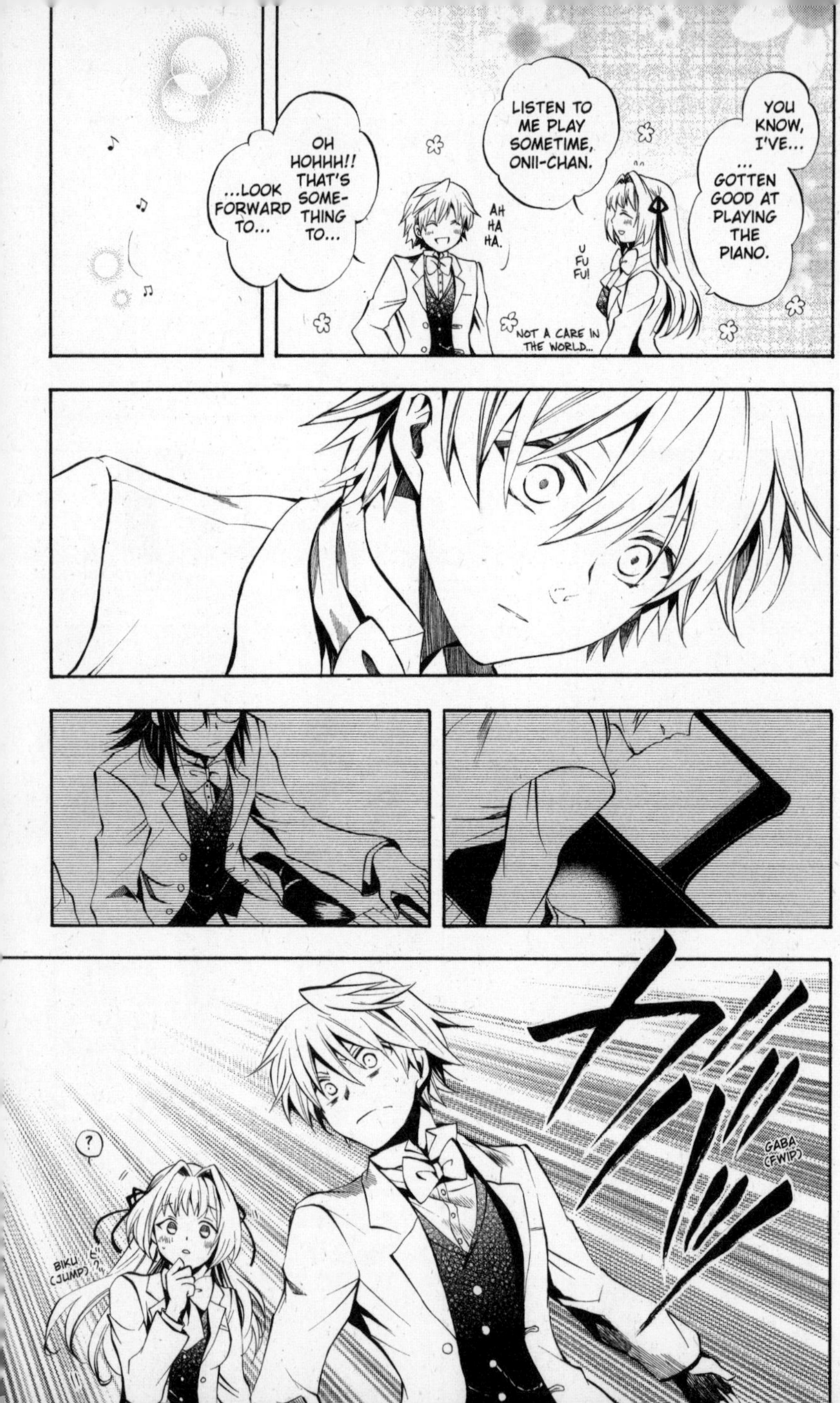
YOU KNOW, I'VE... ... GOTTEN GOOD AT PLAYING THE PIANO.
U FU FU!
LISTEN TO ME PLAY SOMETIME, ONII-CHAN.
AH HA HA.
OH HOHHH!! THAT'S SOME-THING TO...
...LOOK FORWARD TO...
NOT A CARE IN THE WORLD...
GABA (FWIP)
?
BIKU (JUMP)

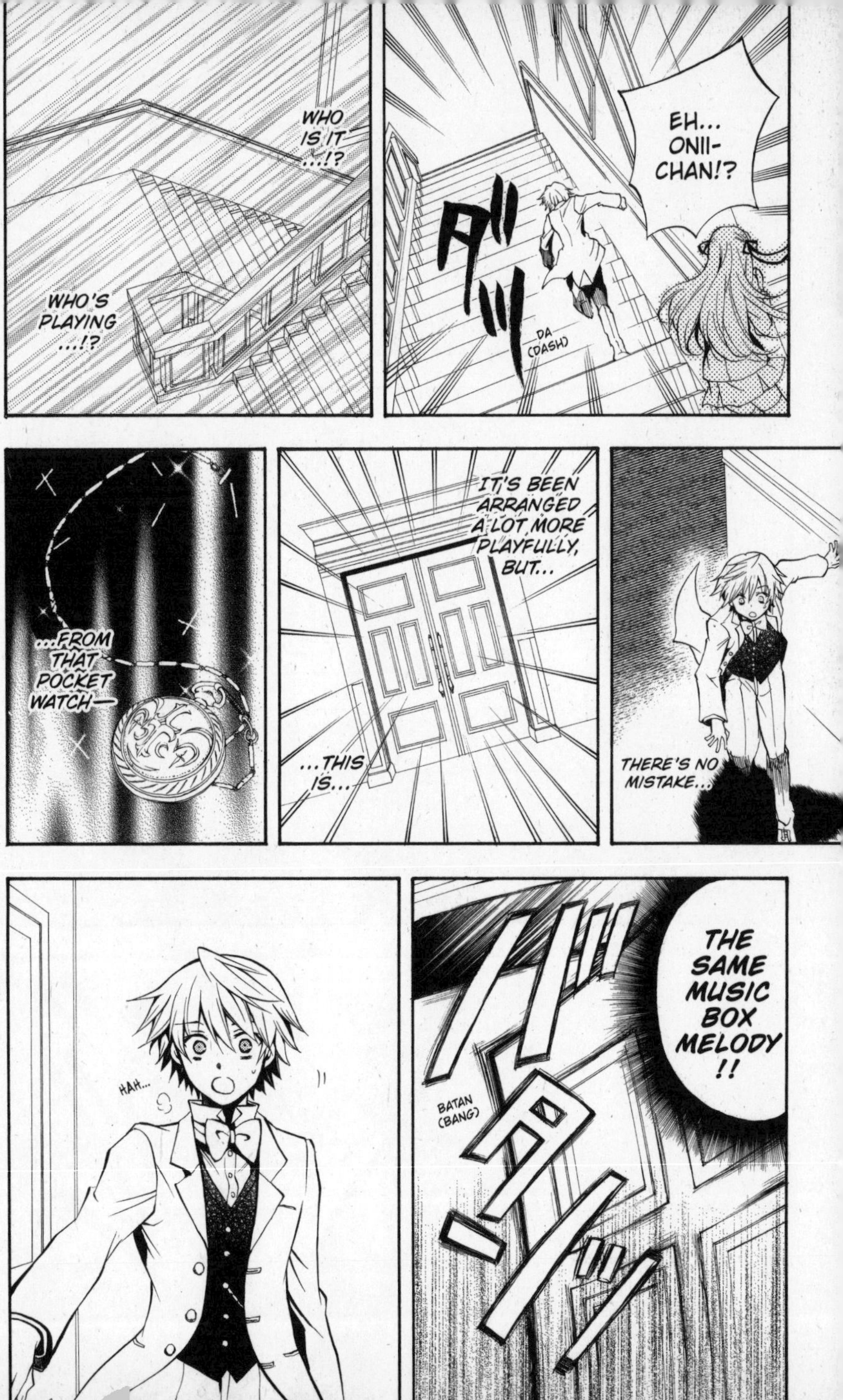
EH... ONII-CHAN!?
DA (DASH)
WHO IS IT ...!?
WHO'S PLAYING ...!?
THERE'S NO MISTAKE...
IT'S BEEN ARRANGED A LOT MORE PLAYFULLY, BUT...
...THIS IS...
...FROM THAT POCKET WATCH—
THE SAME MUSIC BOX MELODY!!
BATAN (BANG)
HAH...

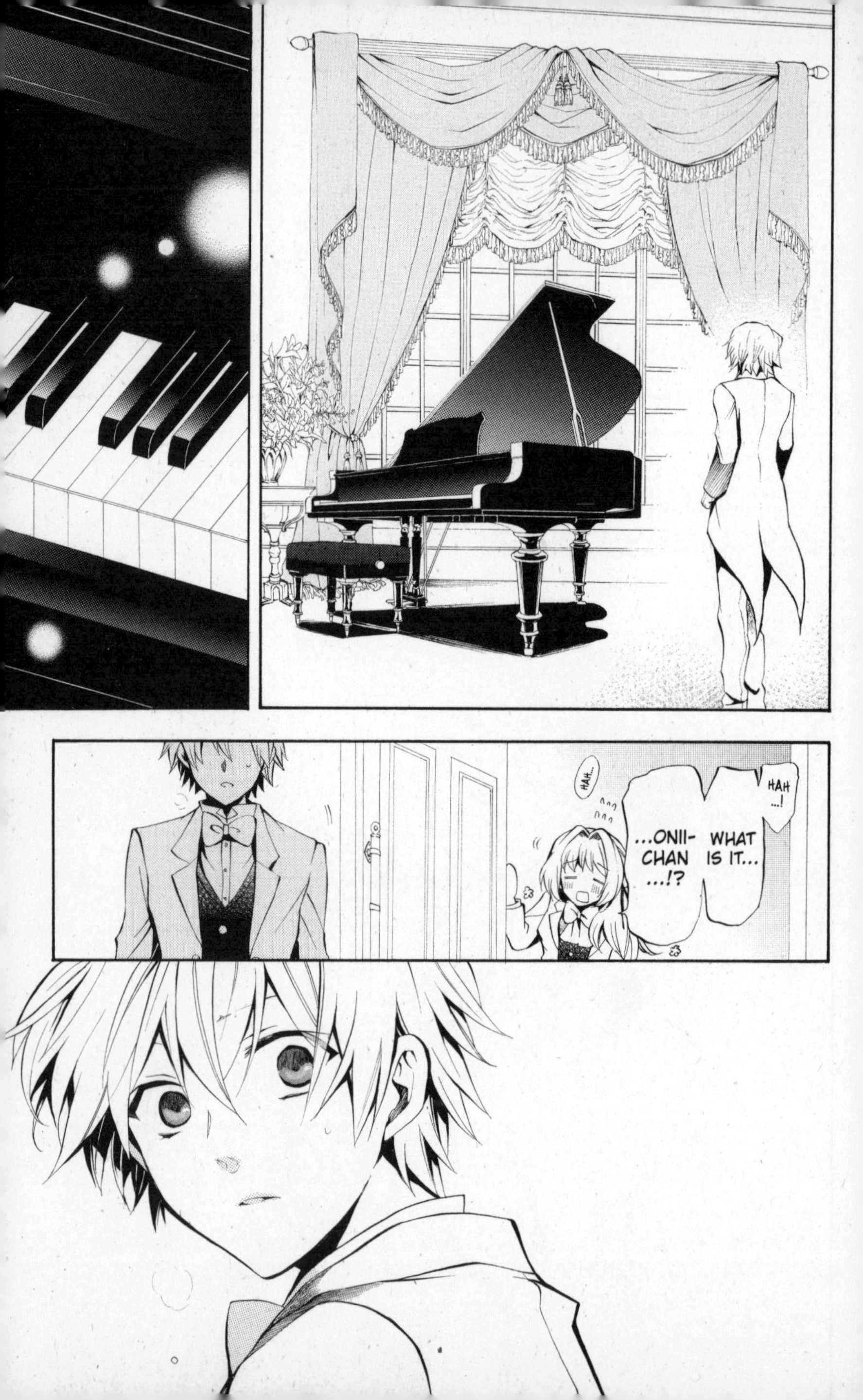
HAH ...!
WHAT IS IT...
...ONII-CHAN ...!?
HAH...

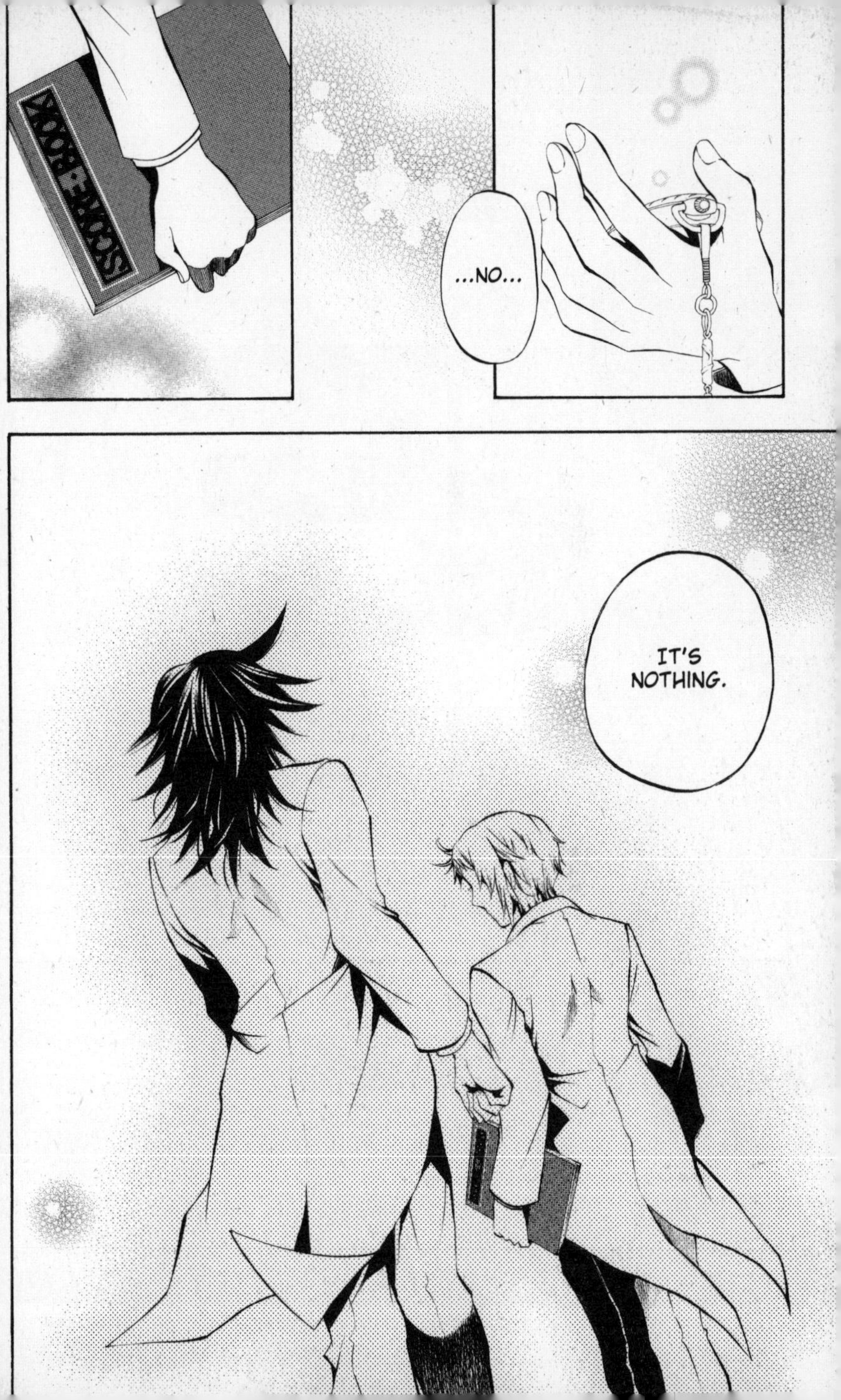
...NO...
SCORE BOOK
IT'S NOTHING.

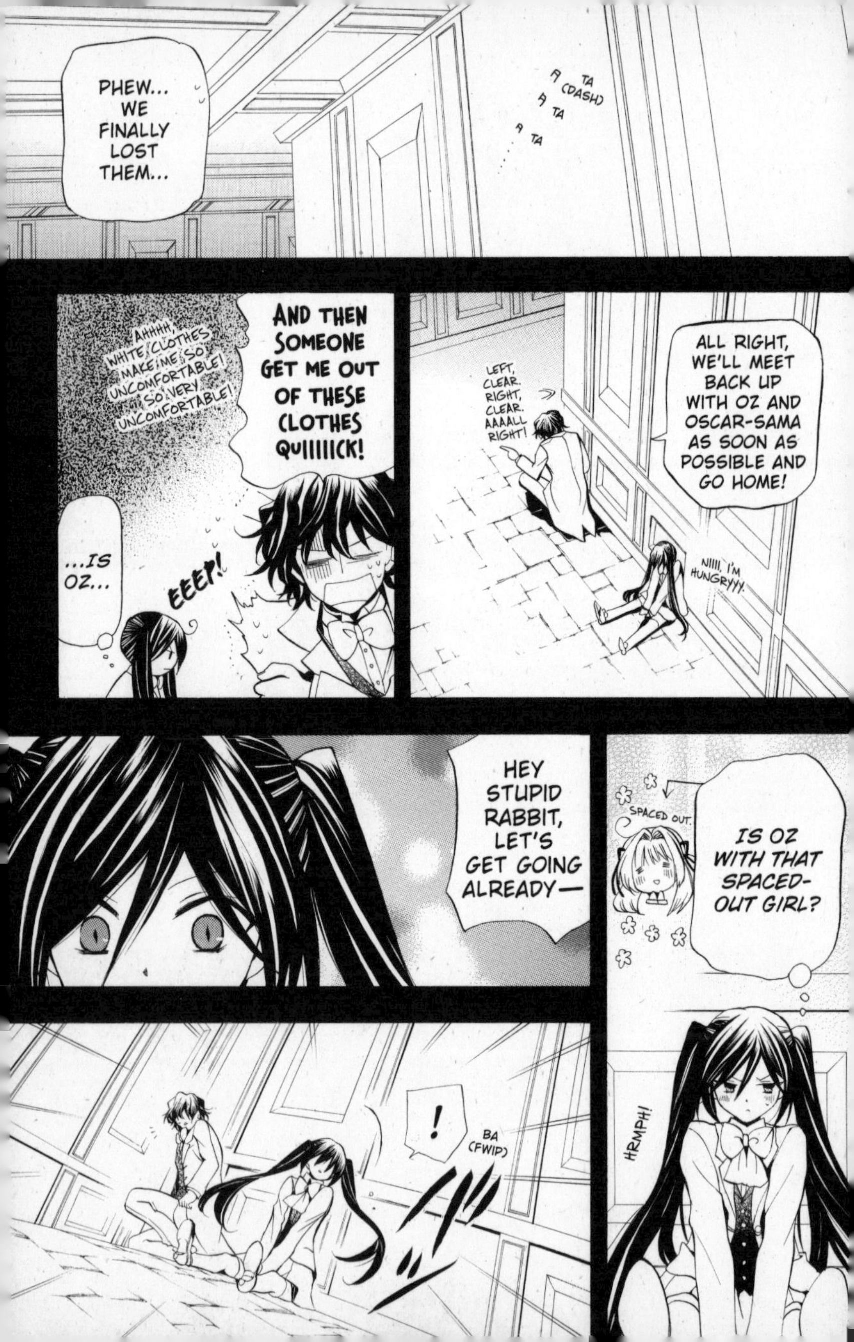
TA (DASH) TA TA
PHEW... WE FINALLY LOST THEM...
ALL RIGHT, WE'LL MEET BACK UP WITH OZ AND OSCAR-SAMA AS SOON AS POSSIBLE AND GO HOME!
LEFT, CLEAR. RIGHT, CLEAR. AAAALL RIGHT!
NIIII, I'M HUNGRYYY.
AND THEN SOMEONE GET ME OUT OF THESE CLOTHES QUIIIIICK!
AHHHH, WHITE CLOTHES MAKE ME SO UNCOMFORTABLE! SO VERY UNCOMFORTABLE!
...IS OZ...
EEEP!
SPACED OUT.
IS OZ WITH THAT SPACED-OUT GIRL?
HRMPH!
HEY STUPID RABBIT, LET'S GET GOING ALREADY—
!
BA (FWIP)

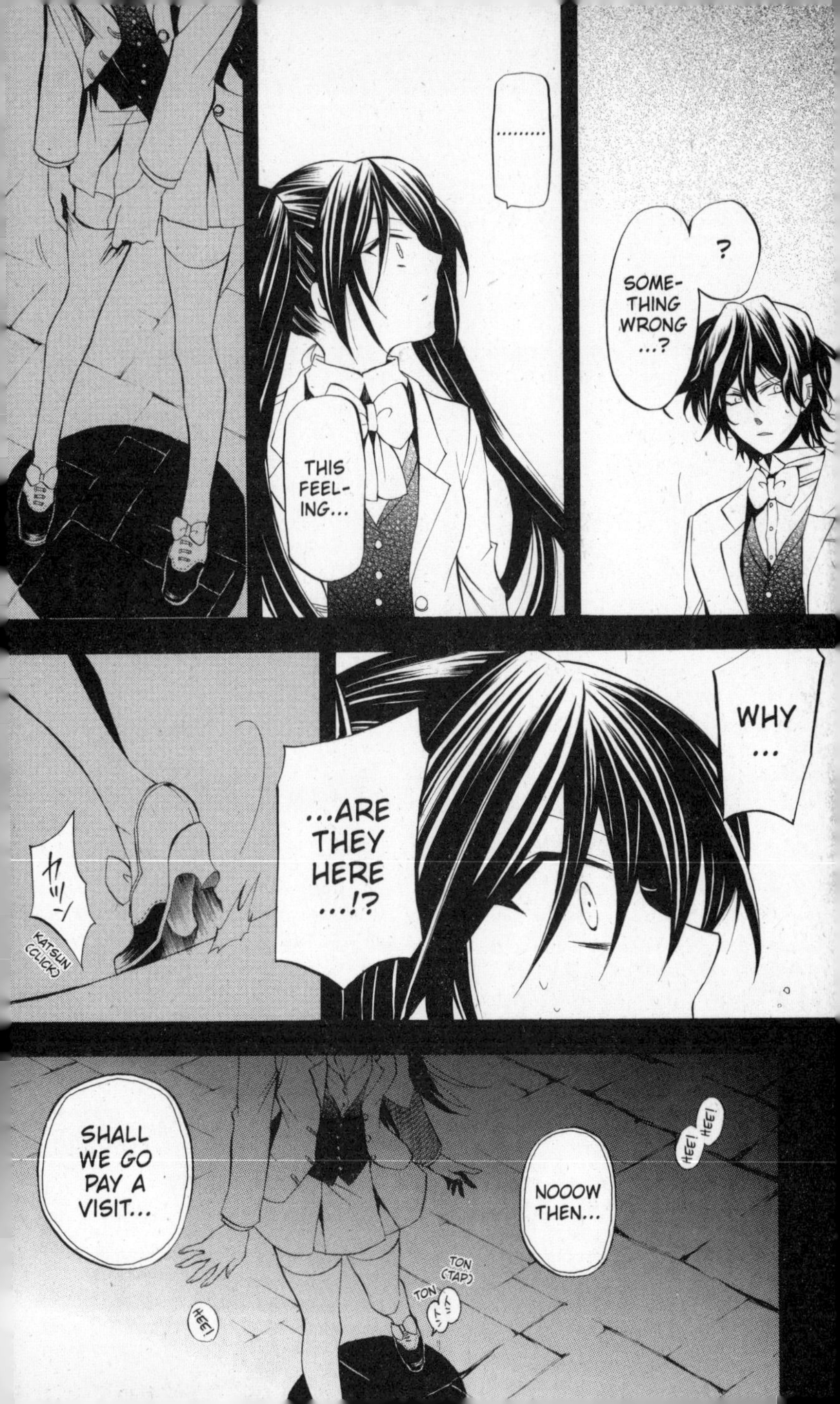
?
SOME-THING WRONG ...?
....
THIS FEEL-ING...
WHY ...
...ARE THEY HERE ...!?
カツン
KATSUN (CLICK)
HEE! HEE!
NOOOW THEN...
SHALL WE GO PAY A VISIT...
TON (TAP)
TON
HEE!

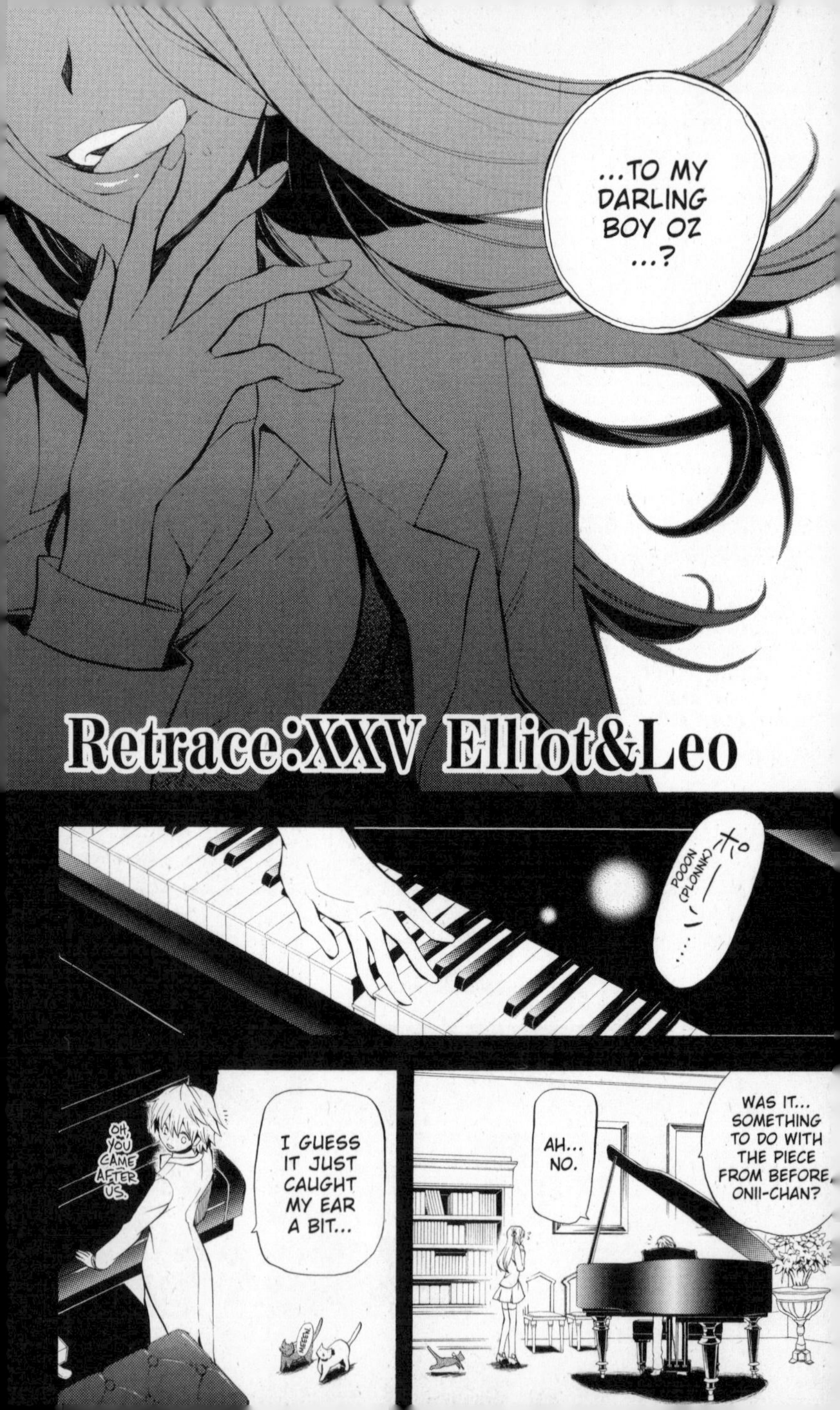
...TO MY DARLING BOY OZ ...?
Retrace:XXV Elliot&Leo
POOOON (PLONK)
WAS IT... SOMETHING TO DO WITH THE PIECE FROM BEFORE, ONII-CHAN?
AH... NO.
I GUESS IT JUST CAUGHT MY EAR A BIT...
OH, YOU CAME AFTER US.
MEEEW

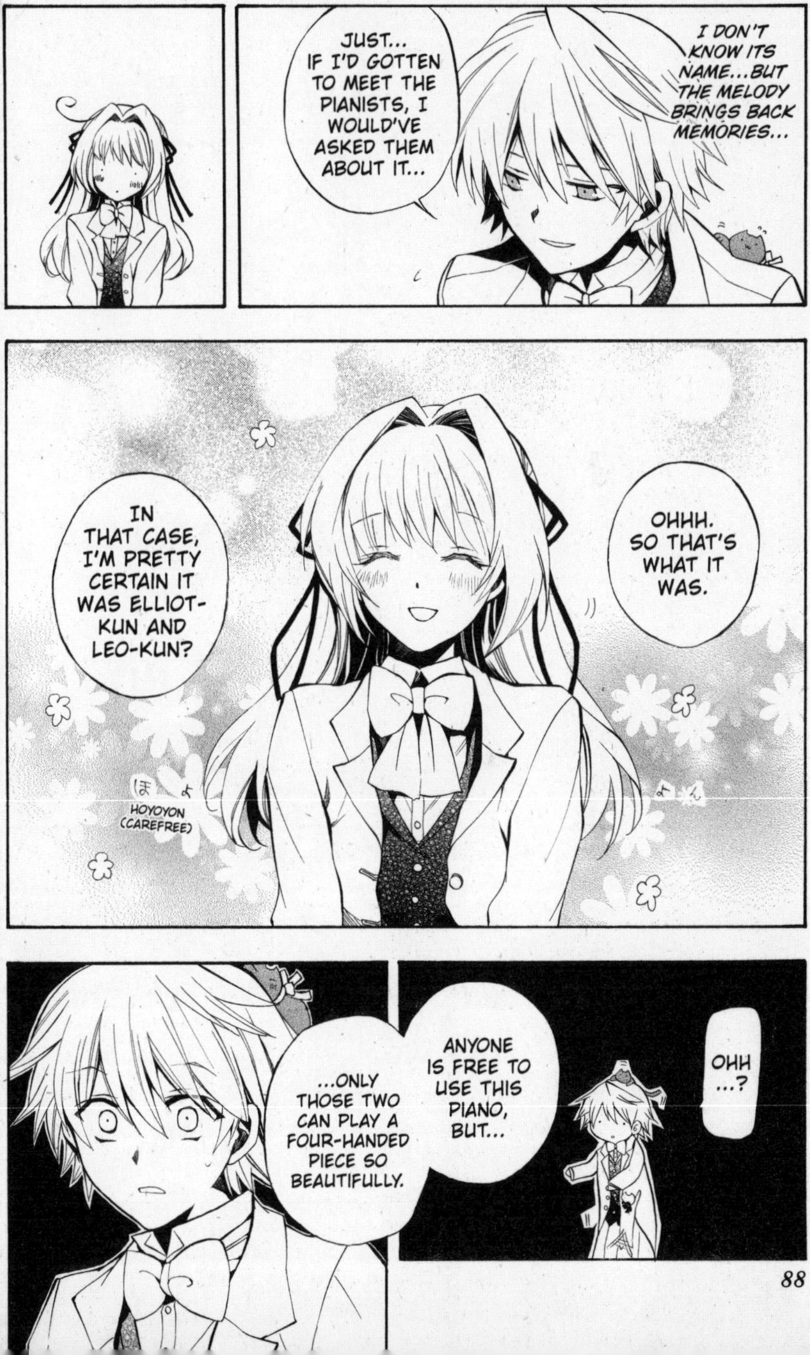
I DON'T KNOW ITS NAME...BUT THE MELODY BRINGS BACK MEMORIES...
JUST... IF I'D GOTTEN TO MEET THE PIANISTS, I WOULD'VE ASKED THEM ABOUT IT...
OHHH. SO THAT'S WHAT IT WAS.
IN THAT CASE, I'M PRETTY CERTAIN IT WAS ELLIOT-KUN AND LEO-KUN?
HOYOYON (CAREFREE)
OHH ...?
ANYONE IS FREE TO USE THIS PIANO, BUT...
...ONLY THOSE TWO CAN PLAY A FOUR-HANDED PIECE SO BEAUTIFULLY.

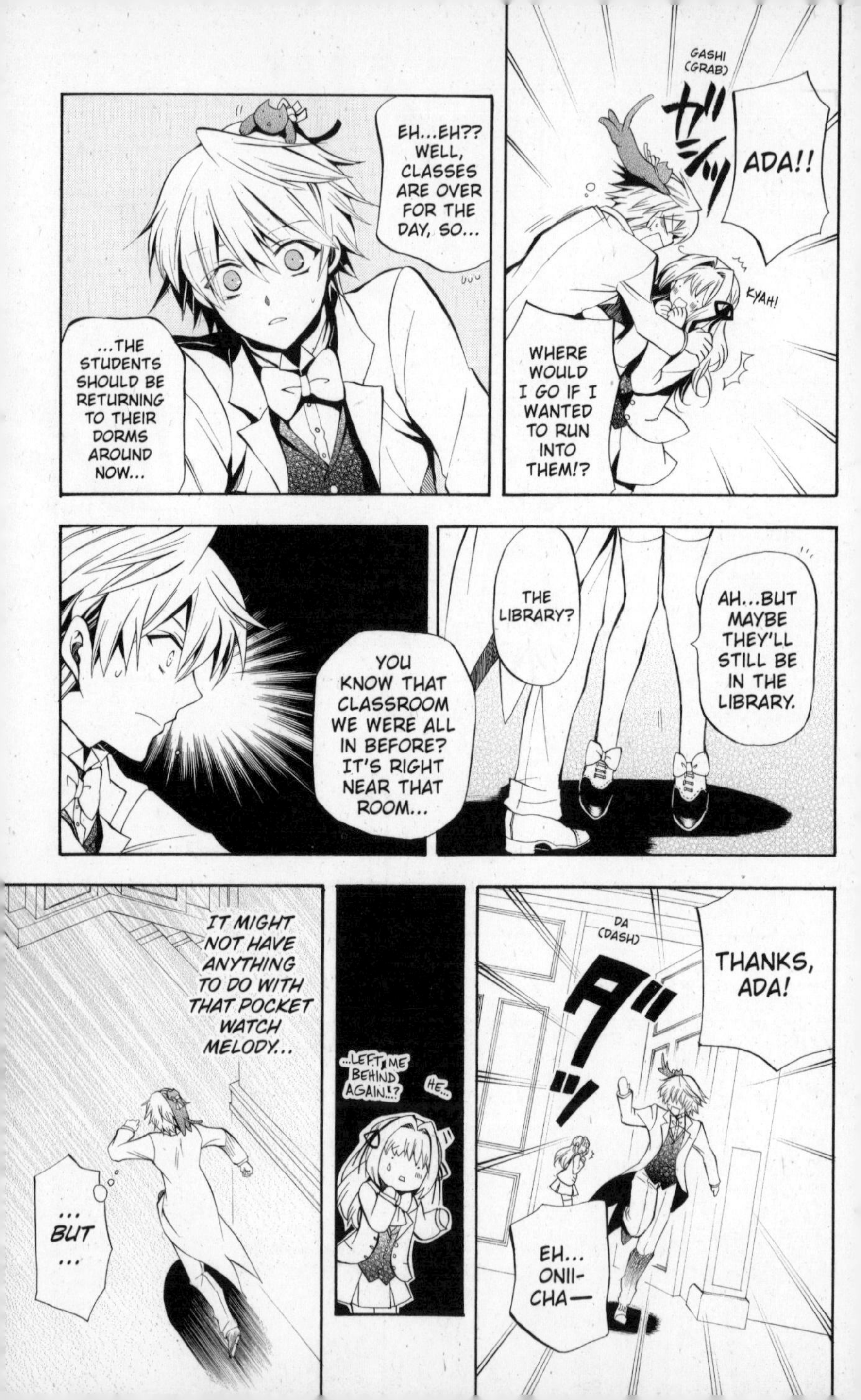
GASHI (GRAB)
ADA!!
KYAH!
WHERE WOULD I GO IF I WANTED TO RUN INTO THEM!?
EH...EH?? WELL, CLASSES ARE OVER FOR THE DAY, SO...
...THE STUDENTS SHOULD BE RETURNING TO THEIR DORMS AROUND NOW...
AH...BUT MAYBE THEY'LL STILL BE IN THE LIBRARY.
THE LIBRARY?
YOU KNOW THAT CLASSROOM WE WERE ALL IN BEFORE? IT'S RIGHT NEAR THAT ROOM...
DA (DASH)
THANKS, ADA!
EH... ONII-CHA—
HE...
...LEFT ME BEHIND AGAIN!?
IT MIGHT NOT HAVE ANYTHING TO DO WITH THAT POCKET WATCH MELODY...
...BUT...

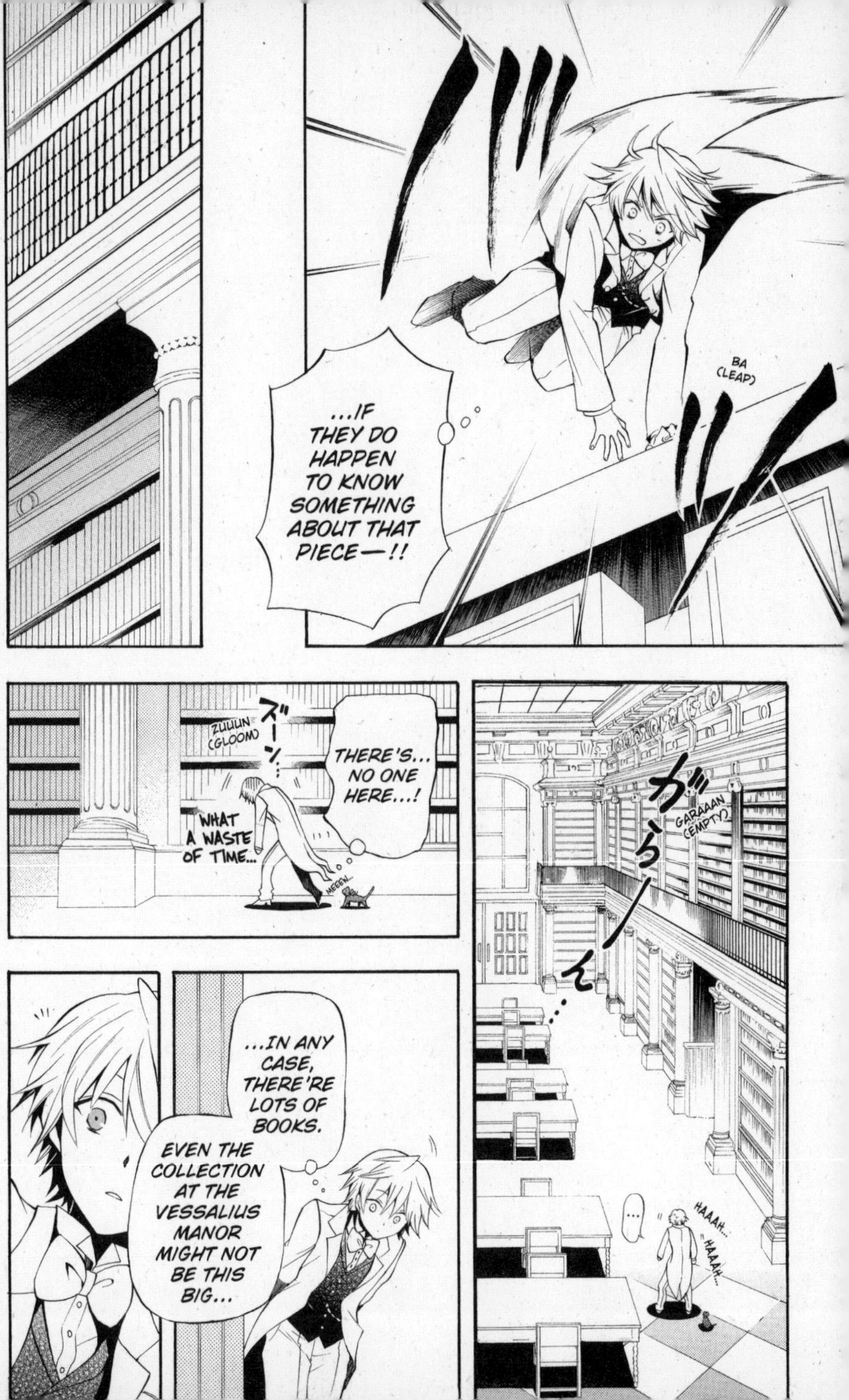

...IF THEY DO HAPPEN TO KNOW SOMETHING ABOUT THAT PIECE—!!
BA (LEAP)
GARAAAN (EMPTY)
...
HAAAH... HAAAH...
ZUUUN (GLOOM)
THERE'S... NO ONE HERE...!
WHAT A WASTE OF TIME...
MEEEW...
...IN ANY CASE, THERE'RE LOTS OF BOOKS.
EVEN THE COLLECTION AT THE VESSALIUS MANOR MIGHT NOT BE THIS BIG...

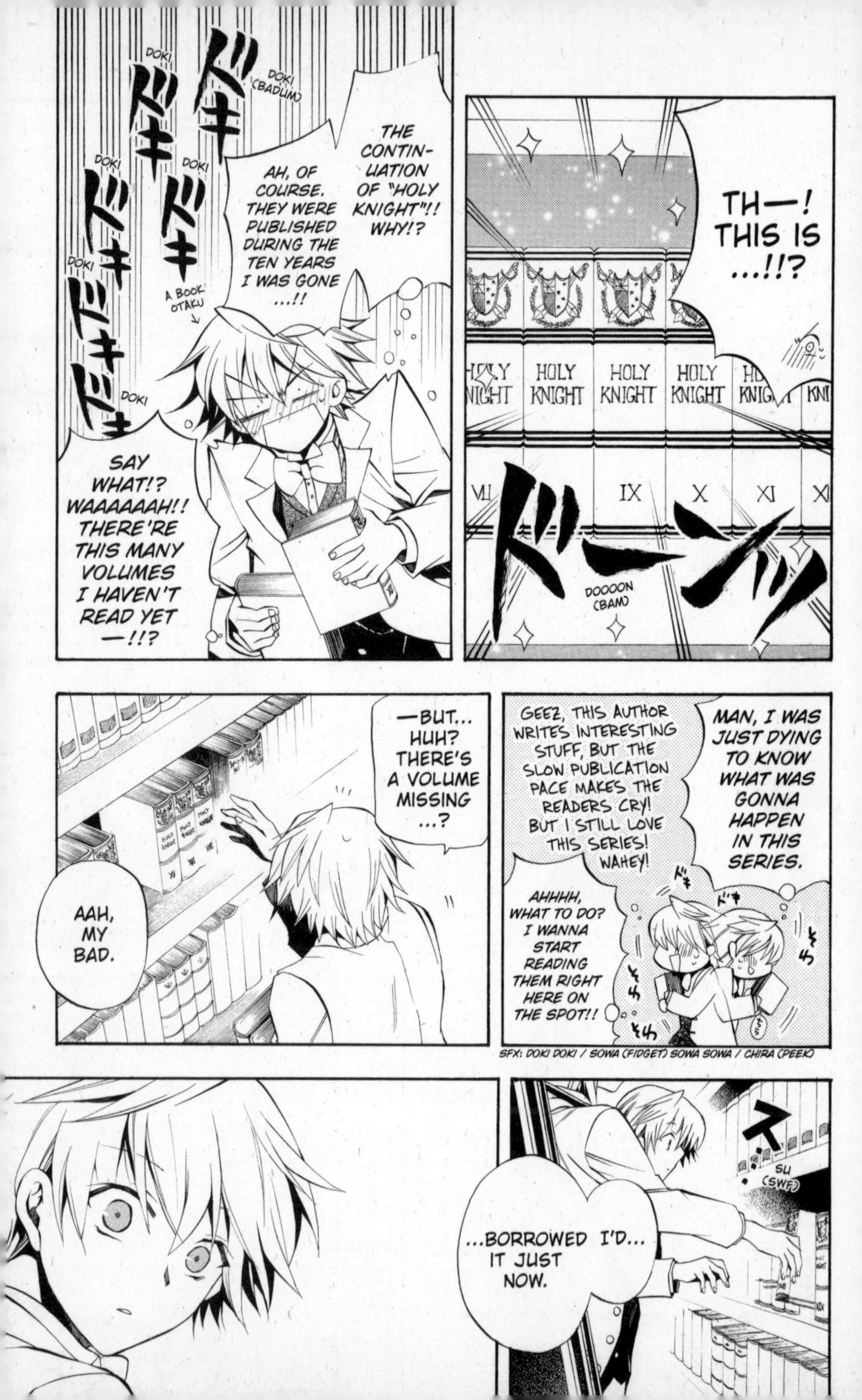
TH—! THIS IS ...!!?
HOLY KNIGHT
VII IX X XI XI
DOOOON (BAM)
THE CONTINUATION OF "HOLY KNIGHT"!! WHY!?
AH, OF COURSE. THEY WERE PUBLISHED DURING THE TEN YEARS I WAS GONE ...!!
DOKI DOKI (BADUM)
DOKI DOKI DOKI DOKI DOKI
A BOOK OTAKU
SAY WHAT!? WAAAAAAH!! THERE'RE THIS MANY VOLUMES I HAVEN'T READ YET —!!?
MAN, I WAS JUST DYING TO KNOW WHAT WAS GONNA HAPPEN IN THIS SERIES.
GEEZ, THIS AUTHOR WRITES INTERESTING STUFF, BUT THE SLOW PUBLICATION PACE MAKES THE READERS CRY! BUT I STILL LOVE THIS SERIES! WAHEY!
AHHHH, WHAT TO DO? I WANNA START READING THEM RIGHT HERE ON THE SPOT!!
—BUT... HUH? THERE'S A VOLUME MISSING ...?
AAH, MY BAD.
SFX: DOKI DOKI / SOWA (FIDGET) SOWA SOWA / CHIRA (PEEK)
SU (SWF)
I'D... BORROWED IT JUST NOW.

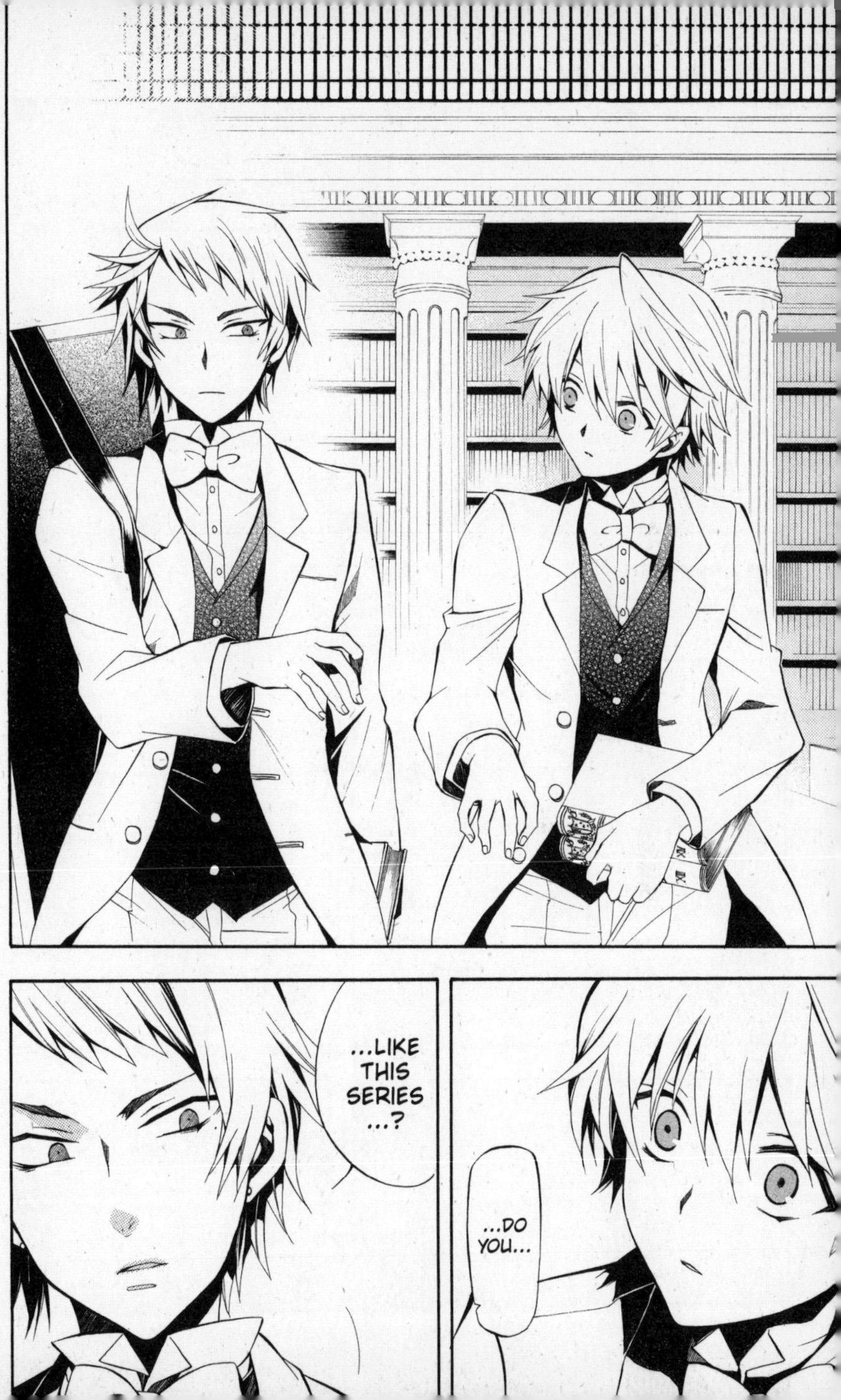
...DO YOU...
...LIKE THIS SERIES ...?

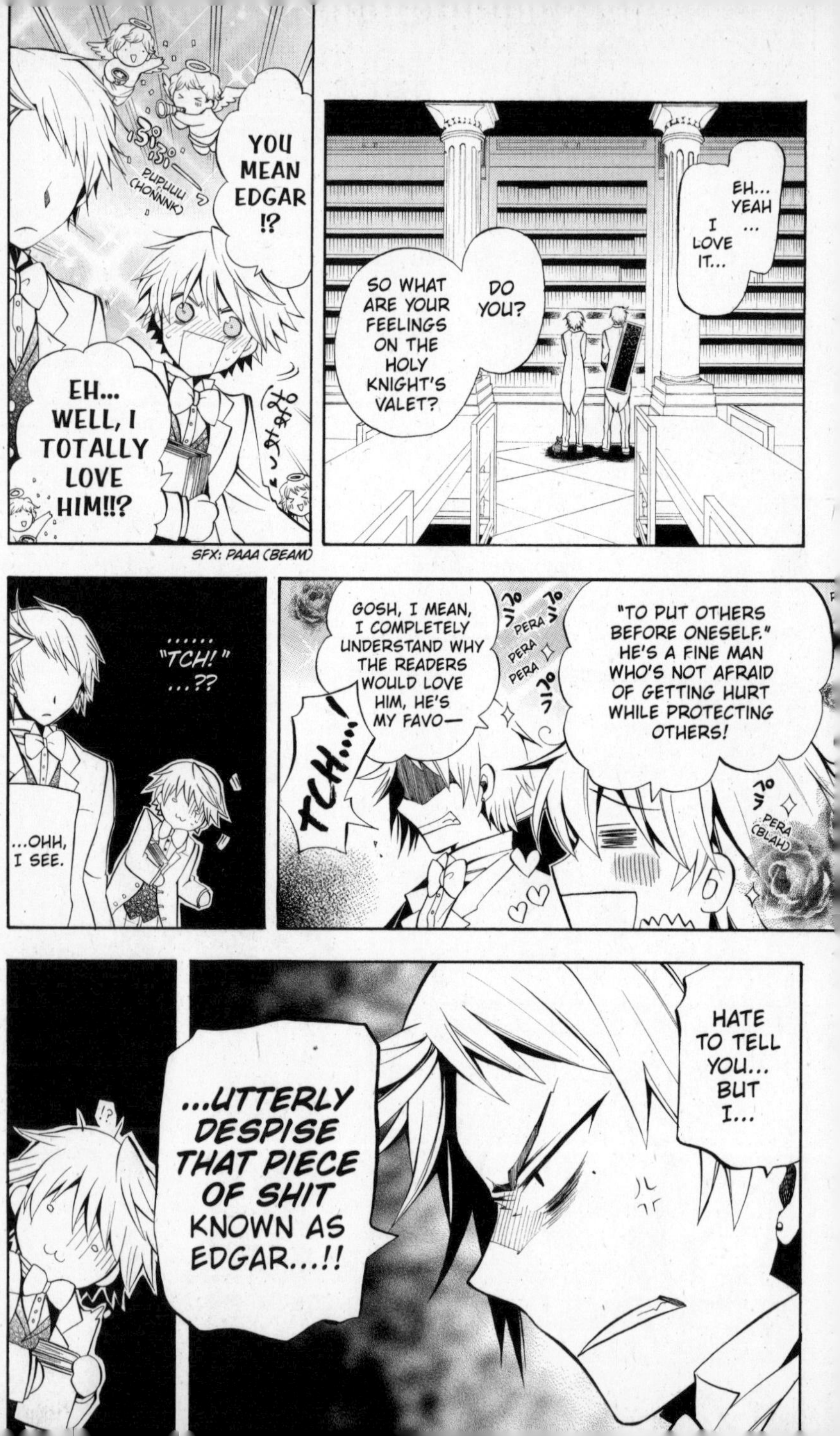
EH... YEAH ... I LOVE IT...
SO WHAT ARE YOUR FEELINGS ON THE HOLY KNIGHT'S VALET?
DO YOU?
YOU MEAN EDGAR !?
PUPULUU (HONNNK)
EH... WELL, I TOTALLY LOVE HIM!!?
SFX: PAAA (BEAM)
"TO PUT OTHERS BEFORE ONESELF." HE'S A FINE MAN WHO'S NOT AFRAID OF GETTING HURT WHILE PROTECTING OTHERS!
PERA PERA PERA
GOSH, I MEAN, I COMPLETELY UNDERSTAND WHY THE READERS WOULD LOVE HIM, HE'S MY FAVO—
TCH...!
PERA (BLAH)
...... "TCH!" ...??
...OHH, I SEE.
HATE TO TELL YOU... BUT I...
...UTTERLY DESPISE THAT PIECE OF SHIT KNOWN AS EDGAR...!!
!?

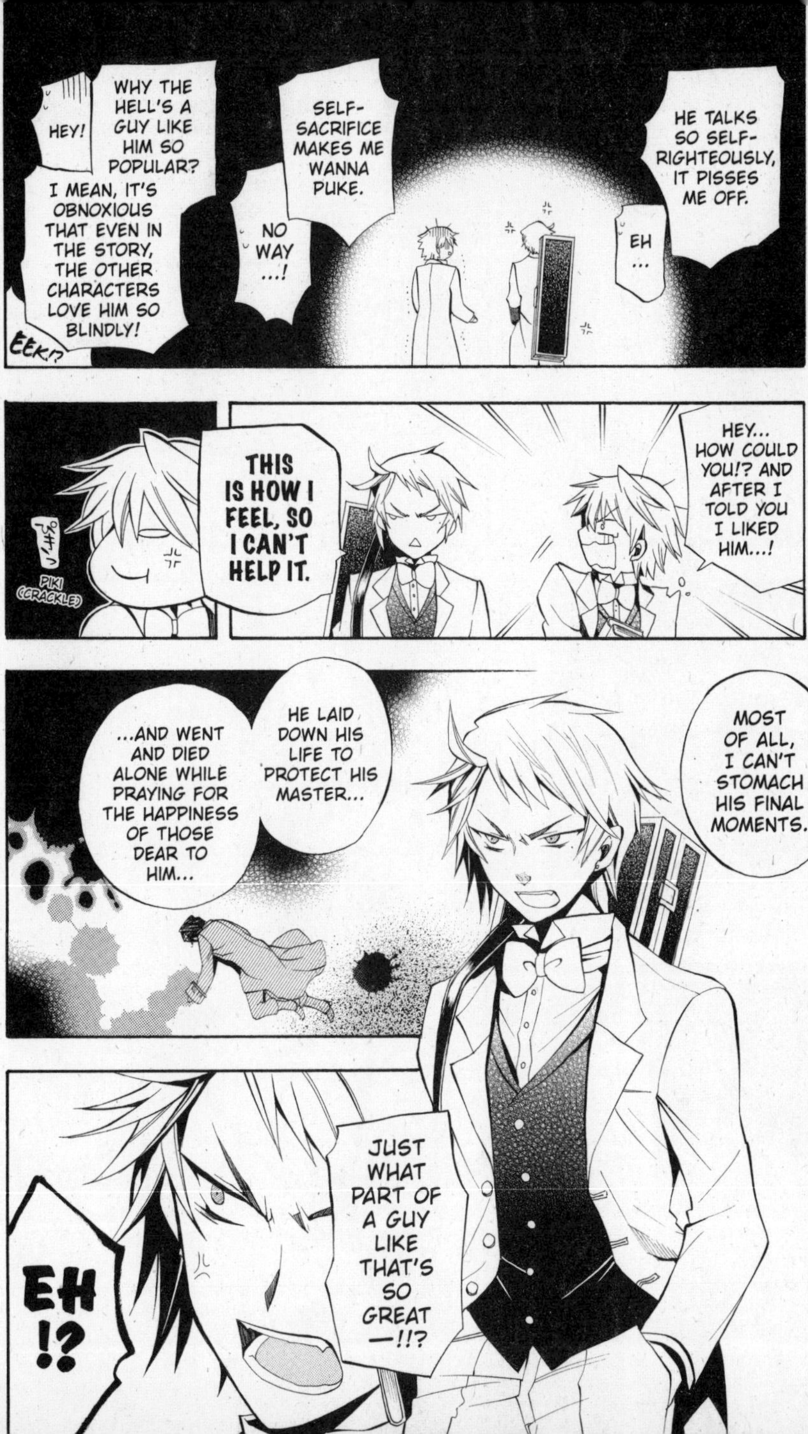
HE TALKS SO SELF-RIGHTEOUSLY, IT PISSES ME OFF.
EH...
SELF-SACRIFICE MAKES ME WANNA PUKE.
NO WAY...!
WHY THE HELL'S A GUY LIKE HIM SO POPULAR?
I MEAN, IT'S OBNOXIOUS THAT EVEN IN THE STORY, THE OTHER CHARACTERS LOVE HIM SO BLINDLY!
HEY!
EEK!?
HEY... HOW COULD YOU!? AND AFTER I TOLD YOU I LIKED HIM...!
THIS IS HOW I FEEL, SO I CAN'T HELP IT.
PIKI (CRACKLE)
MOST OF ALL, I CAN'T STOMACH HIS FINAL MOMENTS.
HE LAID DOWN HIS LIFE TO PROTECT HIS MASTER...
...AND WENT AND DIED ALONE WHILE PRAYING FOR THE HAPPINESS OF THOSE DEAR TO HIM...
JUST WHAT PART OF A GUY LIKE THAT'S SO GREAT—!!?
EH!?

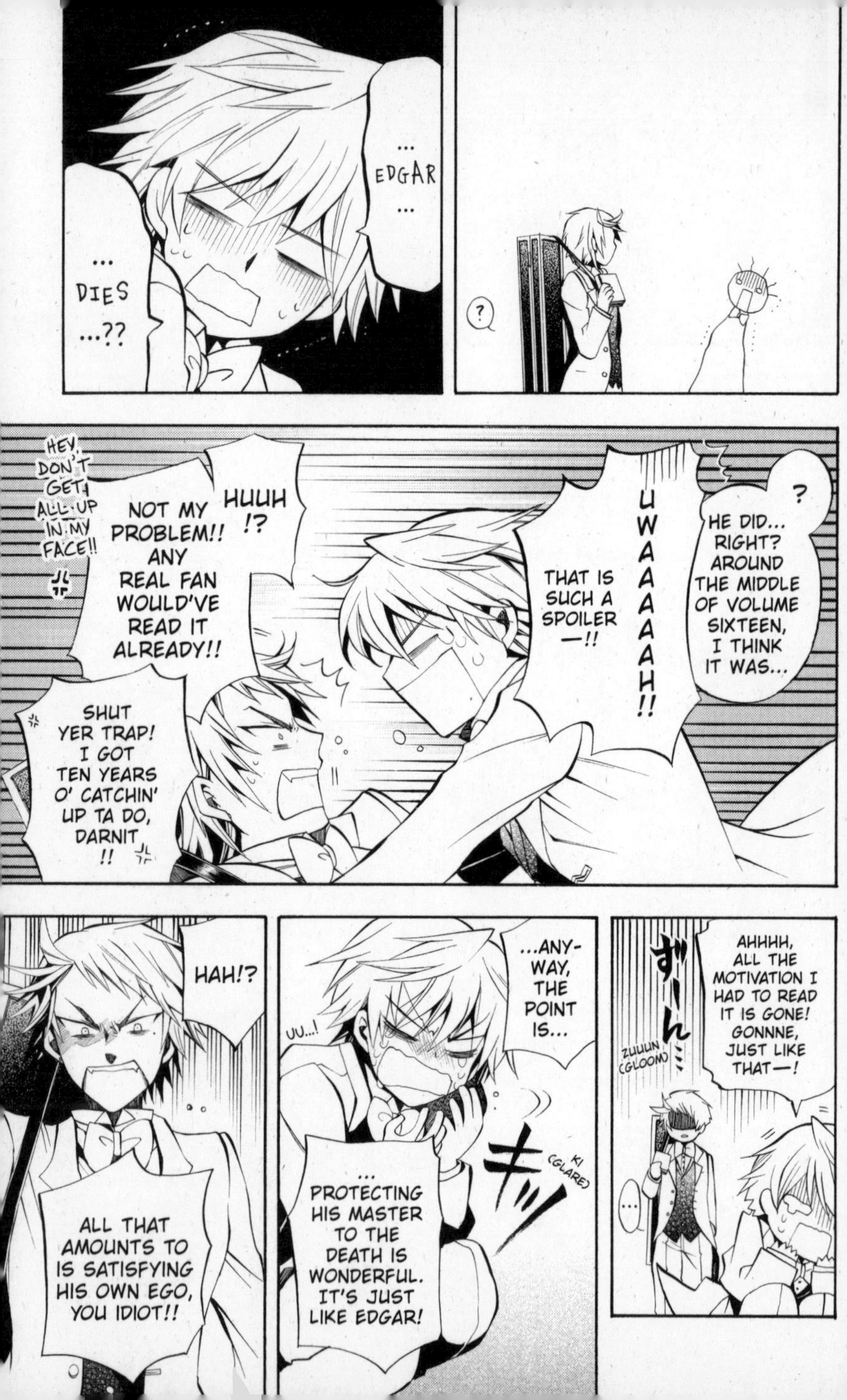
?
...EDGAR...
...DIES...??
?
HE DID... RIGHT? AROUND THE MIDDLE OF VOLUME SIXTEEN, I THINK IT WAS...
UWAAAAAAH!!
THAT IS SUCH A SPOILER—!!
HUUH!?
NOT MY PROBLEM!! ANY REAL FAN WOULD'VE READ IT ALREADY!!
HEY, DON'T GET ALL UP IN MY FACE!!
SHUT YER TRAP! I GOT TEN YEARS O' CATCHIN' UP TA DO, DARNIT!!
AHHHH, ALL THE MOTIVATION I HAD TO READ IT IS GONE! GONNE, JUST LIKE THAT—!
ZUUUN (GLOOM)
...
...ANY-WAY, THE POINT IS...
UU...!
KI (GLARE)
...PROTECTING HIS MASTER TO THE DEATH IS WONDERFUL. IT'S JUST LIKE EDGAR!
HAH!?
ALL THAT AMOUNTS TO IS SATISFYING HIS OWN EGO, YOU IDIOT!!

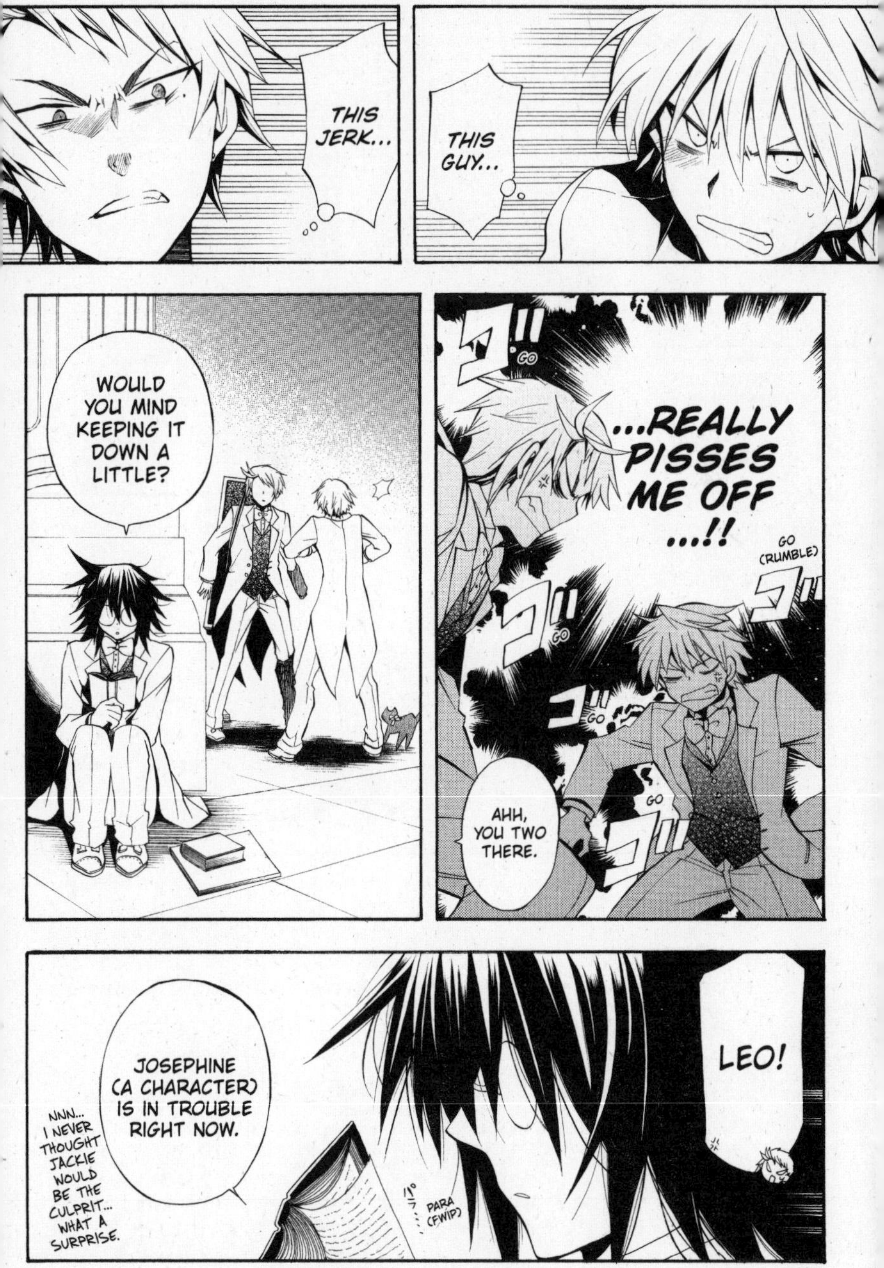
THIS GUY...
THIS JERK...
GO
...REALLY PISSES ME OFF ...!!
GO (RUMBLE)
GO
GO
GO
AHH, YOU TWO THERE.
WOULD YOU MIND KEEPING IT DOWN A LITTLE?
LEO!
PARA (FWIP)
JOSEPHINE (A CHARACTER) IS IN TROUBLE RIGHT NOW.
NNN... I NEVER THOUGHT JACKIE WOULD BE THE CULPRIT... WHAT A SURPRISE.

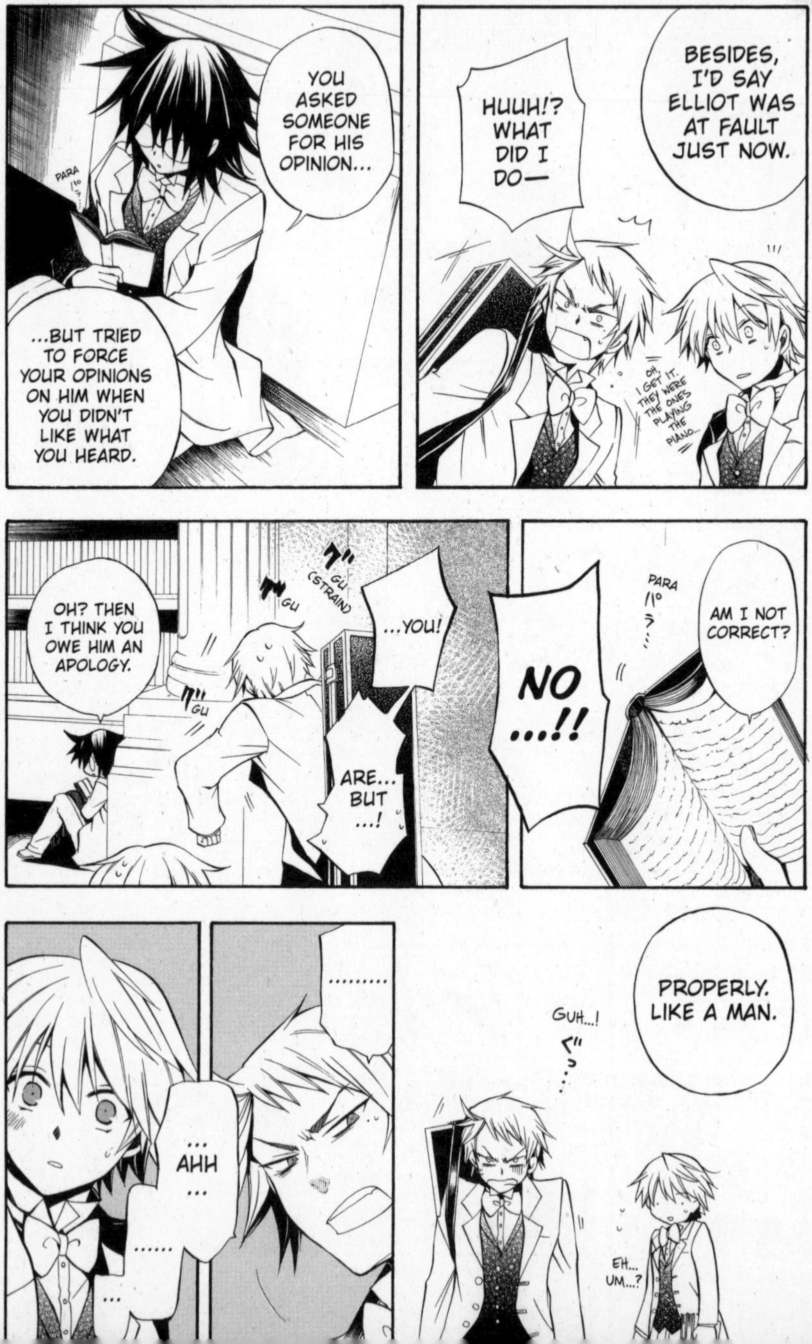
BESIDES, I'D SAY ELLIOT WAS AT FAULT JUST NOW.
HUUH!? WHAT DID I DO—
OH, I GET IT. THEY WERE THE ONES PLAYING THE PIANO...
YOU ASKED SOMEONE FOR HIS OPINION...
PARA
...BUT TRIED TO FORCE YOUR OPINIONS ON HIM WHEN YOU DIDN'T LIKE WHAT YOU HEARD.
PARA
AM I NOT CORRECT?
NO ...!!
...YOU!
GU (STRAIN)
GU
GU
OH? THEN I THINK YOU OWE HIM AN APOLOGY.
ARE... BUT ...!
PROPERLY. LIKE A MAN.
GUH...!
EH... UM...?
....
... AHH ...
......
...

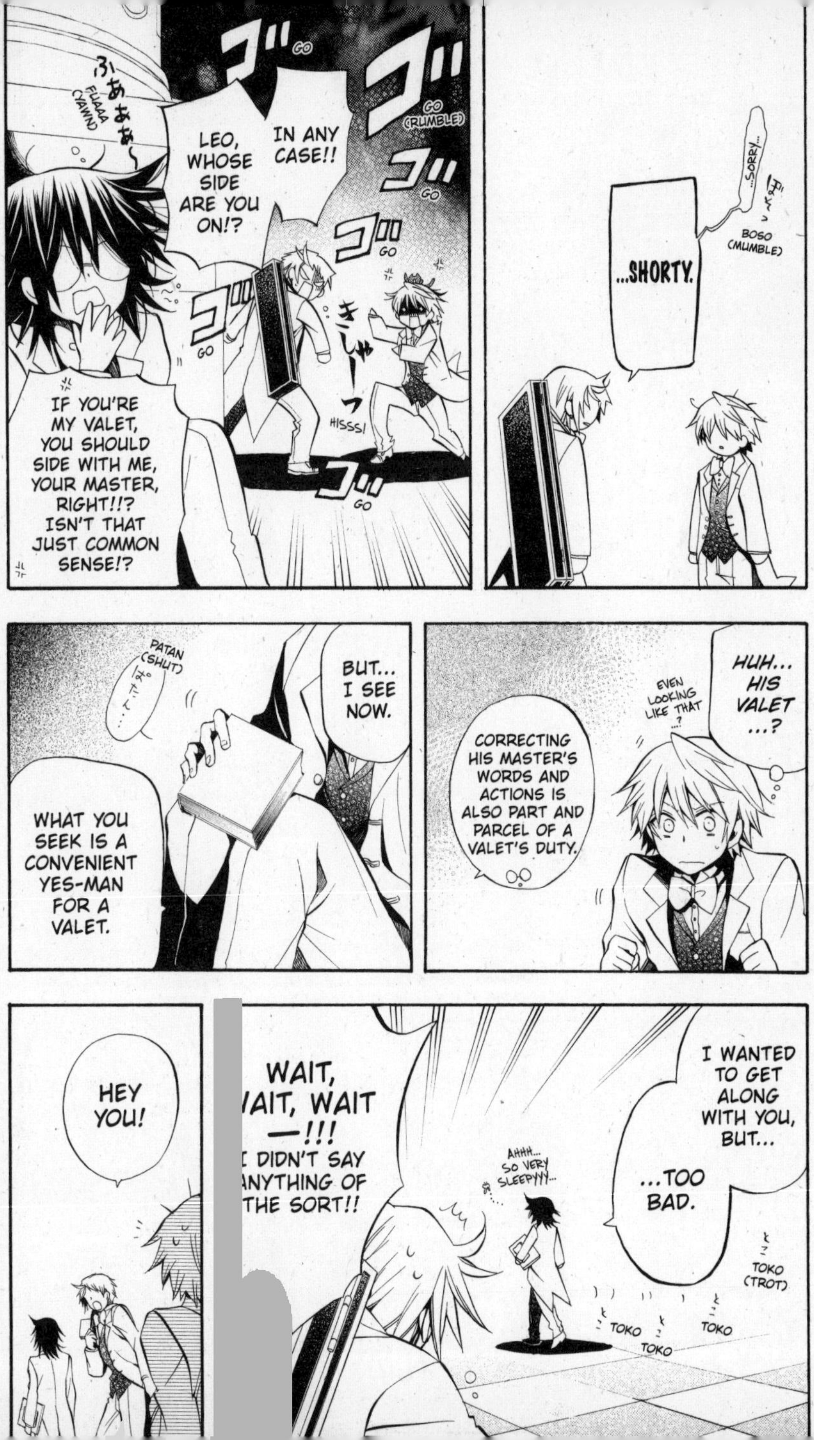
...SORRY...
BOSO (MUMBLE)
...SHORTY.
GO
GO (RUMBLE)
IN ANY CASE!!
LEO, WHOSE SIDE ARE YOU ON!?
GO
GO
FUAAA (YAWN)
GO
HISSS!
GO
IF YOU'RE MY VALET, YOU SHOULD SIDE WITH ME, YOUR MASTER, RIGHT!!? ISN'T THAT JUST COMMON SENSE!?
HUH... HIS VALET ...?
EVEN LOOKING LIKE THAT ...?
CORRECTING HIS MASTER'S WORDS AND ACTIONS IS ALSO PART AND PARCEL OF A VALET'S DUTY.
BUT... I SEE NOW.
PATAN (SHUT)
WHAT YOU SEEK IS A CONVENIENT YES-MAN FOR A VALET.
I WANTED TO GET ALONG WITH YOU, BUT...
...TOO BAD.
TOKO (TROT)
TOKO
TOKO
TOKO
AHHH... SO VERY SLEEPYYY...
WAIT, AIT, WAIT —!!! DIDN'T SAY NYTHING OF THE SORT!!
HEY YOU!

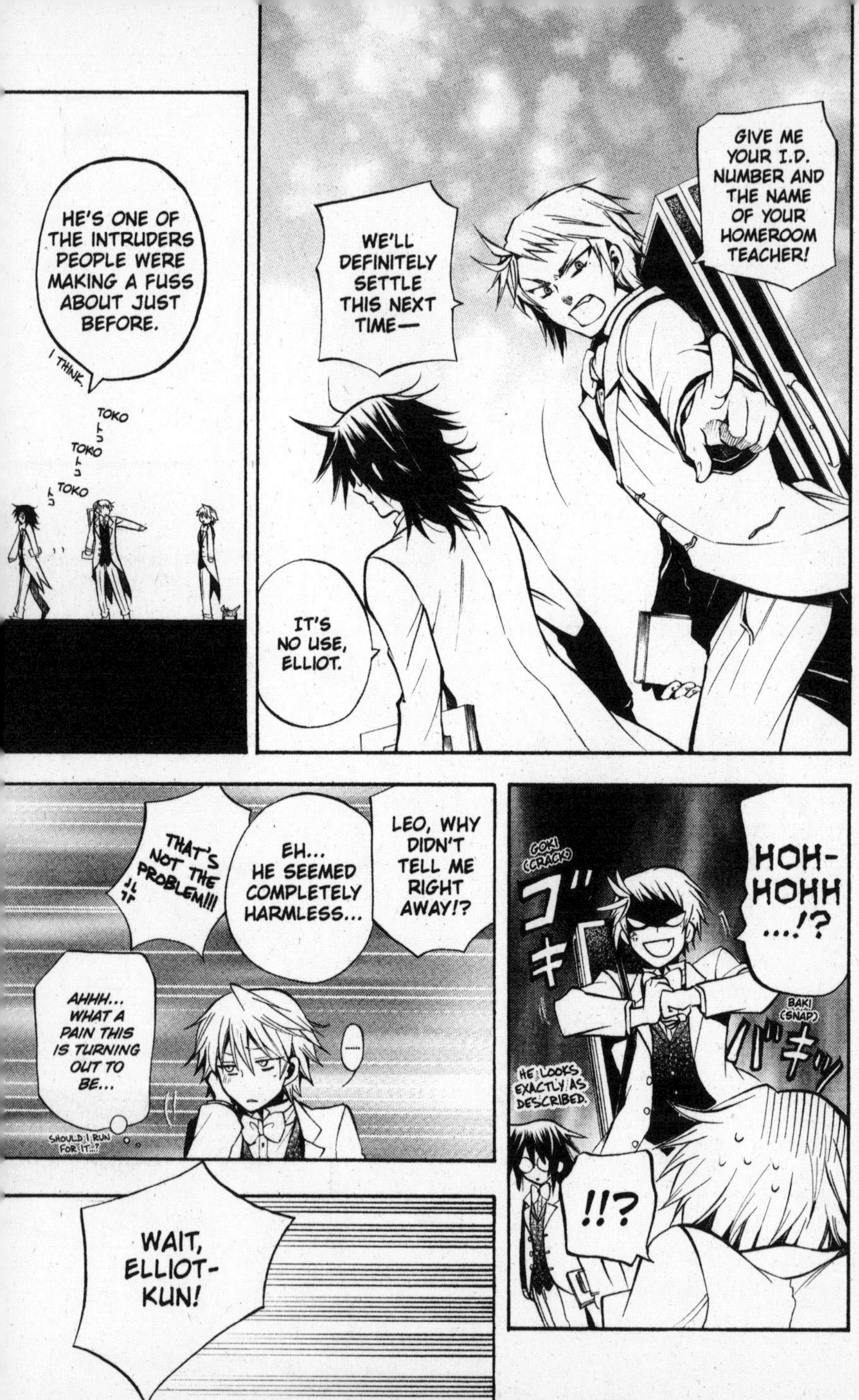
GIVE ME YOUR I.D. NUMBER AND THE NAME OF YOUR HOMEROOM TEACHER!
WE'LL DEFINITELY SETTLE THIS NEXT TIME—
IT'S NO USE, ELLIOT.
HE'S ONE OF THE INTRUDERS PEOPLE WERE MAKING A FUSS ABOUT JUST BEFORE.
I THINK.
TOKO
TOKO
TOKO
HOH-HOHH ...!?
GOKI (CRACK)
BAKI (SNAP)
HE LOOKS EXACTLY AS DESCRIBED.
!!?
LEO, WHY DIDN'T TELL ME RIGHT AWAY!?
EH... HE SEEMED COMPLETELY HARMLESS...
THAT'S NOT THE PROBLEM!!!
AHHH... WHAT A PAIN THIS IS TURNING OUT TO BE...
......
SHOULD I RUN FOR IT...?
WAIT, ELLIOT-KUN!

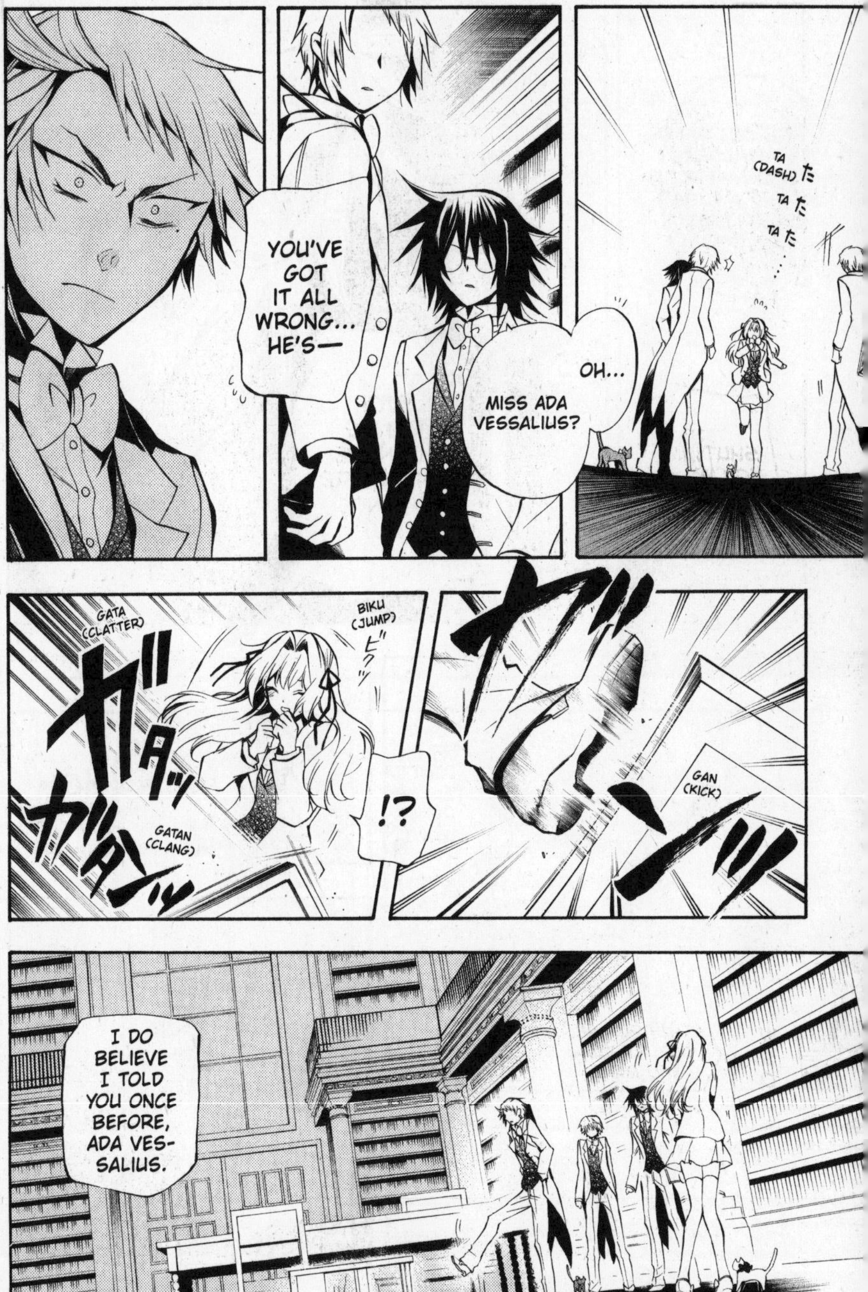
TA (DASH) た
TA た
TA た
YOU'VE GOT IT ALL WRONG... HE'S—
OH...
MISS ADA VESSALIUS?
GAN (KICK)
BIKU (JUMP) ビクッ
!?
GATA (CLATTER) ガタッ
GATAN (CLANG) ガタンッ
I DO BELIEVE I TOLD YOU ONCE BEFORE, ADA VES-SALIUS.

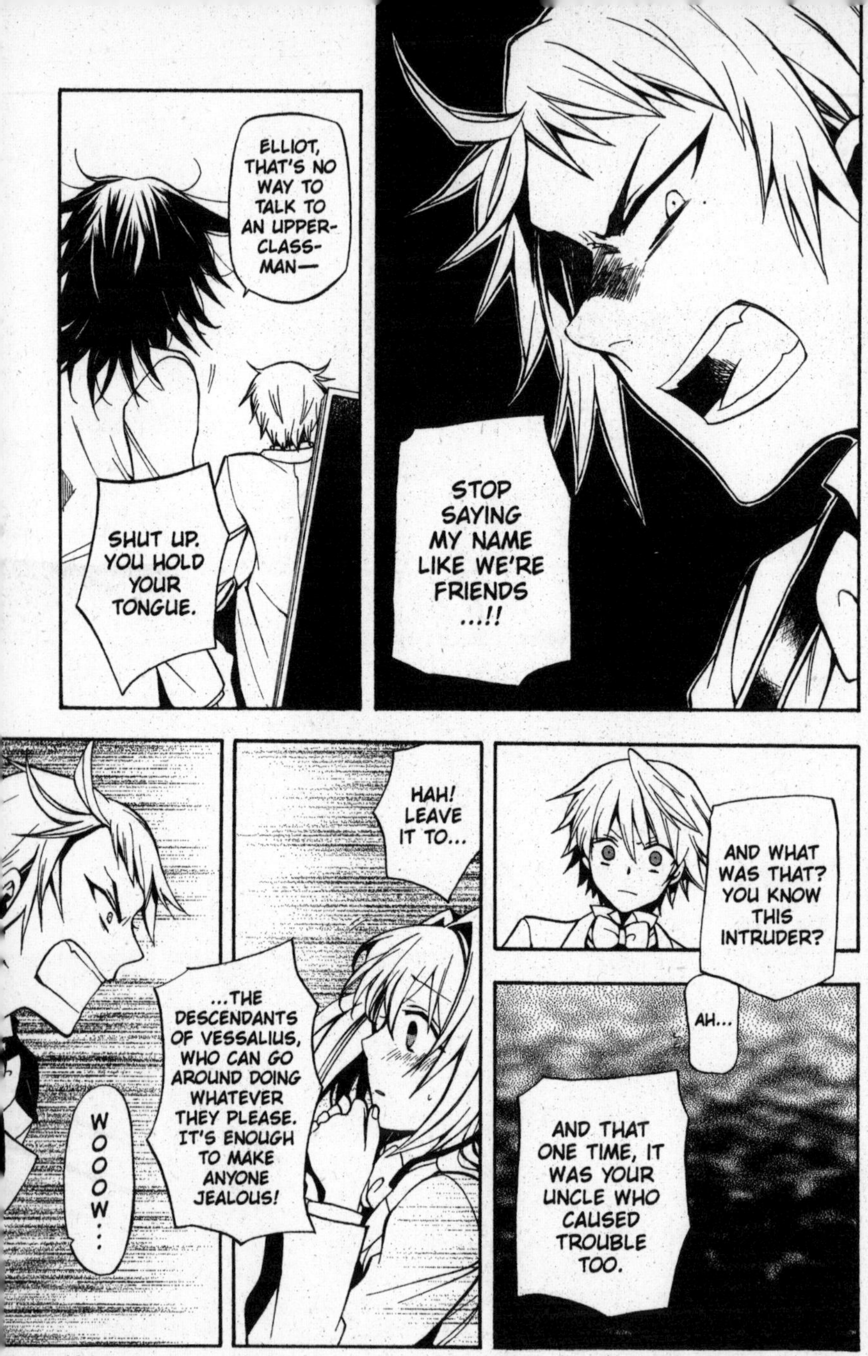
STOP SAYING MY NAME LIKE WE'RE FRIENDS ...!!
ELLIOT, THAT'S NO WAY TO TALK TO AN UPPER-CLASS-MAN—
SHUT UP. YOU HOLD YOUR TONGUE.
AND WHAT WAS THAT? YOU KNOW THIS INTRUDER?
AH...
AND THAT ONE TIME, IT WAS YOUR UNCLE WHO CAUSED TROUBLE TOO.
HAH! LEAVE IT TO...
...THE DESCENDANTS OF VESSALIUS, WHO CAN GO AROUND DOING WHATEVER THEY PLEASE. IT'S ENOUGH TO MAKE ANYONE JEALOUS!
WOOOOW...

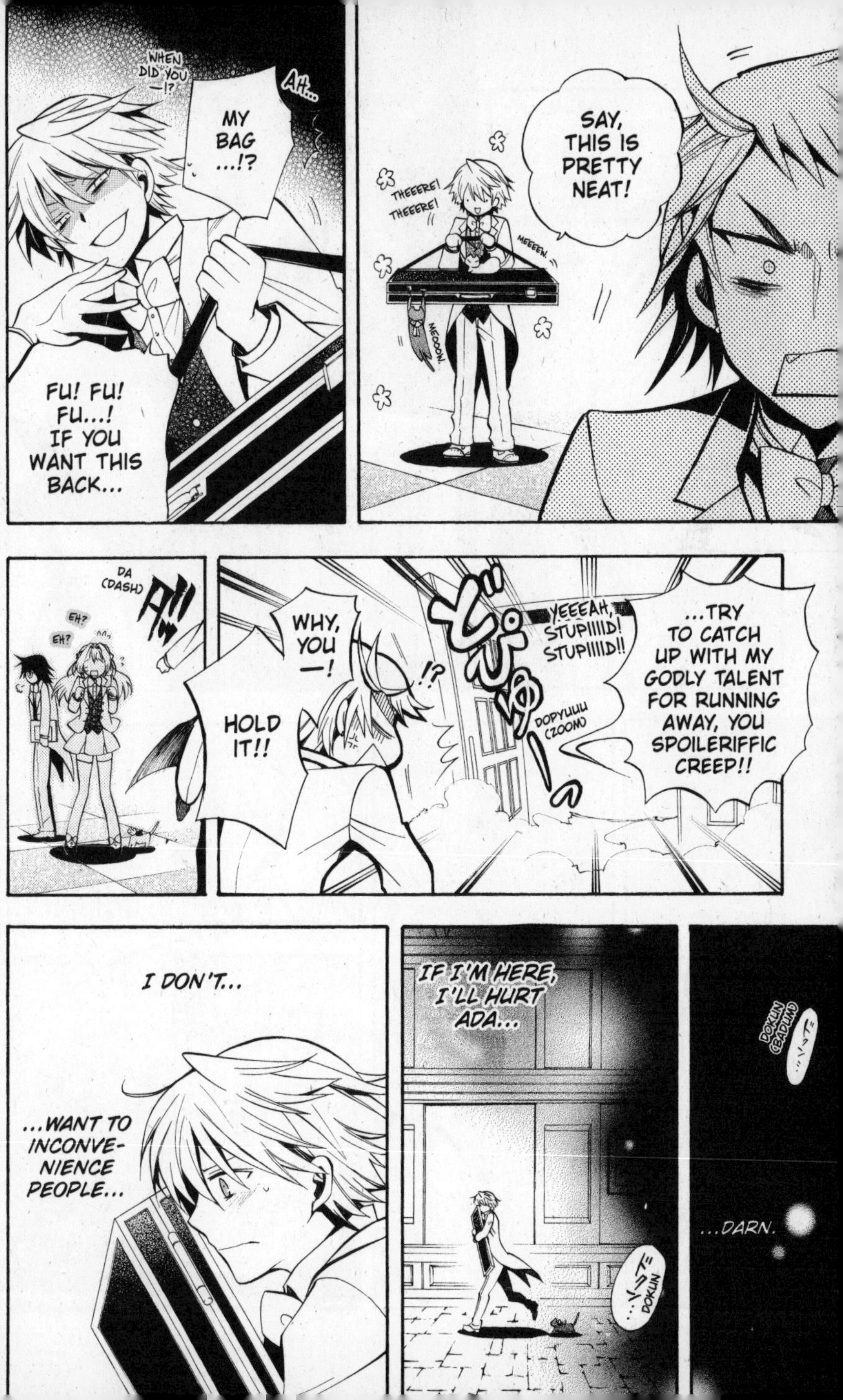
SAY, THIS IS PRETTY NEAT!
THEEERE! THEEERE!
MEEEEN.
MECOON.
WHEN DID YOU —!?
AH...
MY BAG ...!?
FU! FU! FU...! IF YOU WANT THIS BACK...
...TRY TO CATCH UP WITH MY GODLY TALENT FOR RUNNING AWAY, YOU SPOILERIFFIC CREEP!!
YEEEAH, STUPIIIID! STUPIIIID!!
DOPYUUU (ZOOM)
!?
WHY, YOU —!
HOLD IT!!
DA (DASH)
EH?
EH?
DOKUN (BADUMP)
...DARN.
IF I'M HERE, I'LL HURT ADA...
DOKUN
I DON'T...
...WANT TO INCONVENIENCE PEOPLE...

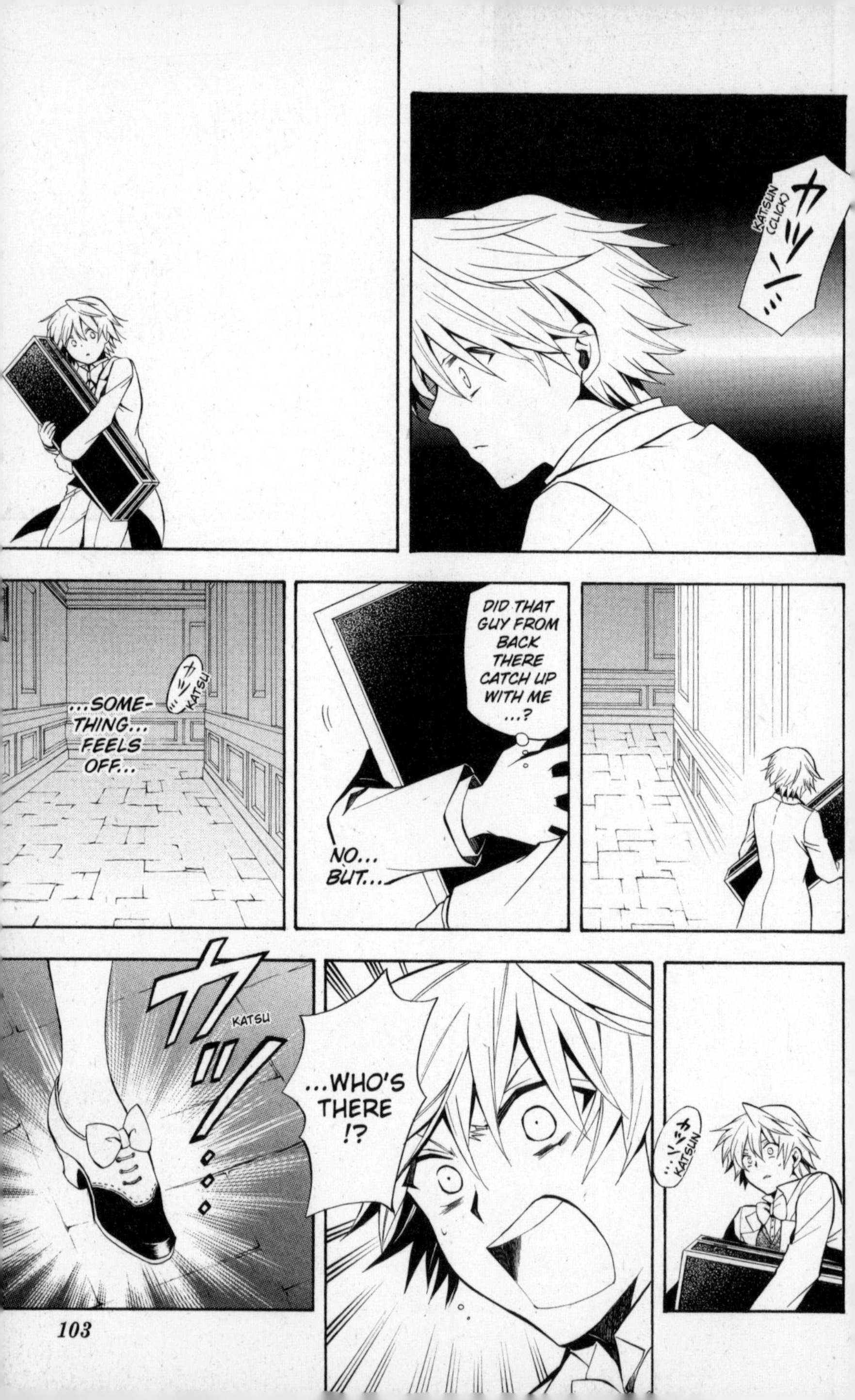
KATSUN (CLICK)
DID THAT GUY FROM BACK THERE CATCH UP WITH ME ...?
NO... BUT...
KATSU
...SOME-THING... FEELS OFF...
KATSUN
...WHO'S THERE !?
KATSU

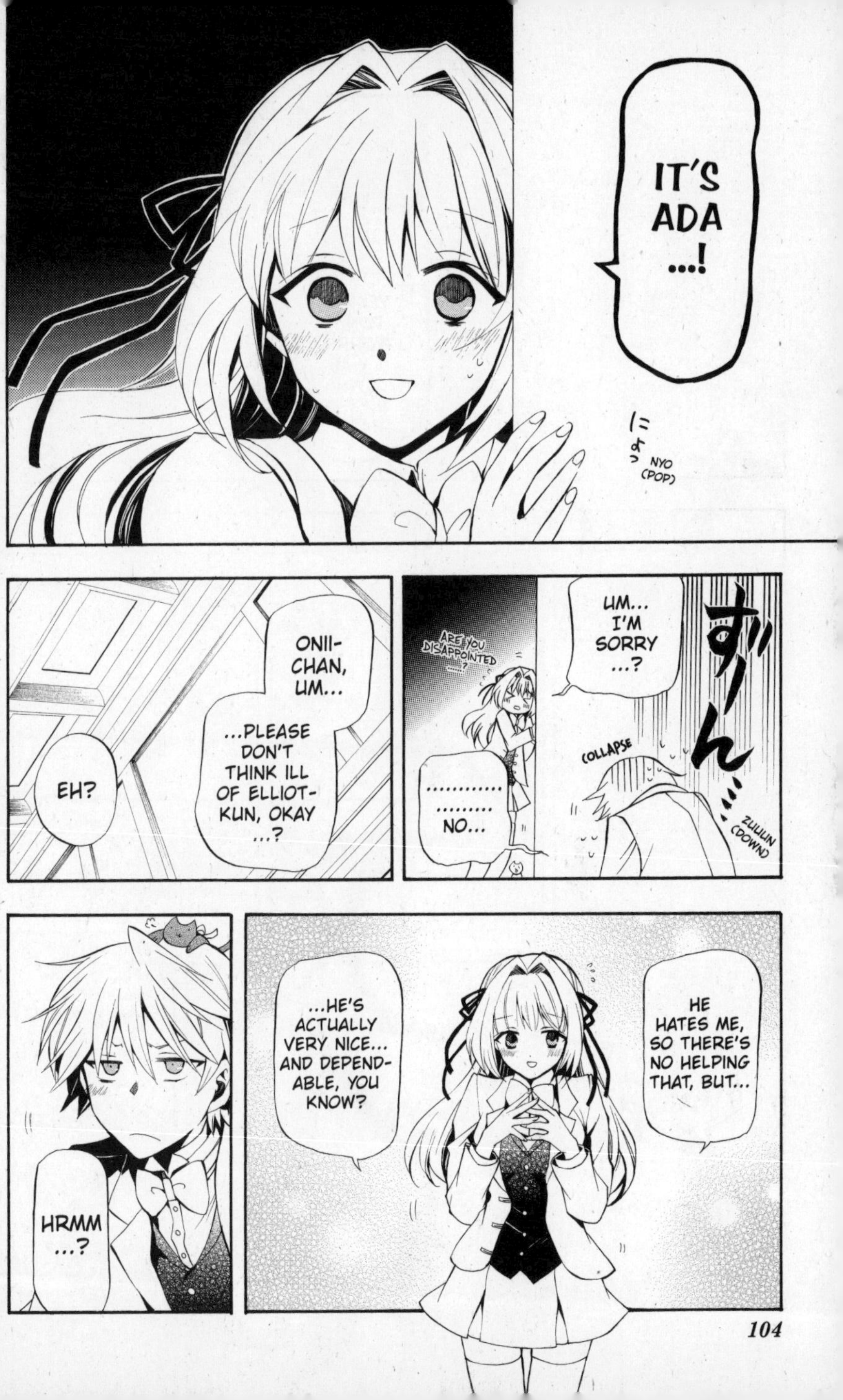
IT'S ADA ...!
にょっ
NYO (POP)
ずーん
UM... I'M SORRY ...?
ARE YOU DISAPPOINTED .....?
COLLAPSE
ZUUUN (DOWN)
.... NO...
ONII-CHAN, UM...
...PLEASE DON'T THINK ILL OF ELLIOT-KUN, OKAY ...?
EH?
HE HATES ME, SO THERE'S NO HELPING THAT, BUT...
...HE'S ACTUALLY VERY NICE... AND DEPENDABLE, YOU KNOW?
HRMM ...?

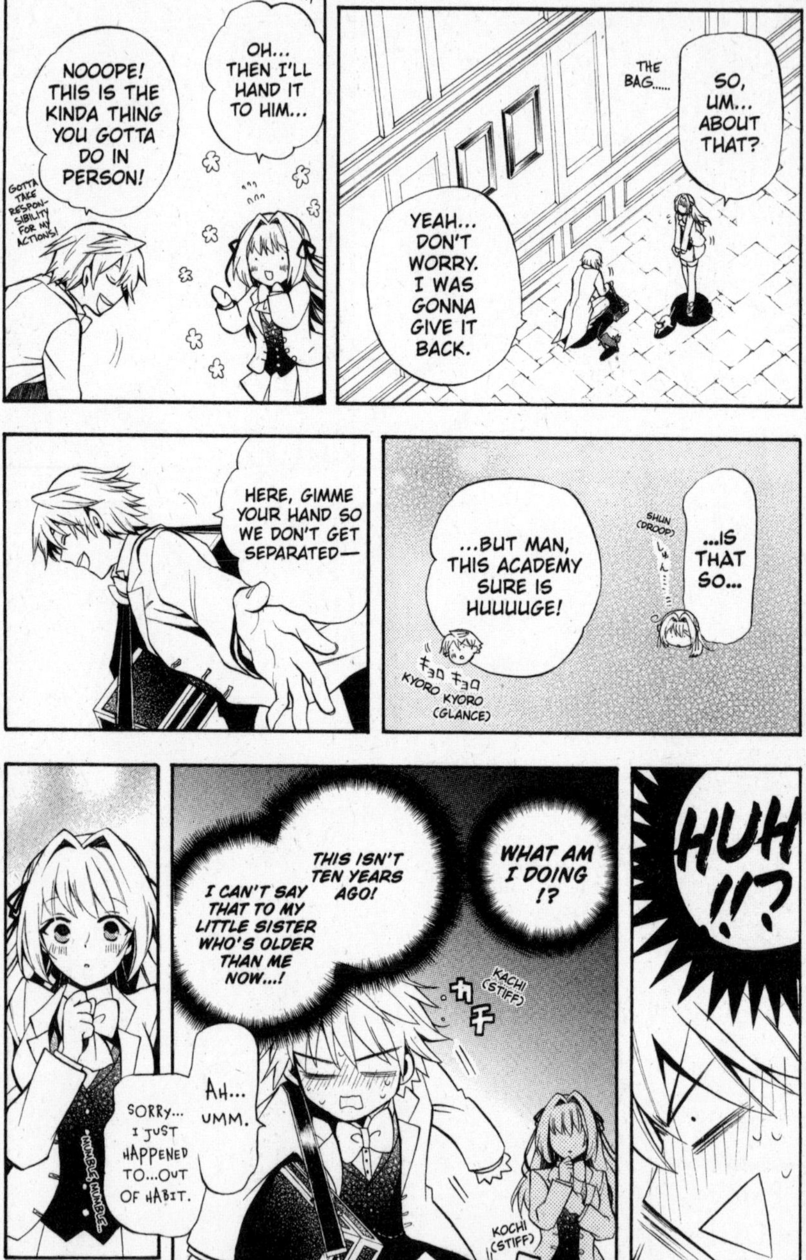
SO, UM... ABOUT THAT?
THE BAG......
YEAH... DON'T WORRY. I WAS GONNA GIVE IT BACK.
OH... THEN I'LL HAND IT TO HIM...
NOOOPE! THIS IS THE KINDA THING YOU GOTTA DO IN PERSON!
GOTTA TAKE RESPONSIBILITY FOR MY ACTIONS!
...IS THAT SO...
しゅん
SHUN (DROOP)
...BUT MAN, THIS ACADEMY SURE IS HUUUUGE!
キョロ キョロ
KYORO KYORO (GLANCE)
HERE, GIMME YOUR HAND SO WE DON'T GET SEPARATED—
HUH!!?
WHAT AM I DOING!?
THIS ISN'T TEN YEARS AGO!
I CAN'T SAY THAT TO MY LITTLE SISTER WHO'S OLDER THAN ME NOW...!
カチ
KACHI (STIFF)
コチ
KOCHI (STIFF)
AAUH...
AH... UMM.
SORRY... I JUST HAPPENED TO...OUT OF HABIT.
MUMBLE, MUMBLE...

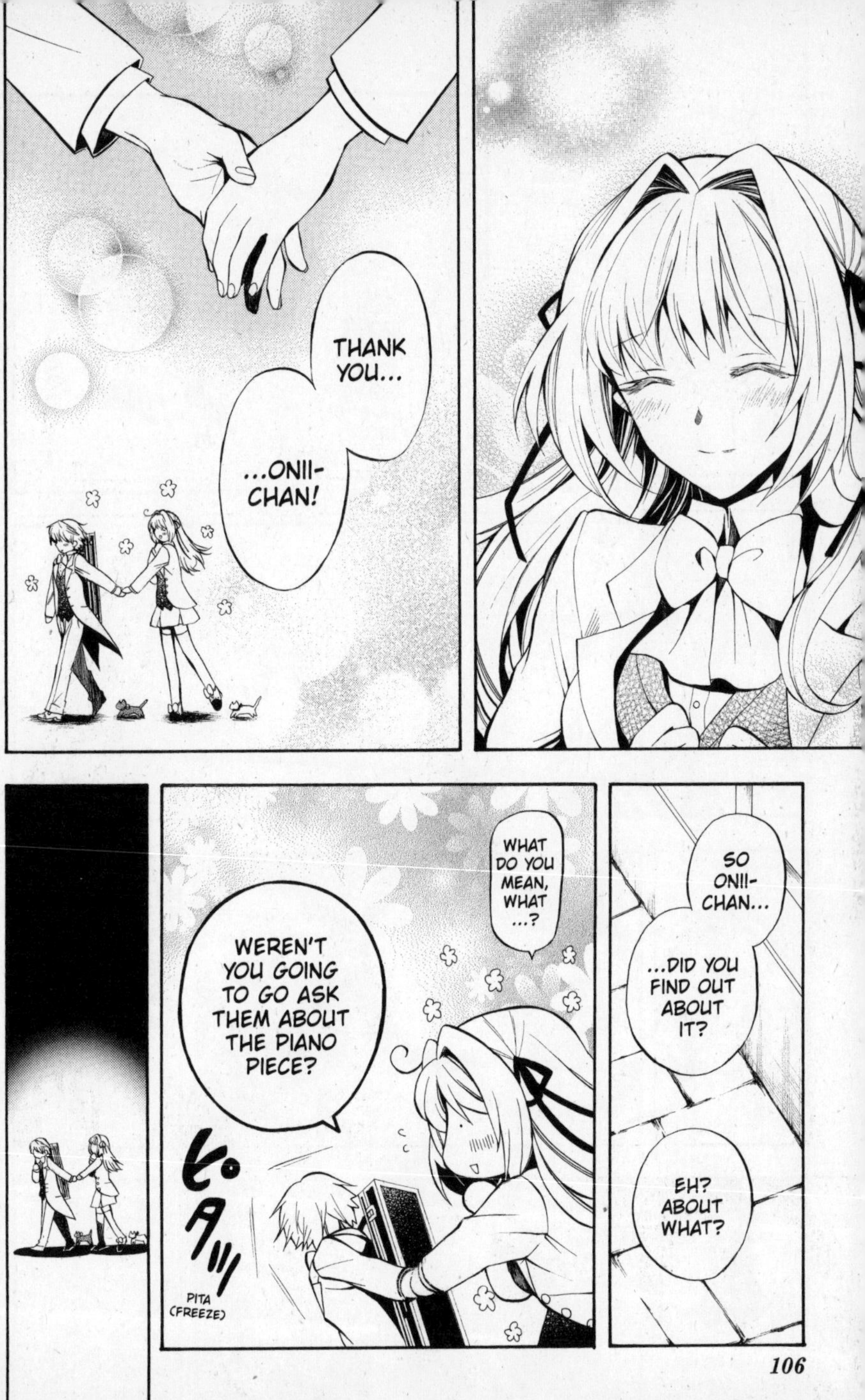
THANK YOU...
...ONII-CHAN!
SO ONII-CHAN...
...DID YOU FIND OUT ABOUT IT?
EH? ABOUT WHAT?
WHAT DO YOU MEAN, WHAT ...?
WEREN'T YOU GOING TO GO ASK THEM ABOUT THE PIANO PIECE?
PITA (FREEZE)

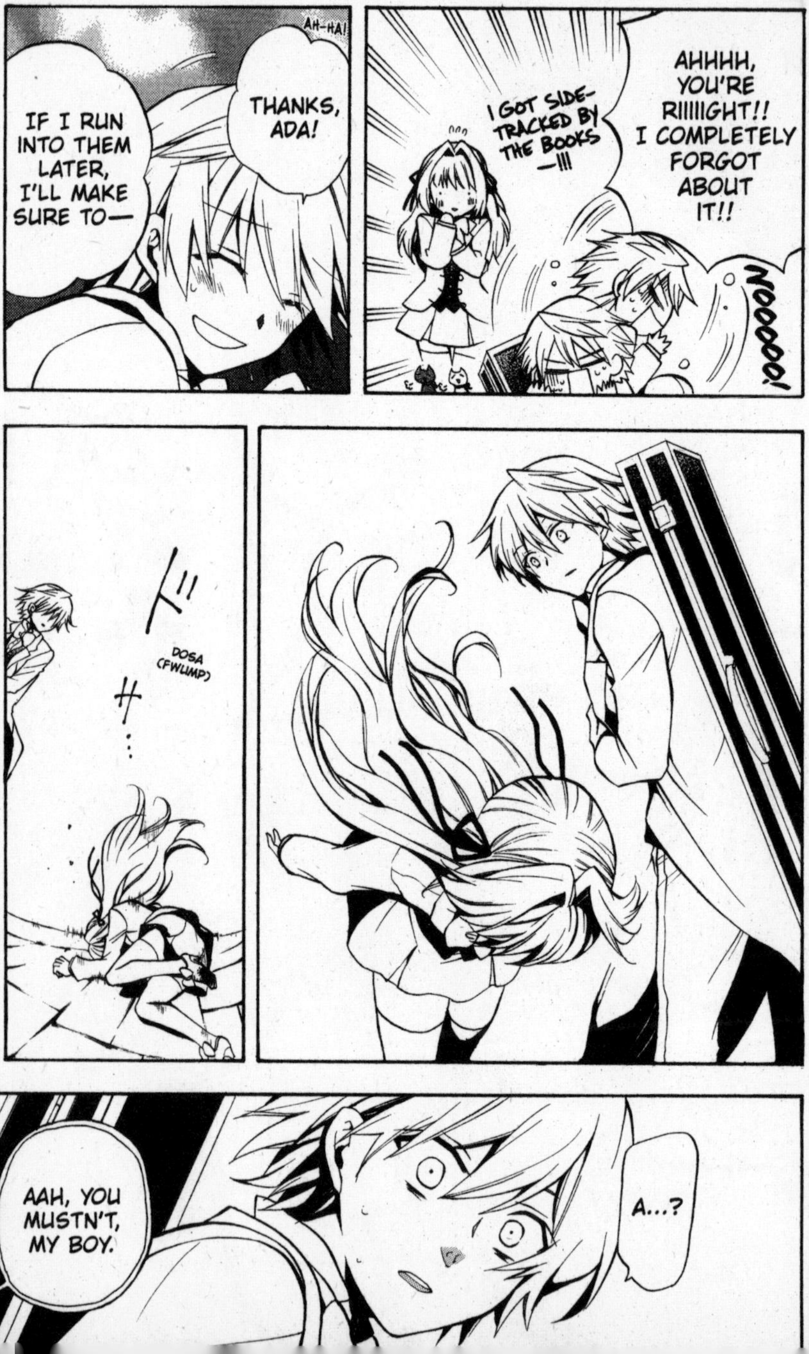
AHHHH, YOU'RE RIIIIIGHT!! I COMPLETELY FORGOT ABOUT IT!!
I GOT SIDE-TRACKED BY THE BOOKS—!!!
NOOOOOO!
AH-HA!
THANKS, ADA!
IF I RUN INTO THEM LATER, I'LL MAKE SURE TO—
DOSA (FWUMP)
A...?
AAH, YOU MUSTN'T, MY BOY.

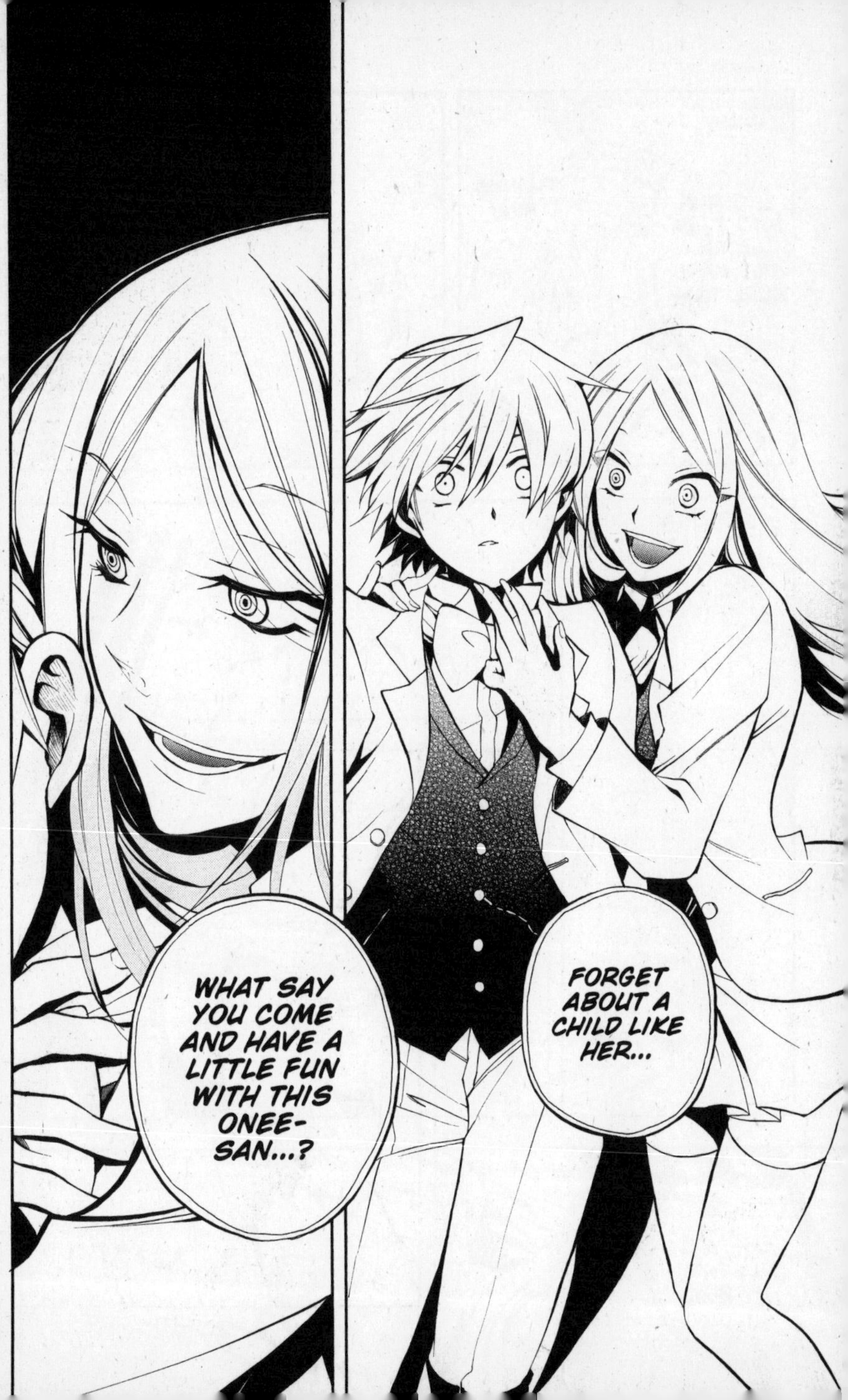
FORGET ABOUT A CHILD LIKE HER...
WHAT SAY YOU COME AND HAVE A LITTLE FUN WITH THIS ONEE-SAN...?

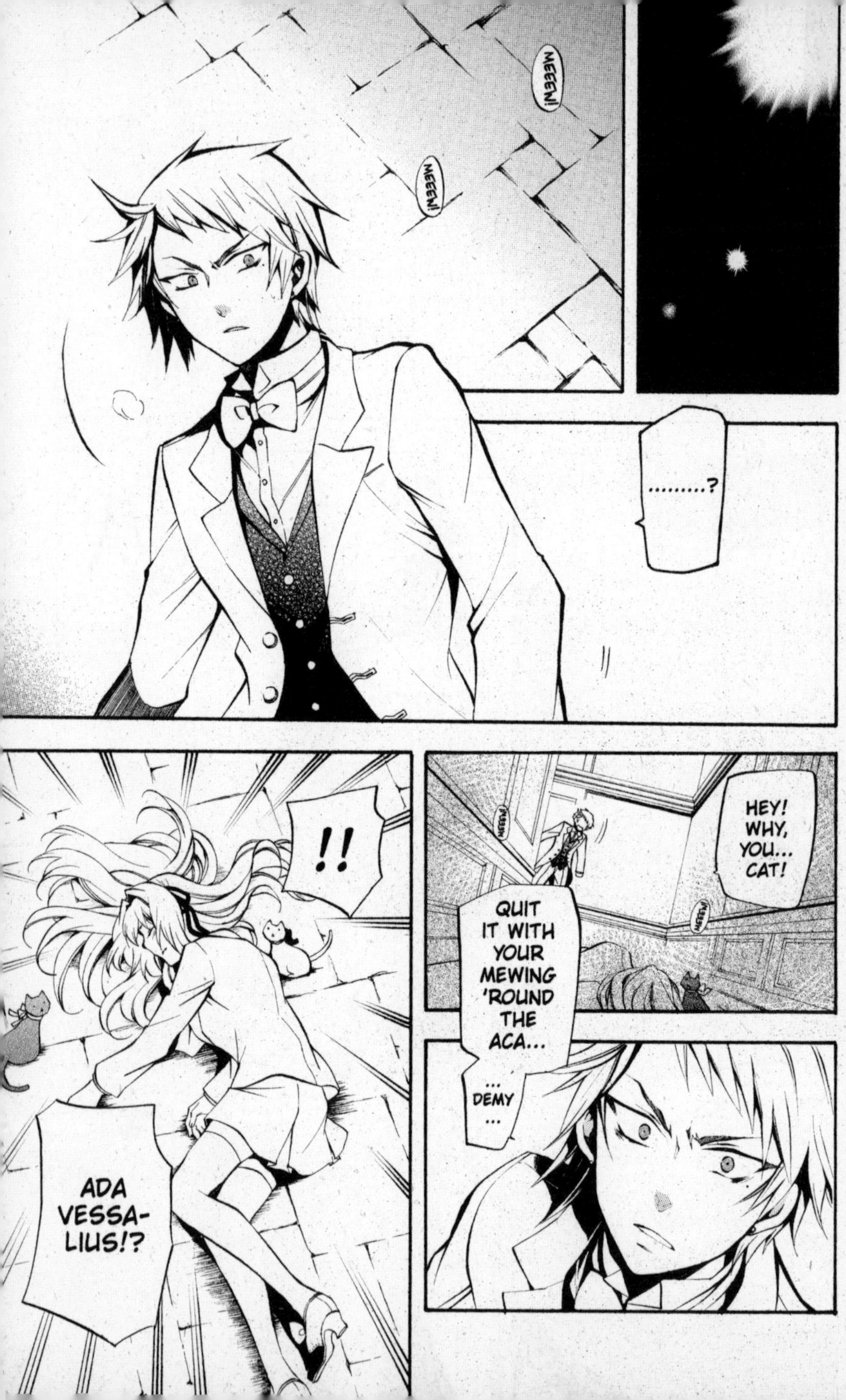
MEEEW!
MEEEW!
.........?
HEY! WHY, YOU... CAT!
MEEEW!
MEEEW!
QUIT IT WITH YOUR MEWING 'ROUND THE ACA...
...DEMY...
!!
ADA VESSA-LIUS!?

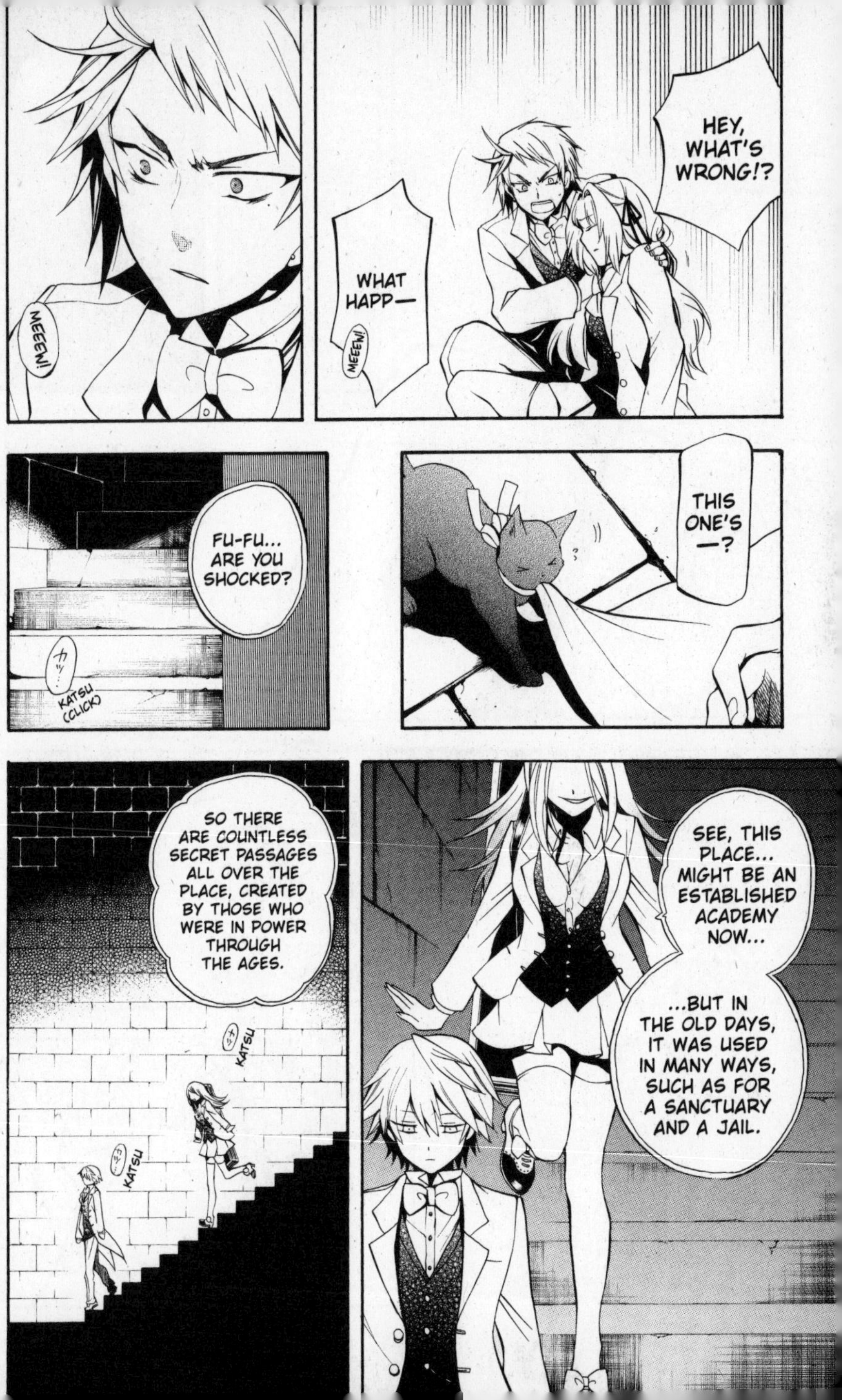
HEY, WHAT'S WRONG!?
WHAT HAPP—
MEEEW!
MEEEW!
THIS ONE'S —?
FU-FU... ARE YOU SHOCKED?
KATSU (CLICK)
SEE, THIS PLACE... MIGHT BE AN ESTABLISHED ACADEMY NOW...
...BUT IN THE OLD DAYS, IT WAS USED IN MANY WAYS, SUCH AS FOR A SANCTUARY AND A JAIL.
SO THERE ARE COUNTLESS SECRET PASSAGES ALL OVER THE PLACE, CREATED BY THOSE WHO WERE IN POWER THROUGH THE AGES.
KATSU
KATSU

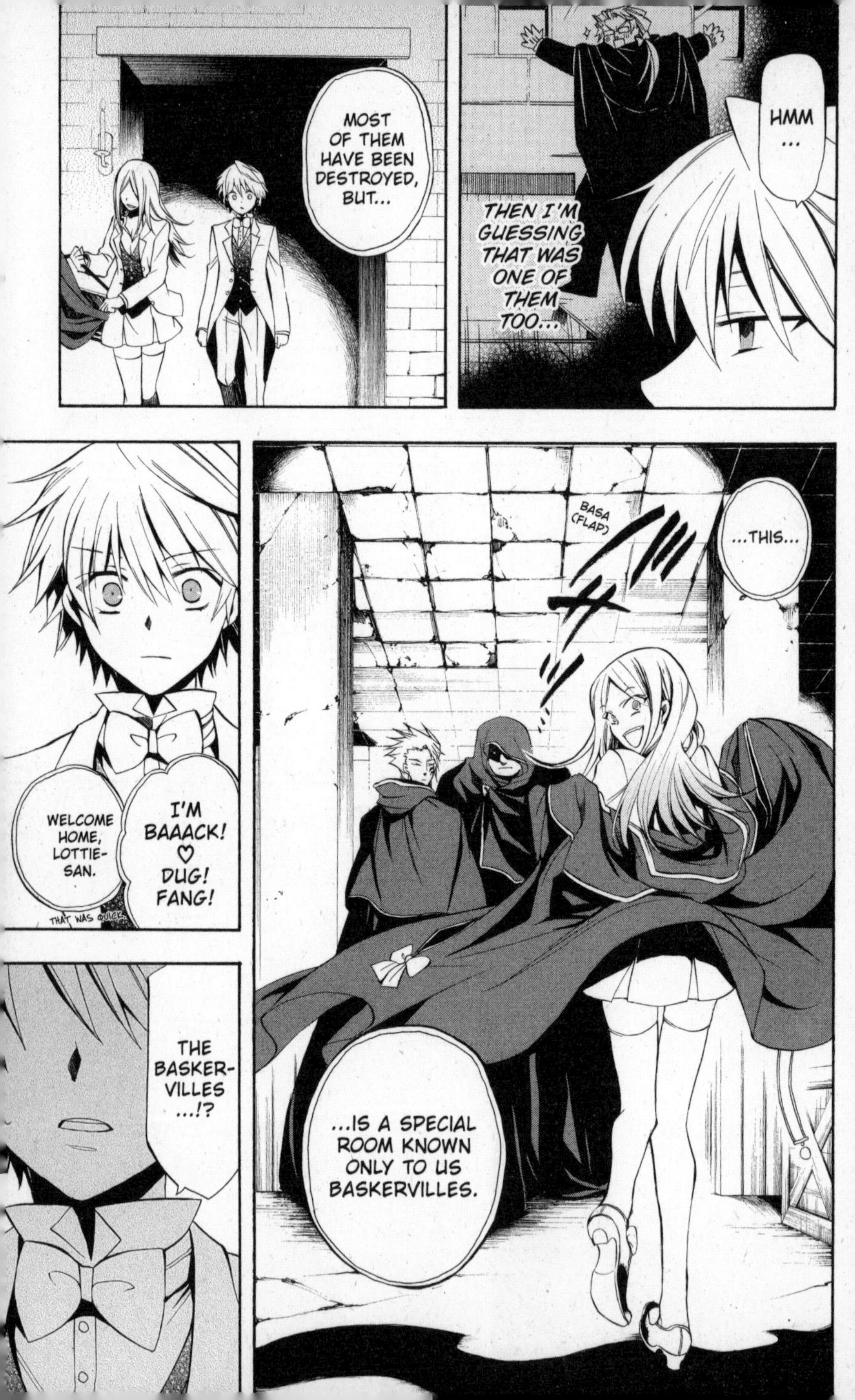
HMM ...
THEN I'M GUESSING THAT WAS ONE OF THEM TOO...
MOST OF THEM HAVE BEEN DESTROYED, BUT...
...THIS...
BASA (FLAP)
...IS A SPECIAL ROOM KNOWN ONLY TO US BASKERVILLES.
I'M BAAACK! ♡ DUG! FANG!
WELCOME HOME, LOTTIE-SAN.
THAT WAS QUICK.
THE BASKER-VILLES ...!?

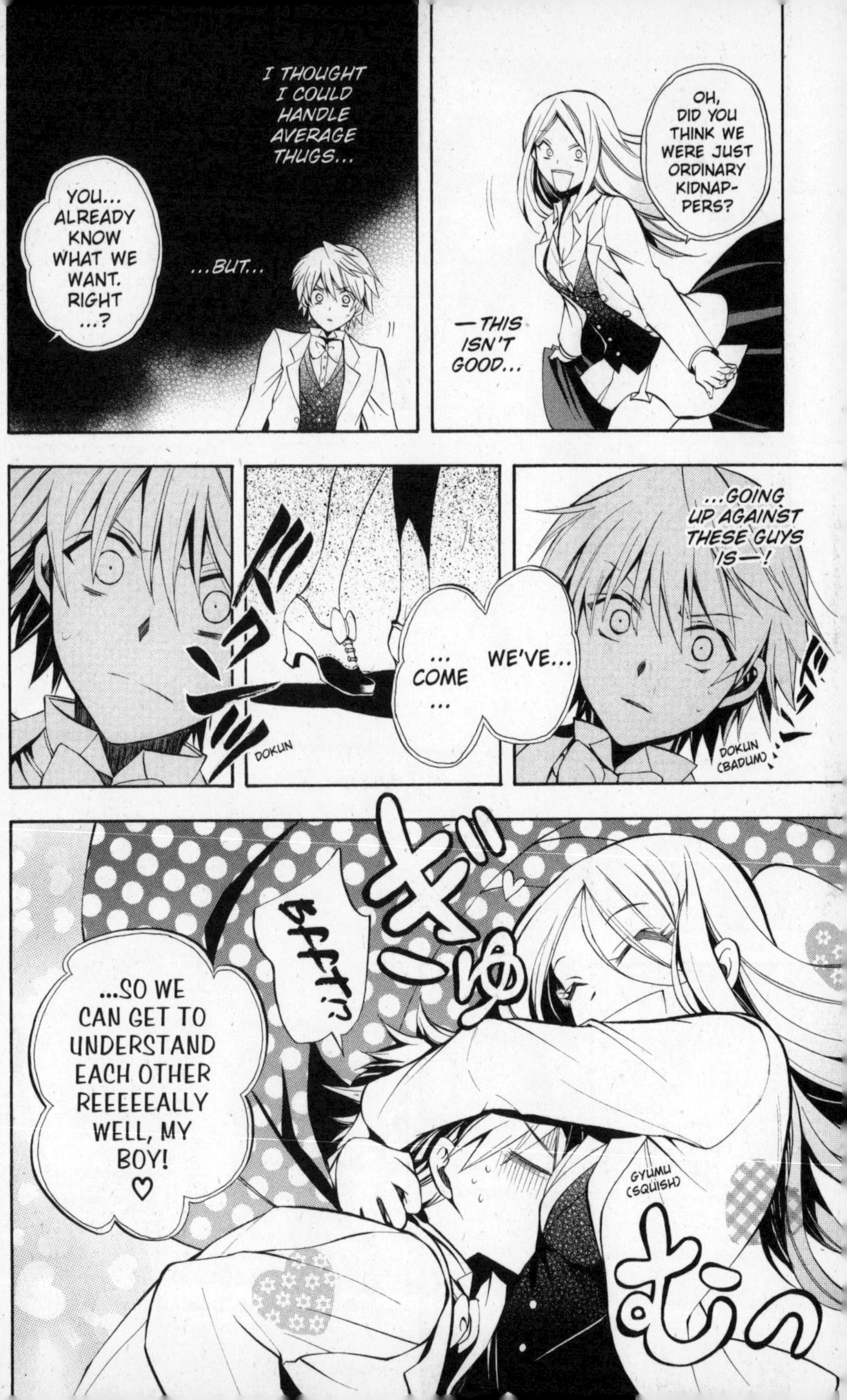
OH, DID YOU THINK WE WERE JUST ORDINARY KIDNAPPERS?
—THIS ISN'T GOOD...
I THOUGHT I COULD HANDLE AVERAGE THUGS...
...BUT...
YOU... ALREADY KNOW WHAT WE WANT. RIGHT ...?
...GOING UP AGAINST THESE GUYS IS—!
DOKUN (BADUM)
WE'VE... ...COME...
DOKUN
BFFT!?
GYUMU (SQUISH)
...SO WE CAN GET TO UNDERSTAND EACH OTHER REEEEEALLY WELL, MY BOY! ♡

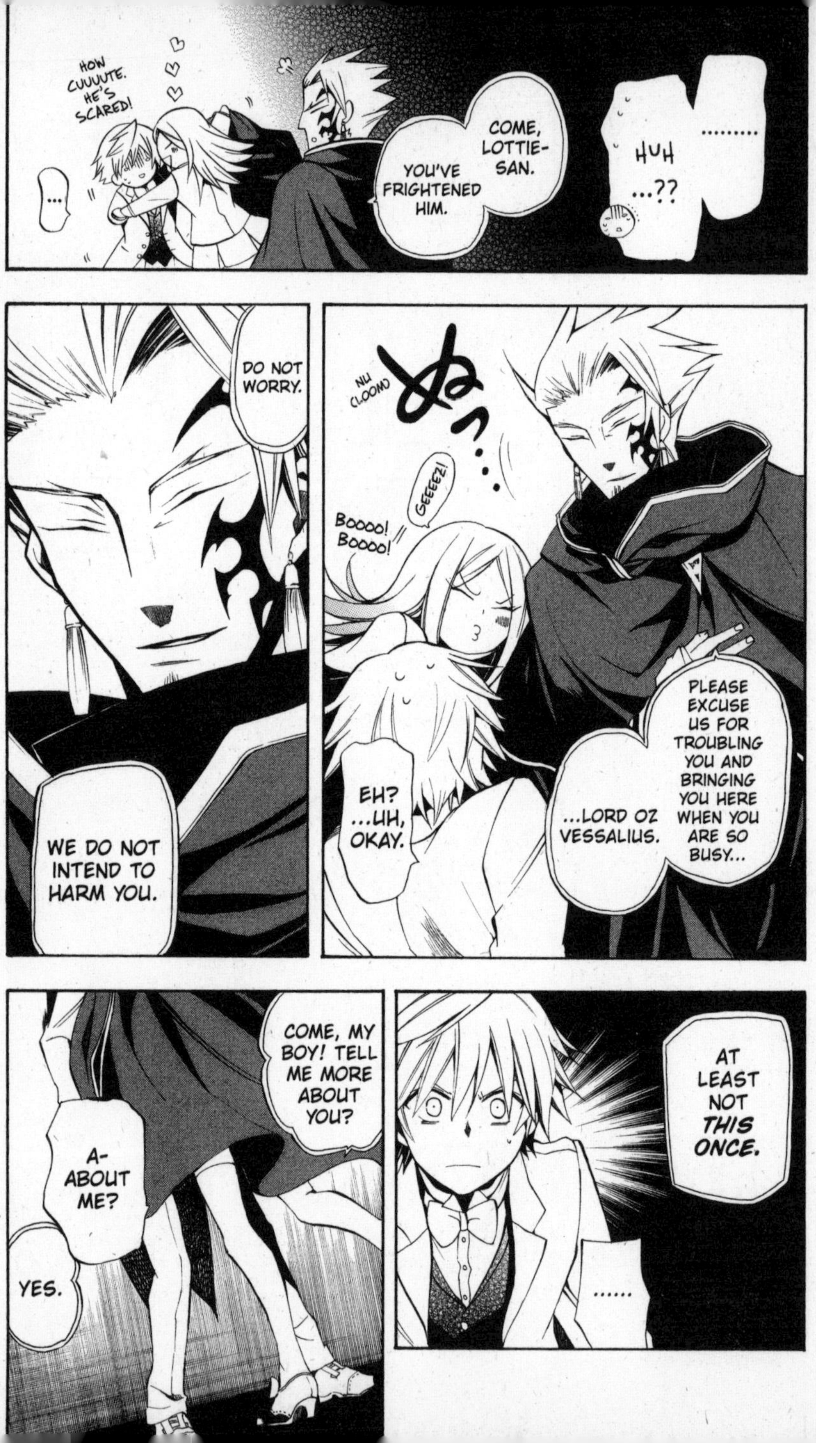
....
HUH ...??
COME, LOTTIE-SAN.
YOU'VE FRIGHTENED HIM.
HOW CUUUUTE. HE'S SCARED!
...
ぬっ...
NU (LOOM)
GEEEEZ!
BOOOO! BOOOO!
PLEASE EXCUSE US FOR TROUBLING YOU AND BRINGING YOU HERE WHEN YOU ARE SO BUSY...
...LORD OZ VESSALIUS.
EH? ...UH, OKAY.
DO NOT WORRY.
WE DO NOT INTEND TO HARM YOU.
AT LEAST NOT *THIS ONCE.*
......
COME, MY BOY! TELL ME MORE ABOUT YOU?
A- ABOUT ME?
YES.

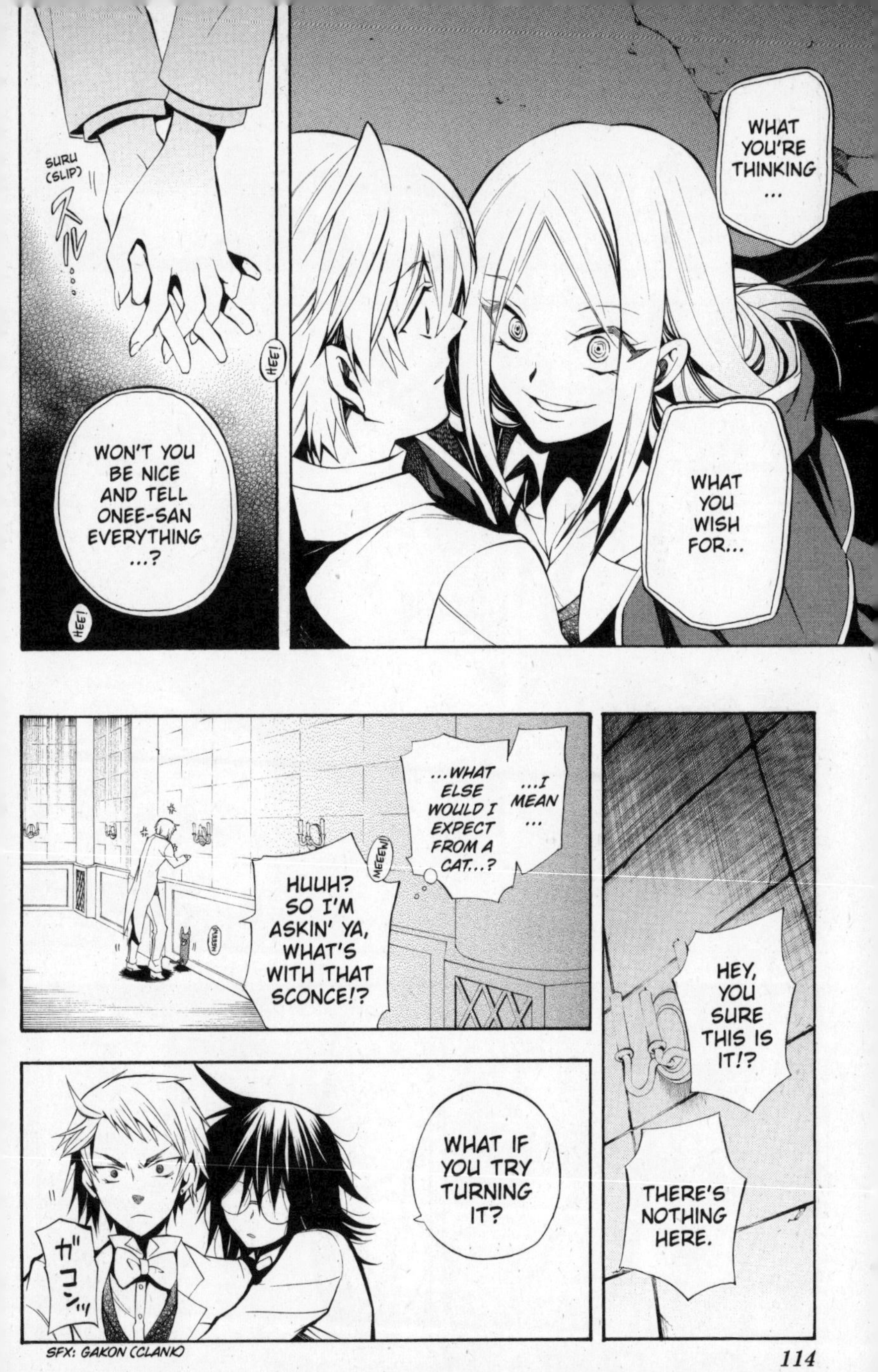
WHAT YOU'RE THINKING ...
HEE!
WHAT YOU WISH FOR...
SURU (SLIP)
スル...
WON'T YOU BE NICE AND TELL ONEE-SAN EVERYTHING ...?
HEE!
HEY, YOU SURE THIS IS IT!?
THERE'S NOTHING HERE.
...I MEAN ...
...WHAT ELSE WOULD I EXPECT FROM A CAT...?
MEEEW!
HUUH? SO I'M ASKIN' YA, WHAT'S WITH THAT SCONCE!?
MEEEW!
WHAT IF YOU TRY TURNING IT?
ガコンッ

SFX: GAKON (CLANK)

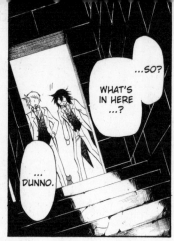

...SO?

WHAT'S IN HERE...?

...DUNNO.

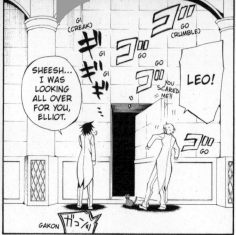

SHEESH... I WAS LOOKING ALL OVER FOR YOU, ELLIOT.

GI (CREAK)

コ゛GO

コ゛GO (RUMBLE)

コ゛GO

YOU SCARED ME!!

LEO!

コ゛GO

GAKON

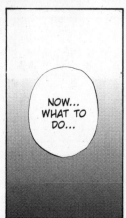

NOW... WHAT TO DO...

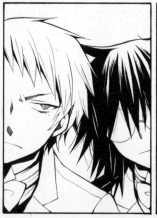

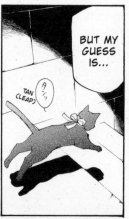

TAN (CLEAP)

BUT MY GUESS IS...

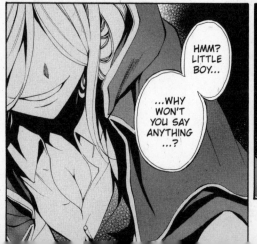

HMM? LITTLE BOY...

...WHY WON'T YOU SAY ANYTHING...?

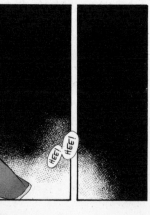

HEE! HEE!

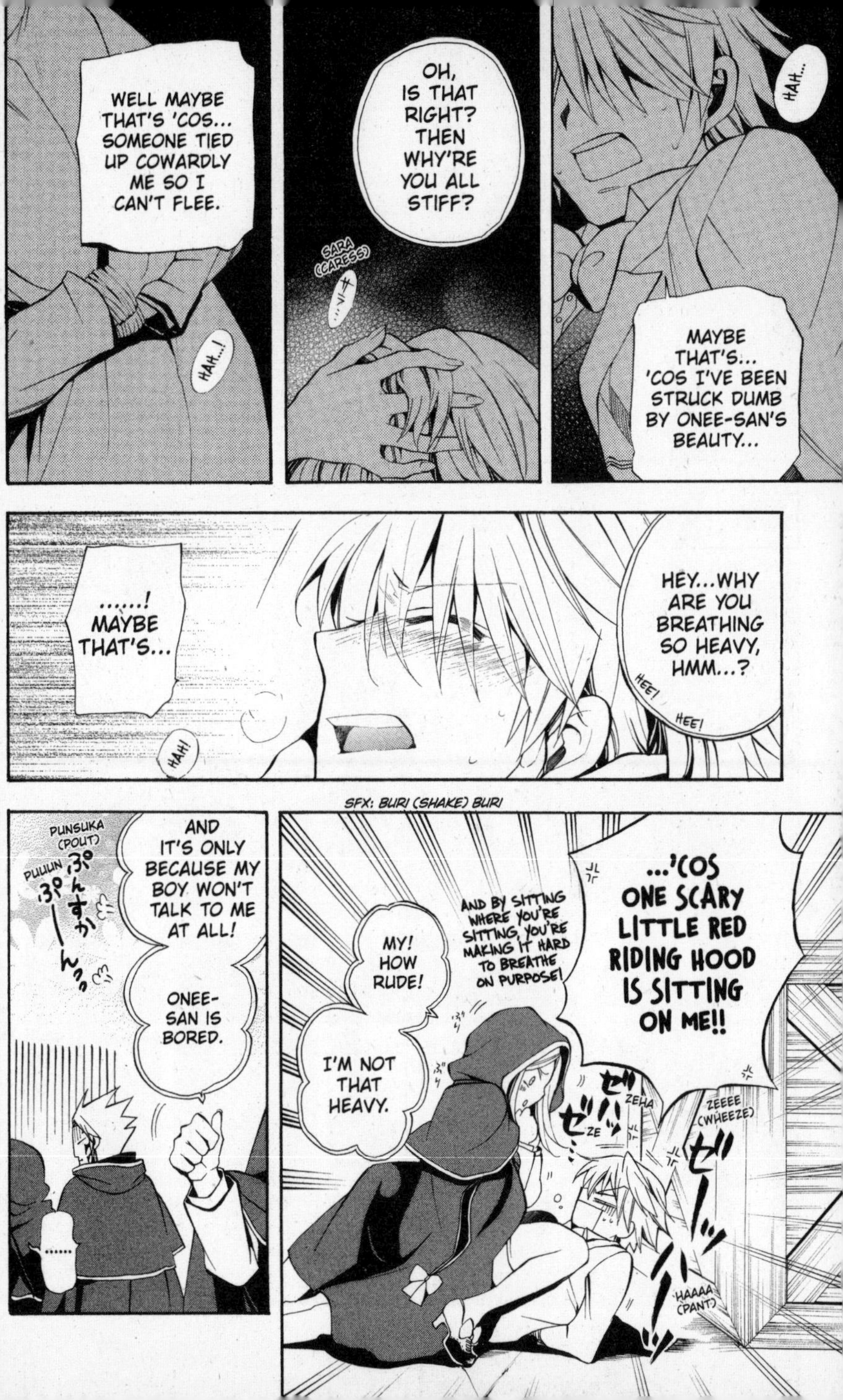
HAH...
MAYBE THAT'S... 'COS I'VE BEEN STRUCK DUMB BY ONEE-SAN'S BEAUTY...
OH, IS THAT RIGHT? THEN WHY'RE YOU ALL STIFF?
SARA (CARESS)
WELL MAYBE THAT'S 'COS... SOMEONE TIED UP COWARDLY ME SO I CAN'T FLEE.
HAH...!
HEY...WHY ARE YOU BREATHING SO HEAVY, HMM...?
HEE! HEE!
......! MAYBE THAT'S...
HAH!
SFX: BURI (SHAKE) BURI
...'COS ONE SCARY LITTLE RED RIDING HOOD IS SITTING ON ME!!
AND BY SITTING WHERE YOU'RE SITTING, YOU'RE MAKING IT HARD TO BREATHE ON PURPOSE!
MY! HOW RUDE!
I'M NOT THAT HEAVY.
ZEHA
ZE
ZEEEE (WHEEZE)
HAAAA (PANT)
AND IT'S ONLY BECAUSE MY BOY WON'T TALK TO ME AT ALL!
ONEE-SAN IS BORED.
PUNSUKA (POUT)
PUUUN
......

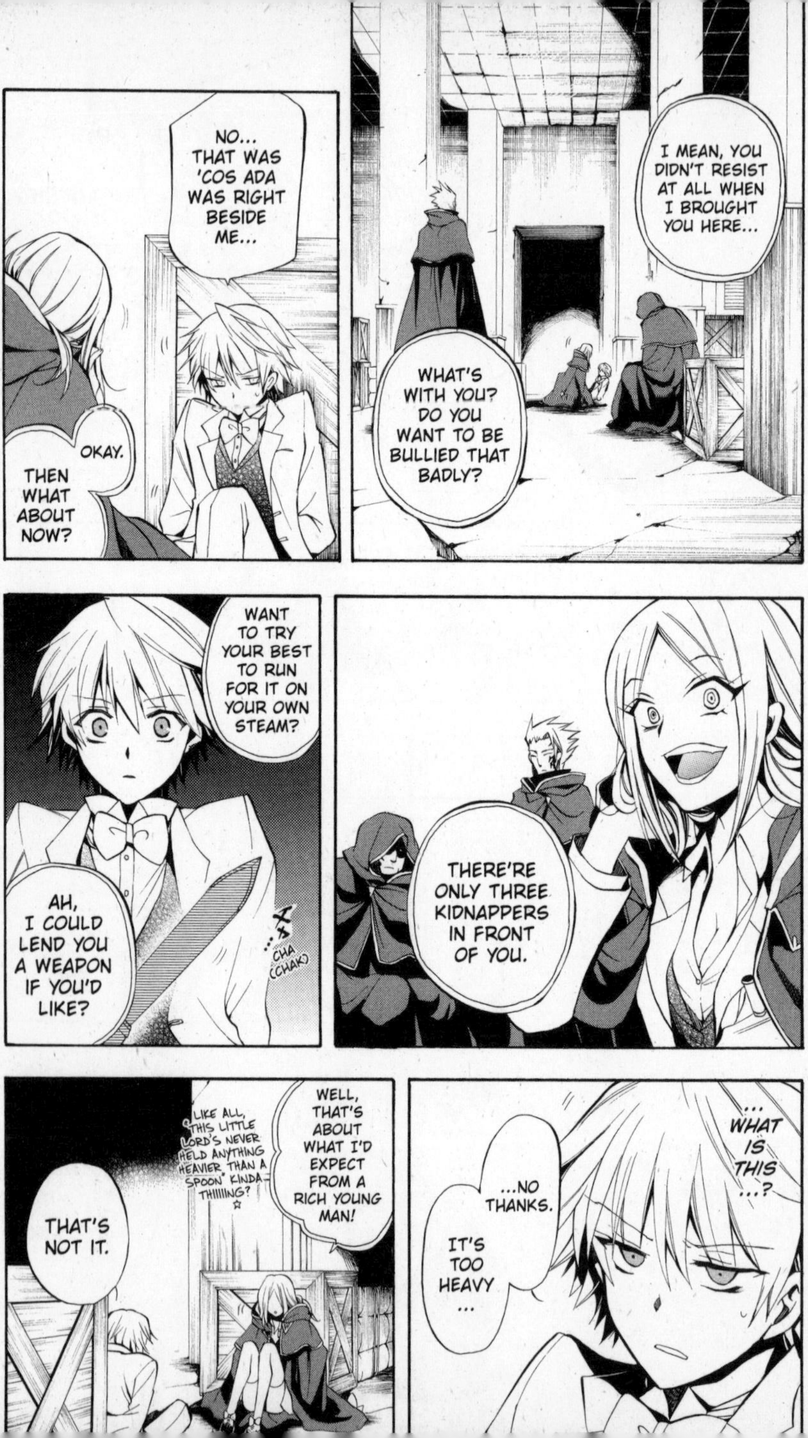
I MEAN, YOU DIDN'T RESIST AT ALL WHEN I BROUGHT YOU HERE...
WHAT'S WITH YOU? DO YOU WANT TO BE BULLIED THAT BADLY?
NO... THAT WAS 'COS ADA WAS RIGHT BESIDE ME...
OKAY.
THEN WHAT ABOUT NOW?
THERE'RE ONLY THREE KIDNAPPERS IN FRONT OF YOU.
WANT TO TRY YOUR BEST TO RUN FOR IT ON YOUR OWN STEAM?
AH, I COULD LEND YOU A WEAPON IF YOU'D LIKE?
CHA (CHAK)
...WHAT IS THIS...?
...NO THANKS.
IT'S TOO HEAVY...
WELL, THAT'S ABOUT WHAT I'D EXPECT FROM A RICH YOUNG MAN!
LIKE ALL, 'THIS LITTLE LORD'S NEVER HELD ANYTHING HEAVIER THAN A SPOON' KINDA THIIIIING? ☆
THAT'S NOT IT.

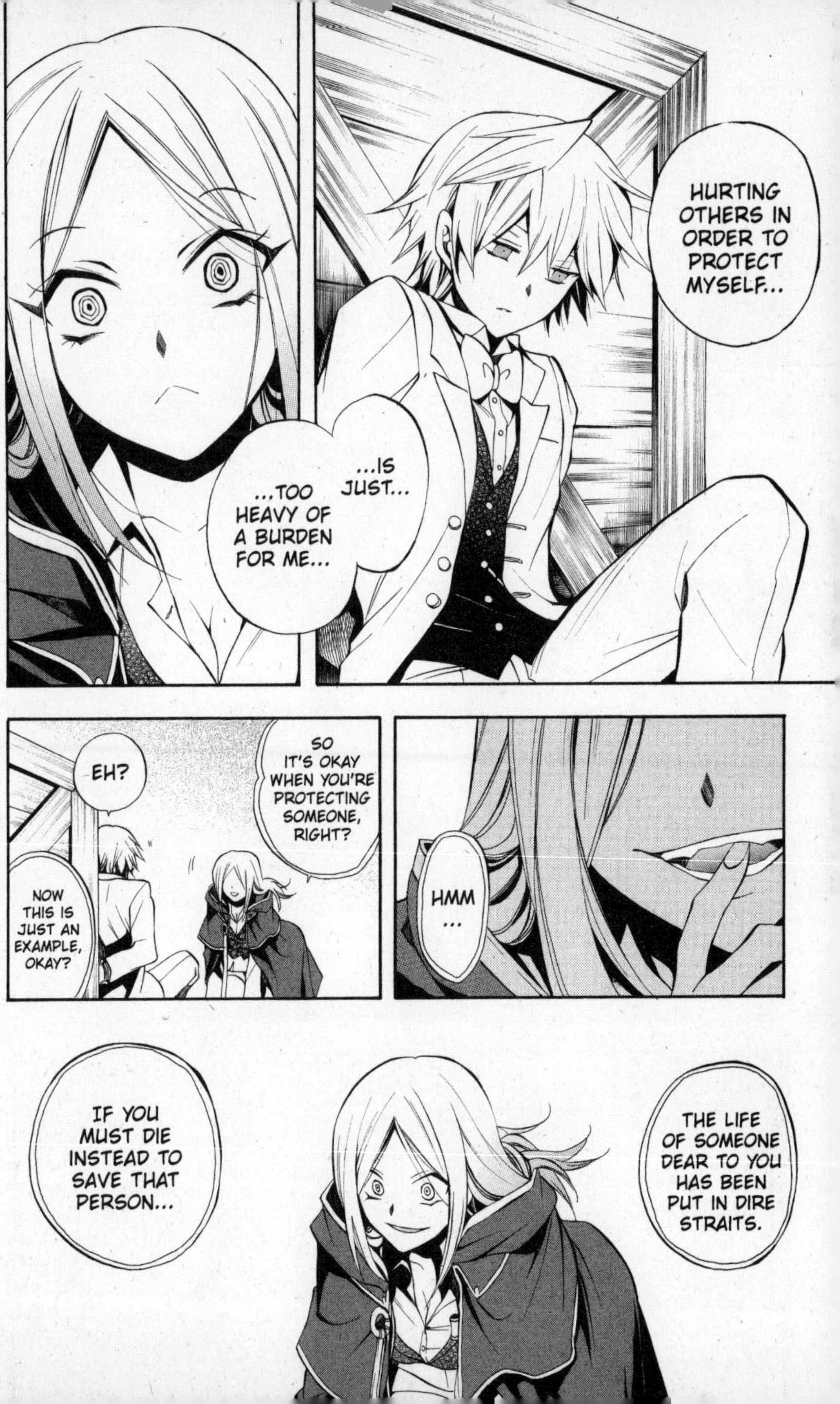
HURTING OTHERS IN ORDER TO PROTECT MYSELF...
...IS JUST...
...TOO HEAVY OF A BURDEN FOR ME...
HMM ...
SO IT'S OKAY WHEN YOU'RE PROTECTING SOMEONE, RIGHT?
EH?
NOW THIS IS JUST AN EXAMPLE, OKAY?
THE LIFE OF SOMEONE DEAR TO YOU HAS BEEN PUT IN DIRE STRAITS.
IF YOU MUST DIE INSTEAD TO SAVE THAT PERSON...

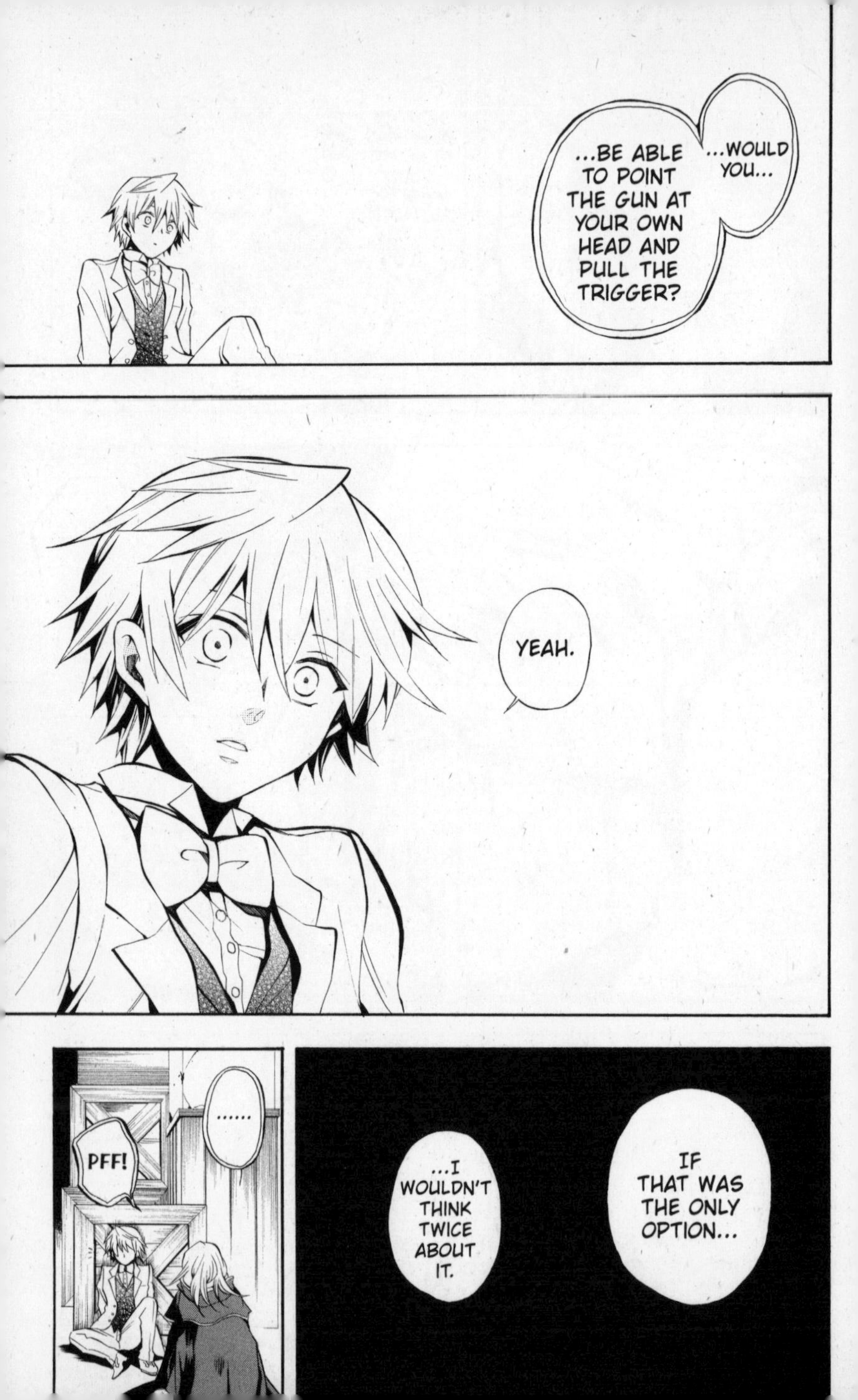
...WOULD YOU...
...BE ABLE TO POINT THE GUN AT YOUR OWN HEAD AND PULL THE TRIGGER?
YEAH.
IF THAT WAS THE ONLY OPTION...
...I WOULDN'T THINK TWICE ABOUT IT.
......
PFF!

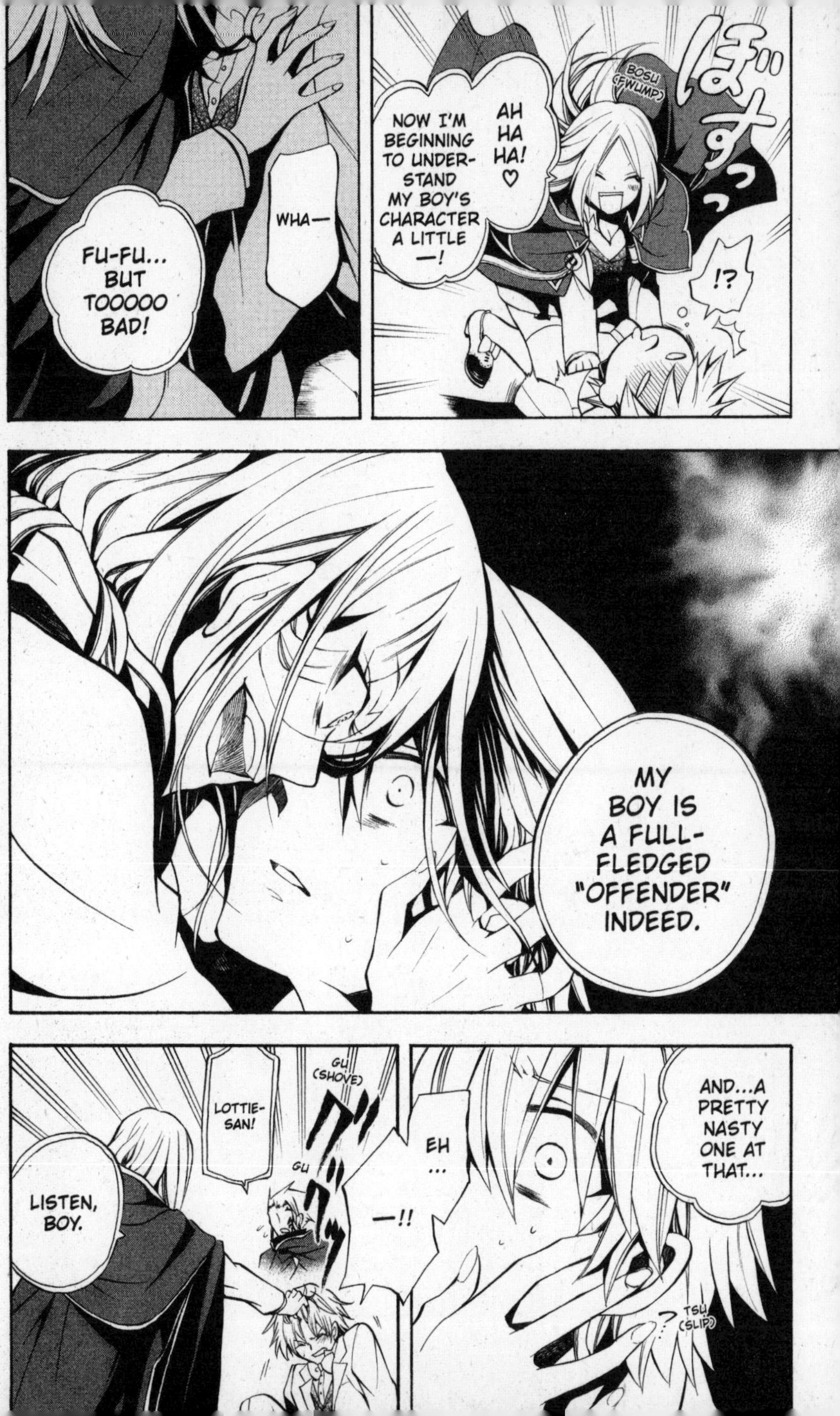
ほすっ
BOSU (FWUMP)
AH HA HA! ♡
NOW I'M BEGINNING TO UNDERSTAND MY BOY'S CHARACTER A LITTLE—!
!?
WHA—
FU-FU... BUT TOOOOO BAD!
MY BOY IS A FULL-FLEDGED "OFFENDER" INDEED.
AND...A PRETTY NASTY ONE AT THAT...
EH...—!!
TSU (SLIP)
GU (SHOVE)
LOTTIE-SAN!
GU
LISTEN, BOY.

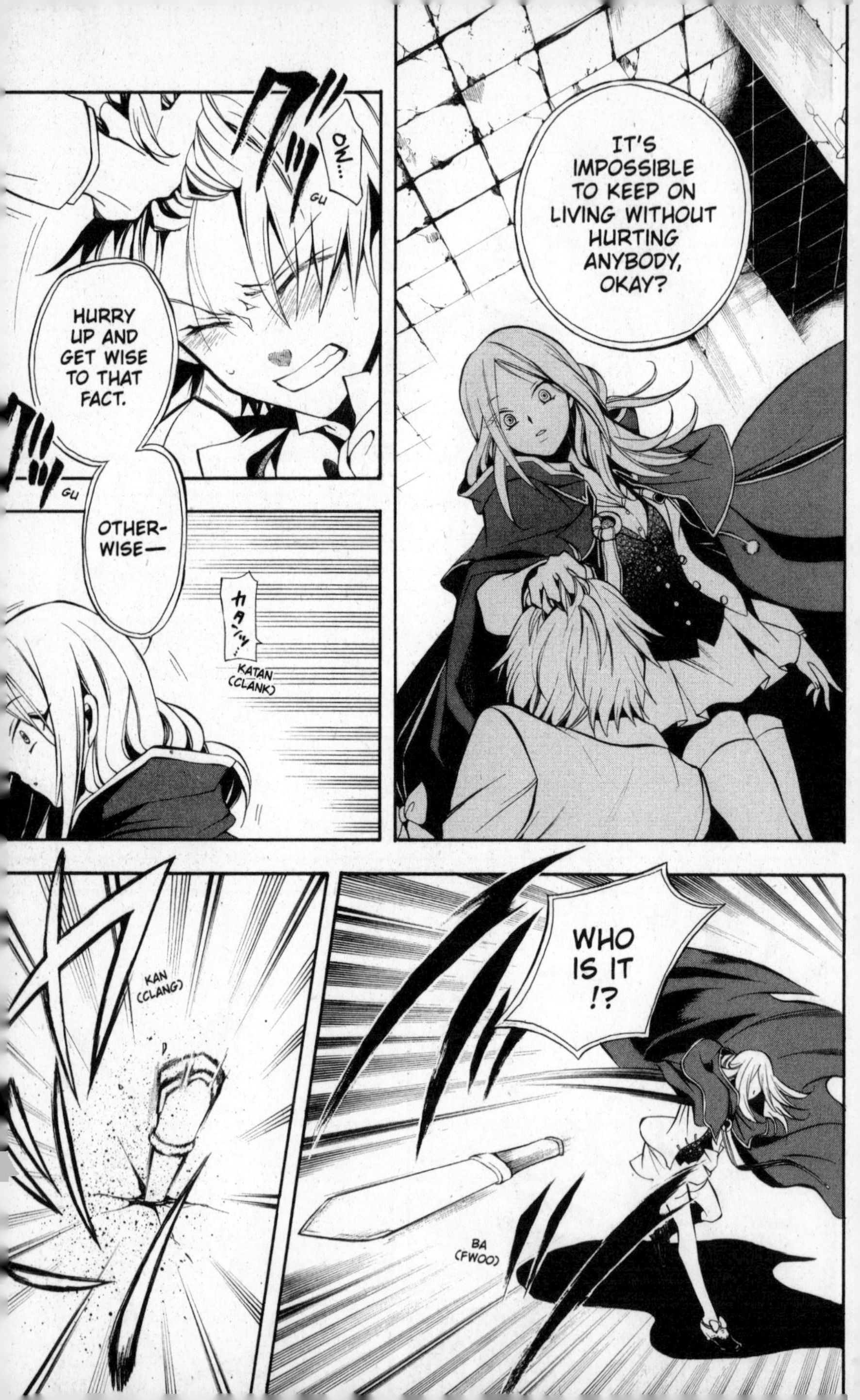
IT'S IMPOSSIBLE TO KEEP ON LIVING WITHOUT HURTING ANYBODY, OKAY?
OW...
GU
HURRY UP AND GET WISE TO THAT FACT.
GU
OTHER-WISE—
カタンッ…
KATAN (CLANK)
WHO IS IT !?
BA (FWOO)
KAN (CLANG)

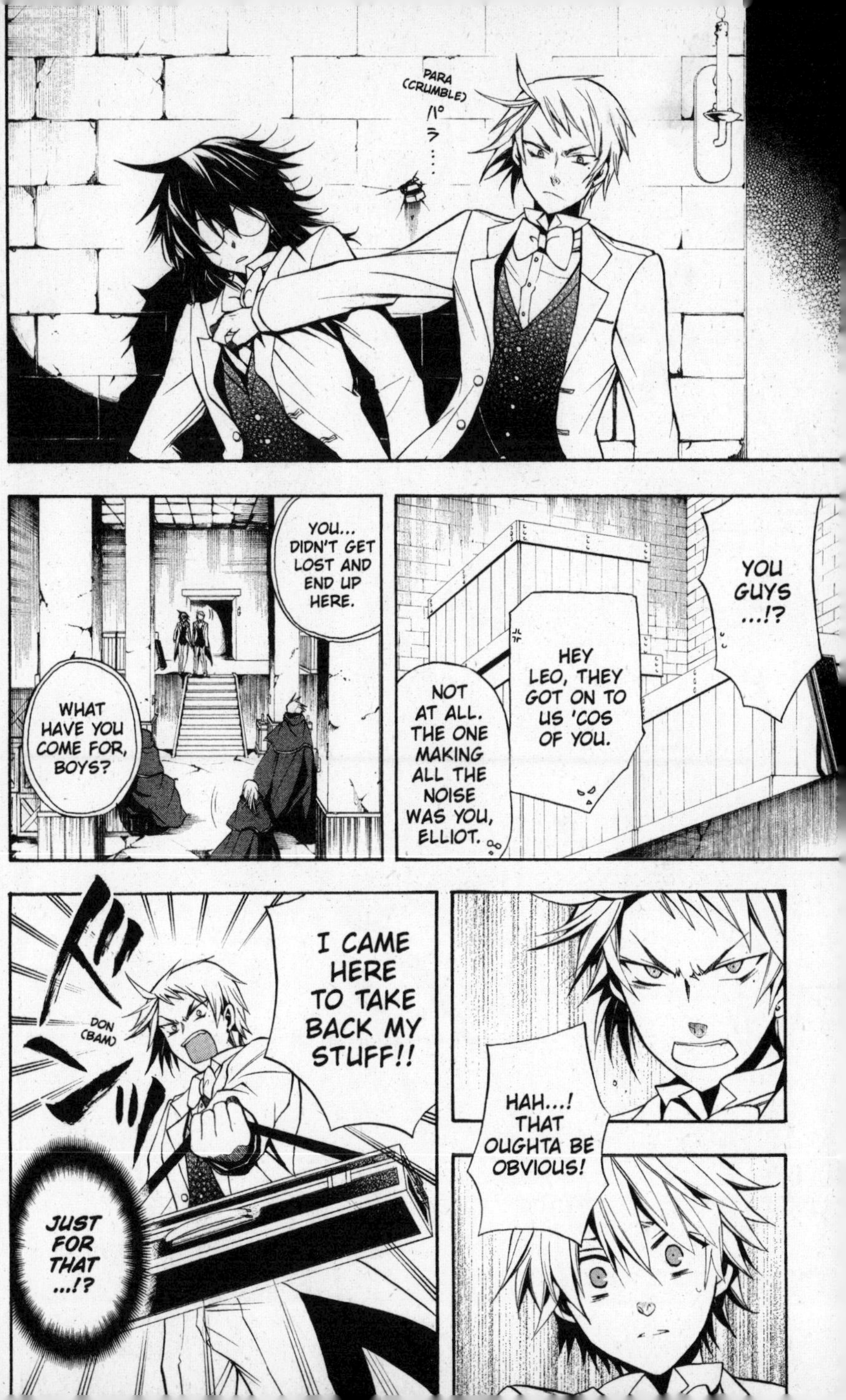
PARA (CRUMBLE)
パラ….
YOU GUYS ...!?
HEY LEO, THEY GOT ON TO US 'COS OF YOU.
NOT AT ALL. THE ONE MAKING ALL THE NOISE WAS YOU, ELLIOT.
YOU... DIDN'T GET LOST AND END UP HERE.
WHAT HAVE YOU COME FOR, BOYS?
HAH...! THAT OUGHTA BE OBVIOUS!
I CAME HERE TO TAKE BACK MY STUFF!!
DON (BAM)
JUST FOR THAT ...!?

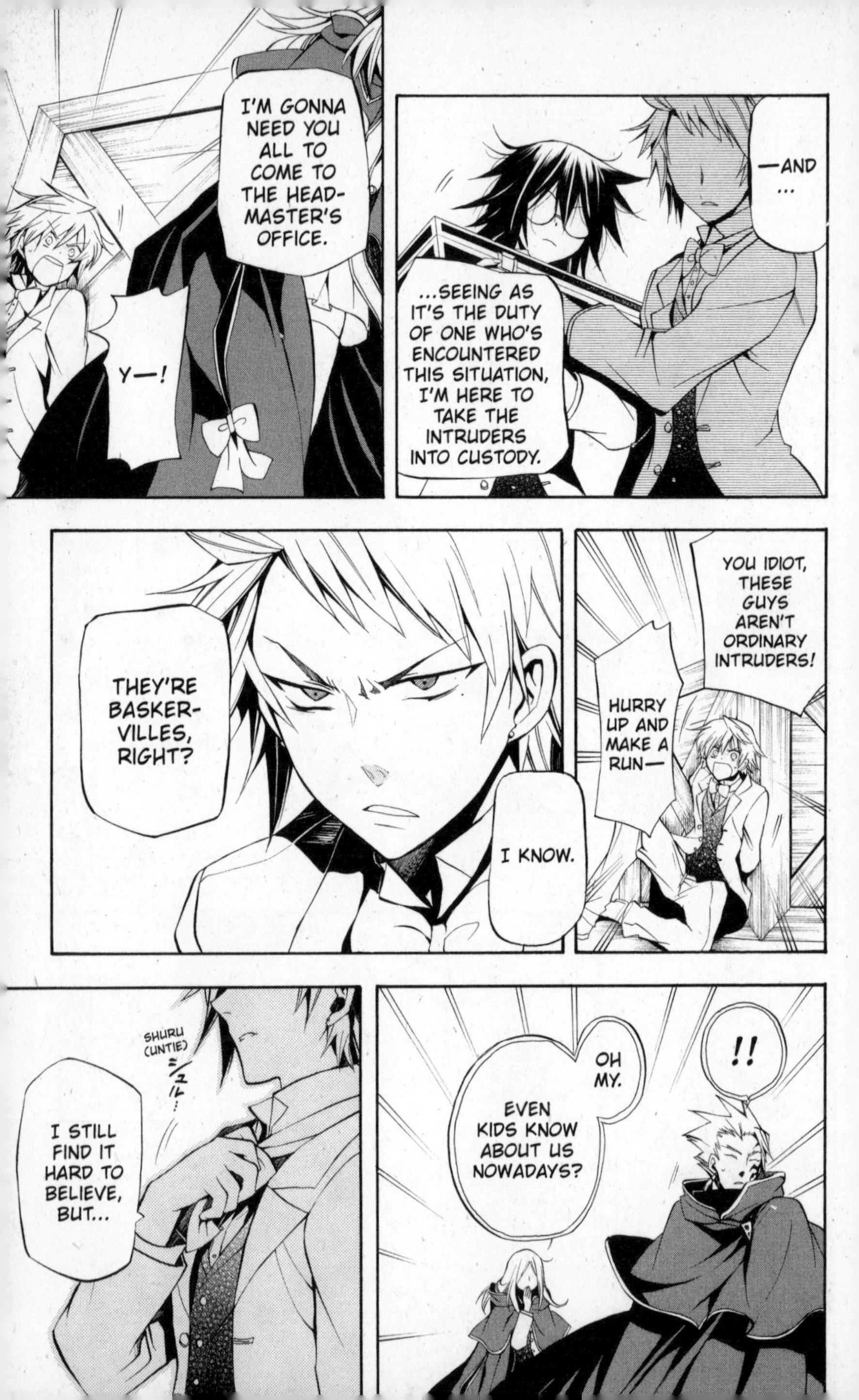
—AND ...
...SEEING AS IT'S THE DUTY OF ONE WHO'S ENCOUNTERED THIS SITUATION, I'M HERE TO TAKE THE INTRUDERS INTO CUSTODY.
I'M GONNA NEED YOU ALL TO COME TO THE HEAD-MASTER'S OFFICE.
Y—!
YOU IDIOT, THESE GUYS AREN'T ORDINARY INTRUDERS!
HURRY UP AND MAKE A RUN—
I KNOW.
THEY'RE BASKER-VILLES, RIGHT?
!!
OH MY.
EVEN KIDS KNOW ABOUT US NOWADAYS?
SHURU (UNTIE)
I STILL FIND IT HARD TO BELIEVE, BUT...

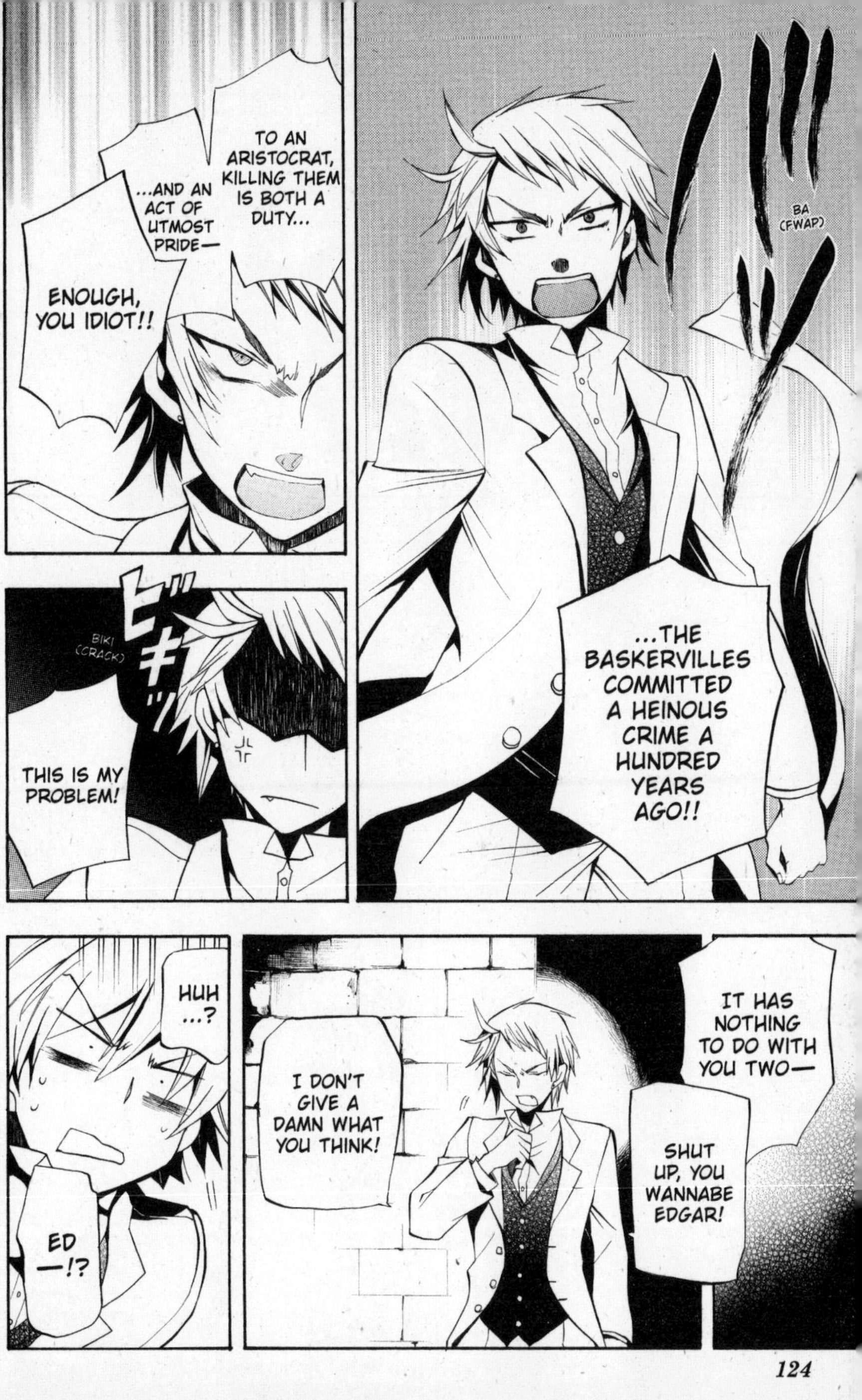
BA (FWAP)
...THE BASKERVILLES COMMITTED A HEINOUS CRIME A HUNDRED YEARS AGO!!
TO AN ARISTOCRAT, KILLING THEM IS BOTH A DUTY...
...AND AN ACT OF UTMOST PRIDE—
ENOUGH, YOU IDIOT!!
BIKI (CRACK)
THIS IS MY PROBLEM!
IT HAS NOTHING TO DO WITH YOU TWO—
SHUT UP, YOU WANNABE EDGAR!
I DON'T GIVE A DAMN WHAT YOU THINK!
HUH ...?
ED —!?

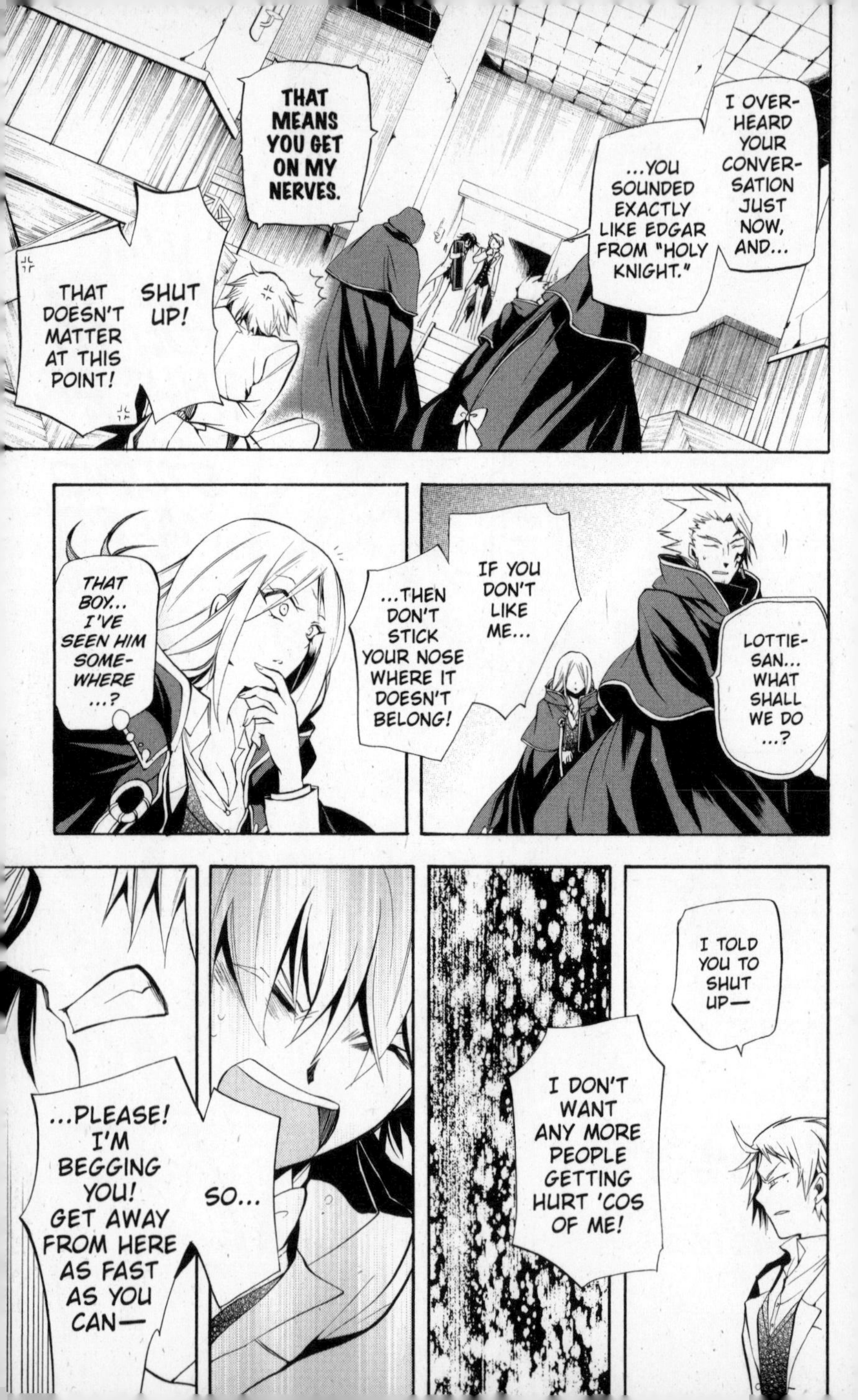
I OVER-HEARD YOUR CONVERSATION JUST NOW, AND...
...YOU SOUNDED EXACTLY LIKE EDGAR FROM "HOLY KNIGHT."
THAT MEANS YOU GET ON MY NERVES.
SHUT UP!
THAT DOESN'T MATTER AT THIS POINT!
IF YOU DON'T LIKE ME...
...THEN DON'T STICK YOUR NOSE WHERE IT DOESN'T BELONG!
LOTTIE-SAN... WHAT SHALL WE DO ...?
THAT BOY... I'VE SEEN HIM SOMEWHERE ...?
I TOLD YOU TO SHUT UP—
I DON'T WANT ANY MORE PEOPLE GETTING HURT 'COS OF ME!
SO...
...PLEASE! I'M BEGGING YOU! GET AWAY FROM HERE AS FAST AS YOU CAN—

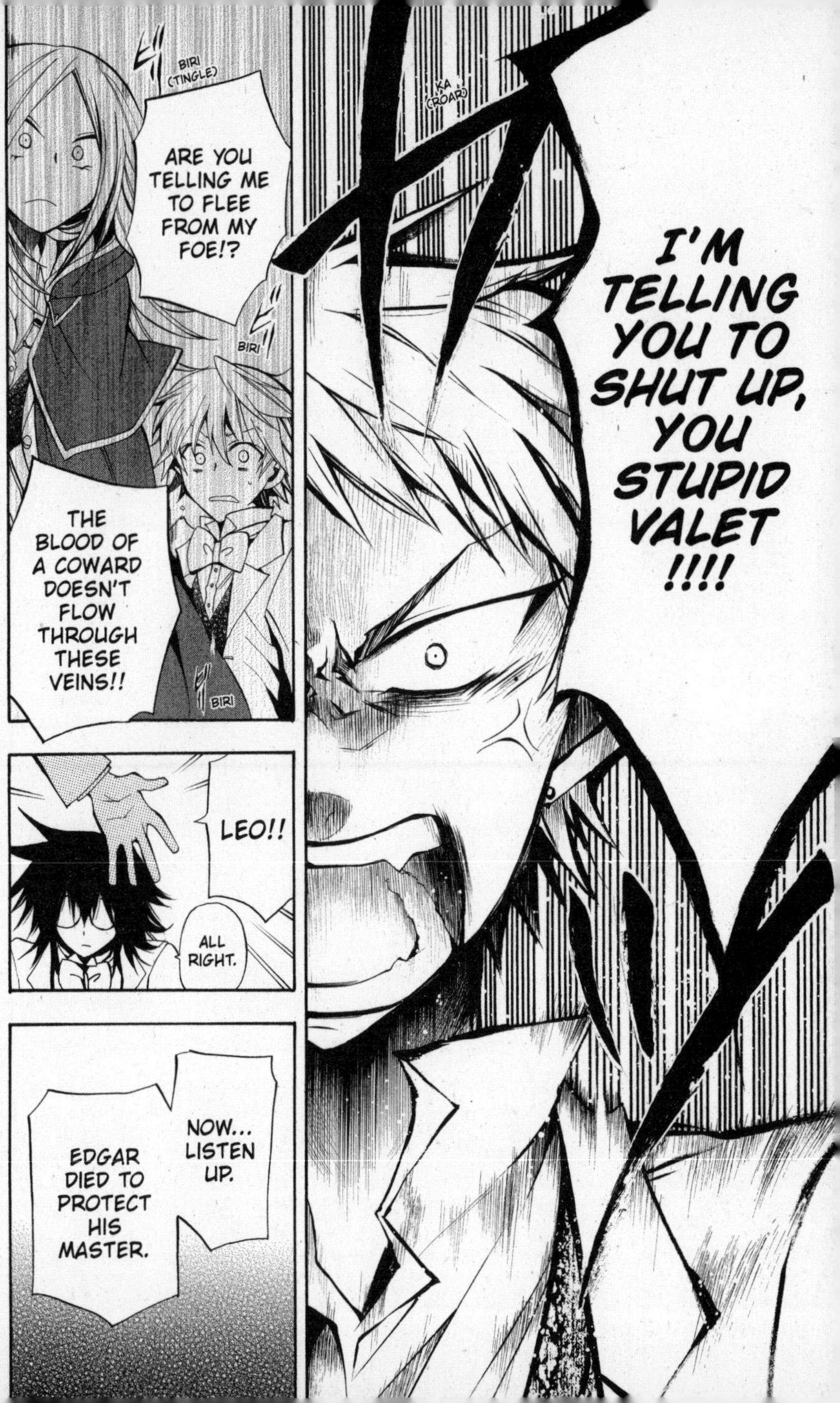
BIRI (TINGLE)
ARE YOU TELLING ME TO FLEE FROM MY FOE!?
BIRI
THE BLOOD OF A COWARD DOESN'T FLOW THROUGH THESE VEINS!!
BIRI
KA (ROAR)
I'M TELLING YOU TO SHUT UP, YOU STUPID VALET !!!!
LEO!!
ALL RIGHT.
NOW... LISTEN UP.
EDGAR DIED TO PROTECT HIS MASTER.

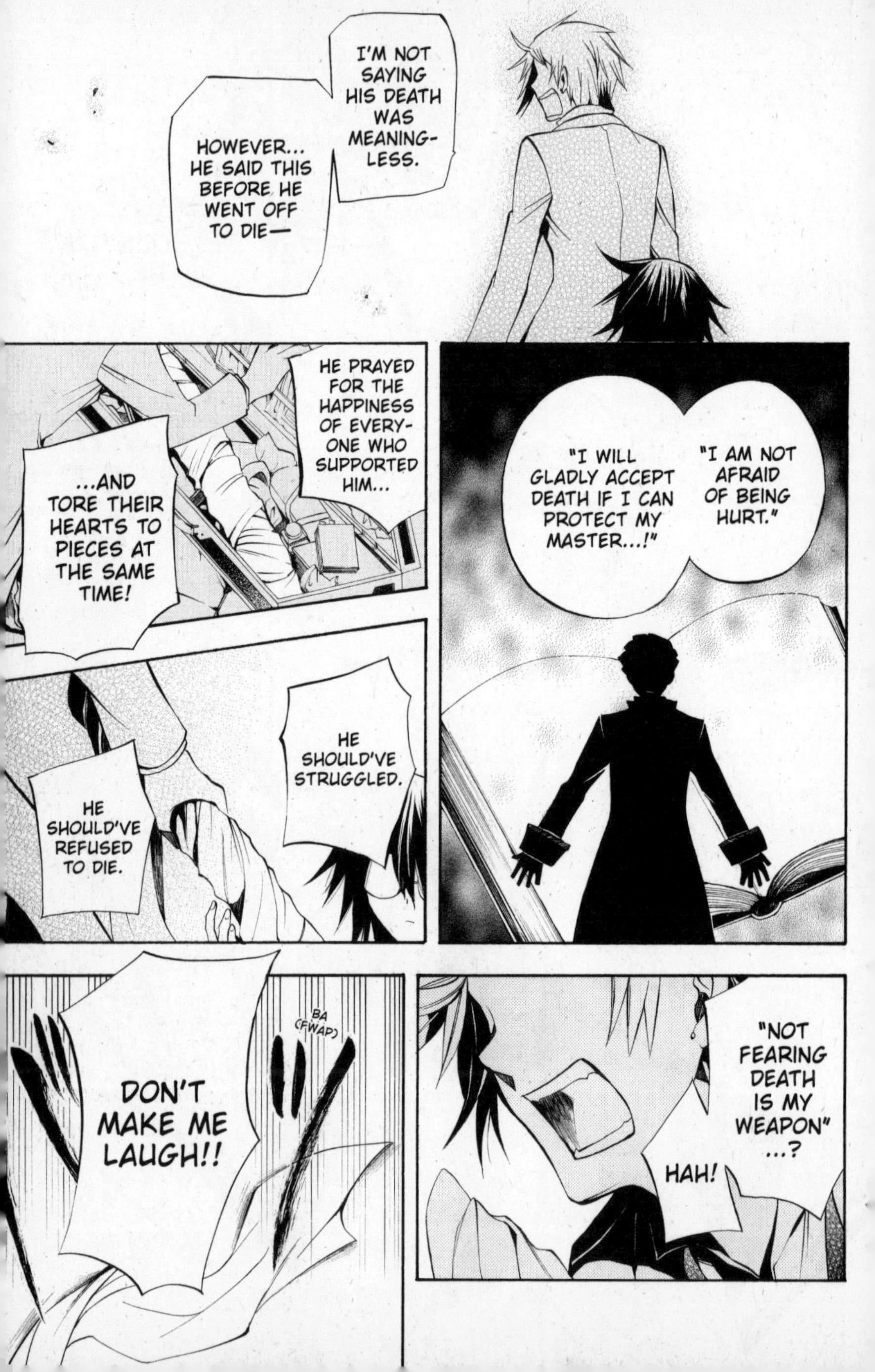
I'M NOT SAYING HIS DEATH WAS MEANINGLESS.
HOWEVER... HE SAID THIS BEFORE HE WENT OFF TO DIE—
"I AM NOT AFRAID OF BEING HURT."
"I WILL GLADLY ACCEPT DEATH IF I CAN PROTECT MY MASTER...!"
HE PRAYED FOR THE HAPPINESS OF EVERYONE WHO SUPPORTED HIM...
...AND TORE THEIR HEARTS TO PIECES AT THE SAME TIME!
HE SHOULD'VE STRUGGLED.
HE SHOULD'VE REFUSED TO DIE.
"NOT FEARING DEATH IS MY WEAPON" ...?
HAH!
BA (FWAP)
DON'T MAKE ME LAUGH!!

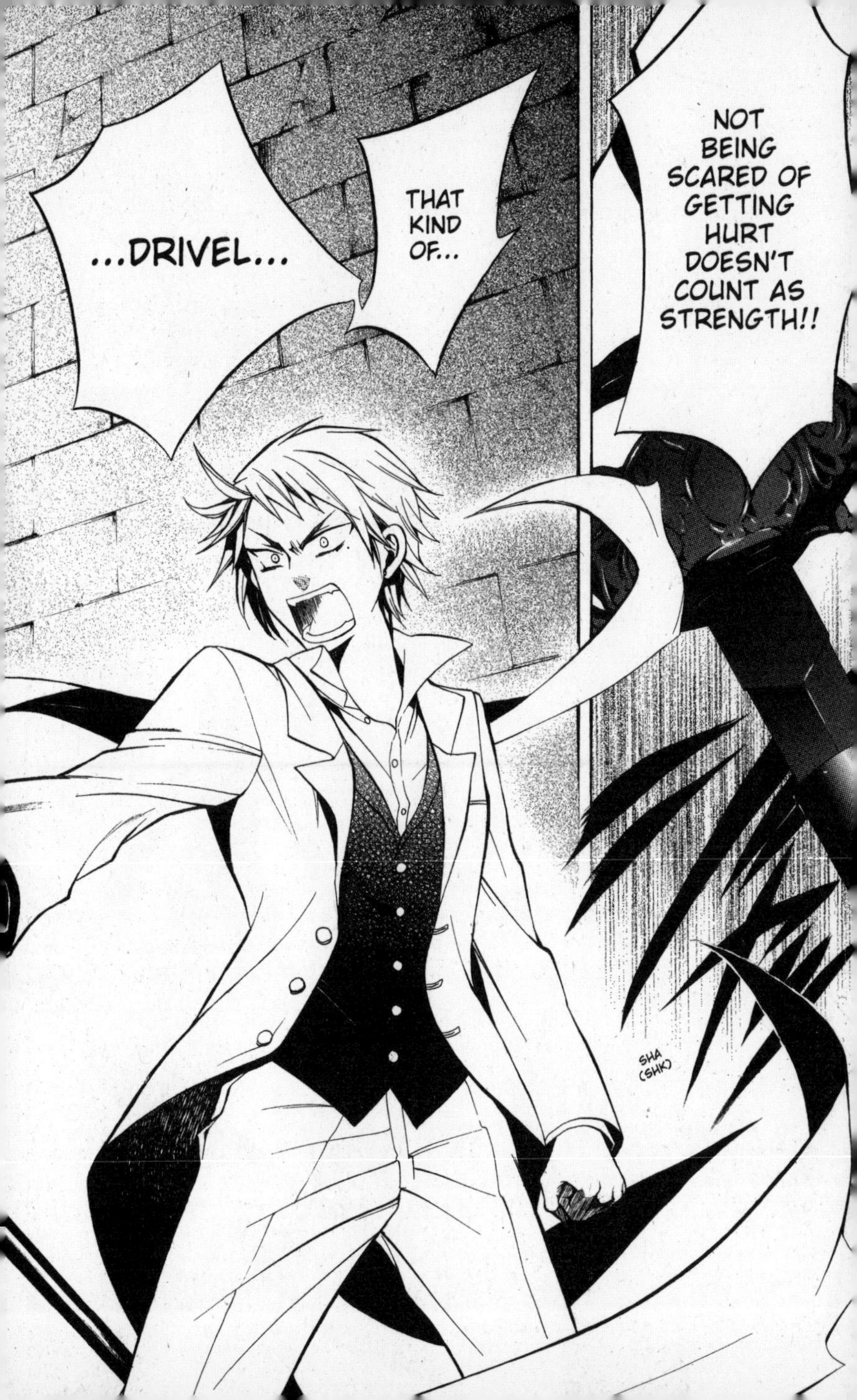
NOT BEING SCARED OF GETTING HURT DOESN'T COUNT AS STRENGTH!!
THAT KIND OF...
...DRIVEL...
SHA (SHK)

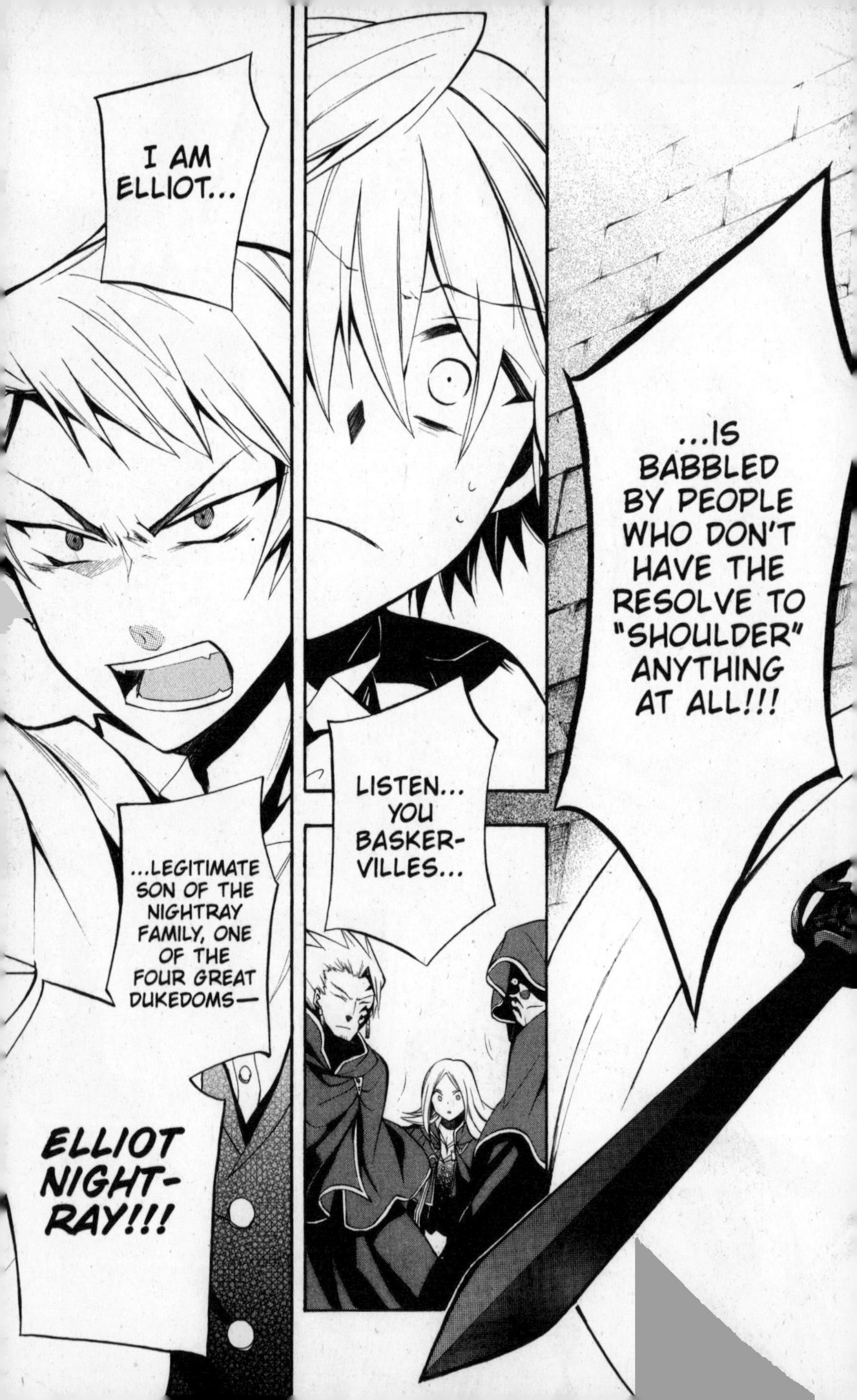
...IS BABBLED BY PEOPLE WHO DON'T HAVE THE RESOLVE TO "SHOULDER" ANYTHING AT ALL!!!
LISTEN... YOU BASKER-VILLES...
I AM ELLIOT...
...LEGITIMATE SON OF THE NIGHTRAY FAMILY, ONE OF THE FOUR GREAT DUKEDOMS—
ELLIOT NIGHT-RAY!!!

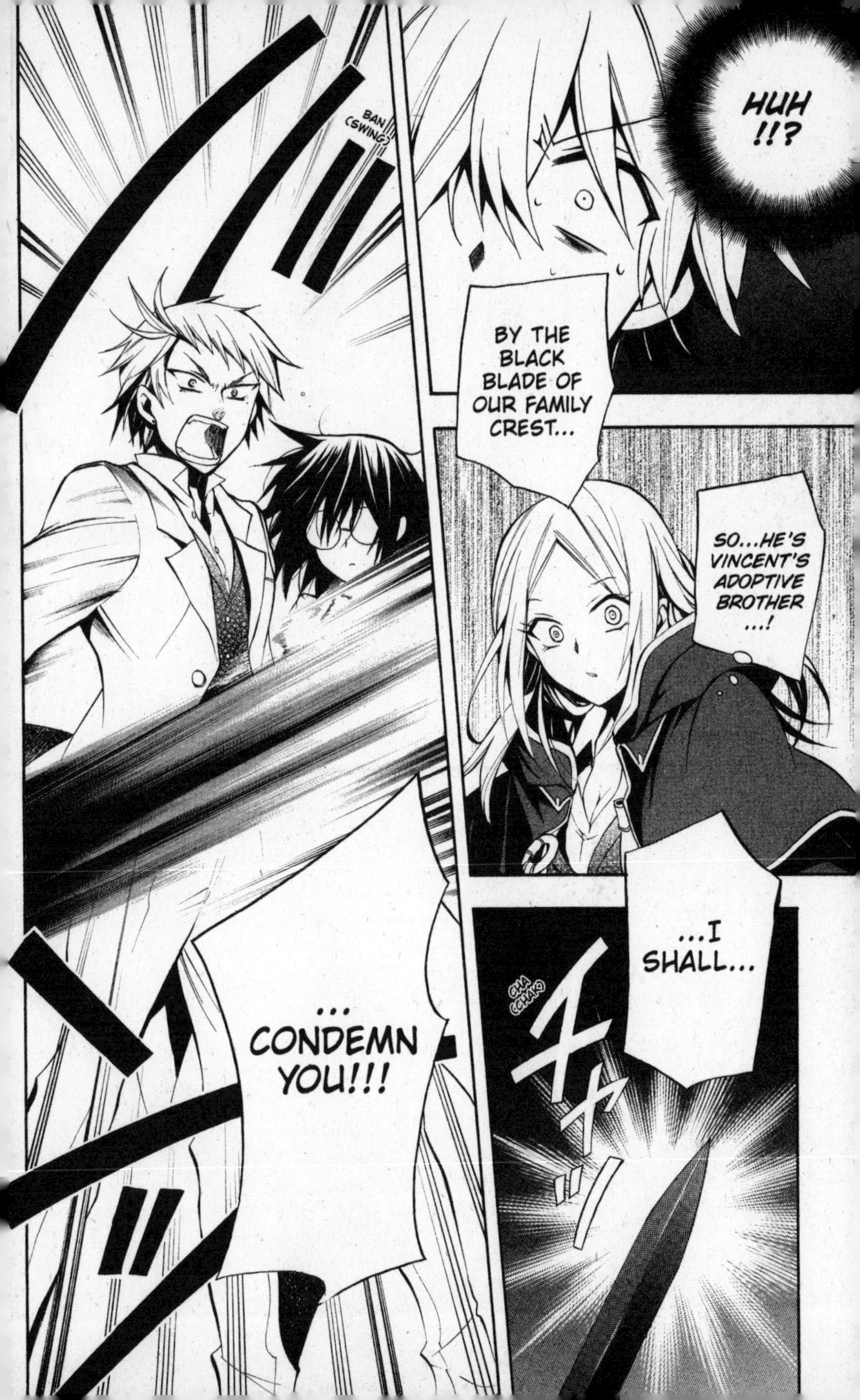
HUH !!?
BY THE BLACK BLADE OF OUR FAMILY CREST...
SO...HE'S VINCENT'S ADOPTIVE BROTHER...!
...I SHALL...
CHA (CHAK)
BAN (SWING)
...CONDEMN YOU!!!

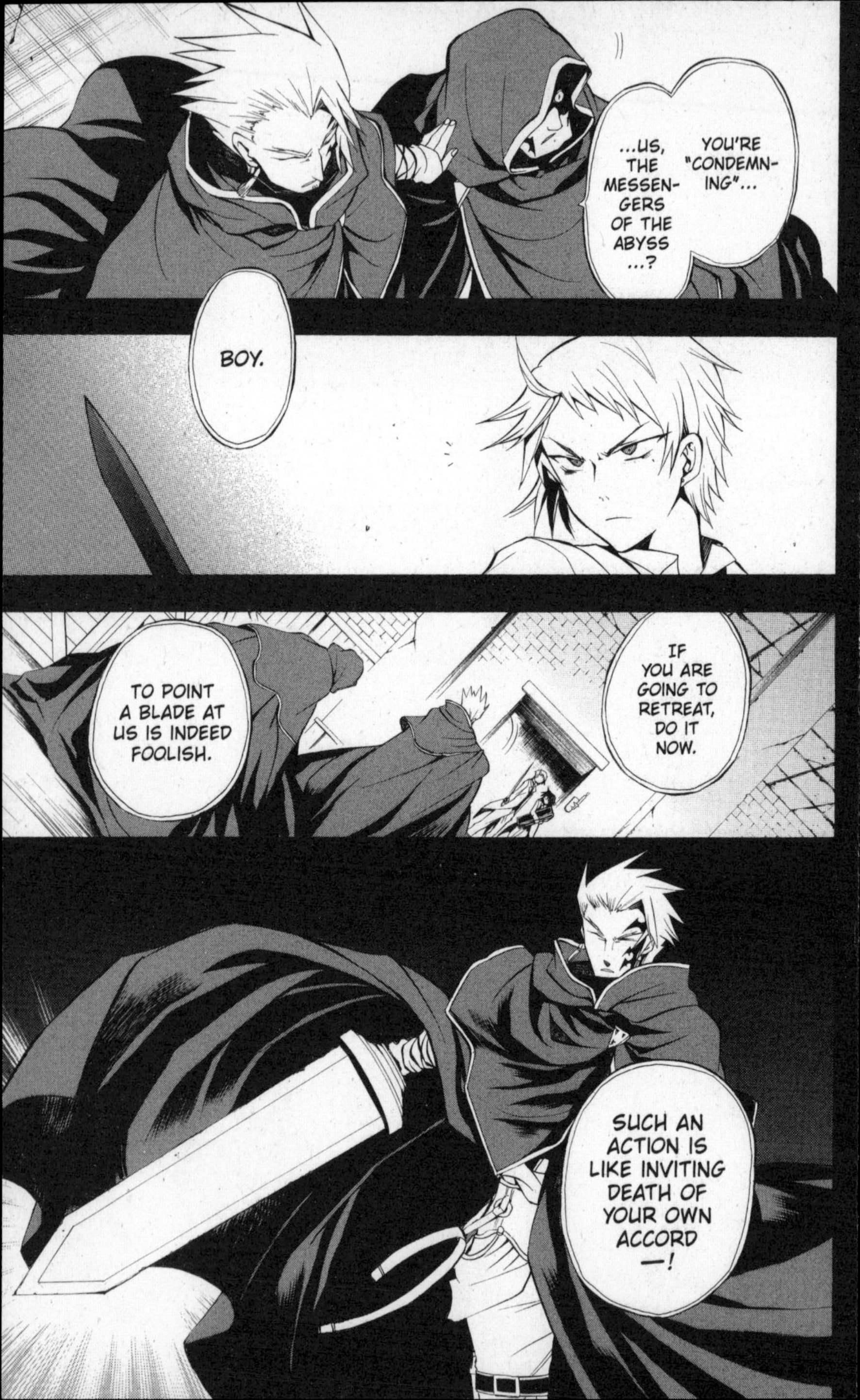
YOU'RE "CONDEMNING"... ...US, THE MESSENGERS OF THE ABYSS...?
BOY.
IF YOU ARE GOING TO RETREAT, DO IT NOW.
TO POINT A BLADE AT US IS INDEED FOOLISH.
SUCH AN ACTION IS LIKE INVITING DEATH OF YOUR OWN ACCORD—!

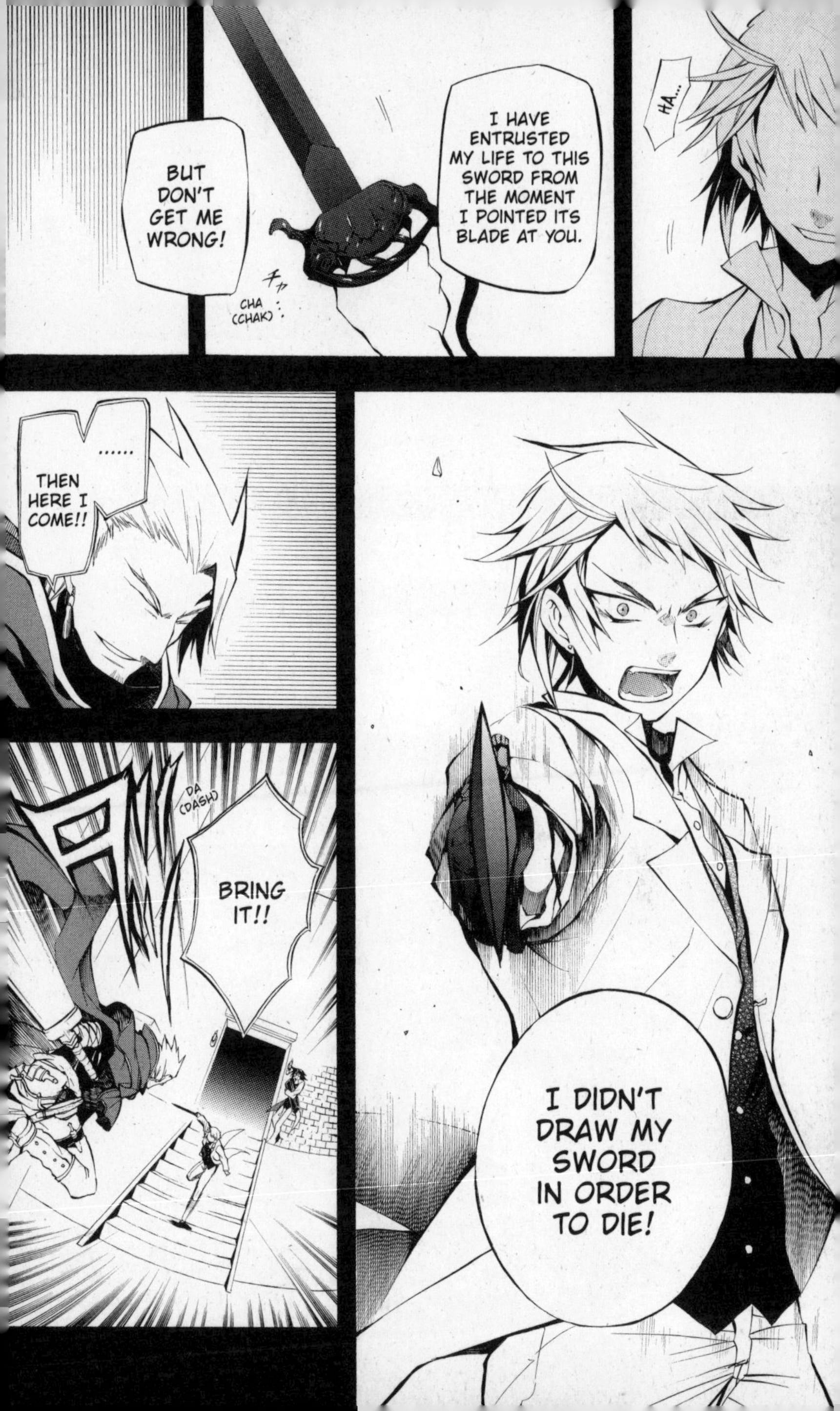
HA...
I HAVE ENTRUSTED MY LIFE TO THIS SWORD FROM THE MOMENT I POINTED ITS BLADE AT YOU.
BUT DON'T GET ME WRONG!
チャ
CHA (CHAK)
I DIDN'T DRAW MY SWORD IN ORDER TO DIE!
......
THEN HERE I COME!!
DA (DASH)
BRING IT!!

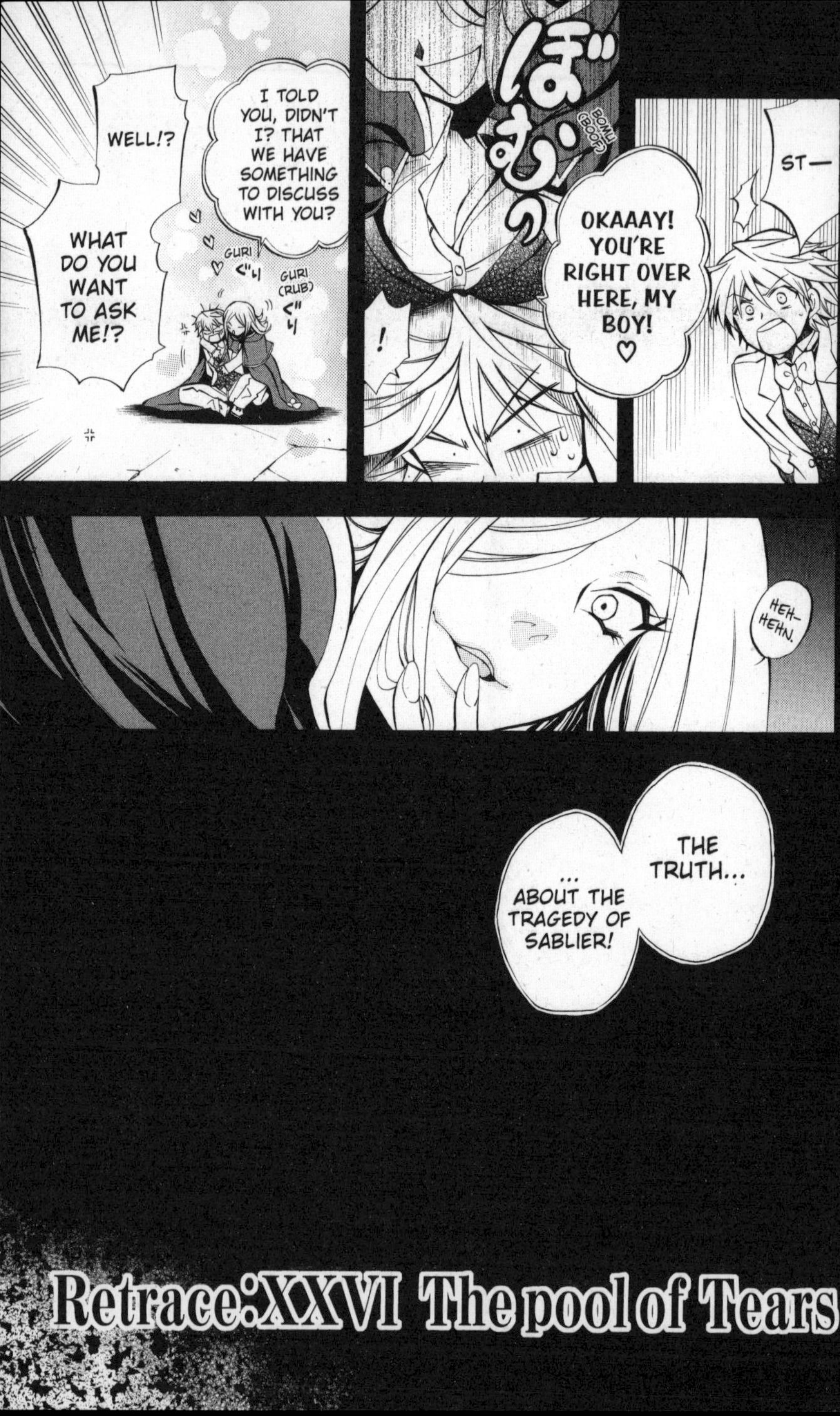
ST—
ぼむっ
BOMU (BOOF)
OKAAAY! YOU'RE RIGHT OVER HERE, MY BOY! ♡
!
I TOLD YOU, DIDN'T I? THAT WE HAVE SOMETHING TO DISCUSS WITH YOU?
WELL!?
WHAT DO YOU WANT TO ASK ME!?
GURI ぐり
GURI (RUB) ぐり
HEH-HEHN.
THE TRUTH...
...ABOUT THE TRAGEDY OF SABLIER!
Retrace:XXVI The pool of Tears

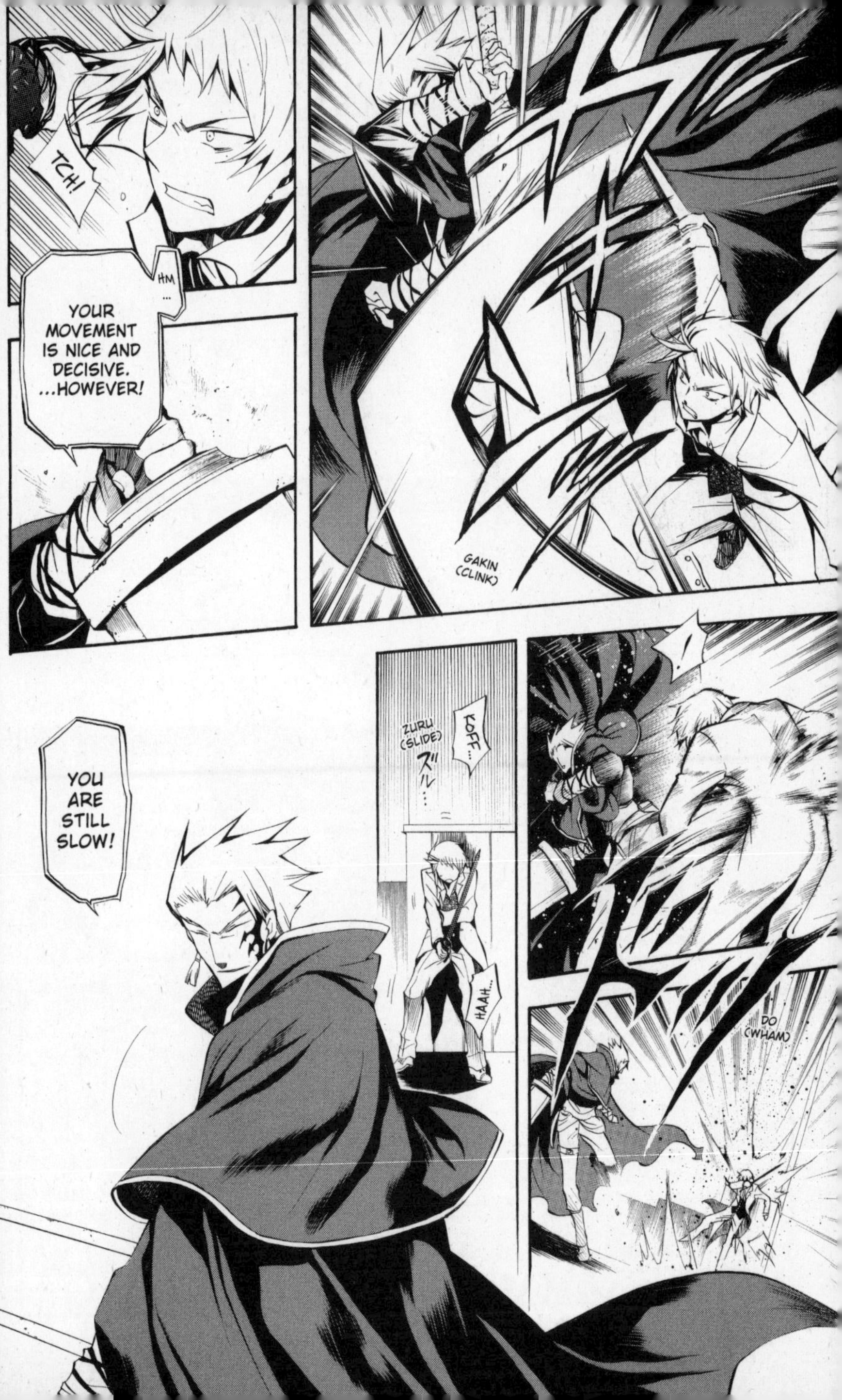
GAKIN (CLINK)
TCH!
HM...
YOUR MOVEMENT IS NICE AND DECISIVE. ...HOWEVER!
!
DO (WHAM)
KOFF...
ZURU (SLIDE) ズル...
HAAH...
YOU ARE STILL SLOW!

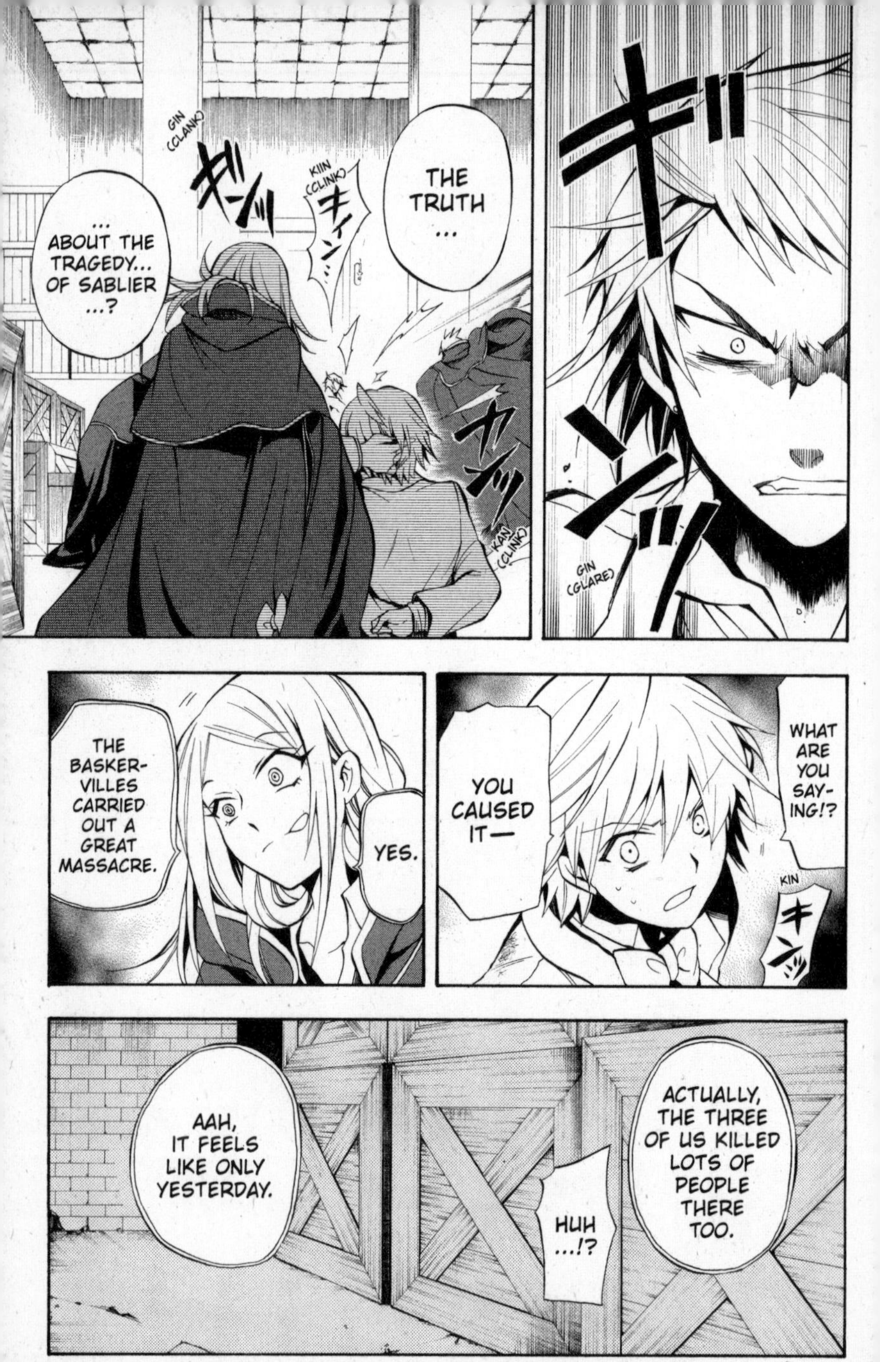
GIN (GLARE)
THE TRUTH ...
KIIN (CLINK)
GIN (CLANK)
... ABOUT THE TRAGEDY... OF SABLIER ...?
KAN (CLINK)
WHAT ARE YOU SAYING!?
YOU CAUSED IT—
KIN
YES.
THE BASKERVILLES CARRIED OUT A GREAT MASSACRE.
ACTUALLY, THE THREE OF US KILLED LOTS OF PEOPLE THERE TOO.
HUH ...!?
AAH, IT FEELS LIKE ONLY YESTERDAY.

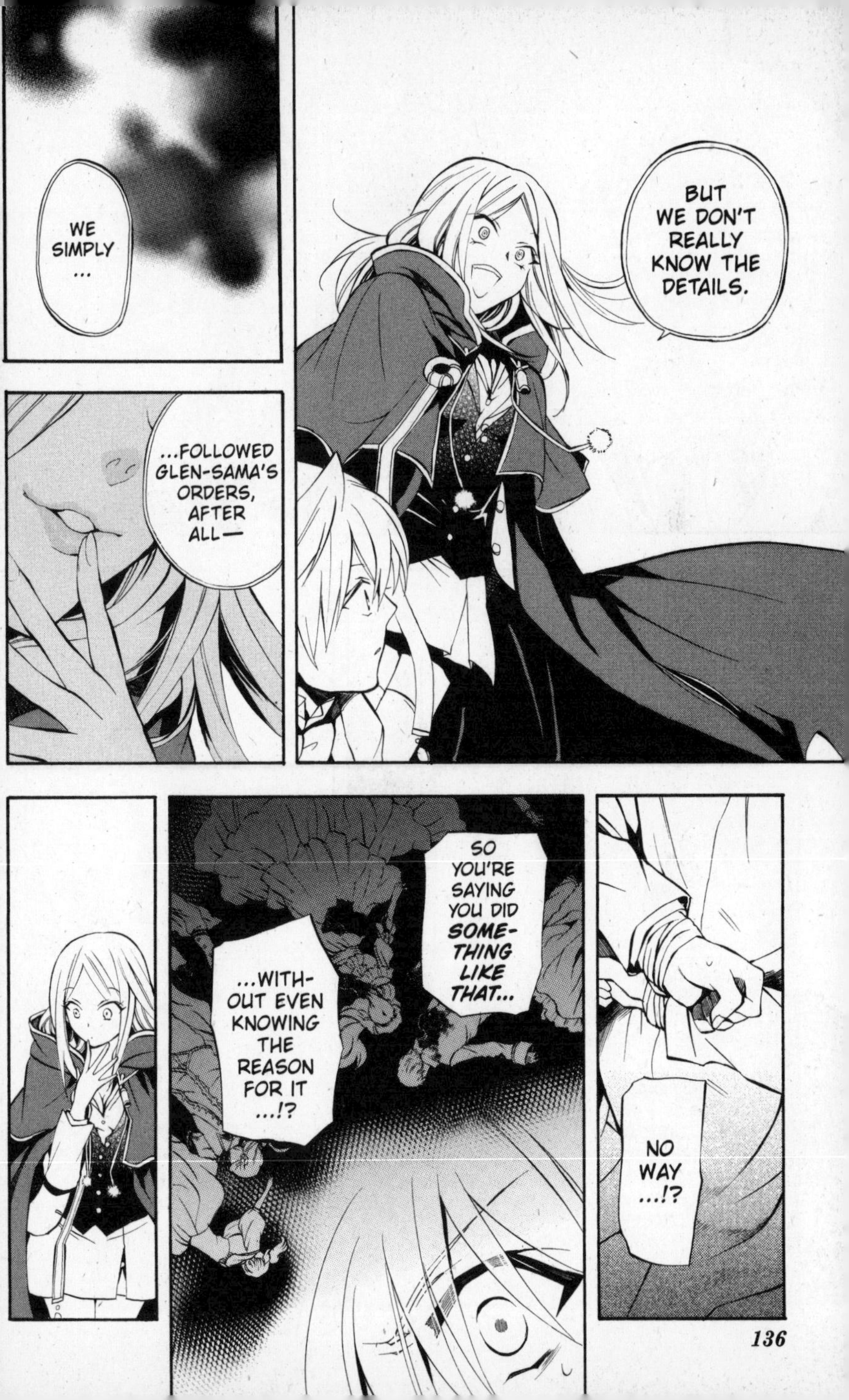
BUT WE DON'T REALLY KNOW THE DETAILS.
WE SIMPLY ...
...FOLLOWED GLEN-SAMA'S ORDERS, AFTER ALL—
NO WAY ...!?
SO YOU'RE SAYING YOU DID *SOMETHING LIKE THAT...*
...WITH-OUT EVEN KNOWING THE REASON FOR IT ...!?

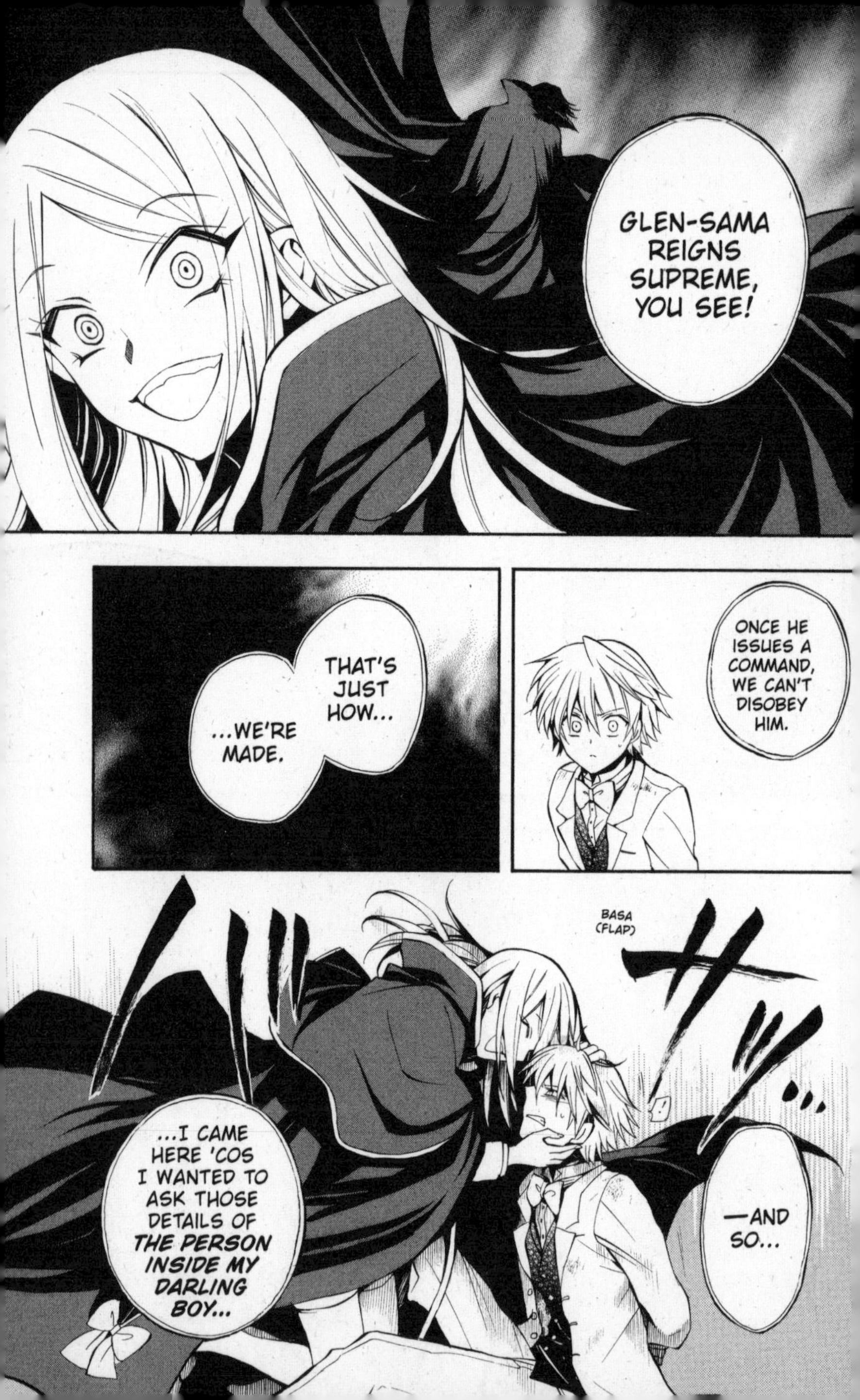
GLEN-SAMA REIGNS SUPREME, YOU SEE!
ONCE HE ISSUES A COMMAND, WE CAN'T DISOBEY HIM.
THAT'S JUST HOW...
...WE'RE MADE.
BASA (FLAP)
—AND SO...
...I CAME HERE 'COS I WANTED TO ASK THOSE DETAILS OF *THE PERSON INSIDE MY DARLING BOY...*

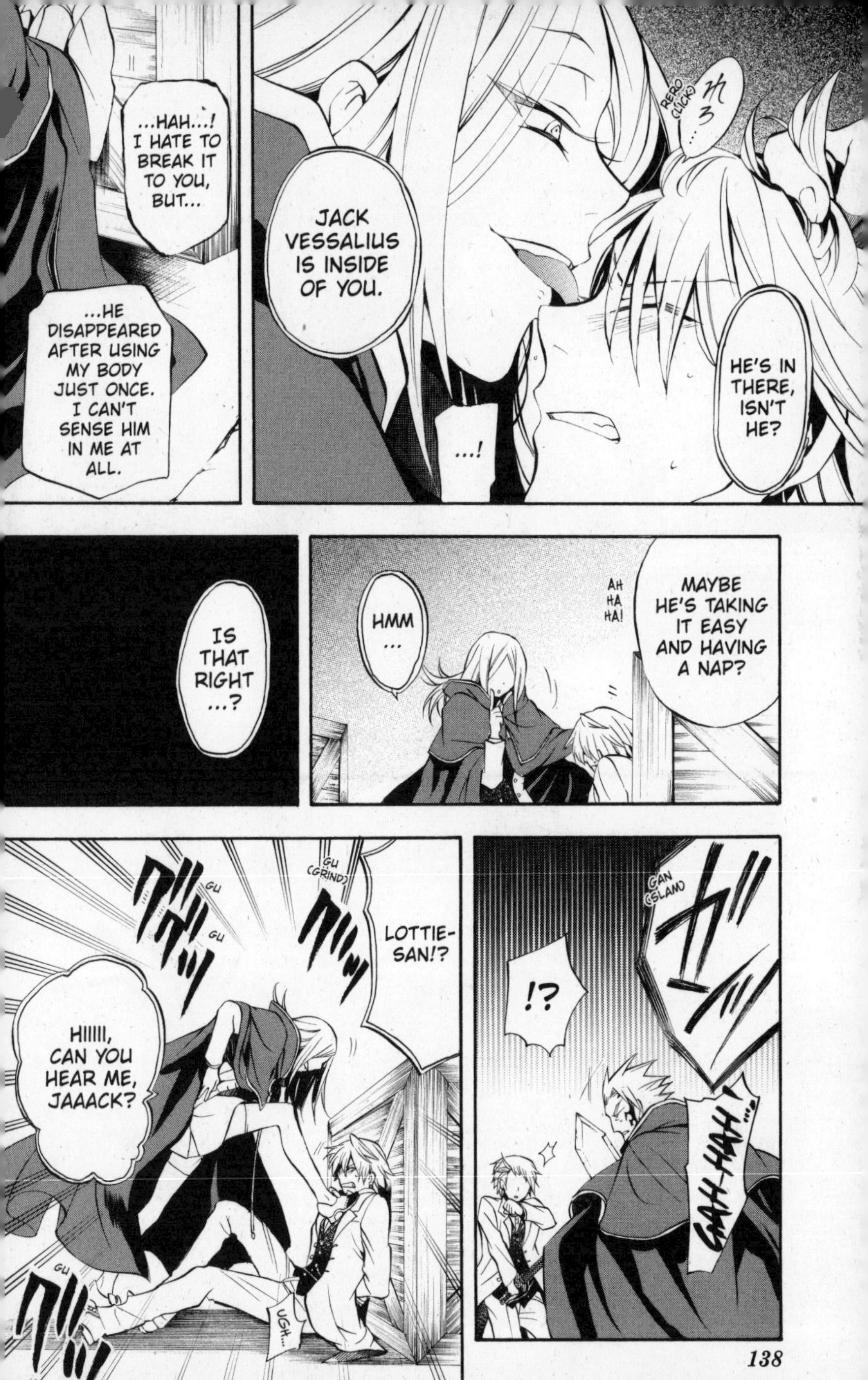

れろ…
RERO (LICK)
JACK VESSALIUS IS INSIDE OF YOU.
HE'S IN THERE, ISN'T HE?
...!
...HAH...! I HATE TO BREAK IT TO YOU, BUT...
...HE DISAPPEARED AFTER USING MY BODY JUST ONCE. I CAN'T SENSE HIM IN ME AT ALL.
MAYBE HE'S TAKING IT EASY AND HAVING A NAP?
AH HA HA!
HMM...
IS THAT RIGHT...?
GAN (SLAM)
!?
GAH-HAH...!
GU (GRIND)
LOTTIE-SAN!?
GU
GU
HIIIII, CAN YOU HEAR ME, JAAACK?
UGH...
GU

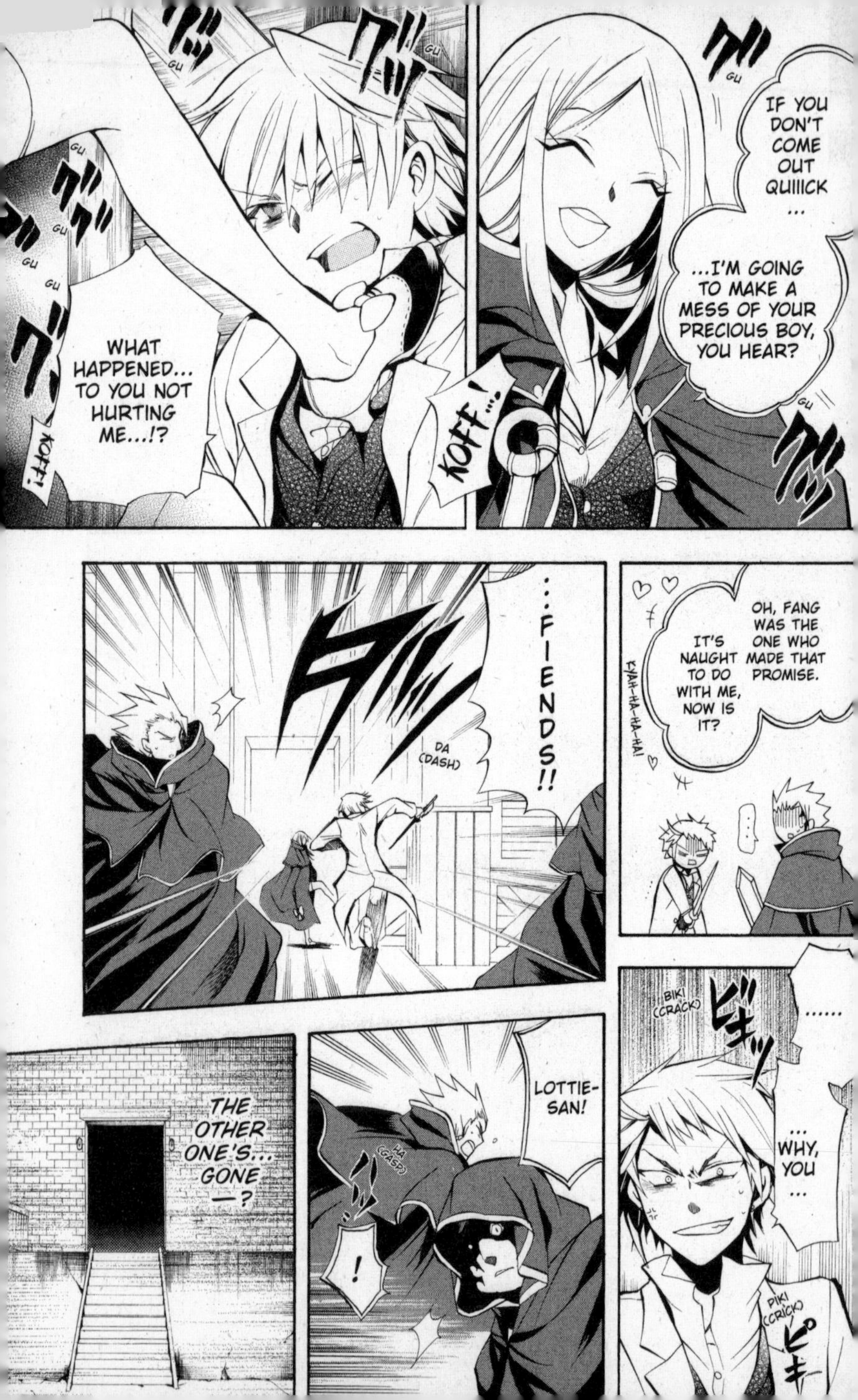
GU
IF YOU DON'T COME OUT QUIIICK...
...I'M GOING TO MAKE A MESS OF YOUR PRECIOUS BOY, YOU HEAR?
GU
GU
GU
KOFF...!
WHAT HAPPENED... TO YOU NOT HURTING ME...!?
GU
GU
GU
KOFF!
OH, FANG WAS THE ONE WHO MADE THAT PROMISE.
IT'S NAUGHT TO DO WITH ME, NOW IS IT?
KYAH-HA-HA-HA!
...
...FIENDS!!
DA (DASH)
BIKI (CRACK)
......
...WHY, YOU...
PIKI (CRICK)
LOTTIE-SAN!
HA (GASP)
!
THE OTHER ONE'S... GONE—?

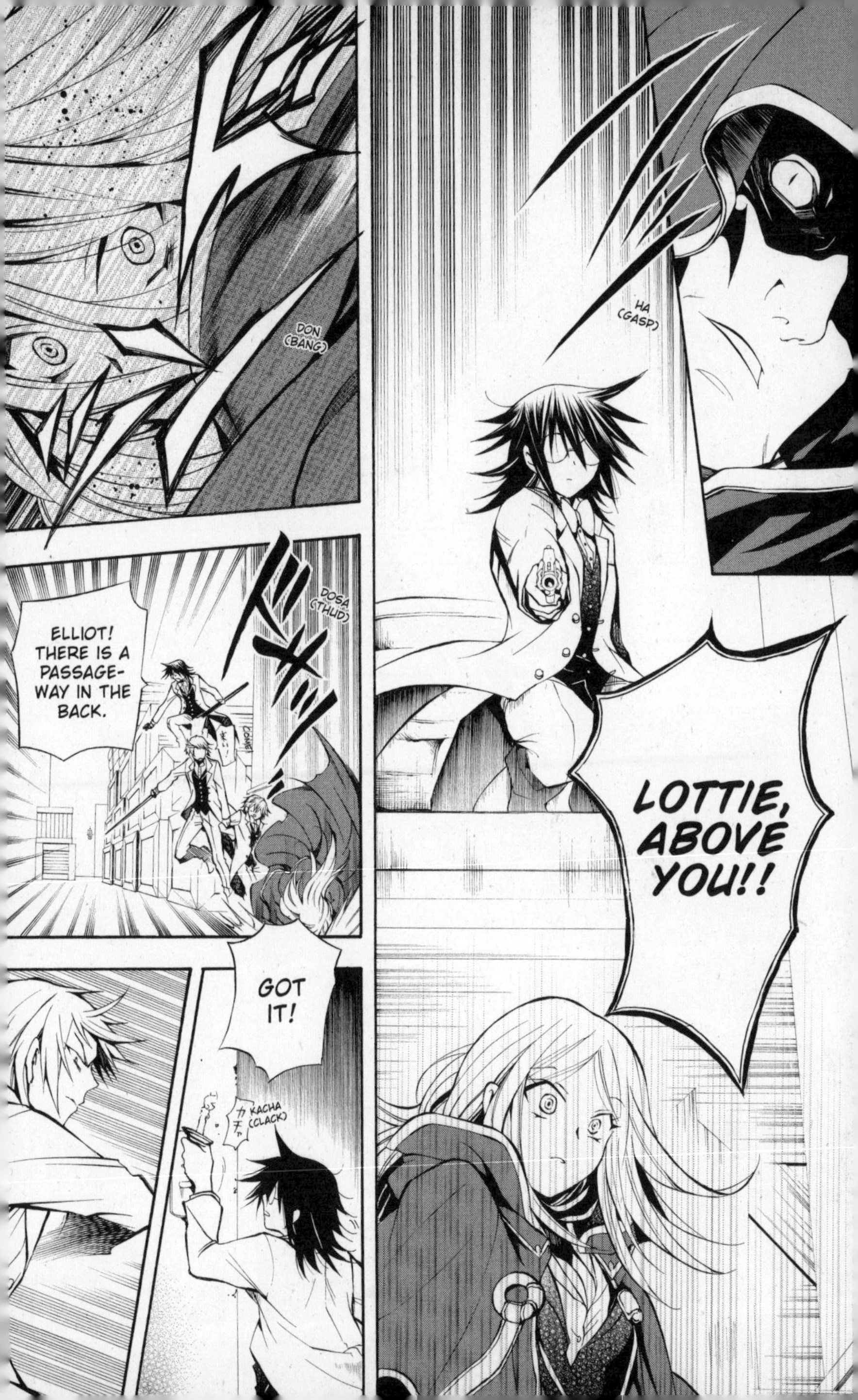
HA (GASP)
LOTTIE, ABOVE YOU!!
DON (BANG)
DOSA (THUD)
ELLIOT! THERE IS A PASSAGEWAY IN THE BACK.
COME!
GOT IT!
KACHA (CLACK)

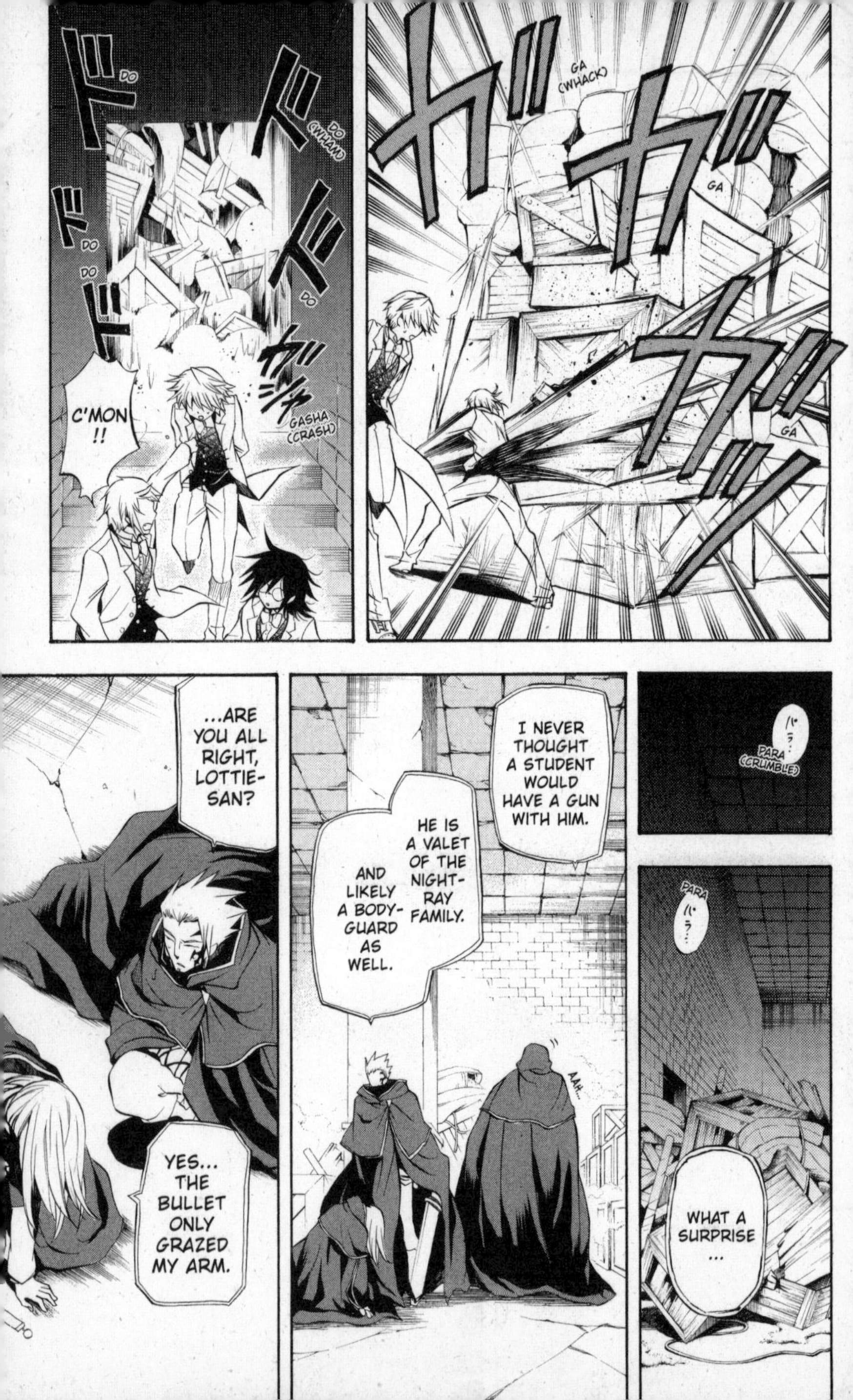
GA (WHACK)
GA
GA
DO
DO (WHAM)
DO
DO
DO
GASHA (CRASH)
C'MON!!
PARA (CRUMBLE)
PARA
WHAT A SURPRISE...
I NEVER THOUGHT A STUDENT WOULD HAVE A GUN WITH HIM.
HE IS A VALET OF THE NIGHTRAY FAMILY.
AND LIKELY A BODYGUARD AS WELL.
AAH...
...ARE YOU ALL RIGHT, LOTTIE-SAN?
YES... THE BULLET ONLY GRAZED MY ARM.

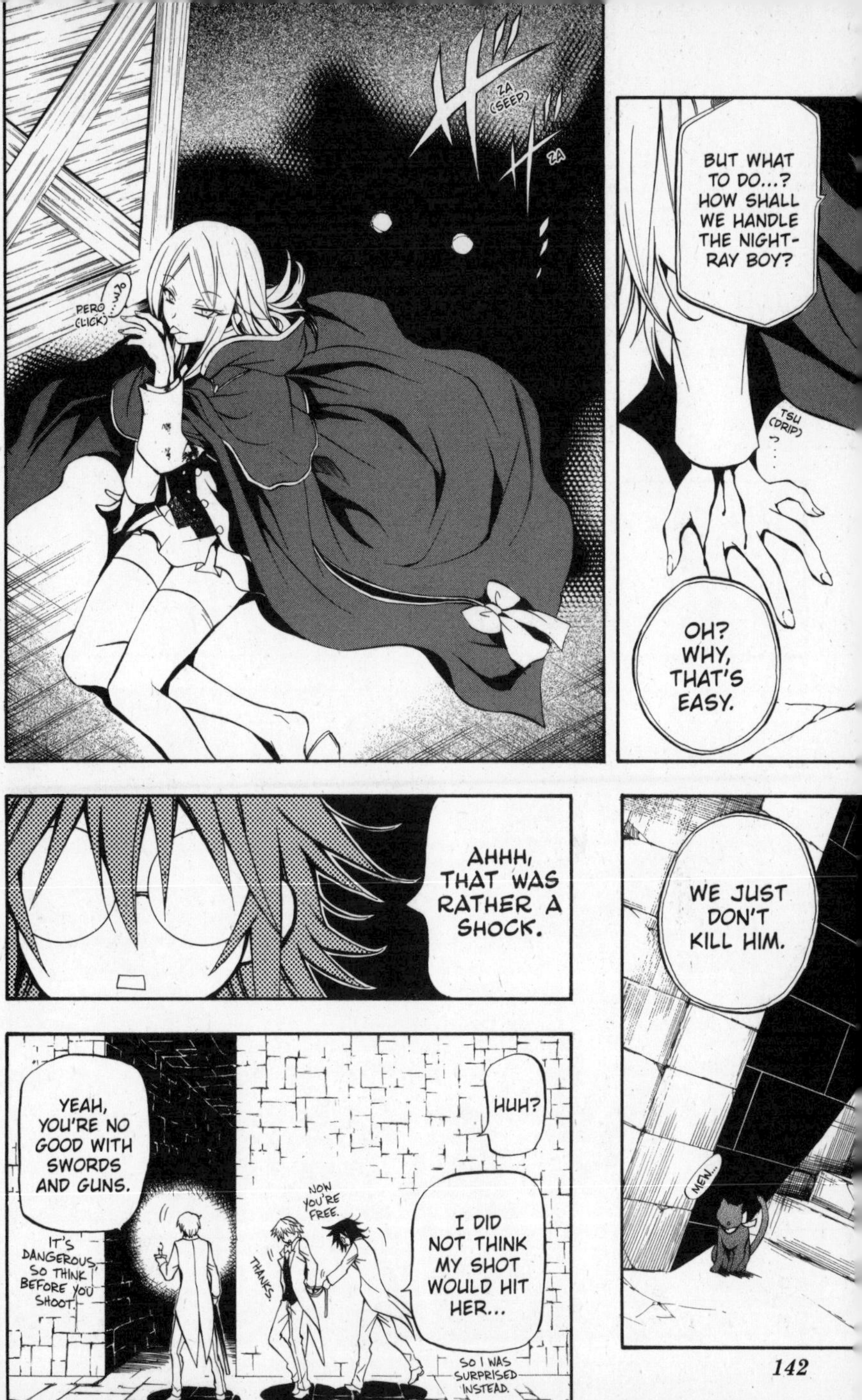
BUT WHAT TO DO...? HOW SHALL WE HANDLE THE NIGHT-RAY BOY?
TSU (DRIP)
OH? WHY, THAT'S EASY.
ZA (SEEP)
ZA
PERO (LICK)
WE JUST DON'T KILL HIM.
MEW...
AHHH, THAT WAS RATHER A SHOCK.
HUH?
I DID NOT THINK MY SHOT WOULD HIT HER...
SO I WAS SURPRISED INSTEAD.
NOW YOU'RE FREE.
THANKS.
YEAH, YOU'RE NO GOOD WITH SWORDS AND GUNS.
IT'S DANGEROUS, SO THINK BEFORE YOU SHOOT.

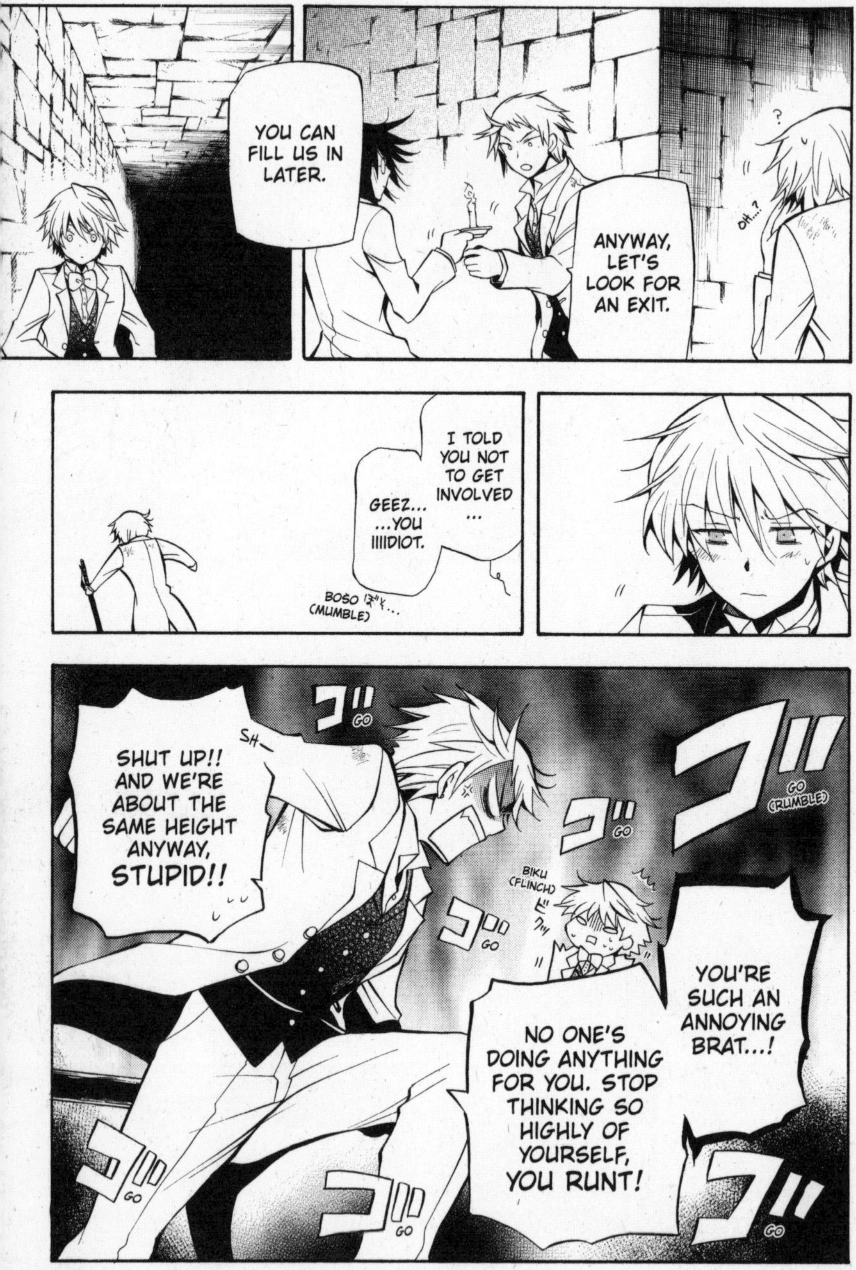
YOU CAN FILL US IN LATER.
ANYWAY, LET'S LOOK FOR AN EXIT.
?
OH...?
I TOLD YOU NOT TO GET INVOLVED ...
GEEZ... ...YOU IIIIDIOT.
BOSO ぼそ… (MUMBLE)
GO (RUMBLE)
GO
YOU'RE SUCH AN ANNOYING BRAT...!
NO ONE'S DOING ANYTHING FOR YOU. STOP THINKING SO HIGHLY OF YOURSELF, YOU RUNT!
BIKU (FLINCH)
SH–
SHUT UP!! AND WE'RE ABOUT THE SAME HEIGHT ANYWAY, STUPID!!
GO
GO
GO
GO

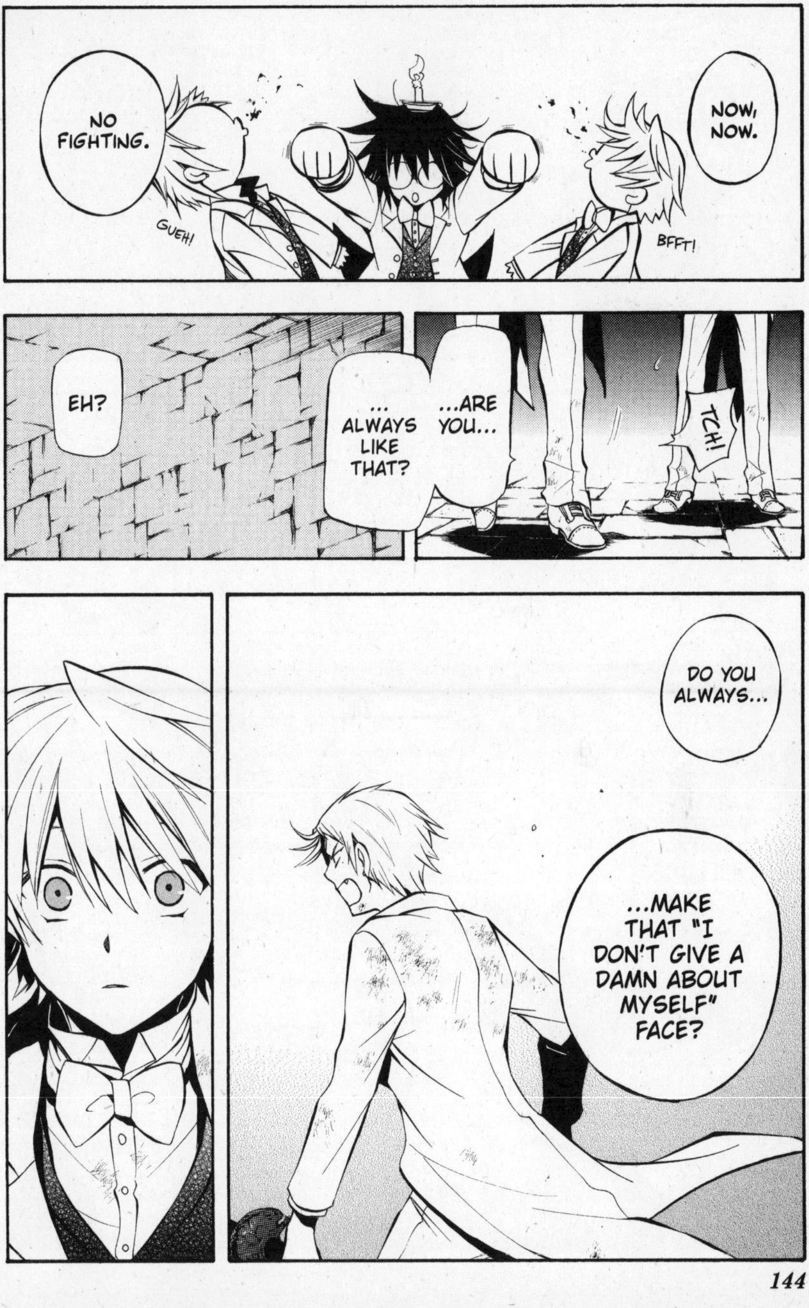
NOW, NOW.
NO FIGHTING.
BFFT!
GUEH!
TCH!
...ARE YOU...
... ALWAYS LIKE THAT?
EH?
DO YOU ALWAYS...
...MAKE THAT "I DON'T GIVE A DAMN ABOUT MYSELF" FACE?

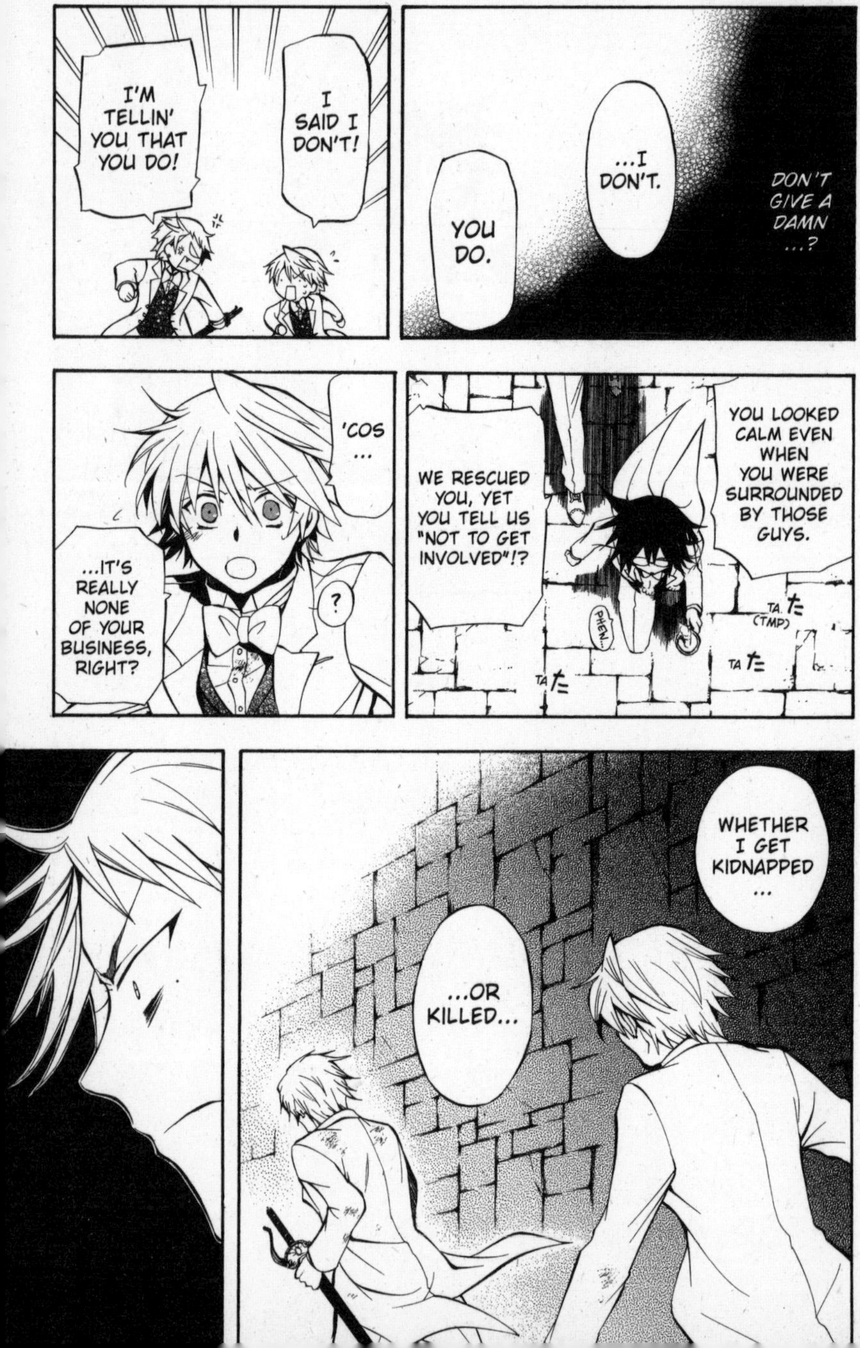
DON'T GIVE A DAMN ...?
...I DON'T.
YOU DO.
I SAID I DON'T!
I'M TELLIN' YOU THAT YOU DO!
YOU LOOKED CALM EVEN WHEN YOU WERE SURROUNDED BY THOSE GUYS.
WE RESCUED YOU, YET YOU TELL US "NOT TO GET INVOLVED"!?
PHEW...
TA (TMP)
TA
TA
'COS ...
?
...IT'S REALLY NONE OF YOUR BUSINESS, RIGHT?
WHETHER I GET KIDNAPPED ...
...OR KILLED...

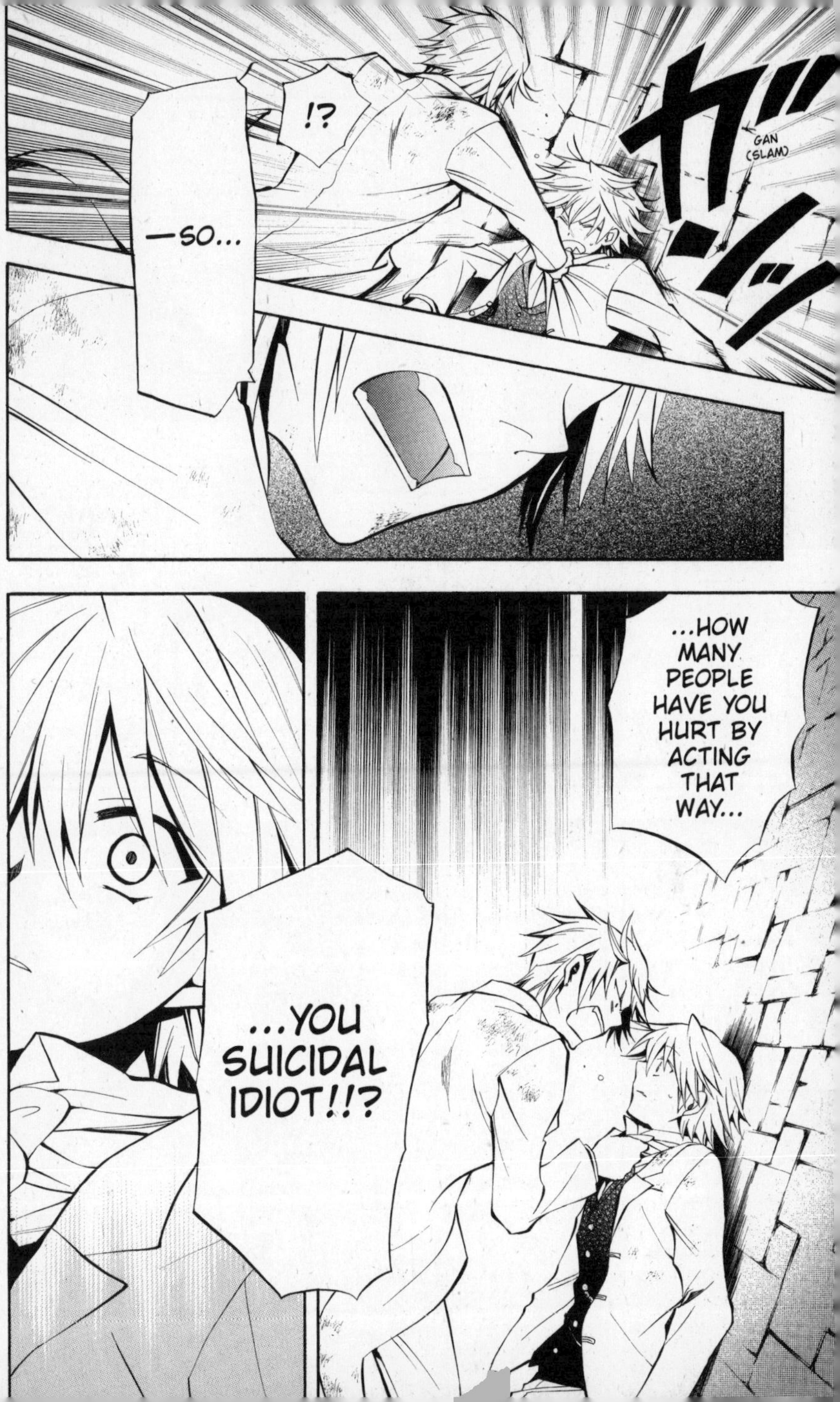
GAN (SLAM)
!?
—SO...
...HOW MANY PEOPLE HAVE YOU HURT BY ACTING THAT WAY...
...YOU SUICIDAL IDIOT!!?

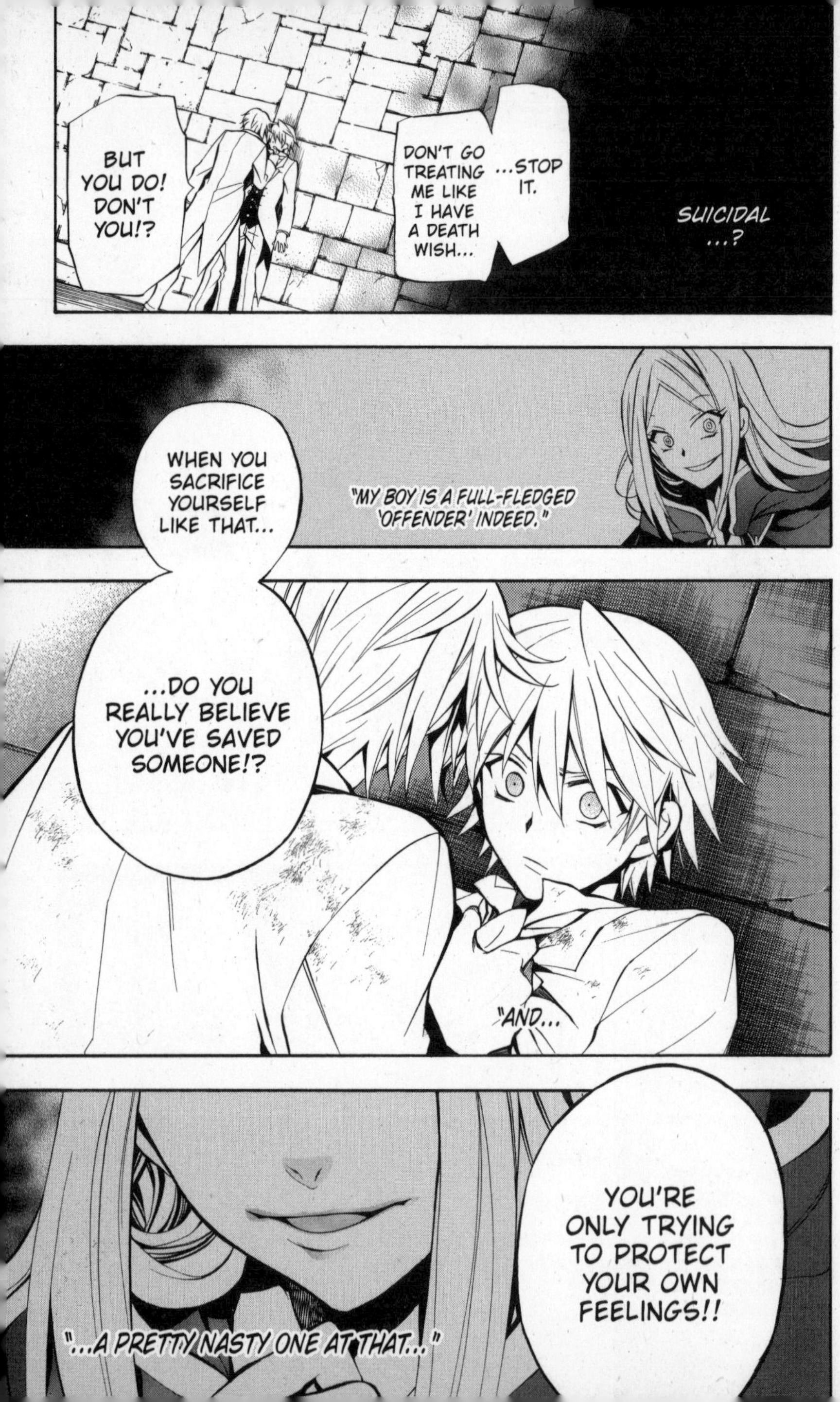
SUICIDAL ...?
...STOP IT.
DON'T GO TREATING ME LIKE I HAVE A DEATH WISH...
BUT YOU DO! DON'T YOU!?
"MY BOY IS A FULL-FLEDGED 'OFFENDER' INDEED."
WHEN YOU SACRIFICE YOURSELF LIKE THAT...
...DO YOU REALLY BELIEVE YOU'VE SAVED SOMEONE!?
"AND...
YOU'RE ONLY TRYING TO PROTECT YOUR OWN FEELINGS!!
"...A PRETTY NASTY ONE AT THAT..."

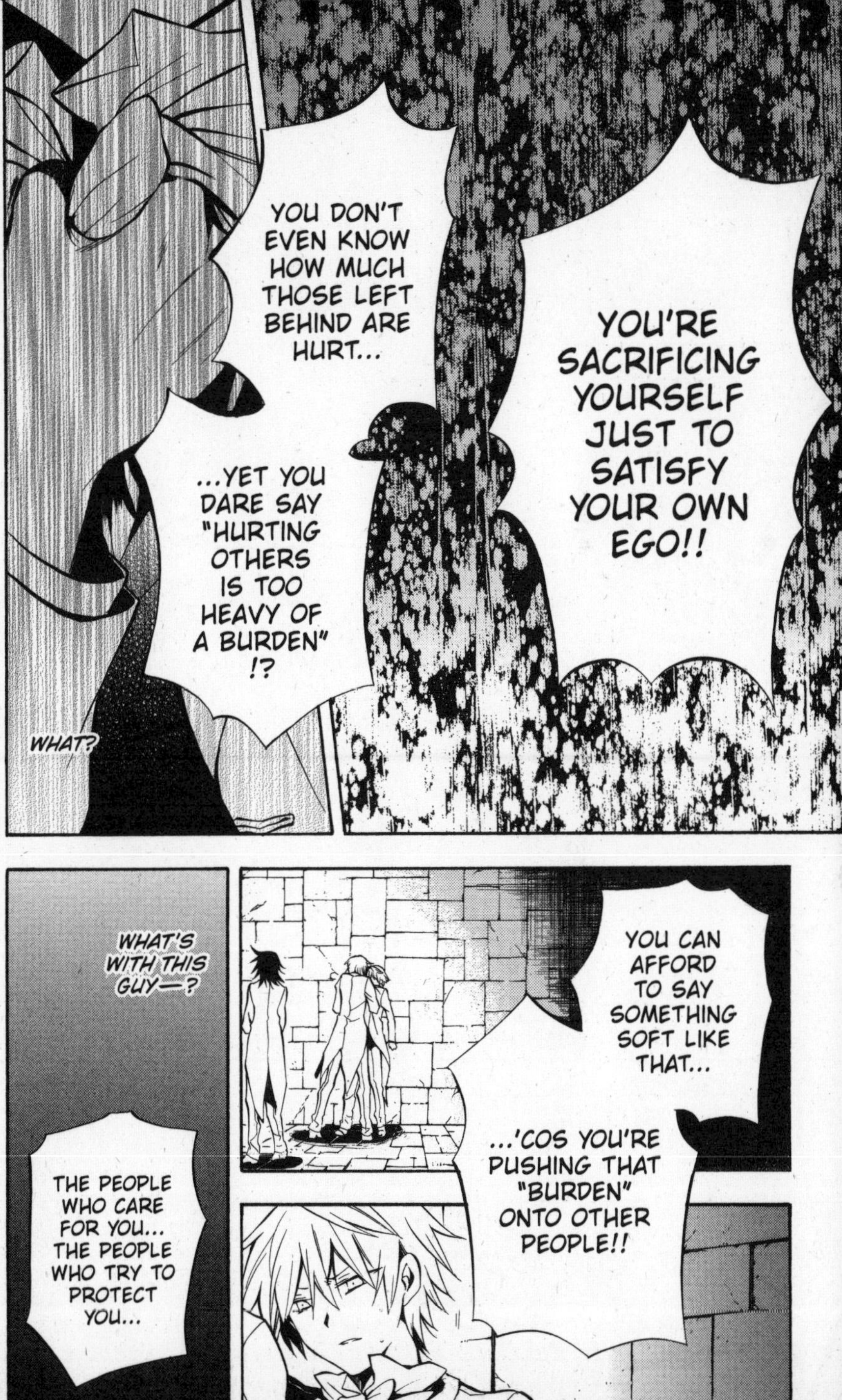
YOU'RE SACRIFICING YOURSELF JUST TO SATISFY YOUR OWN EGO!!
YOU DON'T EVEN KNOW HOW MUCH THOSE LEFT BEHIND ARE HURT...
...YET YOU DARE SAY "HURTING OTHERS IS TOO HEAVY OF A BURDEN" !?
WHAT?
YOU CAN AFFORD TO SAY SOMETHING SOFT LIKE THAT...
...'COS YOU'RE PUSHING THAT "BURDEN" ONTO OTHER PEOPLE!!
WHAT'S WITH THIS GUY—?
THE PEOPLE WHO CARE FOR YOU... THE PEOPLE WHO TRY TO PROTECT YOU...

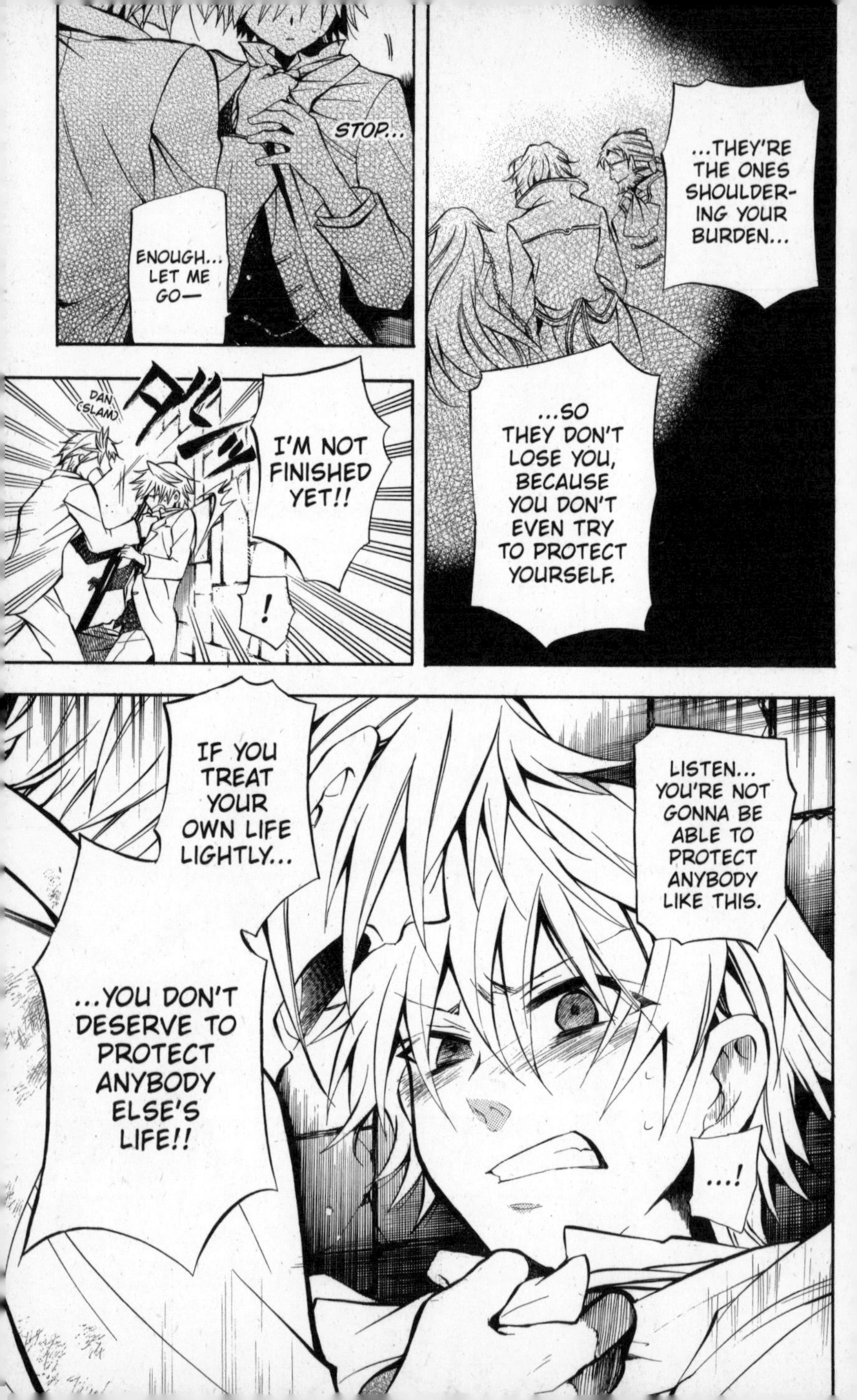
...THEY'RE THE ONES SHOULDERING YOUR BURDEN...
...SO THEY DON'T LOSE YOU, BECAUSE YOU DON'T EVEN TRY TO PROTECT YOURSELF.
STOP...
ENOUGH... LET ME GO—
I'M NOT FINISHED YET!!
DAN (SLAM)
!
LISTEN... YOU'RE NOT GONNA BE ABLE TO PROTECT ANYBODY LIKE THIS.
IF YOU TREAT YOUR OWN LIFE LIGHTLY...
...YOU DON'T DESERVE TO PROTECT ANYBODY ELSE'S LIFE!!
...!

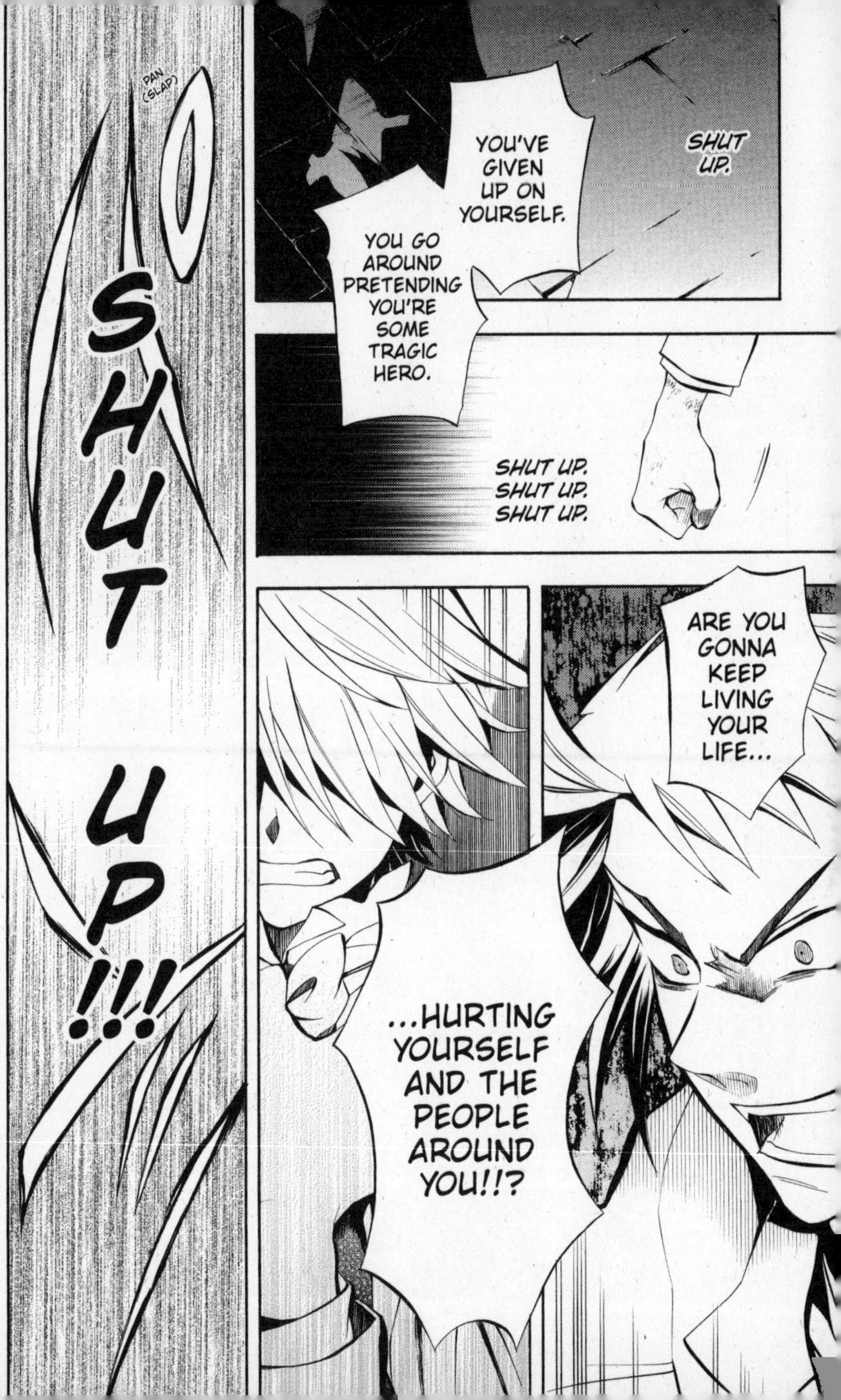
SHUT UP.
YOU'VE GIVEN UP ON YOURSELF.
YOU GO AROUND PRETENDING YOU'RE SOME TRAGIC HERO.
SHUT UP. SHUT UP. SHUT UP.
ARE YOU GONNA KEEP LIVING YOUR LIFE...
...HURTING YOURSELF AND THE PEOPLE AROUND YOU!!?
PAN (SLAP)
SHUT UP!!!

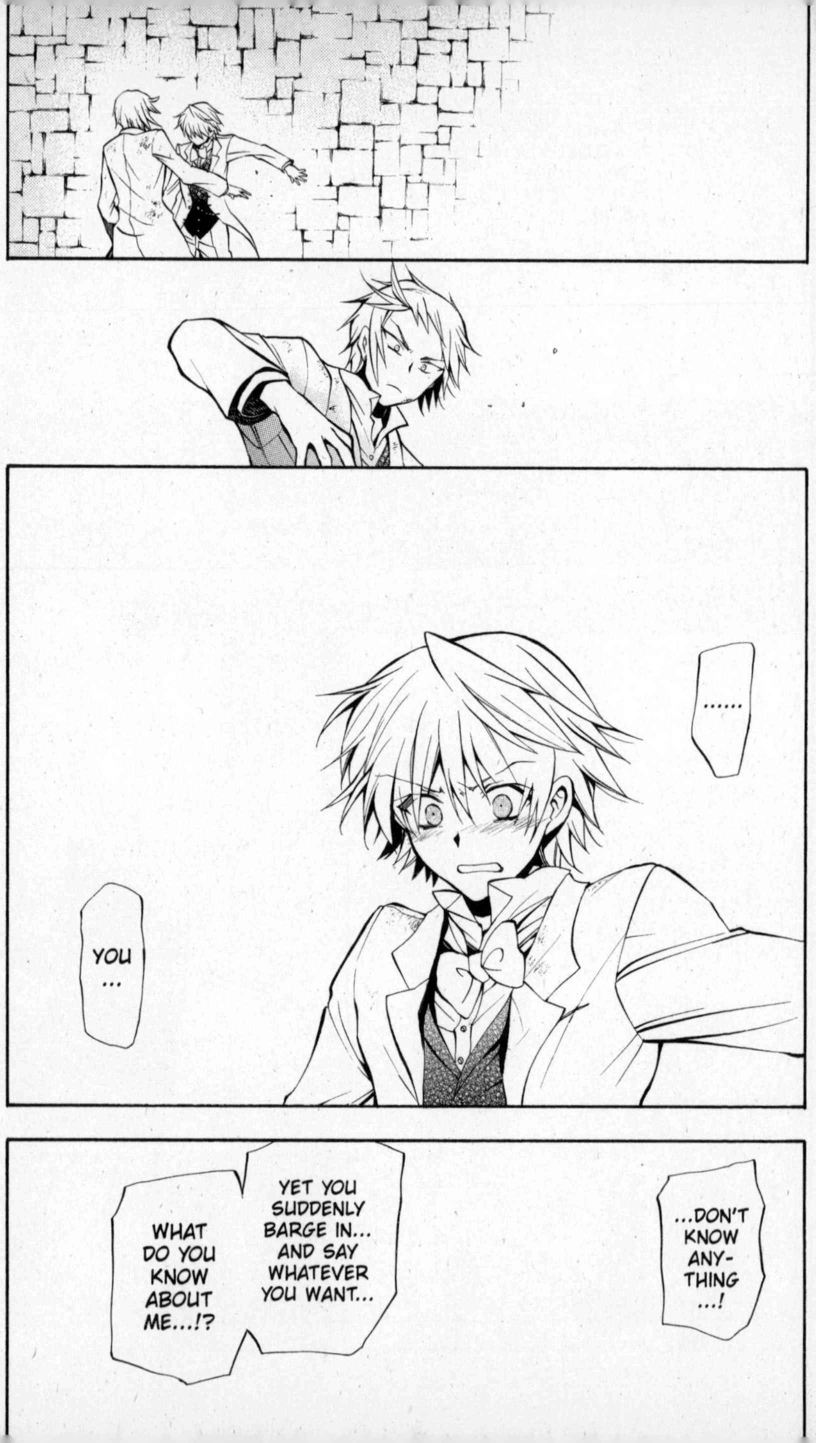
......
YOU ...
...DON'T KNOW ANYTHING ...!
YET YOU SUDDENLY BARGE IN... AND SAY WHATEVER YOU WANT...
WHAT DO YOU KNOW ABOUT ME...!?

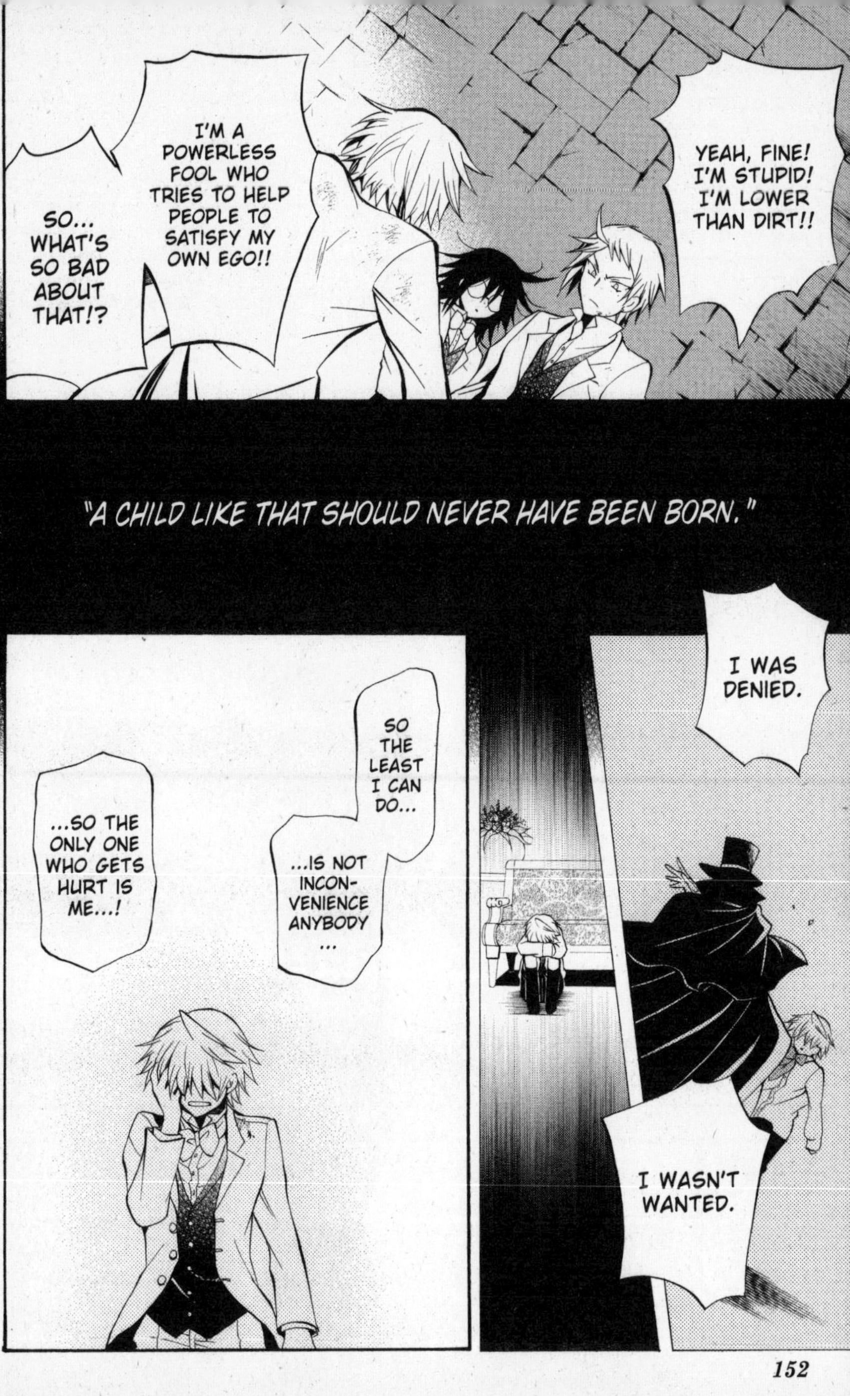
YEAH, FINE! I'M STUPID! I'M LOWER THAN DIRT!!
I'M A POWERLESS FOOL WHO TRIES TO HELP PEOPLE TO SATISFY MY OWN EGO!!
SO... WHAT'S SO BAD ABOUT THAT!?
"A CHILD LIKE THAT SHOULD NEVER HAVE BEEN BORN."
I WAS DENIED.
I WASN'T WANTED.
SO THE LEAST I CAN DO...
...IS NOT INCON-VENIENCE ANYBODY...
...SO THE ONLY ONE WHO GETS HURT IS ME...!

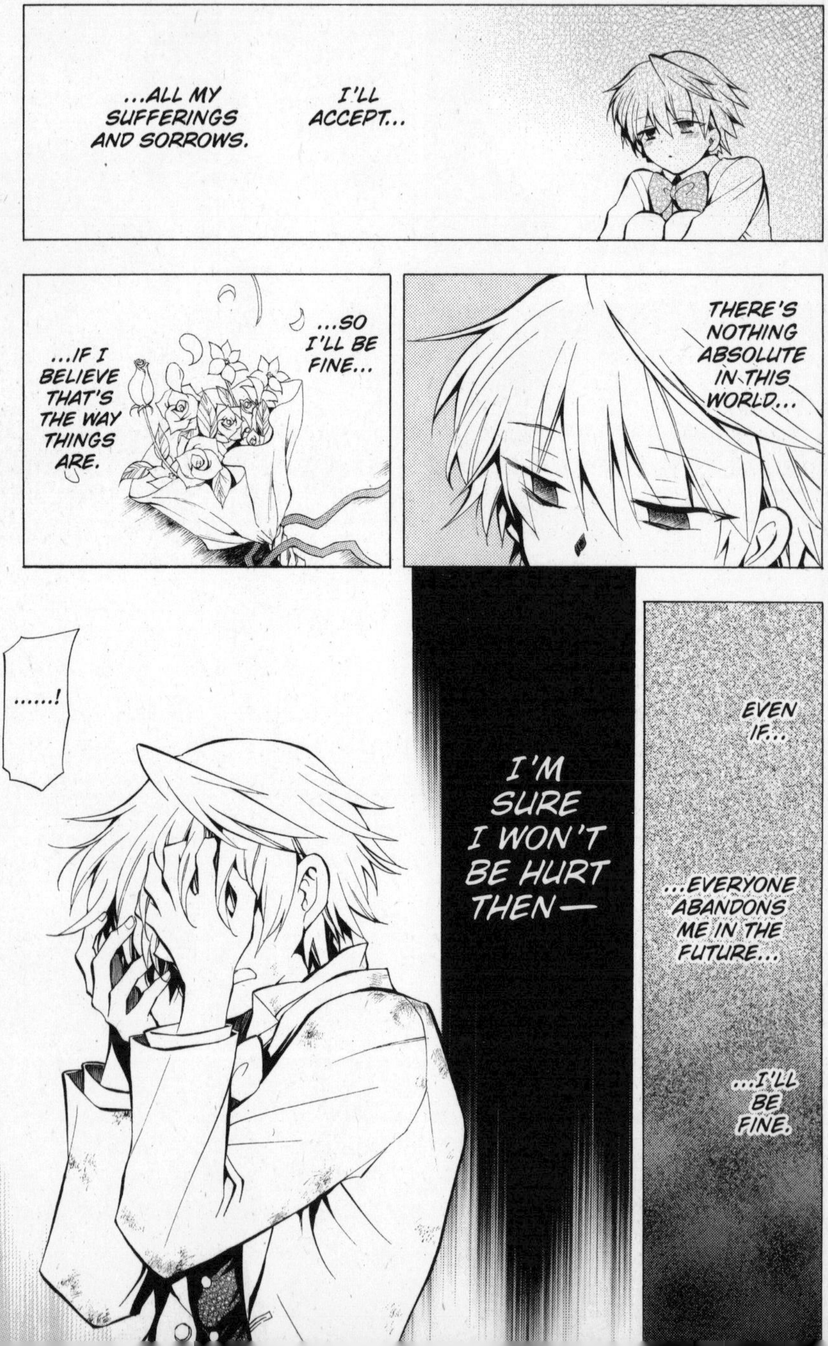
I'LL ACCEPT...
...ALL MY SUFFERINGS AND SORROWS.
THERE'S NOTHING ABSOLUTE IN THIS WORLD...
...SO I'LL BE FINE...
...IF I BELIEVE THAT'S THE WAY THINGS ARE.
EVEN IF...
...EVERYONE ABANDONS ME IN THE FUTURE...
...I'LL BE FINE.
I'M SURE I WON'T BE HURT THEN—
......!

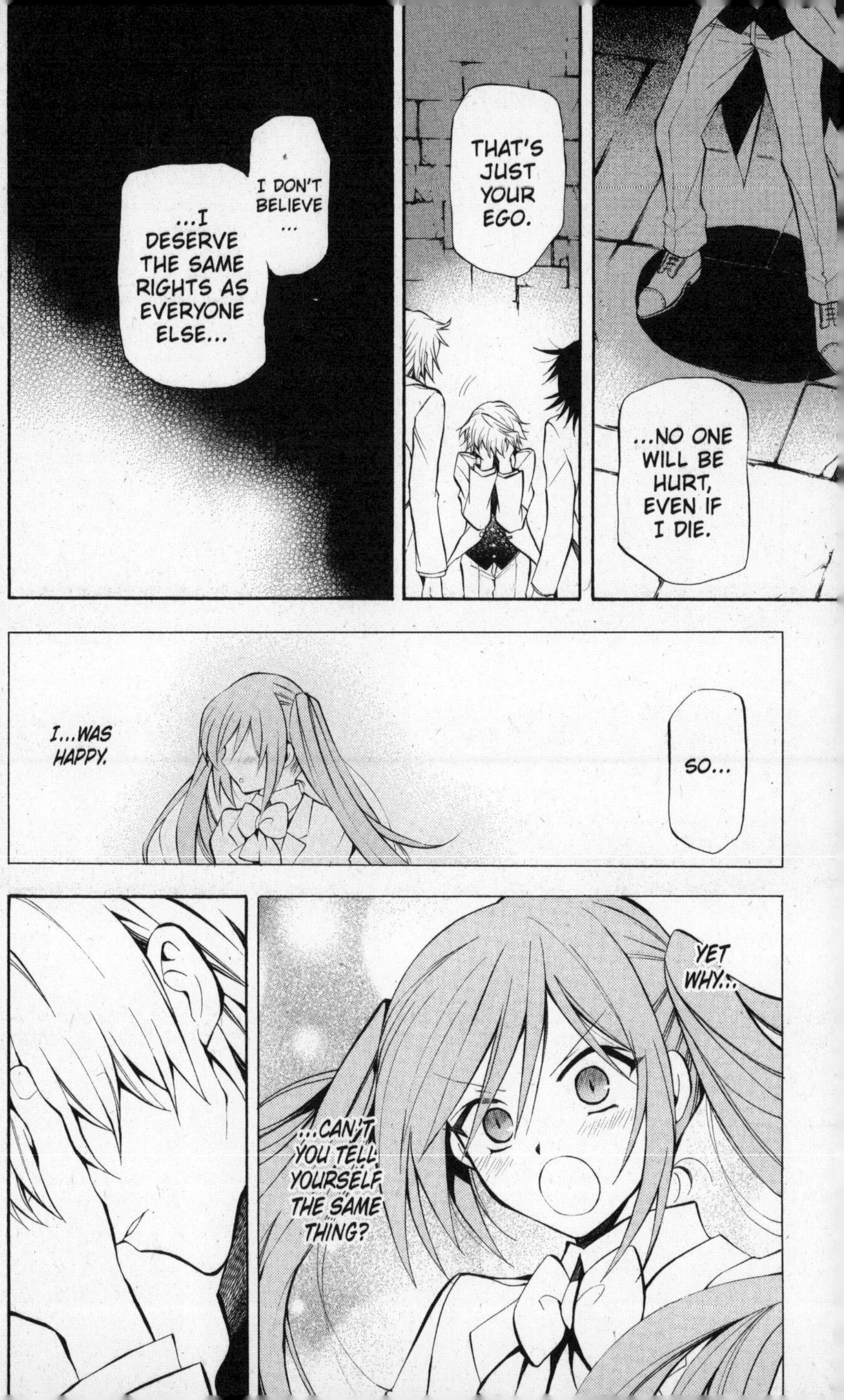
...NO ONE WILL BE HURT, EVEN IF I DIE.
THAT'S JUST YOUR EGO.
I DON'T BELIEVE ...
...I DESERVE THE SAME RIGHTS AS EVERYONE ELSE...
SO...
I...WAS HAPPY.
YET WHY...
...CAN'T YOU TELL YOURSELF THE SAME THING?

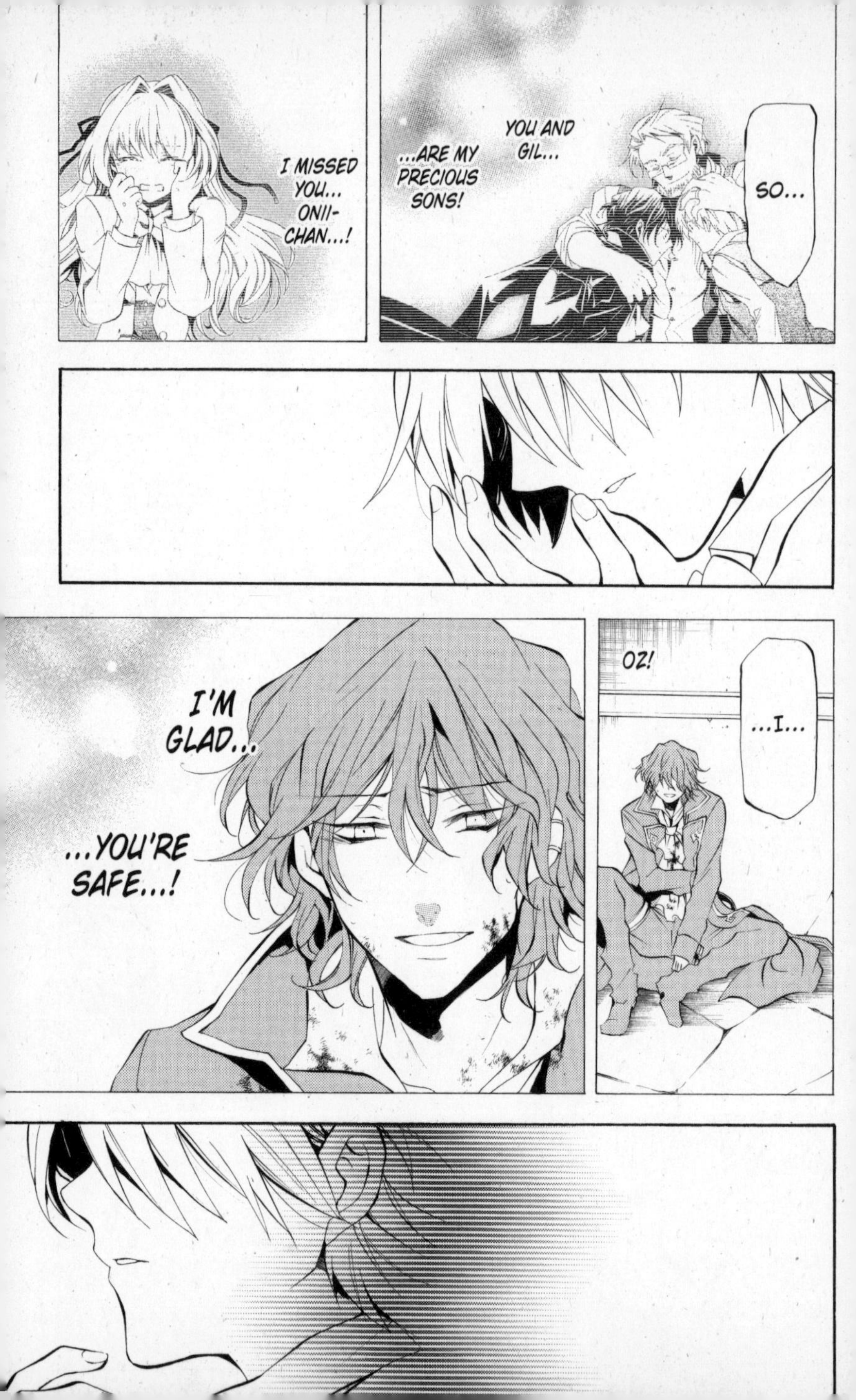
SO...
YOU AND GIL...
...ARE MY PRECIOUS SONS!
I MISSED YOU... ONII-CHAN...!
OZ!
...I...
I'M GLAD...
...YOU'RE SAFE...!

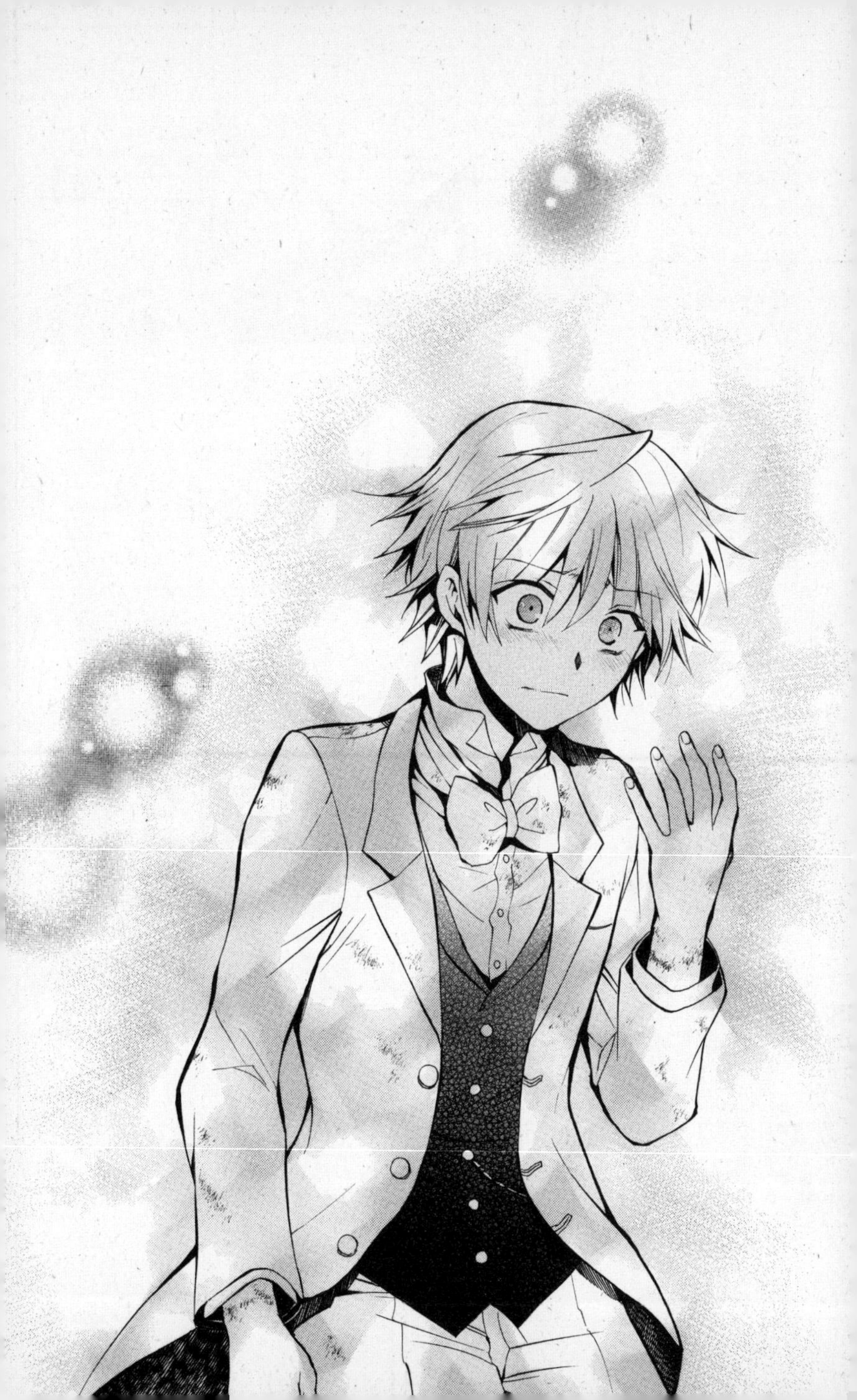

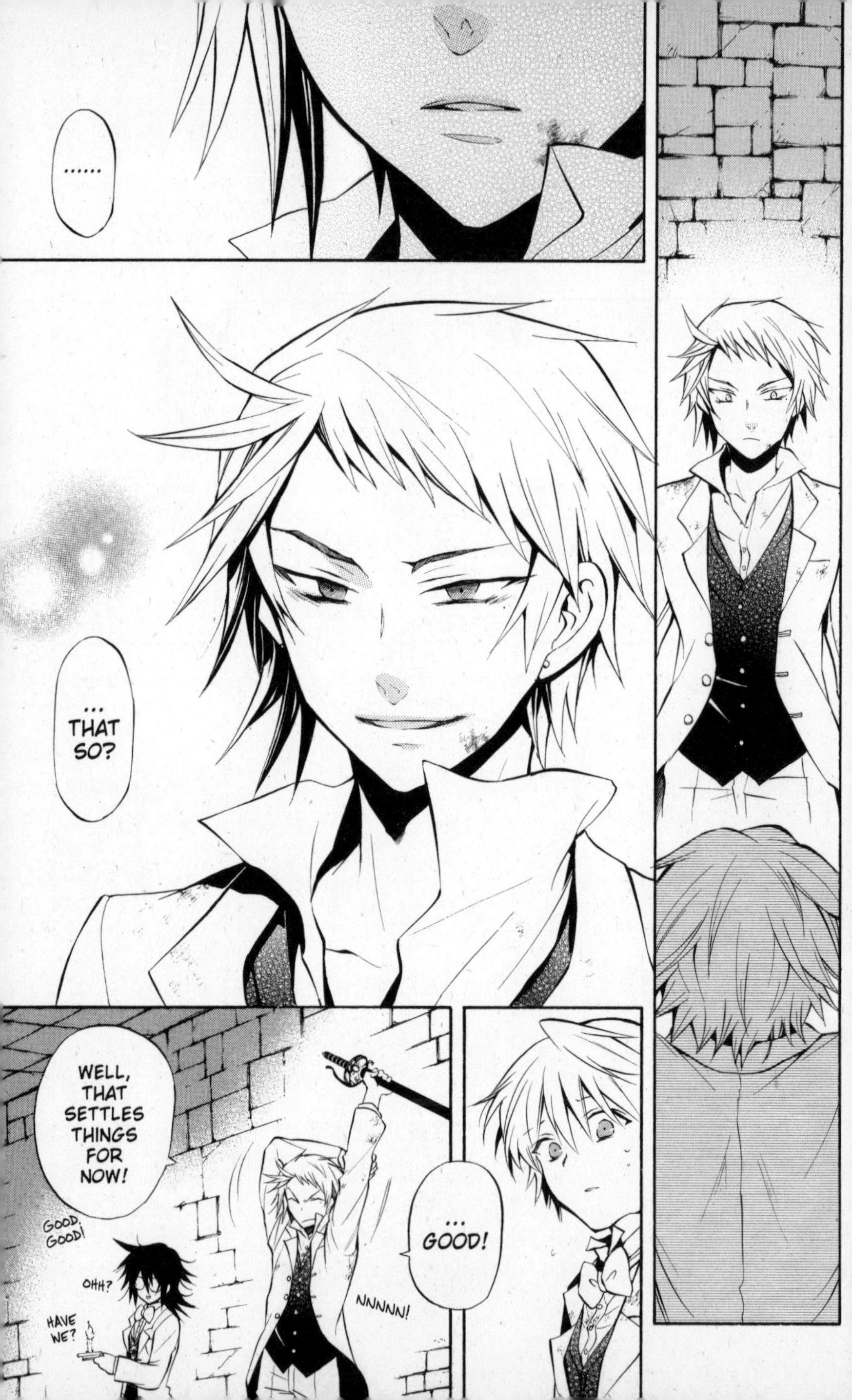
......
... THAT SO?
... GOOD!
WELL, THAT SETTLES THINGS FOR NOW!
NNNNN!
GOOD, GOOD!
OHH?
HAVE WE?

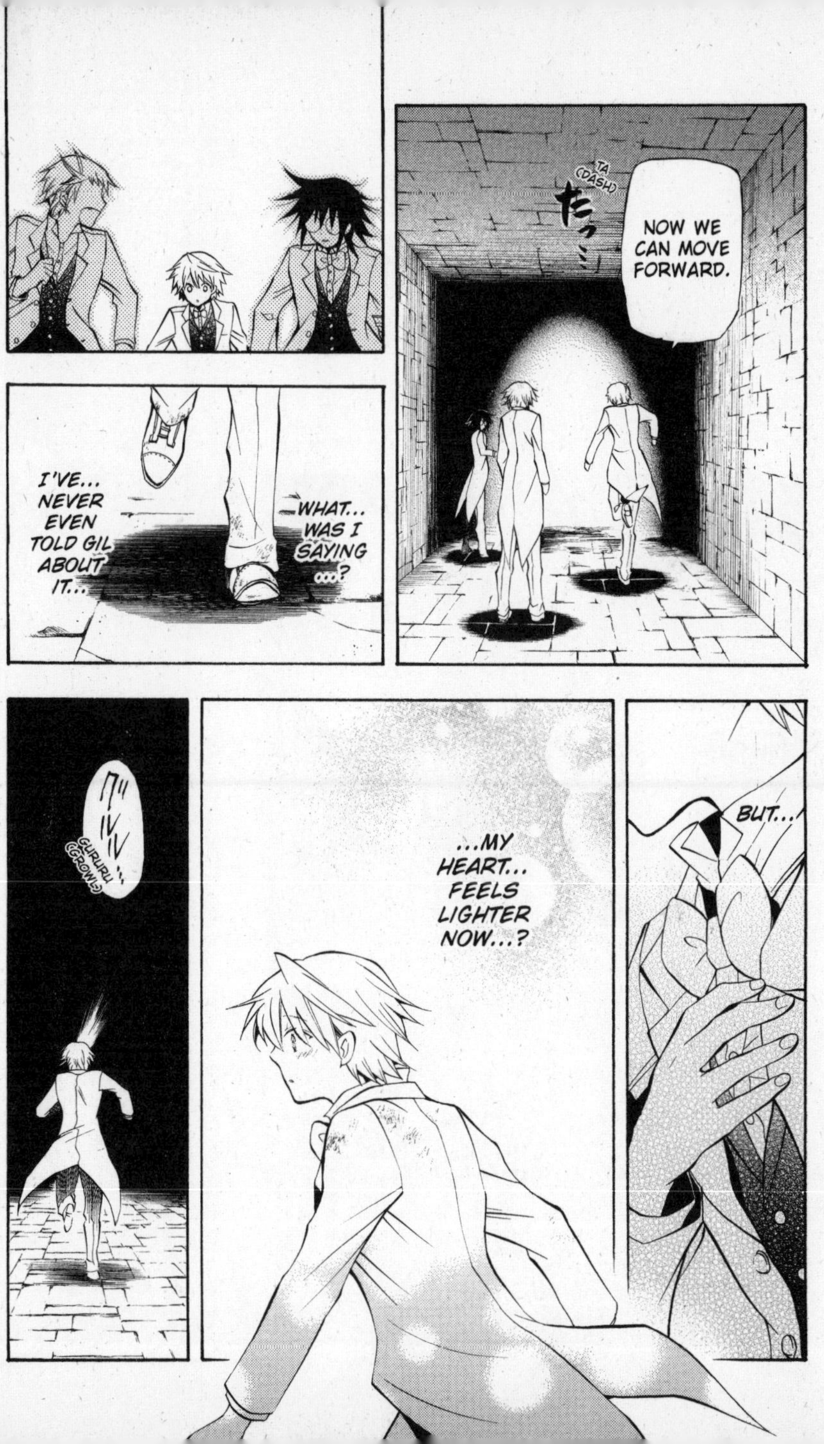

NOW WE CAN MOVE FORWARD.
たっ
TA (DASH)
WHAT... WAS I SAYING...?
I'VE... NEVER EVEN TOLD GIL ABOUT IT...
BUT...
...MY HEART... FEELS LIGHTER NOW...?
グルル…
GURURU (GROWL)

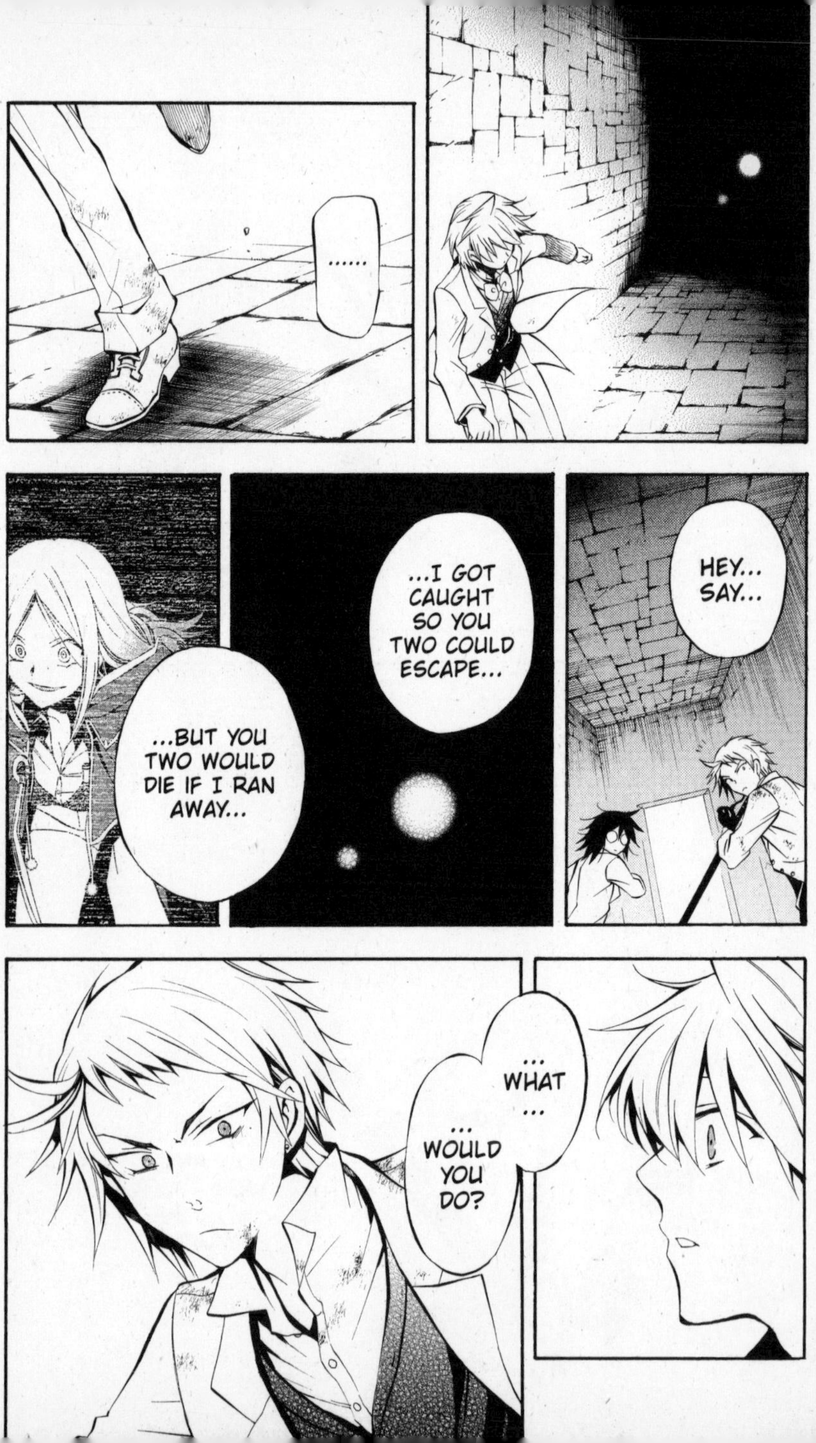
......
HEY... SAY...
...I GOT CAUGHT SO YOU TWO COULD ESCAPE...
...BUT YOU TWO WOULD DIE IF I RAN AWAY...
... WHAT ... ... WOULD YOU DO?

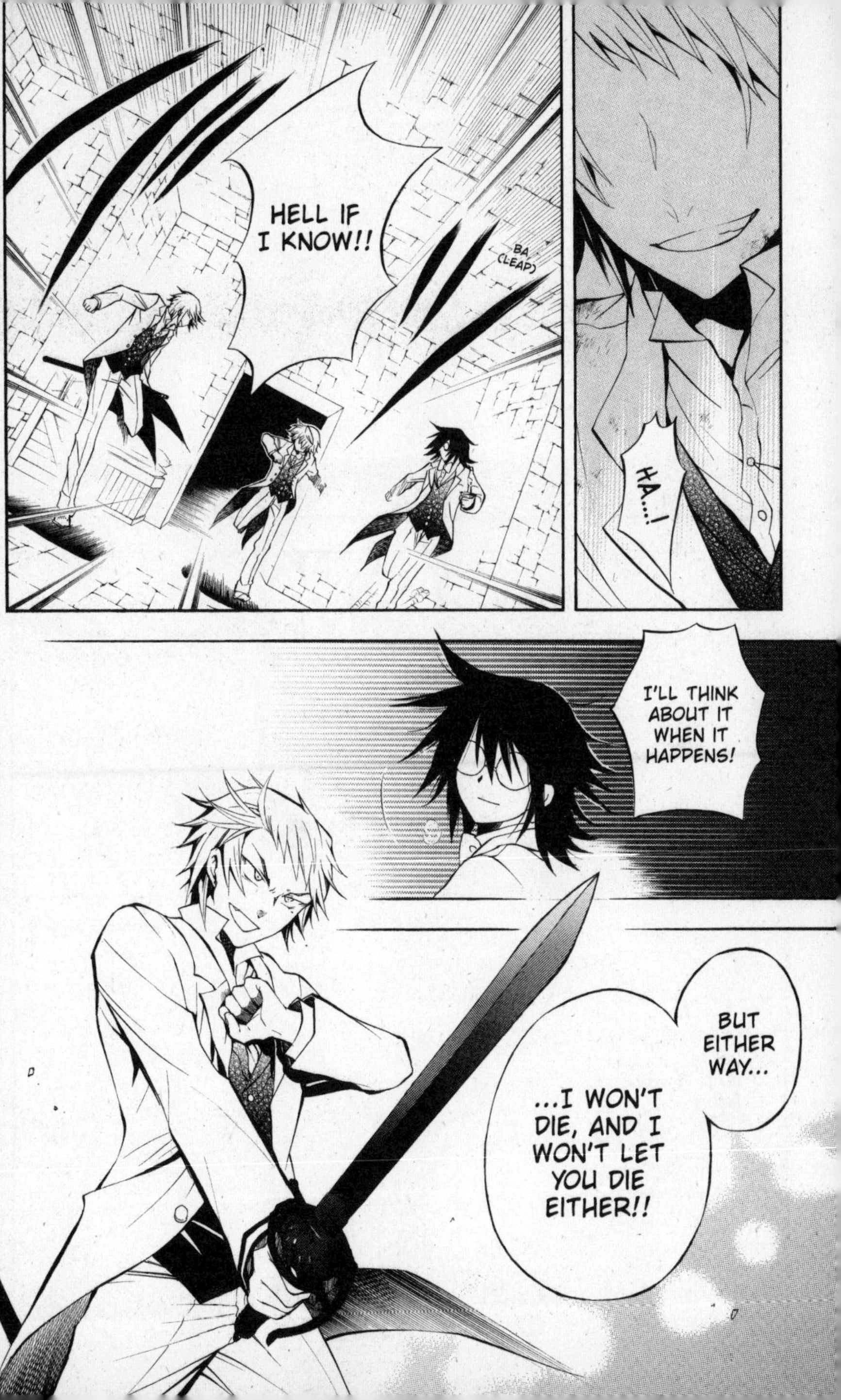
HA...!
HELL IF I KNOW!!
BA (LEAP)
I'LL THINK ABOUT IT WHEN IT HAPPENS!
BUT EITHER WAY...
...I WON'T DIE, AND I WON'T LET YOU DIE EITHER!!

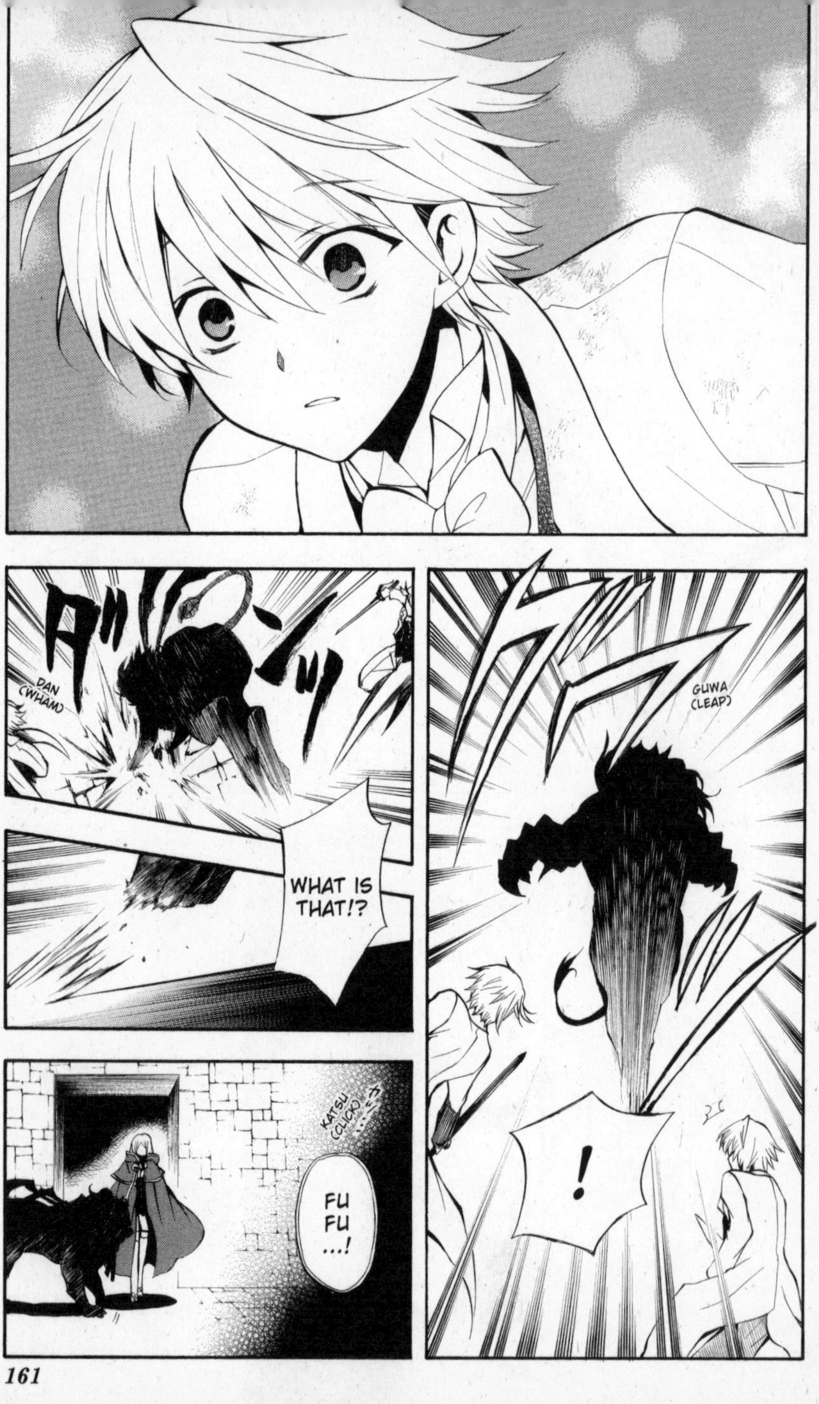
GUWA (LEAP)
!
DAN (WHAM)
WHAT IS THAT!?
KATSU (CLICK)
FU FU ...!

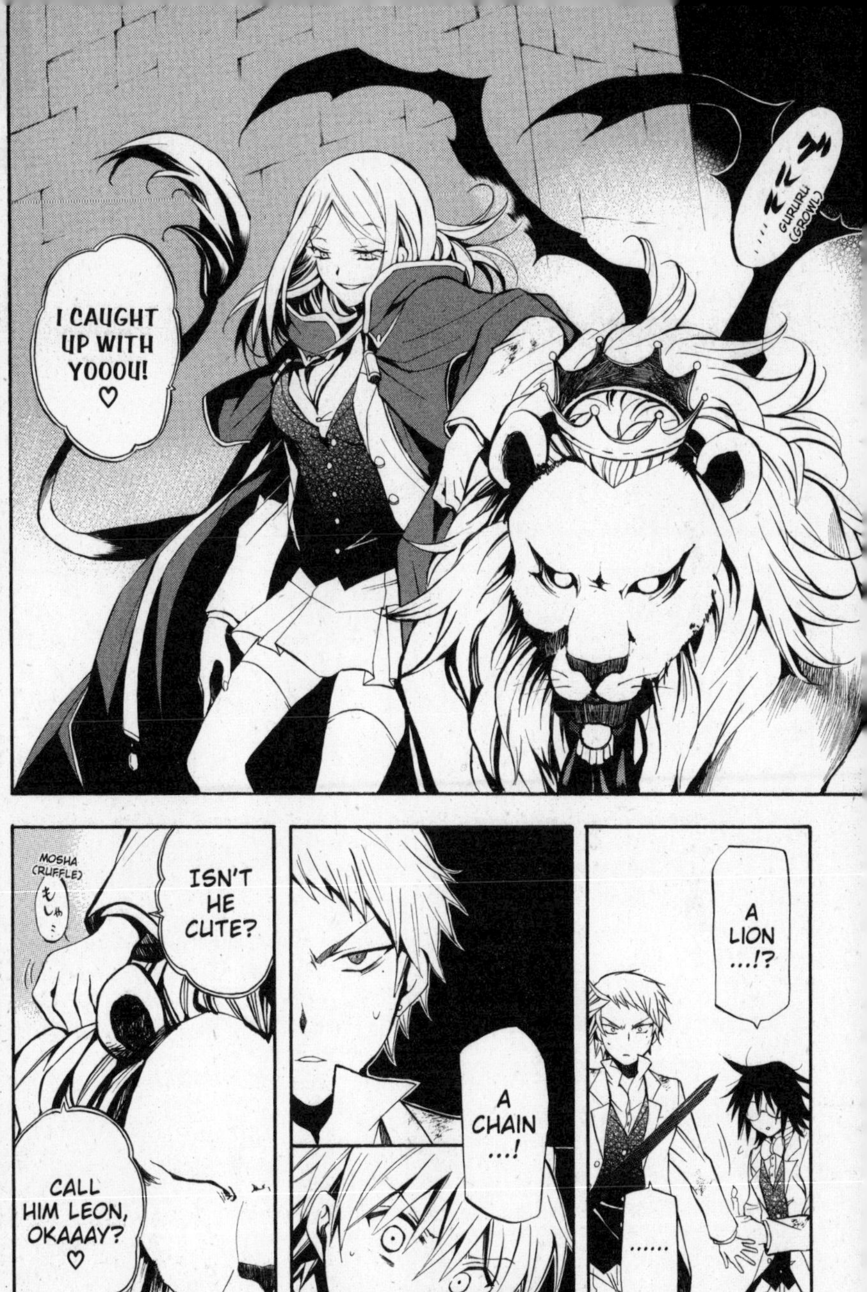
グルル……
GURURU (GROWL)
I CAUGHT UP WITH YOOOU! ♡
A LION ...!?
......
A CHAIN ...!
MOSHA (RUFFLE)
もしゃ
ISN'T HE CUTE?
CALL HIM LEON, OKAAAY? ♡

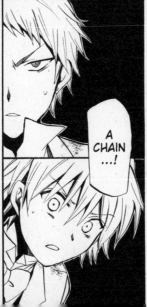

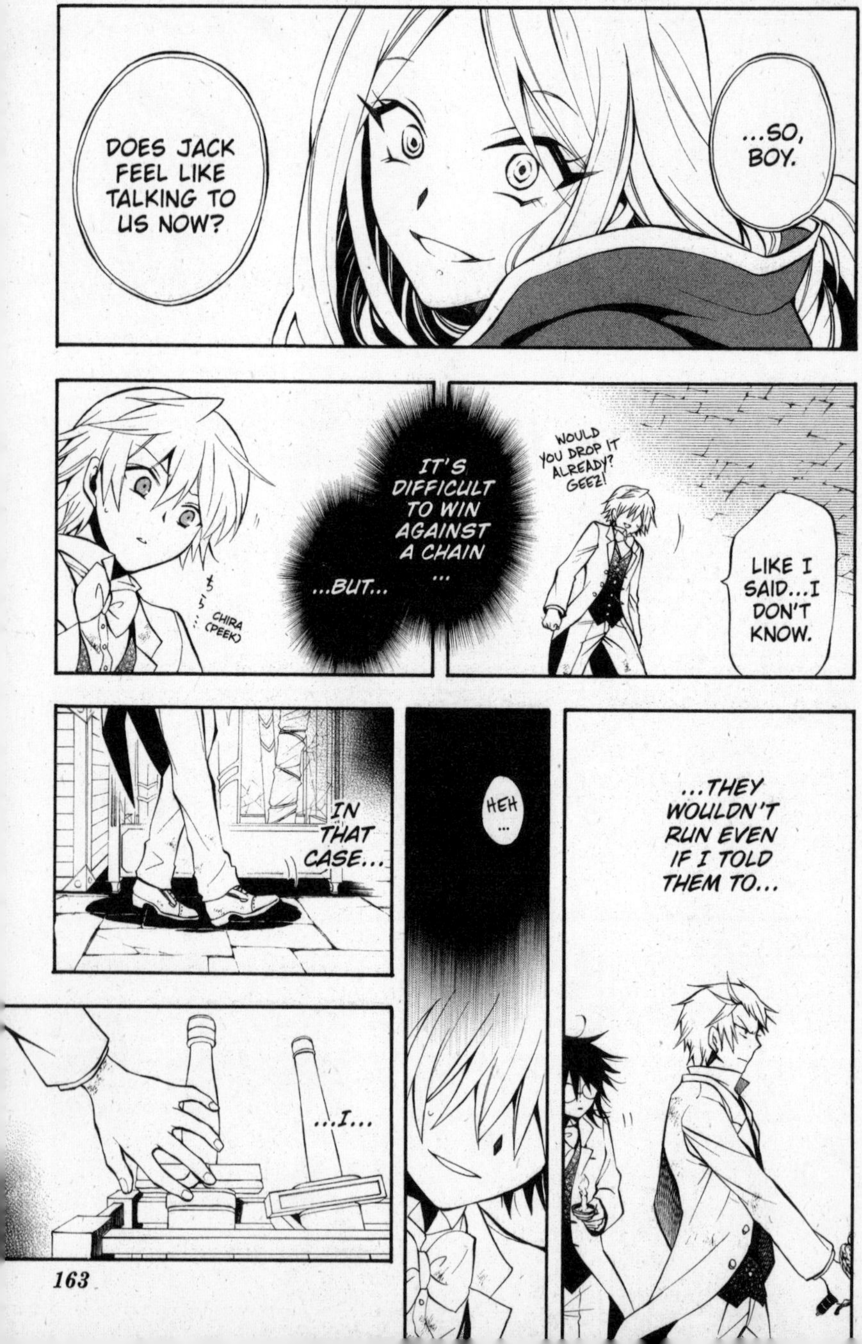
...SO, BOY.
DOES JACK FEEL LIKE TALKING TO US NOW?
LIKE I SAID...I DON'T KNOW.
WOULD YOU DROP IT ALREADY? GEEZ!
IT'S DIFFICULT TO WIN AGAINST A CHAIN...
...BUT...
ちら…
CHIRA (PEEK)
...THEY WOULDN'T RUN EVEN IF I TOLD THEM TO...
HEH...
IN THAT CASE...
...I...

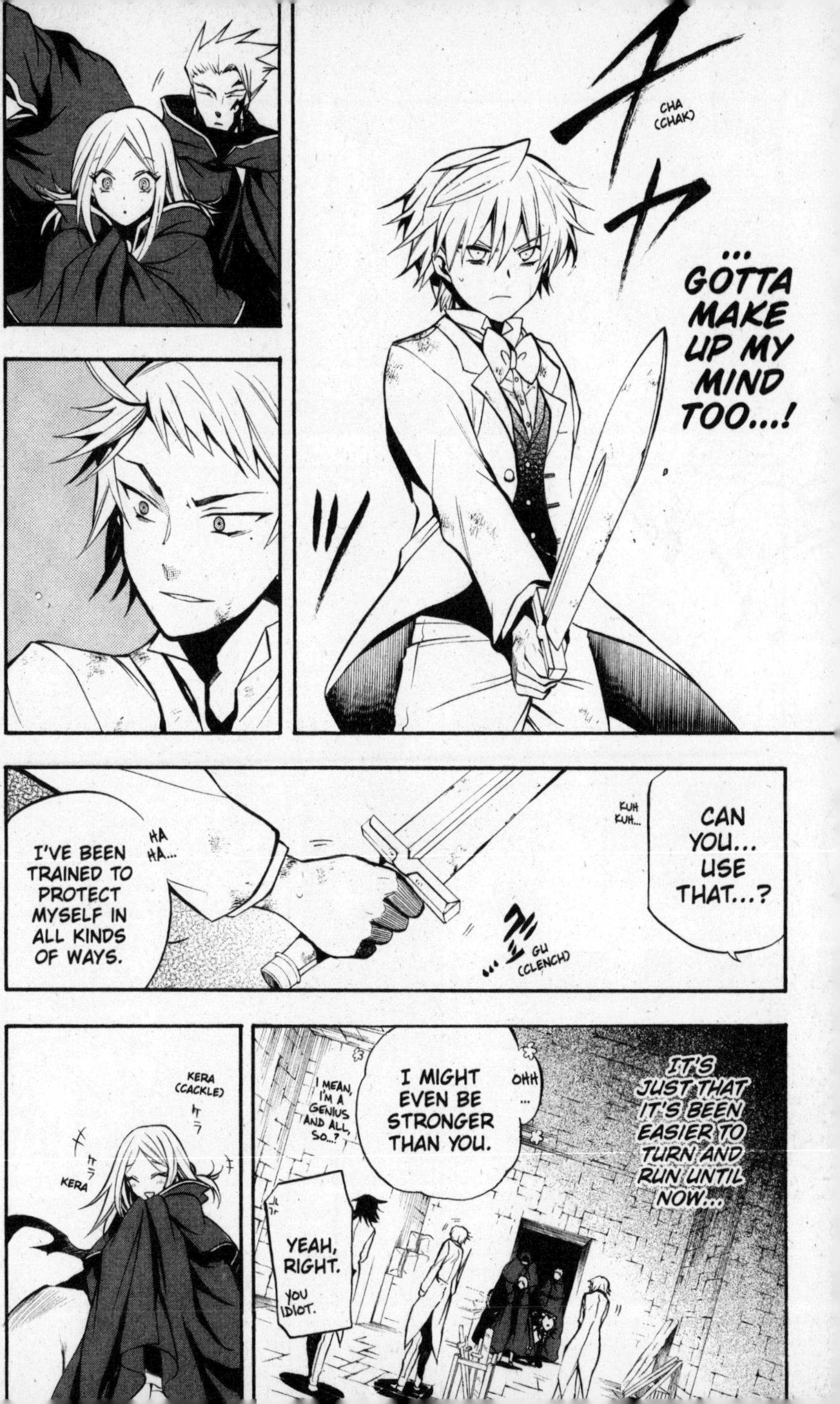
CHA (CHAK)
...GÖTTA MAKE UP MY MIND TOO...!
CAN YOU... USE THAT...?
KUH KUH...
GU (CLENCH)
HA HA...
I'VE BEEN TRAINED TO PROTECT MYSELF IN ALL KINDS OF WAYS.
IT'S JUST THAT IT'S BEEN EASIER TO TURN AND RUN UNTIL NOW...
OHH...
I MIGHT EVEN BE STRONGER THAN YOU.
I MEAN, I'M A GENIUS AND ALL, SO...?
YEAH, RIGHT.
YOU IDIOT.
KERA (CACKLE)
KERA

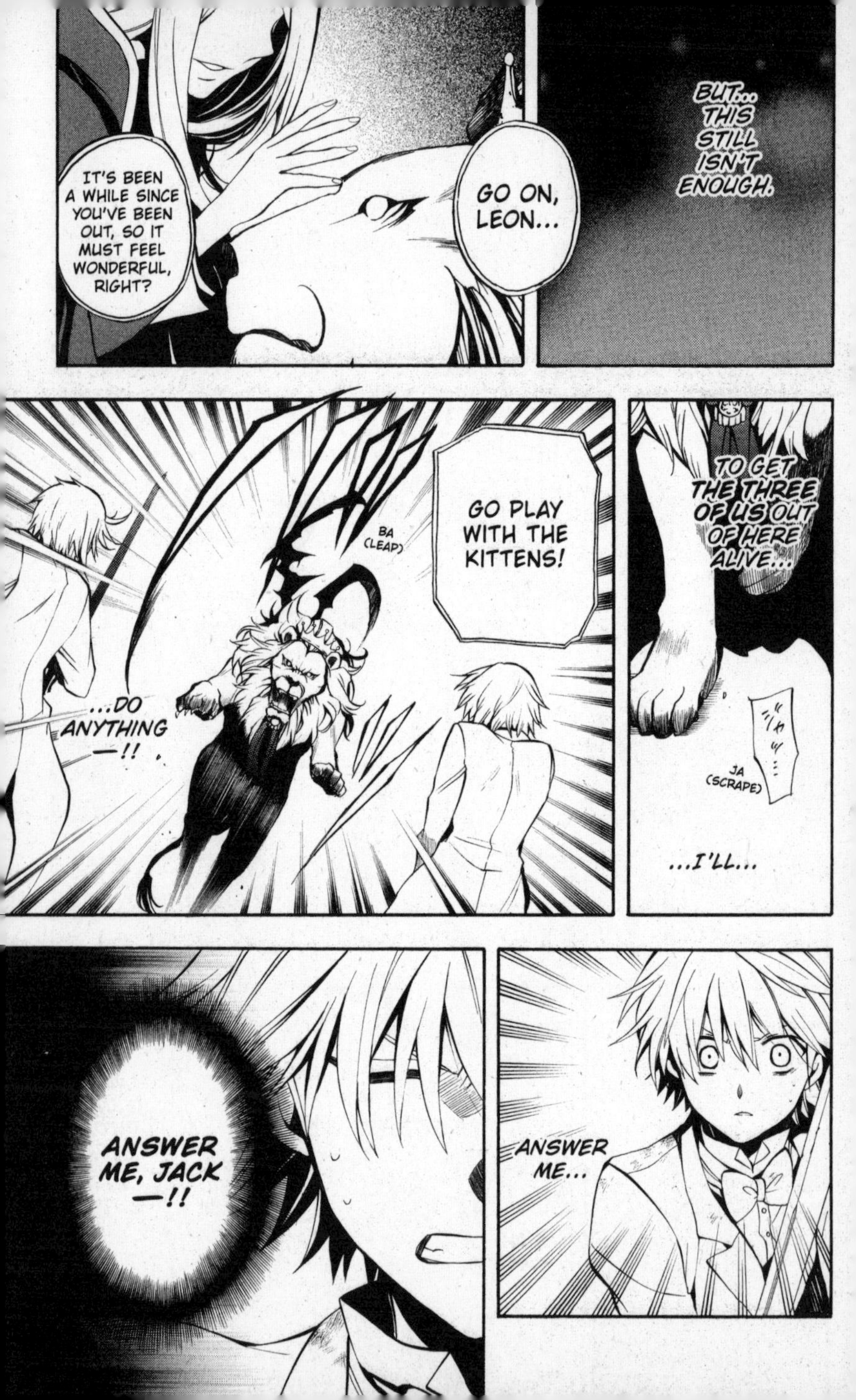
BUT... THIS STILL ISN'T ENOUGH.
GO ON, LEON...
IT'S BEEN A WHILE SINCE YOU'VE BEEN OUT, SO IT MUST FEEL WONDERFUL, RIGHT?
TO GET THE THREE OF US OUT OF HERE ALIVE...
JA (SCRAPE)
...I'LL...
GO PLAY WITH THE KITTENS!
BA (LEAP)
...DO ANYTHING—!!
ANSWER ME...
ANSWER ME, JACK—!!

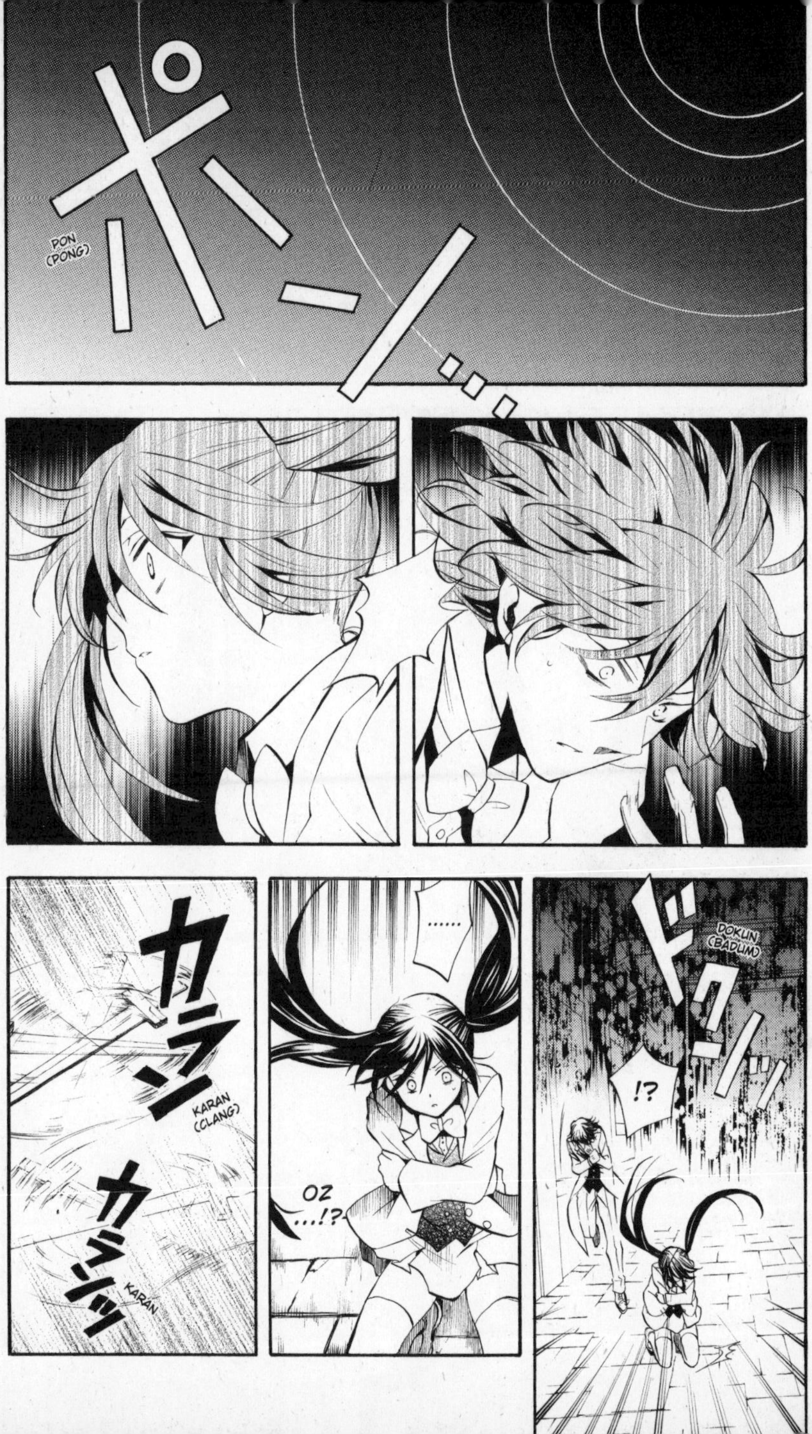
ポーン…
PON
(PONG)
ドクン
DOKUN
(BADUM)
!?
......
OZ
...!?
カラン
KARAN
(CLANG)
カランッ
KARAN

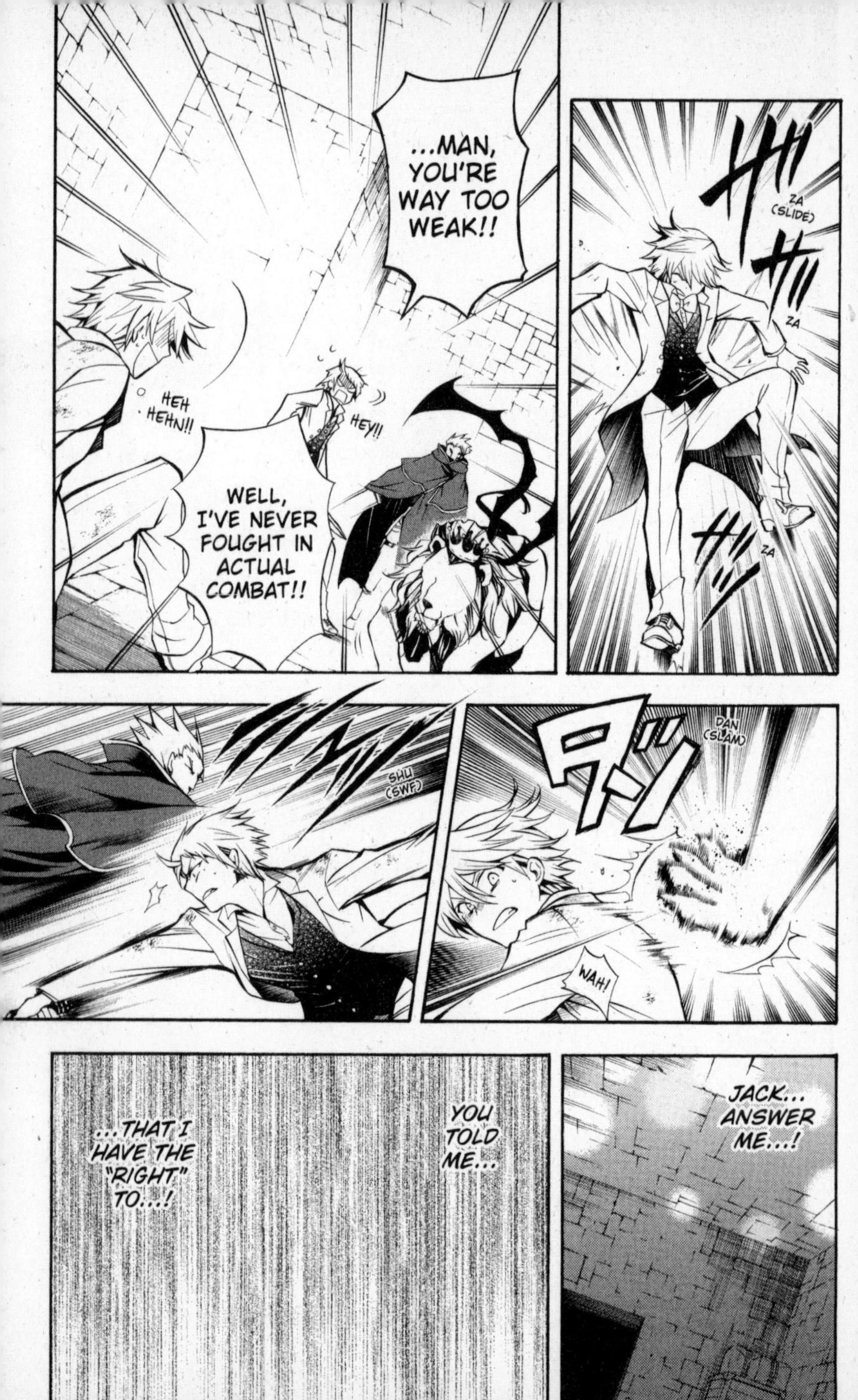
ZA (SLIDE)
ZA
ZA
...MAN, YOU'RE WAY TOO WEAK!!
HEY!!
HEH HEHN!!
WELL, I'VE NEVER FOUGHT IN ACTUAL COMBAT!!
DAN (SLAM)
WAH!
SHU (SWF)
JACK... ANSWER ME...!
YOU TOLD ME...
...THAT I HAVE THE "RIGHT" TO...!

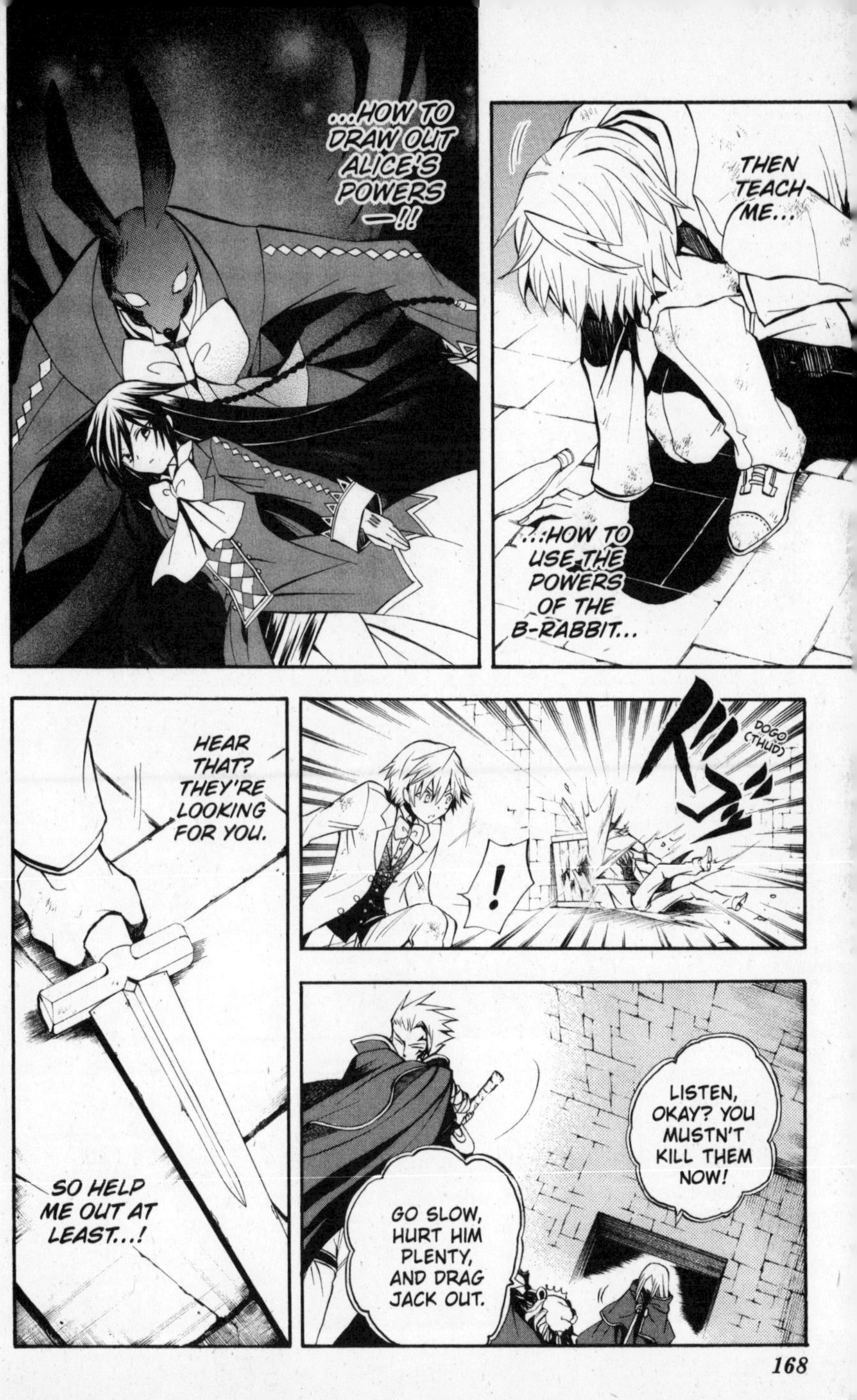
THEN TEACH ME...
...HOW TO USE THE POWERS OF THE B-RABBIT...
...HOW TO DRAW OUT ALICE'S POWERS—!!
DOGO (THUD)
!
LISTEN, OKAY? YOU MUSTN'T KILL THEM NOW!
GO SLOW, HURT HIM PLENTY, AND DRAG JACK OUT.
HEAR THAT? THEY'RE LOOKING FOR YOU.
SO HELP ME OUT AT LEAST...!

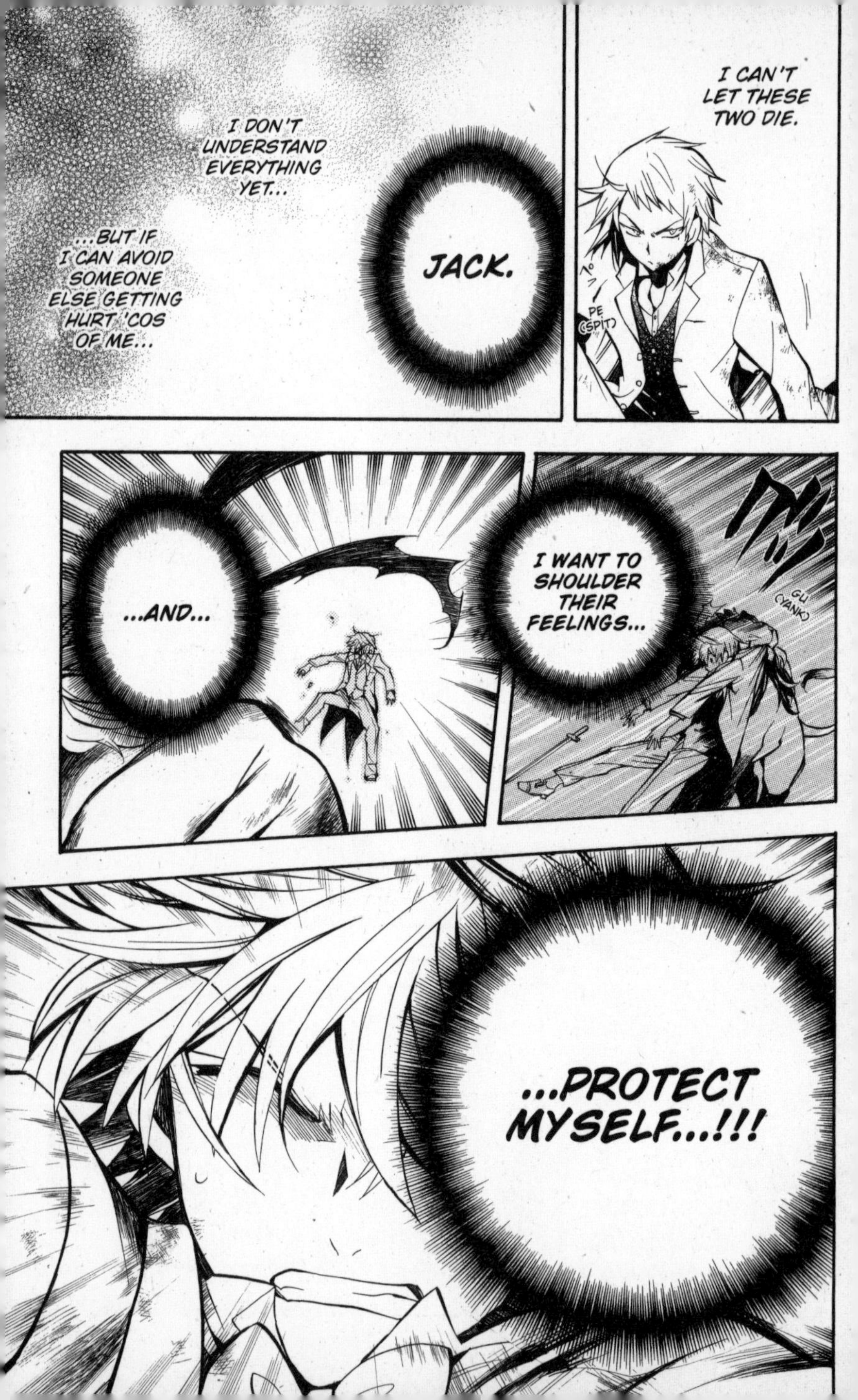
I CAN'T LET THESE TWO DIE.
PE (SPIT)
JACK.
I DON'T UNDERSTAND EVERYTHING YET...
...BUT IF I CAN AVOID SOMEONE ELSE GETTING HURT 'COS OF ME...
I WANT TO SHOULDER THEIR FEELINGS...
GU (YANK)
...AND...
...PROTECT MYSELF...!!!

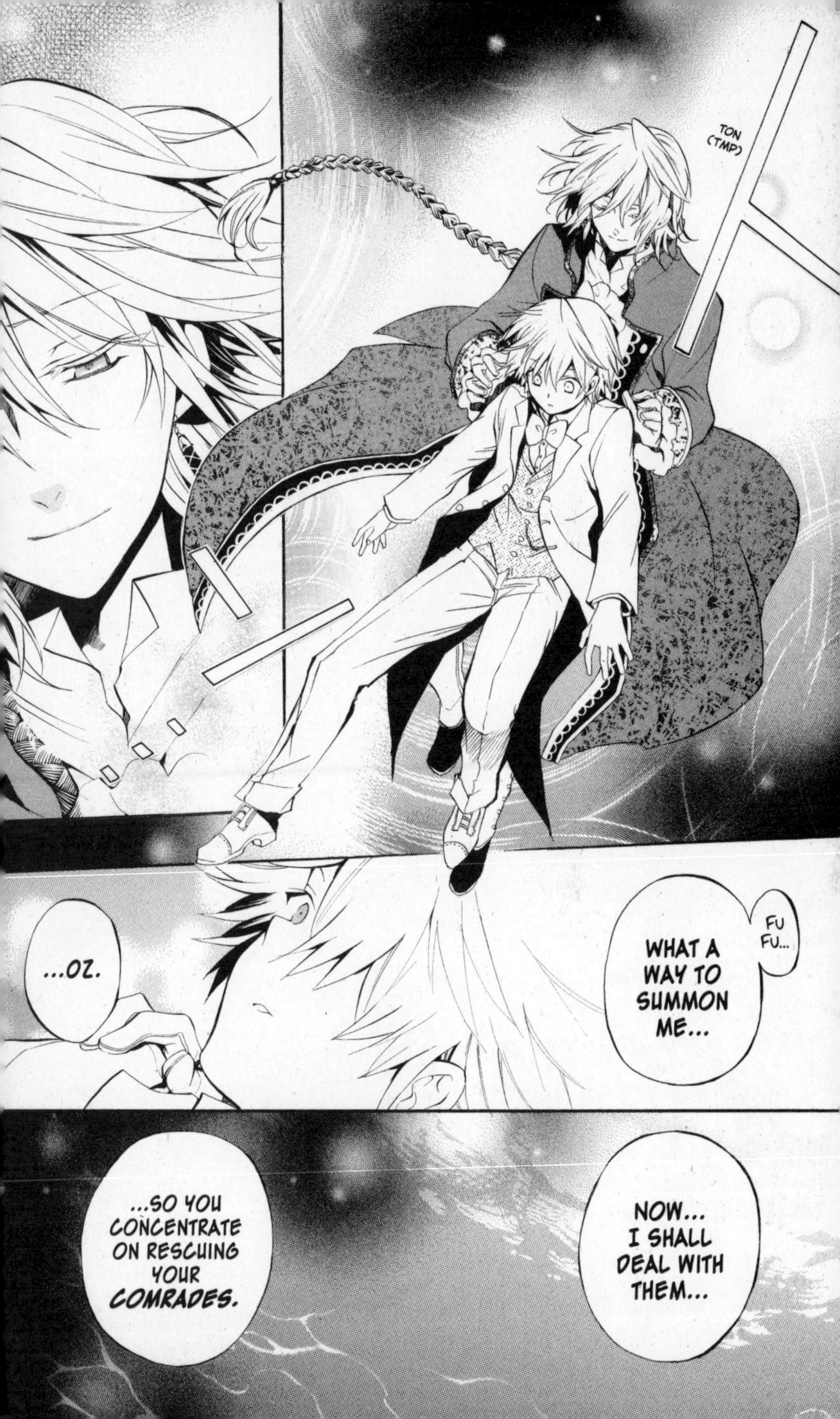
TON (TMP)
FU FU...
WHAT A WAY TO SUMMON ME...
...OZ.
NOW... I SHALL DEAL WITH THEM...
...SO YOU CONCENTRATE ON RESCUING YOUR COMRADES.

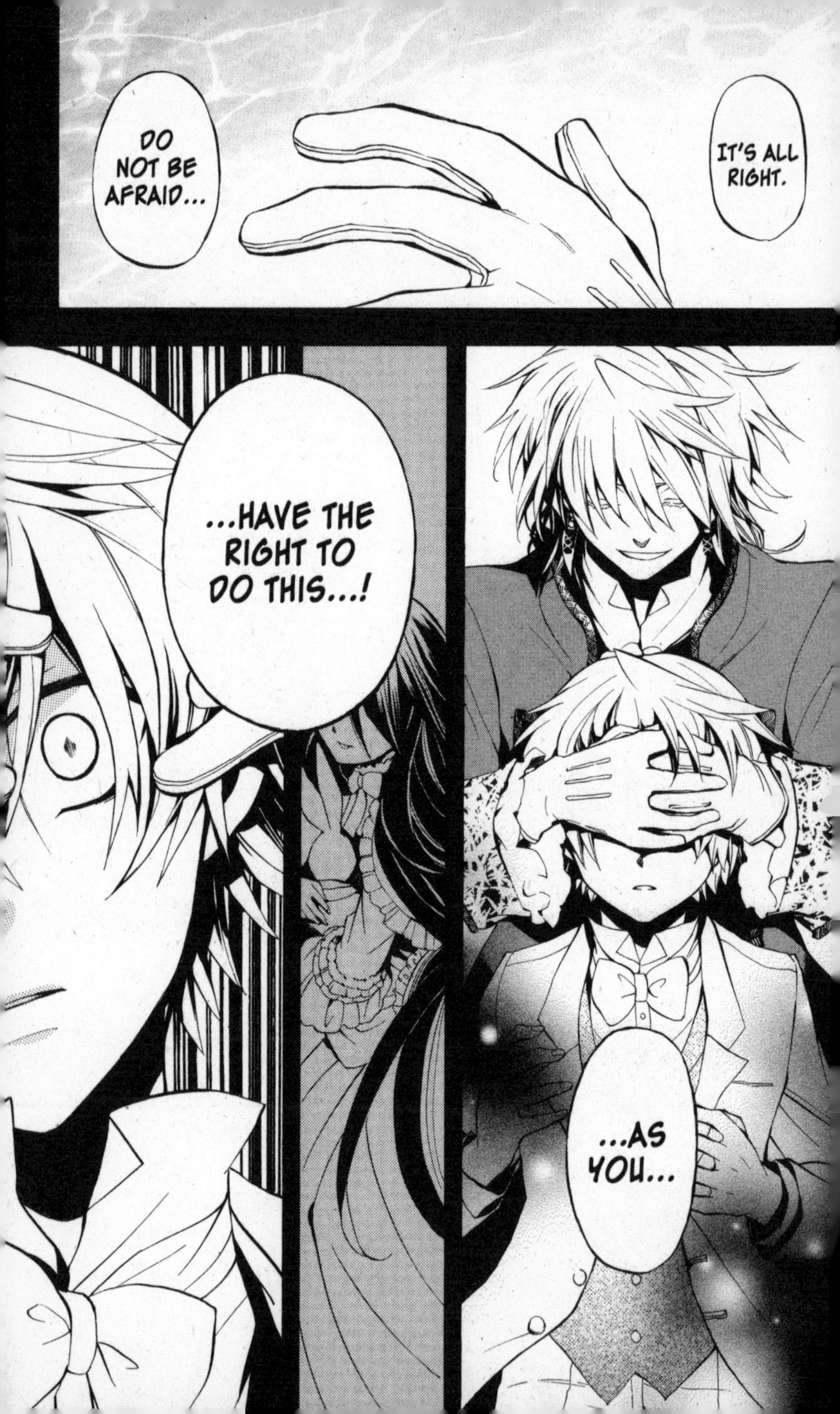
IT'S ALL RIGHT.
DO NOT BE AFRAID...
...AS YOU...
...HAVE THE RIGHT TO DO THIS...!

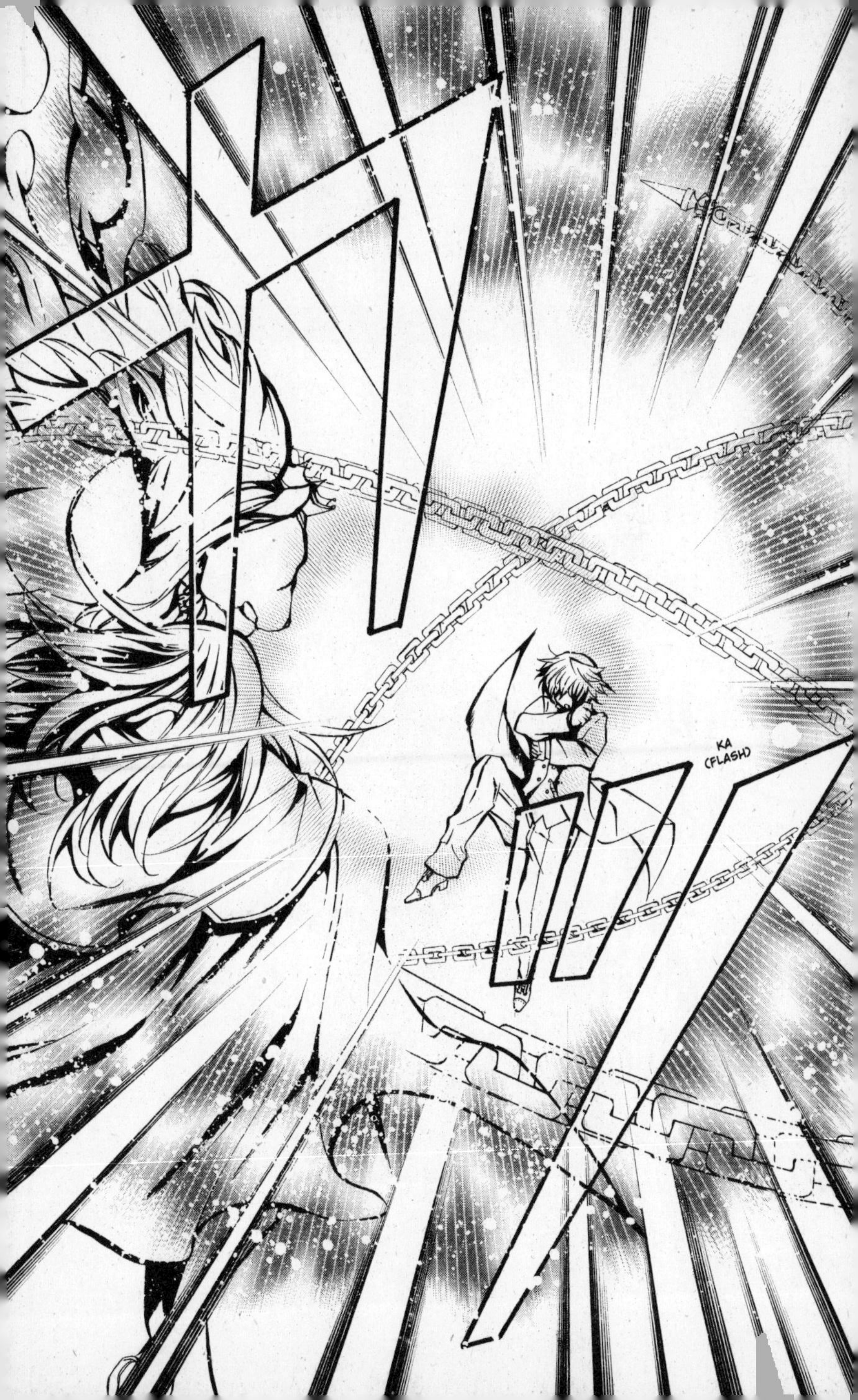
KA
(FLASH)

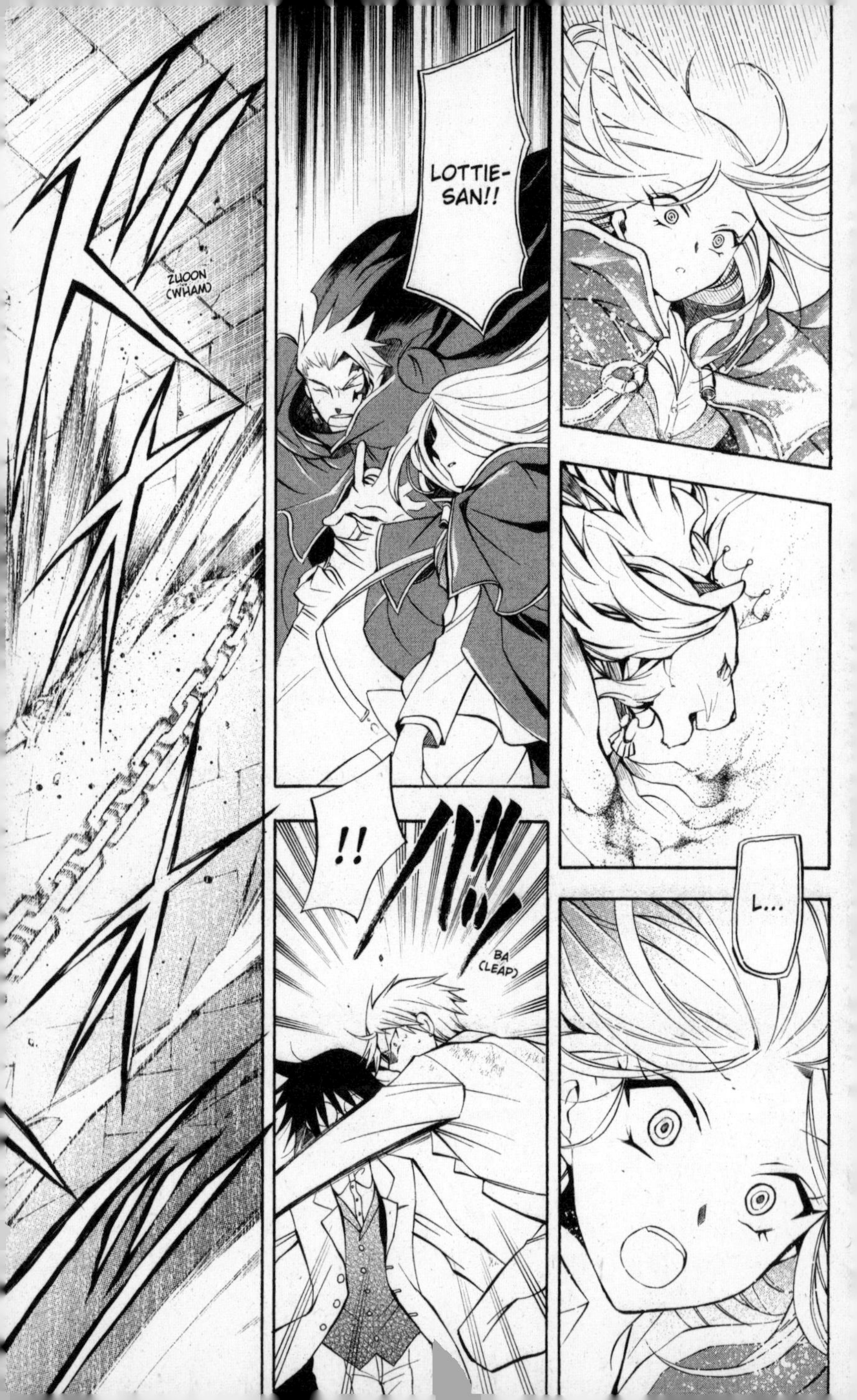
L...
LOTTIE-SAN!!
!!
BA (LEAP)
ZUOON (WHAM)

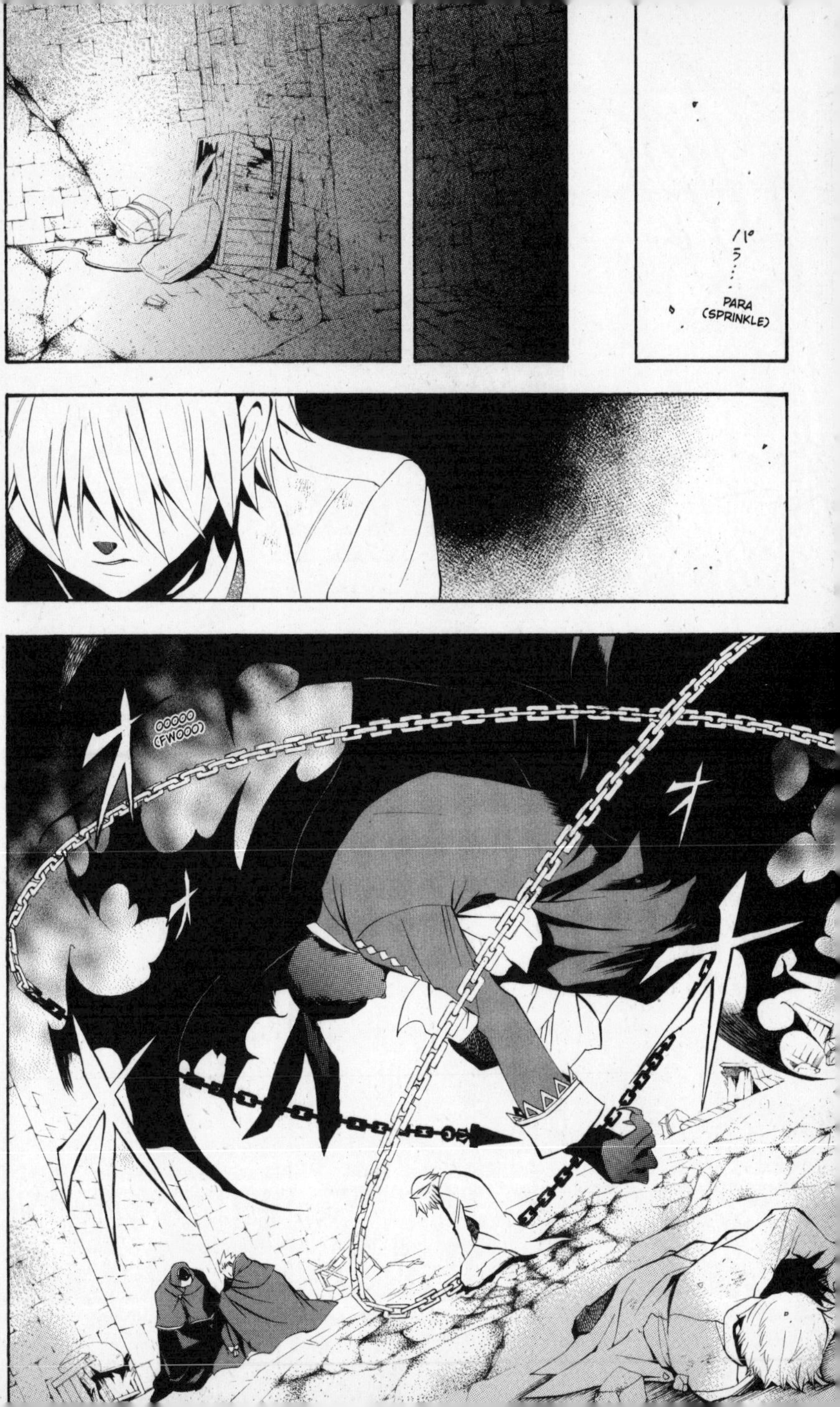
パラ…
PARA (SPRINKLE)
オオオオオ
OOOOO (FWOOO)

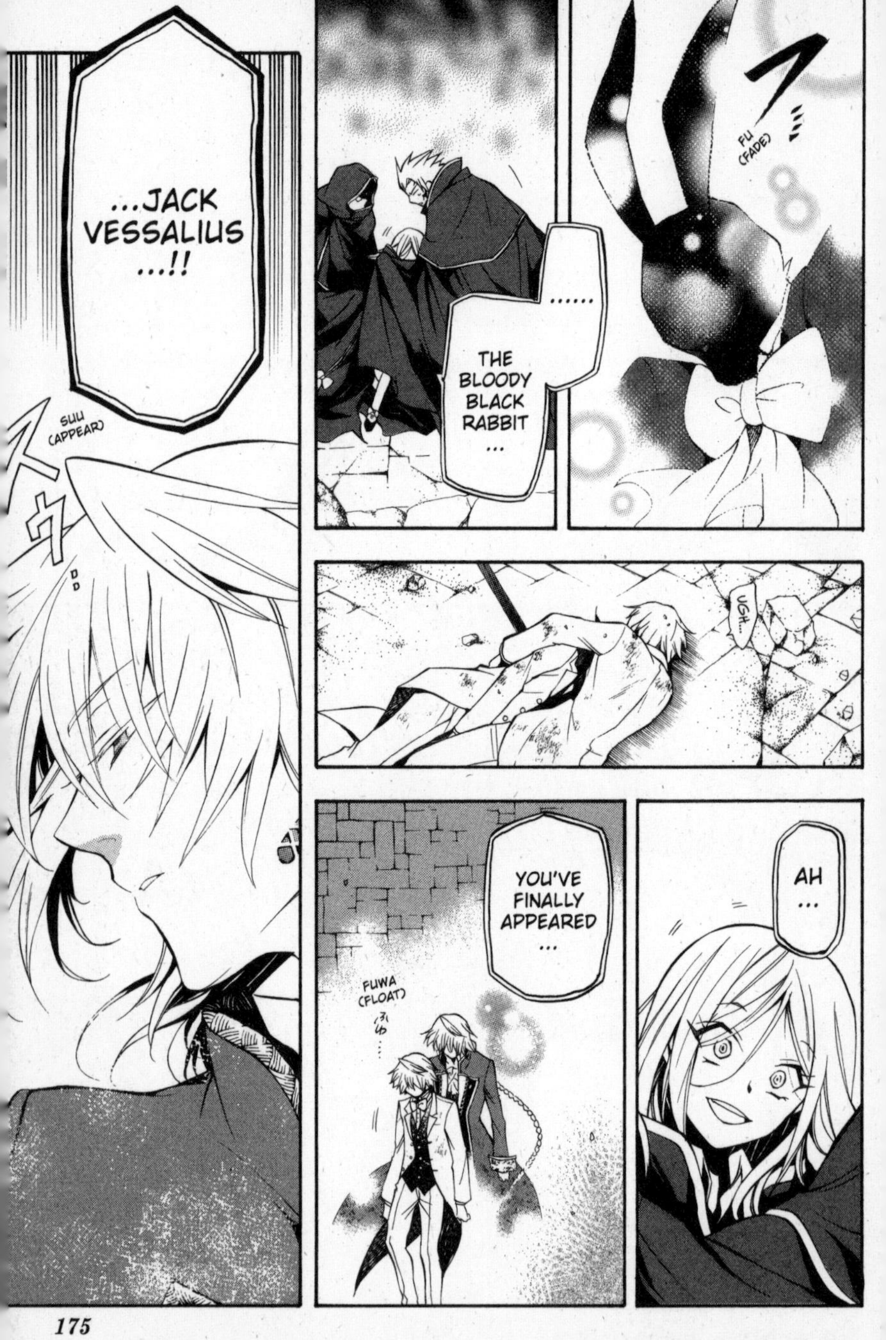
FU (FADE)
......
THE BLOODY BLACK RABBIT ...
UGH...
AH ...
YOU'VE FINALLY APPEARED ...
FUWA (FLOAT)
ふわ...
...JACK VESSALIUS ...!!
SUU (APPEAR)

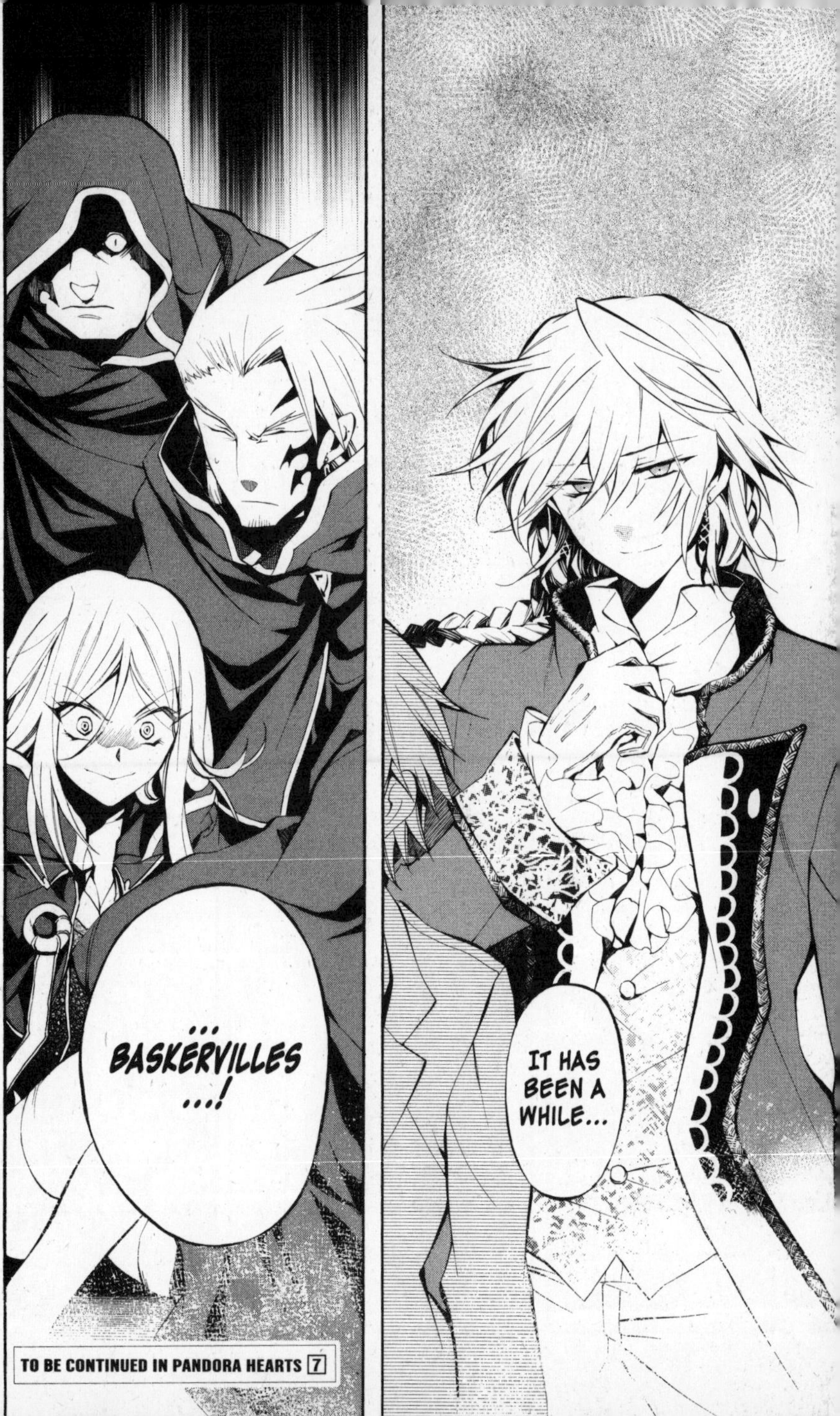
IT HAS BEEN A WHILE...
...BASKERVILLES ...!
TO BE CONTINUED IN PANDORA HEARTS 7

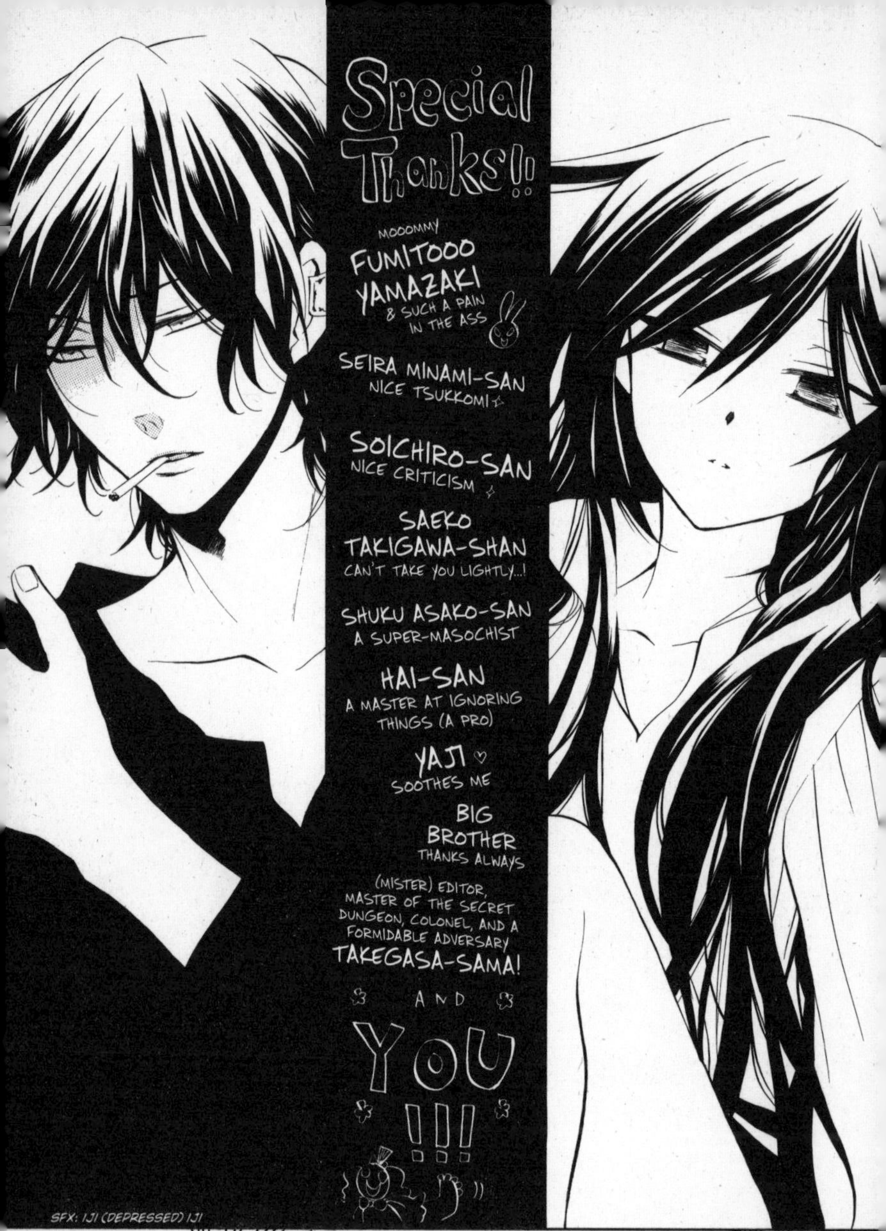
Special Thanks!!
MOOOMMY
FUMITOOO YAMAZAKI
& SUCH A PAIN IN THE ASS
SEIRA MINAMI-SAN
NICE TSUKKOMI
SOICHIRO-SAN
NICE CRITICISM
SAEKO TAKIGAWA-SHAN
CAN'T TAKE YOU LIGHTLY...!
SHUKU ASAKO-SAN
A SUPER-MASOCHIST
HAI-SAN
A MASTER AT IGNORING THINGS (A PRO)
YAJI ♡
SOOTHES ME
BIG BROTHER
THANKS ALWAYS
(MISTER) EDITOR, MASTER OF THE SECRET DUNGEON, COLONEL, AND A FORMIDABLE ADVERSARY
TAKEGASA-SAMA!
AND
YOU!!!
SFX: IJI (DEPRESSED) IJI
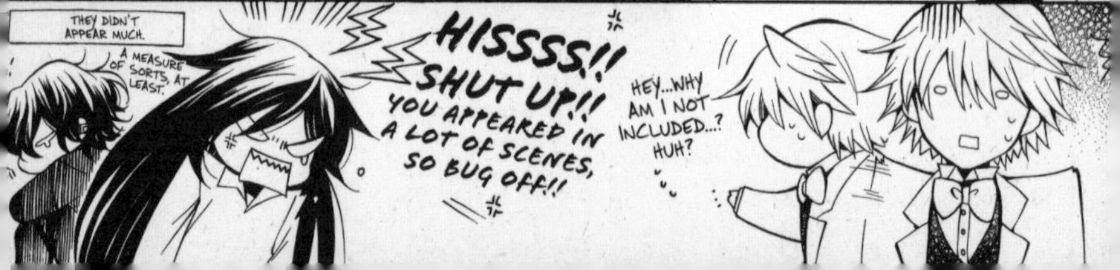
HEY...WHY AM I NOT INCLUDED...? HUH?
HISSSS!!
SHUT UP!! YOU APPEARED IN A LOT OF SCENES, SO BUG OFF!!
THEY DIDN'T APPEAR MUCH.
A MEASURE OF SORTS, AT LEAST.

HOLY KNIGHT

WHAT IS "HOLY KNIGHT"...?

THE HERO EDWIN, WHO WAS BORN AS THE FOURTH SON OF A VISCOUNT (AN AWKWARD POSITION), TAKES ALONG HIS VALET EDGAR, AND KEEPS FORCING HIS WAY UP... THAT'S THE STORY IN A NUTSHELL. THERE'S LAUGHTER, TEARS, BATTLES, POLITICS, ROMANTIC ATTACHMENTS, FRIENDSHIP, LOVE AND HATE, EVERYTHING!...DELICIOUS! SUITABLE FOR THE YOUNG AND OLD, MEN AND WOMEN. TWENTY-ONE VOLUMES HAVE BEEN PUBLISHED SO FAR!

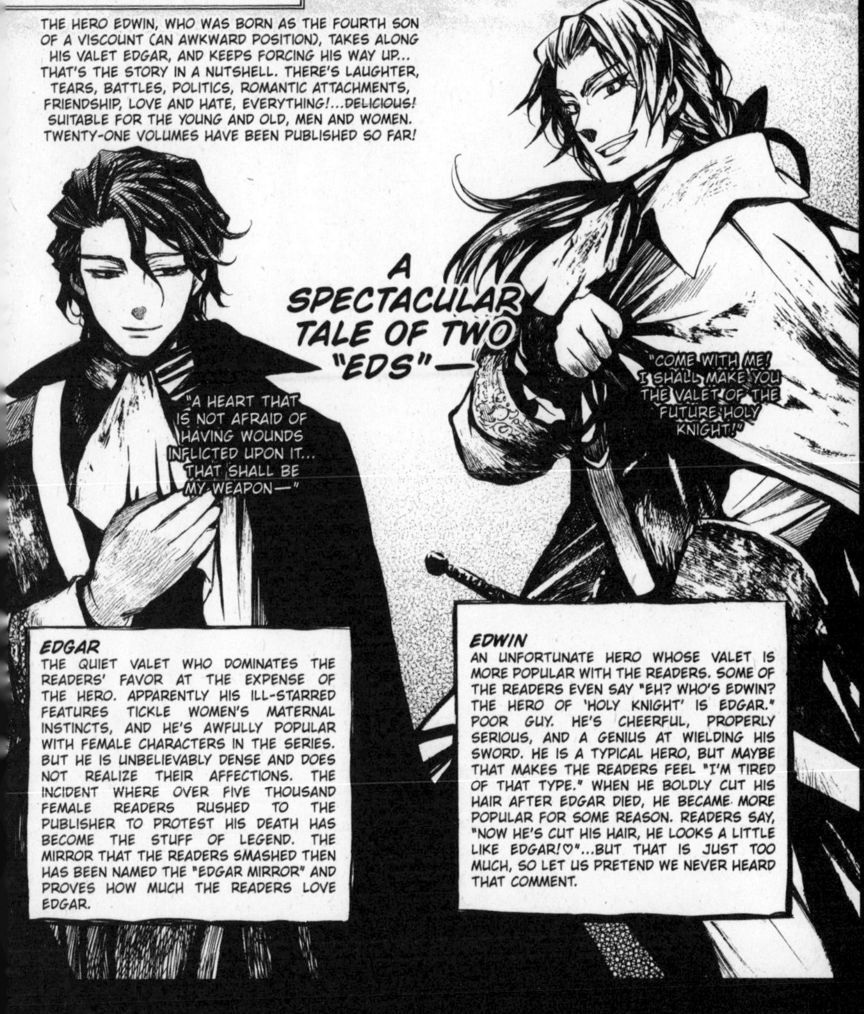
A SPECTACULAR TALE OF TWO "EDS"—
"COME WITH ME! I SHALL MAKE YOU THE VALET OF THE FUTURE HOLY KNIGHT!"
"A HEART THAT IS NOT AFRAID OF HAVING WOUNDS INFLICTED UPON IT... THAT SHALL BE MY WEAPON—"

EDGAR
THE QUIET VALET WHO DOMINATES THE READERS' FAVOR AT THE EXPENSE OF THE HERO. APPARENTLY HIS ILL-STARRED FEATURES TICKLE WOMEN'S MATERNAL INSTINCTS, AND HE'S AWFULLY POPULAR WITH FEMALE CHARACTERS IN THE SERIES. BUT HE IS UNBELIEVABLY DENSE AND DOES NOT REALIZE THEIR AFFECTIONS. THE INCIDENT WHERE OVER FIVE THOUSAND FEMALE READERS RUSHED TO THE PUBLISHER TO PROTEST HIS DEATH HAS BECOME THE STUFF OF LEGEND. THE MIRROR THAT THE READERS SMASHED THEN HAS BEEN NAMED THE "EDGAR MIRROR" AND PROVES HOW MUCH THE READERS LOVE EDGAR.

EDWIN
AN UNFORTUNATE HERO WHOSE VALET IS MORE POPULAR WITH THE READERS. SOME OF THE READERS EVEN SAY "EH? WHO'S EDWIN? THE HERO OF 'HOLY KNIGHT' IS EDGAR." POOR GUY. HE'S CHEERFUL, PROPERLY SERIOUS, AND A GENIUS AT WIELDING HIS SWORD. HE IS A TYPICAL HERO, BUT MAYBE THAT MAKES THE READERS FEEL "I'M TIRED OF THAT TYPE." WHEN HE BOLDLY CUT HIS HAIR AFTER EDGAR DIED, HE BECAME MORE POPULAR FOR SOME REASON. READERS SAY, "NOW HE'S CUT HIS HAIR, HE LOOKS A LITTLE LIKE EDGAR!♡"...BUT THAT IS JUST TOO MUCH, SO LET US PRETEND WE NEVER HEARD THAT COMMENT.

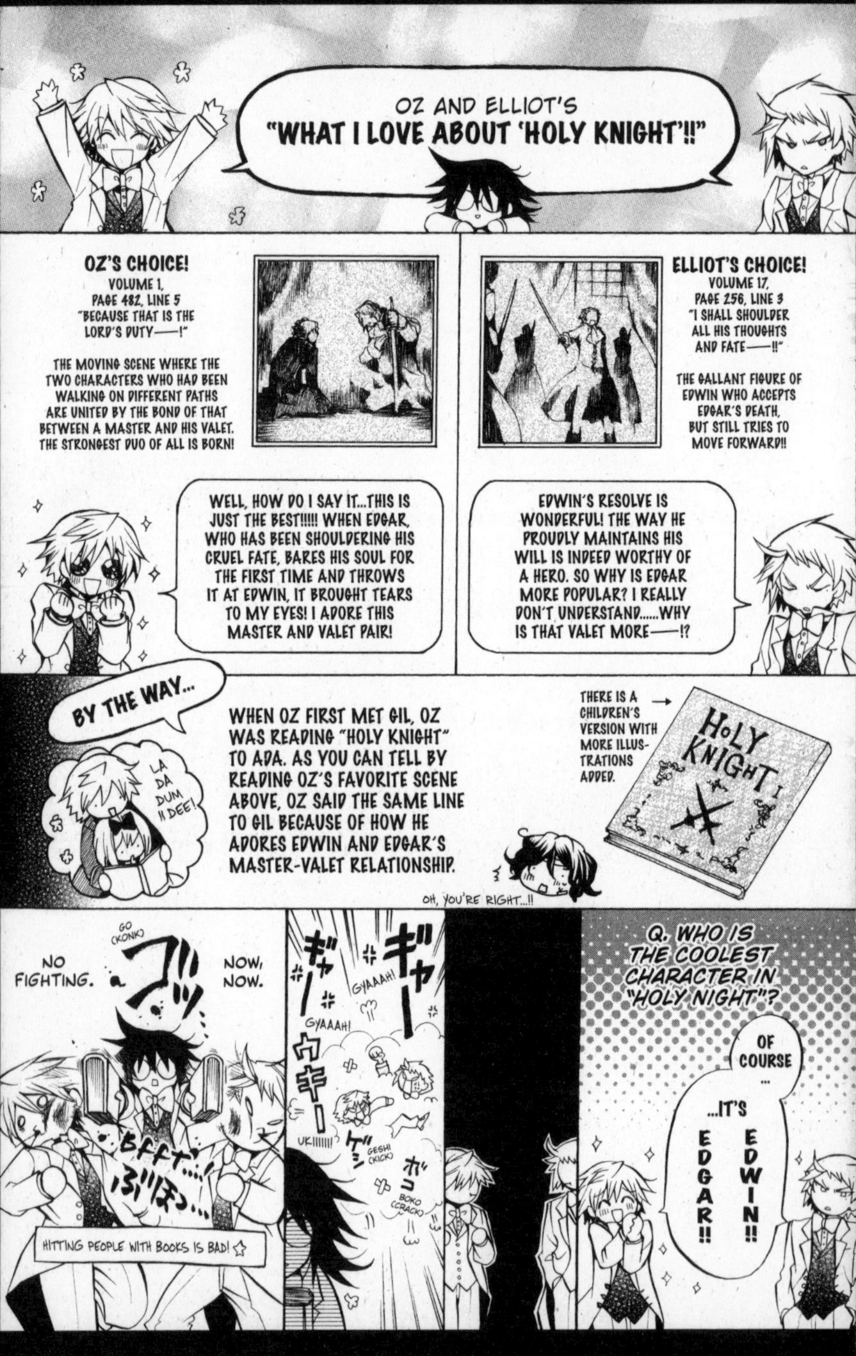
OZ AND ELLIOT'S
"WHAT I LOVE ABOUT 'HOLY KNIGHT'!!"
ELLIOT'S CHOICE!
VOLUME 17, PAGE 256, LINE 3
"I SHALL SHOULDER ALL HIS THOUGHTS AND FATE——!!"
THE GALLANT FIGURE OF EDWIN WHO ACCEPTS EDGAR'S DEATH, BUT STILL TRIES TO MOVE FORWARD!!
OZ'S CHOICE!
VOLUME 1, PAGE 482, LINE 5
"BECAUSE THAT IS THE LORD'S DUTY——!"
THE MOVING SCENE WHERE THE TWO CHARACTERS WHO HAD BEEN WALKING ON DIFFERENT PATHS ARE UNITED BY THE BOND OF THAT BETWEEN A MASTER AND HIS VALET. THE STRONGEST DUO OF ALL IS BORN!
EDWIN'S RESOLVE IS WONDERFUL! THE WAY HE PROUDLY MAINTAINS HIS WILL IS INDEED WORTHY OF A HERO. SO WHY IS EDGAR MORE POPULAR? I REALLY DON'T UNDERSTAND......WHY IS THAT VALET MORE——!?
WELL, HOW DO I SAY IT...THIS IS JUST THE BEST!!!!! WHEN EDGAR, WHO HAS BEEN SHOULDERING HIS CRUEL FATE, BARES HIS SOUL FOR THE FIRST TIME AND THROWS IT AT EDWIN, IT BROUGHT TEARS TO MY EYES! I ADORE THIS MASTER AND VALET PAIR!
THERE IS A CHILDREN'S VERSION WITH MORE ILLUSTRATIONS ADDED.
HOLY KNIGHT I
OH, YOU'RE RIGHT...!!
BY THE WAY...
WHEN OZ FIRST MET GIL, OZ WAS READING "HOLY KNIGHT" TO ADA. AS YOU CAN TELL BY READING OZ'S FAVORITE SCENE ABOVE, OZ SAID THE SAME LINE TO GIL BECAUSE OF HOW HE ADORES EDWIN AND EDGAR'S MASTER-VALET RELATIONSHIP.
LA DA DUM DEE!
Q. WHO IS THE COOLEST CHARACTER IN "HOLY NIGHT"?
OF COURSE...
...IT'S
EDWIN!!
EDGAR!!
GYAAAH!
GYAAAH!
UKI!!!!!!
GESHI (KICK)
BOKO (CRACK)
NOW, NOW.
GO (KONK)
NO FIGHTING.
BFFT...!
HITTING PEOPLE WITH BOOKS IS BAD!

COMMON HONORIFICS

no honorific: Indicates familiarity or closeness; if used without permission or reason, addressing someone in this manner would constitute an insult.

-san: The Japanese equivalent of Mr./Mrs./Miss. If a situation calls for politeness, this is the fail-safe honorific.

-sama: Conveys great respect; may also indicate that the social status of the speaker is lower than that of the addressee.

-kun: Used most often when referring to boys (though it can be applied to girls as well), this indicates affection or familiarity. Occasionally used by older men among their peers, but it may also be used by anyone referring to a person of lower standing.

-chan: An affectionate honorific indicating familiarity used mostly in reference to girls; also used in reference to cute persons or animals of either gender.

harisen   *page 35*

A big fan which is a prop used in Japanese comedy. It makes a loud sound when you whack someone with it, but it doesn't hurt as much as it sounds.

Lutwidge Academy   *page 48*

Alice's Adventures in Wonderland, which *Pandora Hearts* references loosely, was written by Lewis Carroll, the pseudonym of English author Charles Lutwidge Dodgson.

PandoraHearts

Because there were so few girls in the previous volume, Volume 6 contains the most girls ever. Many characters are jumbled together in Volume 6, but the main character is still Oz.

Do your best, hero!!

MOCHIZUKI'S MUSINGS

VOLUME 6

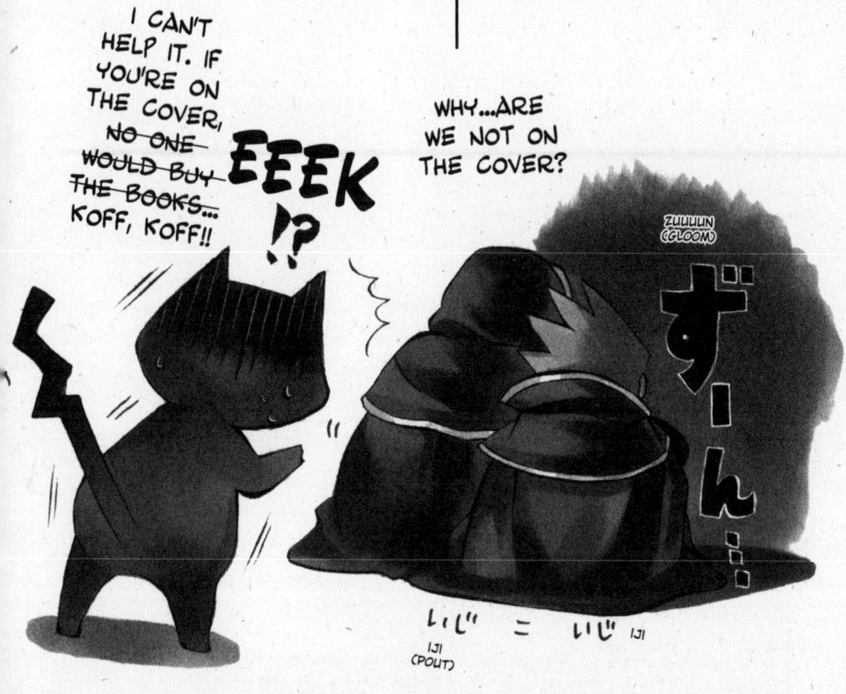
WHY...ARE WE NOT ON THE COVER?
ZUUUUN (GLOOM)
ずーん...
I CAN'T HELP IT. IF YOU'RE ON THE COVER, ~~NO ONE WOULD BUY THE BOOKS...~~ KOFF, KOFF!!
EEEK!?
いじいじ
IJI IJI (POUT)

PandoraHearts

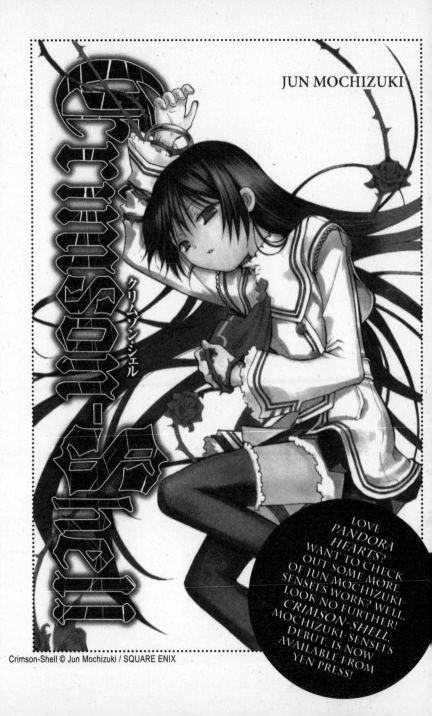

JUN MOCHIZUKI

Crimson-Shell

クリムゾン・シェル

LOVE
*PANDORA
HEARTS?*
WANT TO CHECK
OUT SOME MORE
OF JUN MOCHIZUKI-
SENSEI'S WORK? WELL,
LOOK NO FURTHER!
CRIMSON-SHELL,
MOCHIZUKI-SENSEI'S
DEBUT, IS NOW
AVAILABLE FROM
YEN PRESS!

PandoraHearts

Can't wait for the next volume? You don't have to!

Keep up with the latest chapters of some of your favorite manga every month online in the pages of YEN PLUS!

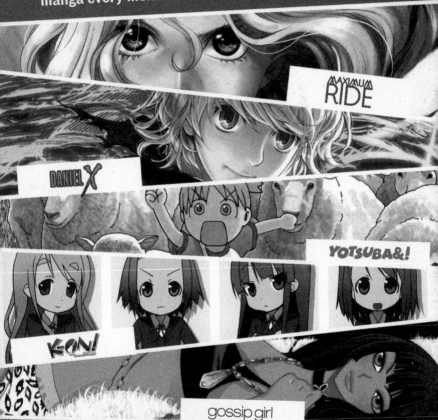

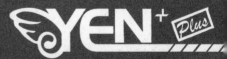

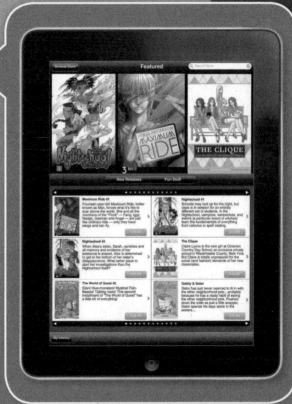
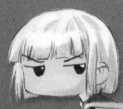

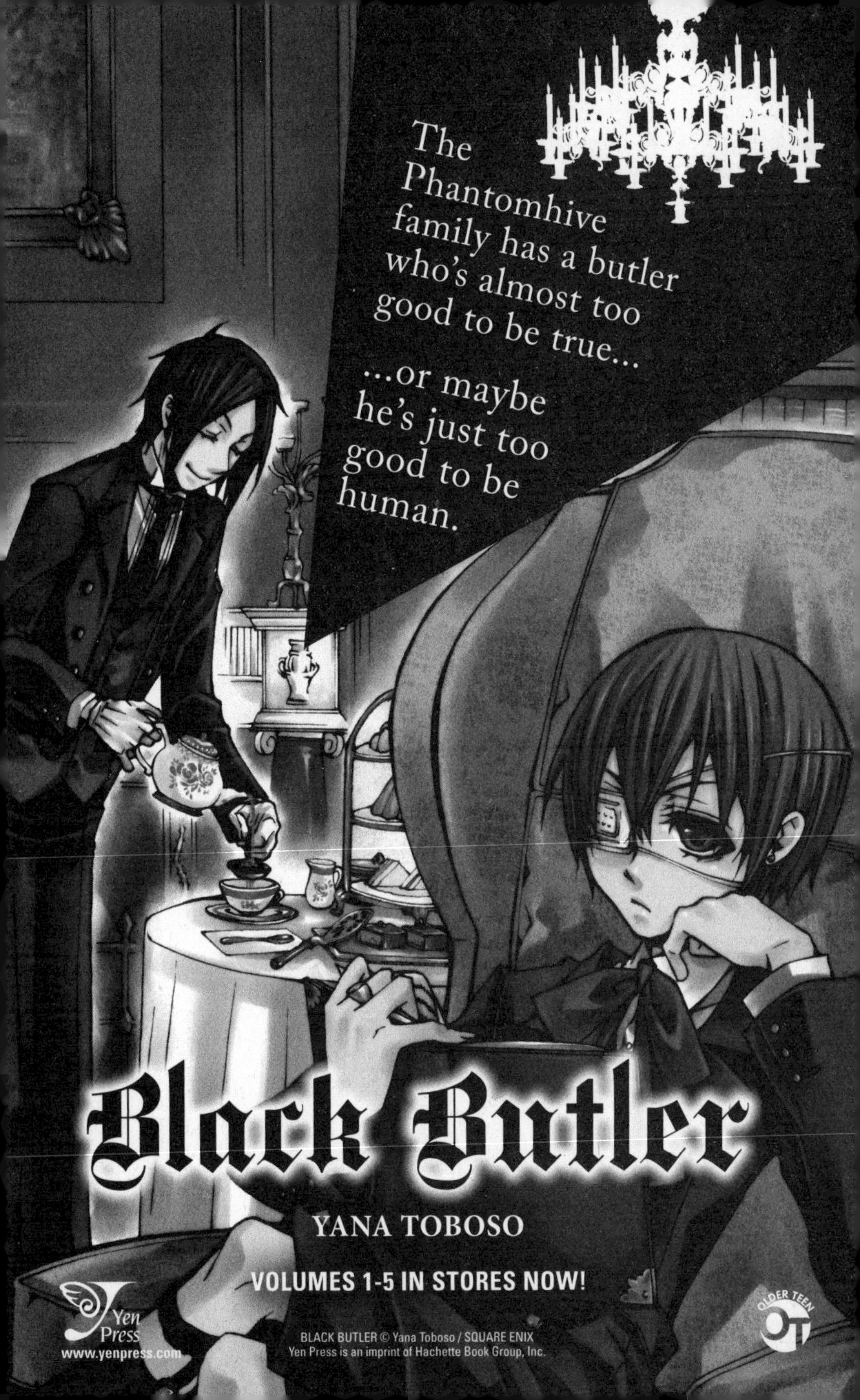

The Phantomhive family has a butler who's almost too good to be true...
...or maybe he's just too good to be human.
Black Butler
YANA TOBOSO
VOLUMES 1-5 IN STORES NOW!
Yen Press
www.yenpress.com
BLACK BUTLER © Yana Toboso / SQUARE ENIX
Yen Press is an imprint of Hachette Book Group, Inc.
OLDER TEEN
OT

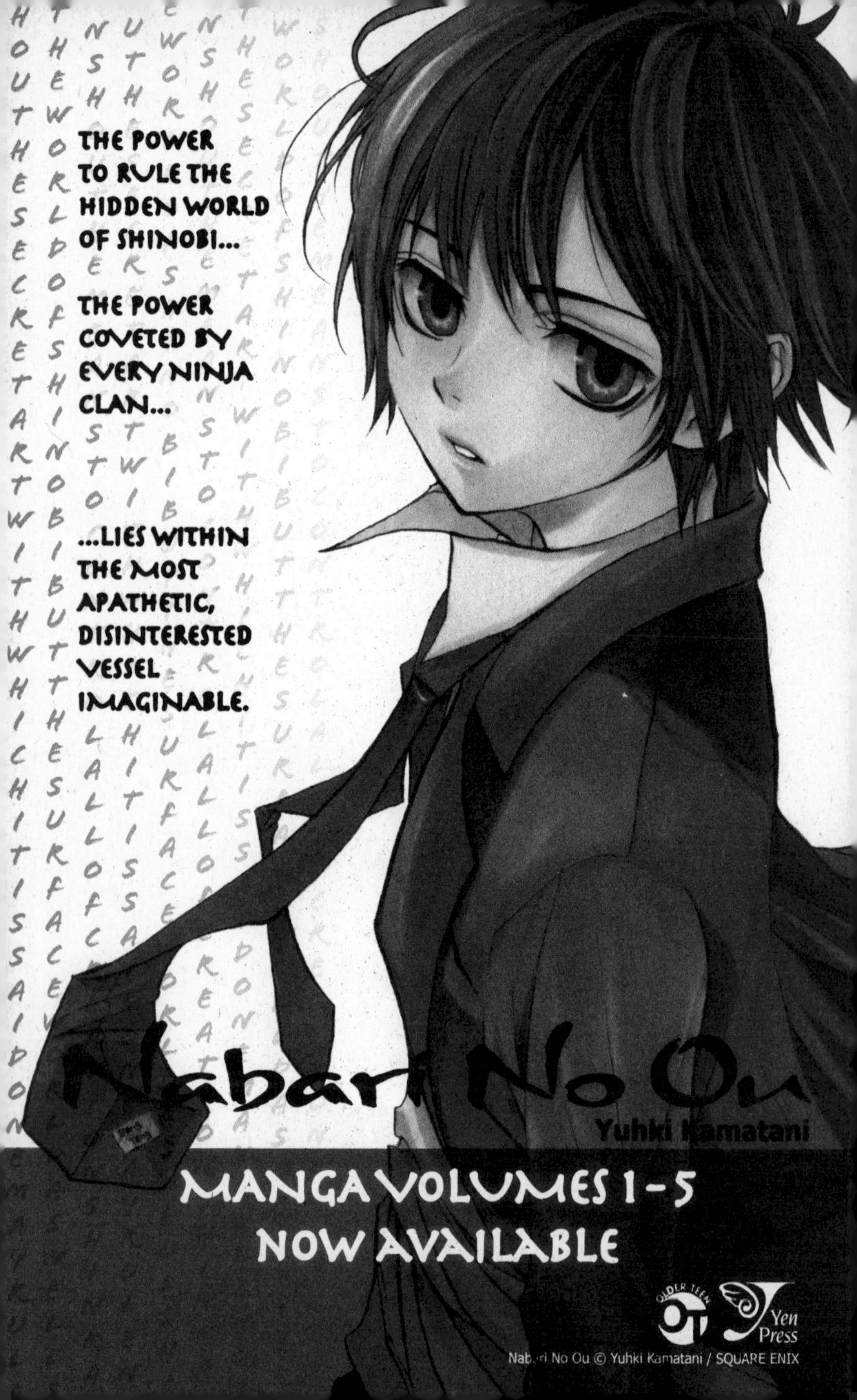
THE POWER TO RULE THE HIDDEN WORLD OF SHINOBI...
THE POWER COVETED BY EVERY NINJA CLAN...
...LIES WITHIN THE MOST APATHETIC, DISINTERESTED VESSEL IMAGINABLE.
Nabari No Ou
Yuhki Kamatani
MANGA VOLUMES 1-5
NOW AVAILABLE
OLDER TEEN
OT
Yen Press
Nabari No Ou © Yuhki Kamatani / SQUARE ENIX

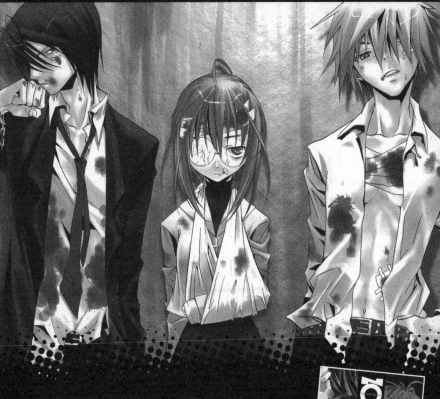
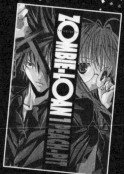

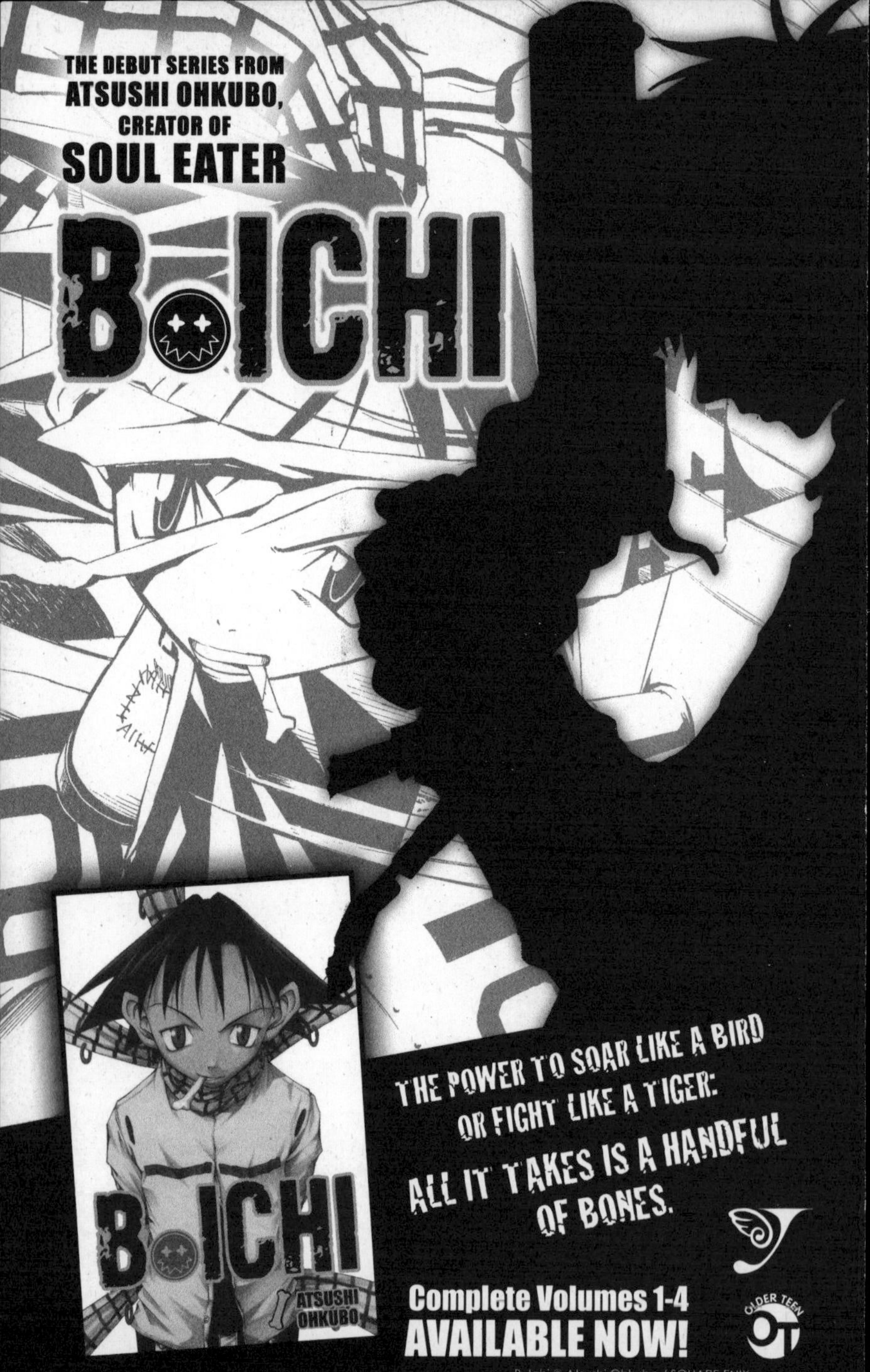
THE DEBUT SERIES FROM
ATSUSHI OHKUBO,
CREATOR OF
SOUL EATER
B. ICHI
B. ICHI
ATSUSHI OHKUBO
THE POWER TO SOAR LIKE A BIRD
OR FIGHT LIKE A TIGER:
ALL IT TAKES IS A HANDFUL
OF BONES.
Complete Volumes 1-4
AVAILABLE NOW!
OLDER TEEN
OT

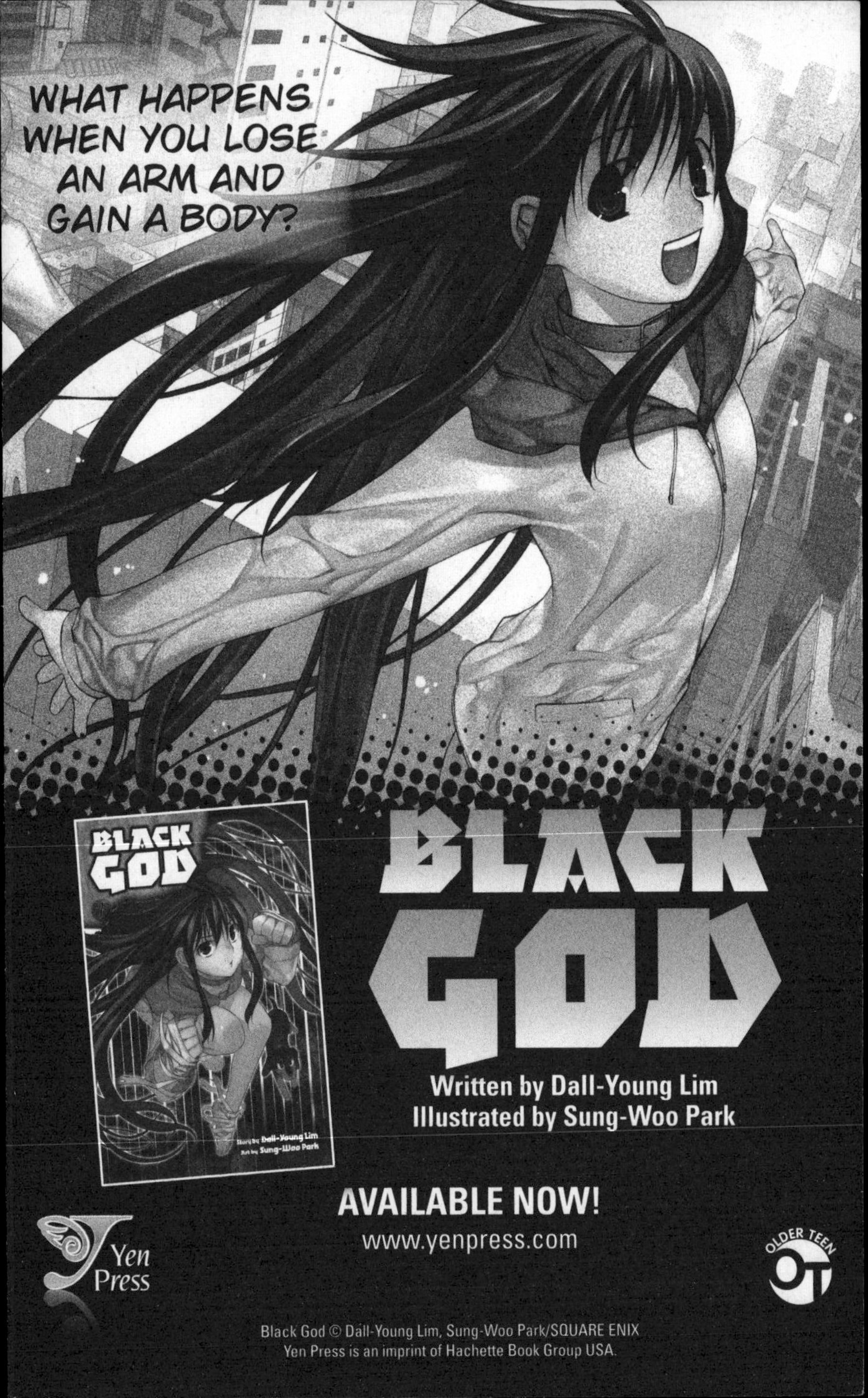
WHAT HAPPENS WHEN YOU LOSE AN ARM AND GAIN A BODY?
BLACK GOD
Story by Dall-Young Lim
Art by Sung-Woo Park
BLACK GOD
Written by Dall-Young Lim
Illustrated by Sung-Woo Park
AVAILABLE NOW!
www.yenpress.com
Yen Press
OLDER TEEN
OT
Black God © Dall-Young Lim, Sung-Woo Park/SQUARE ENIX
Yen Press is an imprint of Hachette Book Group USA.

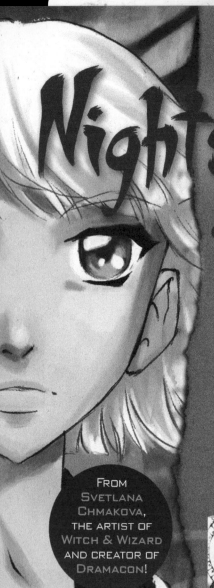
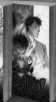

PANDORA HEARTS ❻

JUN MOCHIZUKI

Translation: Tomo Kimura • Lettering: Alexis Eckerman

PANDORA HEARTS Vol. 6 © 2008 Jun Mochizuki / SQUARE ENIX CO.,
LTD. All rights reserved. First published in Japan in 2008 by SQUARE ENIX
CO., LTD. English translation rights arranged with SQUARE ENIX CO., LTD.
and Hachette Book Group through Tuttle-Mori Agency, Inc.

Translation © 2011 by SQUARE ENIX CO., LTD.

Yen Press
Hachette Book Group
237 Park Avenue, New York, NY 10017

www.HachetteBookGroup.com
www.YenPress.com

Yen Press is an imprint of Hachette Book Group, Inc. The Yen Press name
and logo are trademarks of Hachette Book Group, Inc.

First Yen Press Edition: July 2011

ISBN: 978-0-316-07615-9

10 9 8 7 6 5 4 3 2 1

BVG

Printed in the United States of America